RELAX NG

D1091893

Other XML resources from O'Reilly

Related titles

Learning XML,
Second Edition

XML In A Nutshell,
Second Edition

XML Pocket Reference,
Second Edition

XML Schema

Learning XSLT

XSLT

XSLT Cookbook

XPath and XPointer

XML Books Resource Center

xml.oreilly.com is a complete catalog of O'Reilly's books on XML and related technologies, including sample chapters and code examples.

XML.com helps you discover XML and learn how this Internet technology can solve real-world problems in information management and electronic commerce.

Conferences

O'Reilly & Associates brings diverse innovators together to nurture the ideas that spark revolutionary industries. We specialize in documenting the latest tools and systems, translating the innovator's knowledge into useful skills for those in the trenches. Visit *conferences.oreilly.com* for our upcoming events.

Safari Bookshelf (*safari.oreilly.com*) is the premier online reference library for programmers and IT professionals. Conduct searches across more than 1,000 books. Subscribers can zero in on answers to time-critical questions in a matter of seconds. Read the books on your Bookshelf from cover to cover or simply flip to the page you need. Try it today with a free trial.

RELAX NG

WAGGONER LIBRARY
Trevecca Nazarene Univ
DISCARD

Eric van der Vlist

WAGGONER LIBRARY
TREVECCA NAZARENE UNIVERSITY

O'REILLY®

Beijing · Cambridge · Farnham · Köln · Paris · Sebastopol · Taipei · Tokyo

RELAX NG
by Eric van der Vlist

Copyright © 2004 O'Reilly & Associates, Inc. All rights reserved.
Printed in the United States of America.

Published by O'Reilly & Associates, Inc., 1005 Gravenstein Highway North, Sebastopol, CA
95472.

O'Reilly & Associates books may be purchased for educational, business, or sales promotional
use. Online editions are also available for most titles (*safari.oreilly.com*). For more information,
contact our corporate/institutional sales department: (800) 998-9938 or *corporate@oreilly.com*.

Editor:	Simon St.Laurent
Production Editor:	Mary Anne Weeks Mayo
Cover Designer:	Emma Colby
Interior Designer:	Melanie Wang

Printing History:

December 2003: First Edition.

Nutshell Handbook, the Nutshell Handbook logo, and the O'Reilly logo are registered
trademarks of O'Reilly & Associates, Inc. *RELAX NG*, the image of a blood pheasant, and related
trade dress are trademarks of O'Reilly & Associates, Inc.

Many of the designations used by manufacturers and sellers to distinguish their products are
claimed as trademarks. Where those designations appear in this book, and O'Reilly & Associates,
Inc. was aware of a trademark claim, the designations have been printed in caps or initial caps.c.

While every precaution has been taken in the preparation of this book, the publisher and author
assume no responsibility for errors or omissions, or for damages resulting from the use of the
information contained herein.

Permission is granted to copy, distribute, and/or modify this document under the terms of the
GNU Free Documentation License, Version 1.2 or any later version published by the Free
Software Foundation; with the Invariant Sections being no invariant sections, no Front-Cover
Texts, and no Back-Cover Texts. A copy of the license is included in Appendix B, *The GNU Free
Documentation License*. All images are to be included verbatim when the document is copied,
distributed, or modified under the terms of the GFDL.

ISBN: 0-596-00421-4

[M]

Table of Contents

Part II. Reference

Part III. Appendixes

Foreword by James Clark

It is a pleasure to see this first book on RELAX NG, particularly as—at the time of writing—RELAX NG does not enjoy the same level of usage and corporate support as its main rival, W3C XML Schema. Clearly this book is not for those who like their technologies chosen for them by major vendors. But I believe that for those who prefer to select their technologies for themselves, RELAX NG has substantial utility.

Back in February 1998, when the XML 1.0 Recommendation was first introduced, XML was radical in its simplicity compared to SGML. The innovation in XML was not so much in what it added to SGML but rather in what it took away. However, XML is now part of a much larger family of standards from the W3C. Collectively, these are much more complex than SGML ever was. It is hard for a newcomer to understand what is the right way to use XML and what are the core ideas.

RELAX NG is based on a very clear vision of XML processing. XML is useful only because XML processing components can interoperate. Most XML processing components do not input and output arbitrary XML documents. To combine XML processing components reliably, it is therefore essential to be able to specify the inputs and outputs of XML processing components and to verify mechanically that components are behaving according to their specifications. The most important issue in doing this is choosing which abstraction of XML to use for specifying the inputs and outputs of XML processing components.

XML standardizes only a syntax, but if you constrain XML documents directly in terms of the sequences of characters that represent them, the syntactic noise is deafening. On the other hand, if you use an abstraction that incorporates concepts such as object orientation that have no basis in the syntax, then you are coupling your XML processing components more tightly than necessary. What then is the right abstraction? The W3C XML Infoset Recommendation provides a menu of abstractions, but the items on the menu are of wildly differing importance.

I would argue that the right abstraction is a very simple one. The abstraction is a labelled tree of elements. Each element has an ordered list of children in which each child is a Unicode string or an element. An element is labelled with a two-part name consisting of a URI and local part. Each element also has an unordered collection of attributes in which each attribute has a two-part name, distinct from the name of the other attributes in the collection, and a value, which is a Unicode string. That is the complete abstraction. The core ideas of XML are this abstraction, the syntax of XML, and how the abstraction and syntax correspond. If you understand this, then you understand XML.

In my view, the most important lesson to learn from SGML is not the syntax but the concept of generic markup. Generic markup means describing things in terms of their semantics rather than their appearance. Generalizing, the lesson is to keep your data as independent as possible of assumptions about how you are going to process it. The way to do this for XML is to focus on this minimal labelled-tree abstraction. The more you build alternative abstractions on top of that and look at XML instead as a serialization of some other abstraction such as an object or a remote procedure call, the more you build in assumptions about how components will process XML and the less rationale there is for using XML.

RELAX NG is based firmly on the labelled-tree abstraction. All a RELAX NG schema does is provide a way to specify a class of XML documents in terms of this abstraction. Other schema languages, including W3C XML Schema, also provide this capability. Where RELAX NG differs from most other schema languages is in what it leaves out. It leaves out alternative abstractions of XML (such as W3C XML Schema's PSVI) that compete with the fundamental labelled-tree abstraction. It leaves out anything for transforming the document no matter how simple (such as default attributes). It leaves out anything used for parsing the document (such as entity declarations). It leaves out anything for mapping between XML and programming language data structures or relational databases. Just like XML itself, much of the advantage of RELAX NG stems from what it leaves out.

RELAX NG's vision of XML processing is not one that puts RELAX NG at the center of XML processing to the exclusion of other technologies. Rather the RELAX NG vision is one in which XML, or more precisely, the syntax and minimal labelled-tree abstraction implicit in that syntax, is at the center of XML processing. The only thing you are locked into with RELAX NG is XML. This is why a lack of vendor support need not prevent you from using RELAX NG. I hope RELAX NG will not only prove to be useful in itself but also will be an example to the XML community of the benefits of focusing on XML as XML.

Foreword by Murata Makoto

RELAX NG (pronounced *relax-ing*) is an emerging schema language for XML. RELAX NG provides many advantages: simplicity, expressiveness, readability, and reliability, among others, and they are well described in this book. Here I would like to point out one reason behind these advantages. The design of RELAX NG has been guided by tree automaton theory, which is a well-established area in formal computer science, and validators for RELAX NG are typically implemented as tree automata. RELAX NG and validators may be compared to programming languages and compilers, which are grounded on context-free grammars and parsing theory. In both cases, underlying mathematical models provide simplicity, expressiveness, and reliability.

I have studied tree automata for structured documents since 1994. I have come to strongly believe that a schema language for XML should be based on tree automaton theory. Although I was a member of the XML Schema Working Group, I also felt that we need a simpler alternative to W3C XML Schema. I thus designed RELAX Core, which was a simple schema language based on hedge automata, an aspect of tree automation theory. James Clark then designed TREX, which embodied many improvements (see his Foreword to this book). To provide a powerful alternative to W3C XML Schema, RELAX Core and TREX were unified into RELAX NG at OASIS in 2001. Recently ISO/IEC JTC1 has published RELAX NG as a Final Draft International Standard without making any technical changes.

RELAX NG has been successfully used in several projects. Some well-known ones are OASIS DocBook, W3C XHTML 2.0, W3C RDF/XML Syntax Specification (Revised), and Text Encoding Initiative. Although W3C has another schema language—namely, W3C XML Schema—the W3C does not close its doors to RELAX NG but rather recognizes its advantages and uses it for XHTML 2.0, RDF, and so forth. Some people use RELAX NG as well as W3C XML Schema happily, since Trang, a schema converter by James Clark, allows conversion from RELAX NG to W3C XML Schema.

Quite a few implementations of RELAX NG are already available. They include validators, schema converters, schema editors, data binding tools, and so forth. They are written in a variety of programming languages such as Java, C#, and Python and can be used on platforms such as Linux and Windows. Most of the implementations are free software rather than commercial products. With the advent of XHTML 2.0, some commercial products for RELAX NG have started to appear.

As far as I know, this book is the first one dedicated to RELAX NG. Eric van der Vlist gradually introduces basic concepts of RELAX NG with a number of examples. He further provides a reference guide to all features of RELAX NG. I am convinced that every reader will feel comfortable with RELAX NG.

RELAX NG would not be possible without the help of many individuals. Members of the RELAX NG technical committee of OASIS are James Clark (chair), Mike Fitzgerald, David Webber, Josh Lubell, Kohsuke Kawaguchi, Norman Walsh, John Cowan, and me. It was Jon Bosak (the father of XML) who first encouraged the unification of TREX and RELAX Core. Haruo Hosoya has contributed to the mathematical basis of RELAX NG. Kohsuke Kawaguchi, Tomoharu Asami, Masayuki Hiyama, Motohiro Kosaki, Koji Yonekura, Ryosuke Nanba, Daisuke Okajima, Yushi Komachi, and Akira Kawamata contributed to RELAX Core.

Preface

The "X" in XML stands for "Extensible." XML is so extensible that I can invent new elements and attributes as I write XML documents. There is a natural limit to this extensibility; I need to keep track of the elements and attributes that I've created. Then I need to convey to the applications what my document structures will look like. Explaining the new elements and attributes to my application is necessary to help ensure that the application gets information it has a chance of understanding and also to automate some of the most time-consuming (and boring) programming tasks. This is where XML schema languages come into play.

XML schema languages are a nice idea as long as they don't become so complicated that XML vocabularies built using them are difficult to extend. Unfortunately, that's what was starting to happen before RELAX NG (REgular LAnguage for XML, New Generation) appeared. W3C XML Schema, the dominant XML schema language, is so complex and incorporates ideas from so many conflicting fields that it is difficult to learn, difficult to extend—yet its expressive power is still too limited to describe all the possibilities offered by XML! Even though we can expect that many applications will use this mammoth language, many people need a lighter-weight and simpler alternative.

RELAX NG provides that alternative. It is an XML schema language that is:

- Focused on validating the structure of XML documents
- Lightweight enough to be easy to learn, read, and write
- Powerful enough to describe virtually any vocabulary that is based on well-formed XML 1.0 and namespaces in XML

RELAX NG is easier, more reliable, and safer to use than W3C XML Schema because of two things: RELAX NG has a sound mathematical grounding and focuses on doing a single thing perfectly well—validating the structure of XML documents.

RELAX NG won't do fancy tricks or make you coffee, but if you need a schema language that's easy to use and won't leave you in a labyrinth of obscure limitations, this is the language you should be using. Furthermore, an excellent open source tool

(James Clark's Trang) can convert your RELAX NG schemas into other languages, including W3C XML Schema, if you still need to work with W3C XML Schema–based systems. You can work sensibly in RELAX NG but still share your schemas with people who use W3C XML Schema.

Who Should Read This Book?

Read this book if you want to:

- Create RELAX NG schemas
- Understand existing RELAX NG schemas
- Discover that XML schema languages can be simple

To understand this book, you should already have a basic understanding of the structure of XML documents, but do you not need to know any other XML schema language.

Who Shouldn't Read This Book?

You don't need this book if you use only existing RELAX NG schemas to validate XML documents. For that, the documentation for the validator should be enough.

Organization of This Book

Part I, *Tutorial*

Chapter 1, *What RELAX NG Offers*
> This chapter explores XML validation, what schema languages do, and what makes RELAX NG unique.

Chapter 2, *Simple Foundations Are Beautiful*
> This chapter introduces the background of RELAX NG itself and explores the notion of a pattern, the elementary building block on which the whole language is built.

Chapter 3, *First Schema*
> This chapter builds, step by step, a first complete RELAX NG schema using XML syntax.

Chapter 4, *Introducing the Compact Syntax*
> XML syntax is very useful, but it is also verbose. This chapter introduces an alternative, a compact (non-XML) syntax.

Chapter 5, *Flattening the First Schema*
> Chapter 3's schema followed the structure of an instance document to create what is called a Russian doll design. In this chapter, I show how named patterns can limit the depth of a schema, provide reusability, and mimic DTD structures.

Chapter 6, *More Complex Patterns*

Up to now, I've described only ordered sequences of elements. This chapter introduces new compositors for defining choices between patterns.

Chapter 7, *Constraining Text Values*

This chapter introduces the mechanisms that constrain text values and the two datatypes (string and token) built into RELAX NG.

Chapter 8, *Datatype Libraries*

This chapter describes external datatype libraries that may be used in RELAX NG schemas, and spends some time exploring the two datatype libraries that are most frequently used: the W3C XML Schema library and the DTD compatibility library.

Chapter 9, *Using Regular Expressions to Specify Simple Datatypes*

This chapter explores one of the most powerful aspects of datatypes, the pattern facet of the W3C XML Schema datatype library, and its particular flavor of regular expressions.

Chapter 10, *Creating Building Blocks*

Building on previous chapters, this chapter shows how to reuse and redefine the information in grammars that can be merged.

Chapter 11, *Namespaces*

This chapter provides a brief explanation of XML namespaces and how RELAX NG supports their use.

Chapter 12, *Writing Extensible Schemas*

This chapter covers the extensibility of schemas themselves and of the class of instance documents described by a schema.

Chapter 13, *Annotating Schemas*

Schema annotations are useful both for documentation targeted to human users and to provide additional information to software. This chapter explores annotations and their applications, including projects such as embedding Schematron rules in RELAX NG schemas, Bob DuCharme's schema document pipeline proposal, and my own XVIF.

Chapter 14, *Generating RELAX NG Schemas*

This chapter explores how to generate RELAX NG from different sources, including instance documents (Examplotron), UML diagrams, spreadsheets, and literate programming.

Chapter 15, *Simplification and Restrictions*

This chapter goes into the details of the simplification of RELAX NG schemas performed by RELAX NG processors. These details explain some obscure limitations.

Chapter 16, *Determinism and Datatype Assignment*

One strength of RELAX NG is that it allows the creation of nondeterministic schemas. While this is extremely convenient for validation purposes, it creates issues for datatype assignment. This chapter examines schema determinism and ambiguity and their impact on the different uses of RELAX NG.

Part II, *Reference*

Chapter 17, *Element Reference*
This chapter describes all the elements of the XML syntax with descriptions, synopses, and examples.

Chapter 18, *Compact Syntax Reference*
This chapter covers the components of the compact syntax, including descriptions, synopses, and examples.

Chapter 19, *Datatype Reference*
This chapter describes W3C XML Schema datatypes, often used as an external datatype library in RELAX NG schemas.

Part III, *Appendixes*

Appendix A, *DSDL*
This appendix presents the ISO DSDL project, which includes RELAX NG as its Part 2.

Appendix B, *The GNU Free Documentation License*
This book is being made available under the GNU Free Documentation License, which provides certain freedoms related to copying, modifying, and distributing this book. This appendix contains pointers to the online version of the book (which includes additional examples and errata), as well as the text of the license.

Glossary
This glossary provides a concise explanation of terms used throughout the book.

Conventions Used in This Book

The following typographical conventions are used in this book:

Italic
New terms where they are defined, pathnames, filenames, program names, hostnames, domain names, and URLs

`Constant width`
Code examples and fragments, element names, tags, attribute values, entity references, processing instructions, keywords, operators, method names, class names, and literals

`Constant width bold`
User input

`Constant width italic`
Replaceable elements in code examples and fragments

This icon signifies a tip, suggestion, or general note.

This icon indicates a warning or caution.

Comments and Questions

Please address comments and questions concerning this book to the publisher:

O'Reilly & Associates, Inc.
1005 Gravenstein Highway North
Sebastopol, CA 95472
(800) 998-9938 (in the United States or Canada)
(707) 829-0515 (international or local)
(707) 829-0104 (fax)

There's a web page for this book that lists errata, examples, and any additional information. You can access this page at:

http://www.oreilly.com/catalog/relax

To comment or ask technical questions about this book, send email to:

bookquestions@oreilly.com

For more information about books, conferences, Resource Centers, and the O'Reilly Network, see the O'Reilly web site at:

http://www.oreilly.com

The GFDL release of this book, along with updates, is available at:

http://books.xmlschemata.org/relaxng

Powered by WikiML

Most of this book has been edited in a WikiWikiWeb powered by PhpWiki. PhpWiki is a PHP implementation of the concept of WikiWikiWeb, invented by Ward Cunningham in 1995, and famous for the simplicity of its text-based markup. The WikiWikiWeb pages have been converted to XHTML pages using the parser developed by the WikiML project, and these pages have been transformed through XSLT into DocBook for production at O'Reilly.

This is probably one of the first attempts to leverage something as simple to use as a WikiWikiWeb to produce something as complex as a whole book marked up as DocBook. I have been surprised by the smoothness of the whole process.

To learn more about these subjects, consult these sites:

- *http://c2.com/cgi-bin/wiki?WikiWikiWeb* (WikiWikiWeb)
- *http://phpwiki.sourceforge.net* (PhpWiki)
- *http://wikiml.org* (WikiML)
- *http://www.w3.org/TR/xslt* (XSLT)
- *http://www.oasis-open.org/docbook* (DocBook)

Acknowledgments

I would like to thank the RELAX NG OASIS Technical Committee for having created the subject of this book, and especially Murata Makoto, James Clark, and John Cowan for the timely and highly accurate answers they have provided to my many questions.

My own implementation of RELAX NG has proven to be most useful in gaining a deep understanding of the language. I would also like to thank Uche Ogbuji, who has been my Python mentor during this project and again James Clark for his detailed instructions of how RELAX NG can be implemented using the derivative algorithm.

This book is the result of a collaborative work, and I thank all the people who contributed comments and annotations, including J. David Eisenberg, John Cowan, and Dave Pawson, who have extended their comments well beyond the scope of simple tech review and have significantly improved its level of quality, as well as Tracey Cranston, who reviewed and edited the prose. This collaborative work would never have started without my editor, Simon St.Laurent, who has believed in this book since before its beginning and made it happen.

Finally, I need to thank my wife and children for their patience and moral support while I was busy writing this book. Unlike in the preface of my previous book, I won't dare to promise that they will recover their husband and father now that this book is over, as I fear that a new challenging project might swallow me in the near future!

Tutorial

PART I

Tutorial

CHAPTER 1

What RELAX NG Offers

RELAX NG emerged from many years of XML development in an attempt to solve a variety of common problems raised in the creation and sharing of XML vocabularies. RELAX NG is not the only option for solving many of these problems, but the way in which it addresses them makes it an excellent candidate for many kinds of XML vocabulary development and processing.

Diversity

I have heard people jest that XML stood for Excellent Marketing Language and I often felt that, unfortunately, this had become a very accurate definition. Nevertheless, the official meaning of XML is Extensible Markup Language, which remains slightly more accurate.

XML is extensible in the sense that it lets you define your own sets of elements and attributes which can be used to express virtually any hierarchical structure. The extensibility of XML has been widely used; some would even say overused. I've long since lost count of the different sets of XML elements and attributes (let's call them XML vocabularies) used by different people for different applications. Applications need to be able to tell whether documents conform to their expectations; this need creates a need for validation tools capable of representing and testing each of these vocabularies.

Keeping Documents Independent of Applications

In the XML world, XML documents can live their own lives independently of programs: they can be edited, read, displayed, and transformed using generic tools independent of any particular application. It's also vitally important that they can be validated independently of any application. This validation requirement presents a serious challenge. The diversity of XML vocabularies is virtually infinite. We certainly don't want to limit XML's extensibility because of the tools used to validate XML documents. But that brings us to the next problem: there is diversity in what we can call *validation*.

 This application independence raises some difficult issues in XML design and usage. Some people have focused on the surface parallels between XML document structures and object hierarchies. They say that XML is in the same paradigm for data as object orientation and that XML is a perfect serialization format for object systems. While that assessment is not completely without basis, XML reintroduces a clean separation between data and processing. This is the complete opposite of the basic object-oriented principle of encapsulating both data and behavior into objects.

Validation Has Many Aspects

Validation can be about checking the structure of XML documents. It can be about checking the content of each text node and attribute independently of each other (datatype checking). It can be about checking constraints on relationships between nodes. It can be about checking constraints between nodes and external information such as lookup tables or links. It can be about checking business rules. Taken liberally, it can be almost anything else, even spell checking.

All of these aspects are important for improving the level of quality of XML-based information systems. I recently heard two presentations about two independent projects in very different domains. Both came out with this alarming ratio: one out of ten real-world XML documents contains errors. With such a high proportion, validation is not only useful but indispensable! The word "alarming" is not overstating the case—imagine a banking system where 10% of the transactions contain errors. Calling validation important, therefore, is an understatement.

The Best Way to Validate XML Document Structures

RELAX NG won't solve all issues by itself. It isn't designed to solve every conceivable validation problem. RELAX NG is, however, designed to be the best tool to solve two key pieces of the problem: validating the structure of XML document and providing a connection to datatype libraries that validate the content of text nodes and attributes. It's also designed to be used as a part of the ISO DSDL framework, which deals with the larger issues surrounding validation. (DSDL is described in Appendix A).

This tight focus makes RELAX NG very different from its main rival, W3C XML Schema. One of the reasons for the complexity of W3C XML Schema is that it includes many features that have been kept out of RELAX NG. W3C XML Schema cares not only about validating the structure of XML documents, but also about validating the content of text nodes and attributes and checking the integrity between keys and references. More importantly, W3C XML Schema addresses many issues beyond validation. It attempts to be a modeling language that can classify the elements and attributes of XML documents, identify their semantics, use these semantics as extensible object-like models, and perform automatic binding between XML documents and objects. All these goals are admirable, but too many of them are stuffed into a single technology.

During the development of RELAX NG, XML structure validation remained the focus. No compromises were made in deference to other features. The result is that RELAX NG appears to be the logical successor of XML DTDs and the best tool available to validate the structure of XML documents. RELAX NG's expressive power is such that virtually any XML vocabulary may be described with RELAX NG. That isn't true of W3C XML Schema, nor of DTDs. Perhaps most important for people who have to write schemas, RELAX NG is also very simple: because it does less, the syntax is intuitive. It has been kept simple. It isn't cluttered with complex limitations that take too much time to learn and remember.

RELAX NG's Diverse Applications

RELAX NG's tight focus doesn't mean that RELAX NG is a niche language meant to be limited to its original goal. RELAX NG may well follow the path of XSLT (also developed by James Clark). While XSLT's development was focused strictly on document transformation for formatting, it has become the Swiss Army knife of XML developers. XSLT use has gone well beyond its expected boundaries, in large part because it solves key problems effectively.

The same will likely happen with RELAX NG.

Recently, I had to write a converter for a flat, non-XML format into XML. The structure of the resulting document was described by a non-RELAX NG schema. After various hacks to map the 400 different bits of information of this flat structure into elements and attributes, I found that the easiest way to map them to XML was by using a RELAX NG schema.

I transformed the schema of the destination XML vocabulary into a simple RELAX NG schema. A Python program then walked through that structure, parsing the flat document and dispatching the information items to where they belonged. This was made easy by the uncluttered simplicity of the syntax of RELAX NG. The process would have taken much more time with any other schema language.

Another example is taken from RELAX NG itself. As you will discover in Chapter 4, a non-XML compact syntax is available for RELAX NG. This syntax is defined using an EBNF (Extended Backus-Naur Form) grammar. Knowing James Clark, I was sure he had generated it from XML. When I wrote the reference guide for this syntax (Chapter 18), I asked him to send me the source of this grammar as XML. I was expecting a format like the DocBook EBNF module, but instead, of course, he sent a RELAX NG schema! The syntax of RELAX NG is flexible enough to describe the productions of an EBNF grammar. Chapter 18 was generated using this schema. It's a summary that doesn't completely respect the semantics and restrictions of RELAX NG, but RELAX NG is still a useful way to describe this EBNF.

RELAX NG as a Pivot Format

These last two examples are a little bit extreme, but nevertheless RELAX NG appears to be the perfect pivot format for tasks related to XML schema work in any schema language, providing a useful common ground that developers can use to convert material between various schema forms. Kohsuke Kawaguchi's work on the Sun Multi-Schema Validator (MSV) takes advantage of this capability. Kawaguchi explained that the grammar-based schema languages supported by MSV (DTDs, RELAX NG, Relax and W3C XML Schema) were all translated into a common data model by the validator. The validation algorithm relied on this single data model. That data model is simply RELAX NG. This clearly demonstrates that the expressive power of RELAX NG is so useful and flexible that 99% of the constraints that can be described with other schema languages can be described with RELAX NG.

RELAX NG's advantages can also be a major drawback: if RELAX NG has so much more expressive power than other languages, it could mean that a schema written with RELAX NG would be impossible to translate.

Fortunately, this issue is more theoretical than practical. Although there are situations in which RELAX NG can't be translated into W3C XML Schema, they aren't likely to happen often in real-life schemas. If you can imagine a situation in which it would happen in real life, you can always balance your need to express such a schema in RELAX NG against your need to be able to publish a W3C XML Schema schema. I am confident that most RELAX NG schemas can be translated into other schema languages—even automatically. James Clark has developed Trang, a magic tool that takes a RELAX NG schema and converts it into W3C XML Schema or a DTD (*http://www.thaiopensource.com/relaxng/trang.html*).

RELAX NG's structures support both creation by hand and by auto-generation. RELAX NG can support the growing number of applications that generate their schemas from logical models using high levels of abstraction rather creating them from scratch. Whether you are using as your design tool UML, a simple spreadsheet such as the OASIS UBL project, or sample documents like my Examplotron, it's easier to derive a RELAX NG schema than to derive a schema using any other schema language.

Why Use Other Schema Languages?

There are tools to convert to and from other schema languages; however RELAX NG is easier to write, it's easier to generate, and it's easier for applications to use. As far as validation is concerned, I see no good reason to use another tool. Even if your tools support only XML 1.0 DTDs or W3C XML Schema, you can automatically generate those formats from RELAX NG.

RELAX NG is still a little bit behind, however, in datatype assignment and data binding. Datatype assignment appears to be increasingly important for a whole set of applications, including many new features of the XPath 2.0, XSLT 2.0, and XQuery 1.0 family of future W3C recommendations. Because datatype assignment was out of the scope for RELAX NG during its development, RELAX NG is very permissive about *nondeterministic* schemas. This permissiveness can lead to unpredictable type assignment during processing. This is something worth keeping in mind when writing RELAX NG schemas that will later be transformed into W3C XML Schema schemas. I will explain this subject in detail in Chapter 16.

CHAPTER 2

Simple Foundations Are Beautiful

RELAX NG is built using a set of simple pieces. Before proceeding into the details of how RELAX NG assembles these pieces, it's worth exploring what these pieces are and what they'll contribute.

Documents and Infosets

RELAX NG is an XML-based technology. RELAX NG schemas are commonly stored in XML documents (called *schema documents*) and used to validate other XML documents (called *instance documents*). While RELAX NG works with and uses XML documents, RELAX NG processors operate at a slightly higher level of abstraction, called an *infoset*, rather than processing the actual text of the XML document, which is called *lexical processing*.

An *infoset* is a logical view of the XML document, rather than the document as stored in a text file. Most XML processors read (or generate) XML syntax but work internally on a representation that omits a lot of details. To take a brief example, from a lexical perspective, which looks at the actual contents of an XML document, `<book id='b0836217462' available="true"/>` is an empty tag containing two attributes named `id` and `available`. The value of `id` is delimited with single quotes, while the value of `available` is delimited with double quotes. Yet, from an infoset perspective, this isn't an empty tag with particular syntax; the kind of quotation marks don't matter. It's a `book` element with an attribute named `id` and a value of `b0836217462`, as well as an attribute named `available` with a value of `true`. Elements, attributes, and text are often referred to as *nodes* in this perspective, like nodes in an object tree.

There are a variety of different models for XML documents—specifications such as the Simple API for XML (SAX), the Document Object Model (DOM), and XPath all have slightly different takes on what an infoset is. As a first step toward coordinating these perspectives, the W3C created a Recommendation: the XML Information Set (Infoset), which is available at *http://www.w3.org/TR/xml-infoset/*. The XML Infoset defines an abstract model of XML documents that uses a hierarchical structure described in terms generic and neutral enough to be acceptable for use with a diverse range of specifications.

 The XML Information Set describes elements as "element information items," attributes as "attribute information items," and so on. For convenience, this book uses the RELAX NG convention—inspired by XPath—that refers to element nodes, attribute nodes, and so on, rather than information items.

Schema languages work at the level of the XML Infoset, and their main goal is to define constraints on a subset of the XML Infoset. Because they work at the XML Infoset level, they can't be used to express constraints on things that don't belong to the XML Infoset. Thus such things as the order of the attributes, their quotation style, or the number of spaces between them can't be constrained by schemas. In addition, RELAX NG, like most schema languages, won't let you define constraints on XML comments, processing instructions, or entity references. Schema languages focus on a core set of features: elements, attributes, and textual content.

 Some schema languages, notably the W3C XML Schema (WXS) and the Document Type Definitions (DTDs), also let you augment the infoset of a given instance document with additional information. Both WXS and DTDs let you specify default values for attributes. WXS also provides the ability to add additional type information (the Post-Schema Validation Infoset, or PSVI), while DTDs provide the opportunity to include entity definitions and ID information. While RELAX NG does use the infoset as a base, it doesn't perform these kinds of infoset augmentation.

Different Types of Schema Languages

While the different schema languages all operate on infoset views of documents, they have chosen different ways of defining constraints:

- Constraints may be expressed as rules. In Schematron, for instance, a schema is a set of rules like "the element named book must have an attribute named id and this attribute's content must match this specific rule...."

- Constraints may be expressed as a thorough description of each element and attribute like DTDs and W3C XML Schema: "it's an element named book, and it has two attributes named id and available, which look like this...."

- Constraints may be expressed as *patterns*. Patterns are used to match the structures of permissible elements, attributes, and text nodes, much as the regular expressions used in programming can be used to match characters in text. I will cover this third way of defining constraints in detail in this book because this is the method that RELAX NG uses.

The first XML schema language was the Document Type Definition (DTD), which was part of XML 1.0. DTDs provide more than just schema validation features—they include the definition of internal and external entities—but their schema features focus on describing elements. Every element and attribute used by the document type defined by the DTD must be described. Each element must have a content model, identifying which child elements or text nodes are allowed, as well as a list of permissible attributes, if any attributes are allowed. To avoid redundant declarations, DTD developers may use *parameter entities*, which describe larger pieces of content models and work like a kind of macro processing.

W3C XML Schema extends this foundation and defines several kind of *components*, including elements, attributes, datatypes, groups of elements, and groups of attributes. (*Datatypes* are containers for various kinds of content, from text to integers to dates.) The approach is still very focused on elements and attributes, which are clearly differentiated.

RELAX NG, on the other hand, is based on the generic concept of patterns. Patterns are similar to the XPath *node sets*, a collection of nodes with an internal structure. To begin with, a pattern can be defined as the description of a set of valid node sets.

The difference between patterns and the other approaches may seem subtle, but a DTD or W3C XML Schema element definition tries to give a description of the element itself. When RELAX NG defines the same element, a pattern is defined that is checked against elements in the instance document to see if they match, much as if it were a regular expression being used to match text. The difference is miniscule on the surface, but the pattern approach gives far more flexibility to write, maintain, and combine schemas.

A Simple Example

Let's take a look at an example. Figure 2-1 shows the book element with its two attributes and four different subelements:

```
<book id="b0836217462" available="true">
  <isbn>0836217462</isbn>
  <title xml:lang="en">Being a Dog Is a Full-Time Job</title>
- <author id="CMS"></author>
- <character id="PP"></character>
- <character id="Snoopy"></character>
- <character id="Schroeder"></character>
- <character id="Lucy"></character>
</book>
```

Figure 2-1. A complete example of the book element

With a DTD and, to a lesser extent, with W3C XML Schema, you are stuck defining lists of attributes and elements you can't mix or combine. W3C XML Schema has introduced the concept of *types*, abstract descriptions that have no direct corollary in the contents of XML documents. Types provide descriptions of the contents of elements or attributes, but types still can't be freely combined together. This means that you can split the description of elements into blocks such as those shown in Figure 2-2, but can mix the blocks in a limited number of ways.

```
<book id="b0836217462" available="true">
  <isbn>0836217462</isbn>
  <title xml:lang="en">Being a Dog Is a Full-Time Job</title>
  <author id="CMS"></author>
  <character id="PP"></character>
  <character id="Snoopy"></character>
  <character id="Schroeder"></character>
  <character id="Lucy"></character>
</book>
```

Figure 2-2. The blocks of the book element, seen from a W3C XML Schema perspective

RELAX NG patterns, however, can freely mix different types of nodes (elements, text and attributes). Figure 2-3 shows how, if you want to, you can use RELAX NG to split the definition of the book element into a first pattern composed of the attributes id, title, and author and the element character, and then a second pattern composed of the available attribute and the other character elements.

```
<book id="b0836217462" available="true">
  <isbn>0836217462</isbn>
  <title xml:lang="en">Being a Dog Is a Full-Time Job</title>
  <author id="CMS"></author>
  <character id="PP"></character>
  <character id="Snoopy"></character>
  <character id="Schroeder"></character>
  <character id="Lucy"></character>
</book>
```

Figure 2-3. An alternate approach to the document structure, made possible with RELAX NG

The flexibility just demonstrated isn't only useful for combining complex patterns. It also maintains the simplicity desired by RELAX NG schema designers who don't need or want to learn a long list of design limitations that must be checked when they write and combine their schemas.

This generic concept of patterns is powerful enough to replace the specialized containers of DTDs and W3C XML Schema. RELAX NG has no need for (and no notion of) specially reusable components. Elements, attributes, and types are all embedded in patterns. These patterns are the reusable building blocks of RELAX NG. They can be named, reused, and even redefined at will, combined through operators to group them or to provide alternatives among them.

The benefit of having nonspecialized patterns is increased flexibility. These benefits are similar to those seen in manufacturing: repeatedly using a small number of generic parts to create a unique whole provides more flexibility and a higher number of possible combinations than using more specialized pieces. This works for XML schema languages, too.

A Strong Mathematical Background

This pattern-based approach is both new and old. It's new in the sense that the idea of patterns has been applied to XML in RELAX and now in RELAX NG. It's old because it is the adaptation of techniques and theories developed around regular expressions in the 1960s. The name "RELAX," which stands for REgular LAnguage for XML, suggests this related nature. ("NG" stands for New Generation.) RELAX NG relies on both the strong mathematical theory underlying regular expressions and on additional work done by Murata Makoto, which adapts the mathematical concept of "hedges" to XML.

When I asked Murata Makoto, one of the fathers of RELAX NG, my first questions, he kindly pointed me to the details of his work. I was shocked to see that I had forgotten all the mathematics I had learned at school. I couldn't understand a word of it. Fortunately, I can assure you that you won't need to understand hedges or any of the other math behind RELAX NG. Nevertheless, it's very comforting to know that the schema language you are using has an elegant mathematical background. It ensures that the design will work, and work well. While the math behind it is difficult, the results it produces are surprisingly intuitive.

In keeping with its mathematical foundation, RELAX NG patterns are defined as logical operations performed on sets of XML structures. This gives the specification a formalism that removes any possibility of ambiguous interpretation. The lack of ambiguity is incredibly helpful for ensuring the interoperability of different implementations of RELAX NG.

The strong mathematical background of RELAX NG didn't mean that everything needed to be reinvented for RELAX NG implementers. On the contrary, the *derivative algorithm* used by James Clark in his Jing RELAX NG processor was inspired by work done in 1964 on the *derivation* of regular expressions. It recursively removes the nodes found in the instance documents from the patterns: the document is valid if the patterns left after the last node are all optional.

Murata Makoto has adapted the well-known algorithm of finite state machines to cope with the level of nondeterminism accepted by RELAX NG. He has, for example, used this to develop a RELAX NG validator that is lightweight enough to be used in a mobile phone.

Apart from the fact that it can be implemented with well-known and well-documented algorithms, developers of RELAX NG processors also appreciate the simplicity of its underlying model. This simplicity should also guarantee a strong interoperability between implementations, unlike with some more complex schema languages.

Patterns, and Only Patterns

In science, strong theories tend to be simple, yet have almost infinite potential for complexity in application. RELAX NG is, because of its simplicity, one of those theories that is easy to explain, easy to implement, and generic and flexible enough to meet the most stringent requirements.

I'll present the RELAX NG patterns throughout this book, but I'd like to make a brief introduction here. In RELAX NG, there are three basic patterns that match the three types of XML nodes:

- Text nodes
- Elements
- Attributes

These basic patterns can be combined into ordered or nonordered groups and used in choices defining alternatives among several patterns. The cardinality of a pattern (i.e., the number of times it can appear in an instance document) can also be controlled. Text nodes can be also be constrained as data, which can be limited to particular datatypes and possibly be split into list items. Lastly, a whole set of features supports the creation of reusable libraries of patterns. Similar to patterns, *name classes* define sets of elements and attributes that can be used to open a schema and control where elements and attributes with unknown names may be included in the instance documents.

Some of these features have been defined to facilitate the work of writing RELAX NG schemas and go beyond the basic (sometimes called "atomic") patterns. To avoid complicating the basic model with these convenience features, the RELAX NG specification describes a *simplification algorithm*. This algorithm is used internally by RELAX NG processors to transform a full schema into a simpler form with fewer and simpler patterns. This algorithm is presented in Chapter 15.

 RELAX NG doesn't pay attention to XML processing instructions and comments.

CHAPTER 3
First Schema

Throughout the book, we will work with variations of a document that describes a library. For a first project, we will create a map from the document to the RELAX NG constructs that will create your first RELAX NG schema.

Getting Started

Example 3-1 shows the instance document used throughout the book as a foundation for RELAX NG experimentation and development.

Example 3-1. Sample instance document

```
<?xml version="1.0"?>
<library>
  <book id="b0836217462" available="true">
    <isbn>0836217462</isbn>
    <title xml:lang="en">Being a Dog Is a Full-Time Job</title>
    <author id="CMS">
      <name>Charles M Schulz</name>
      <born>1922-11-26</born>
      <died>2000-02-12</died>
    </author>
    <character id="PP">
      <name>Peppermint Patty</name>
      <born>1966-08-22</born>
      <qualification>bold, brash and tomboyish</qualification>
    </character>
    <character id="Snoopy">
      <name>Snoopy</name>
      <born>1950-10-04</born>
      <qualification>extroverted beagle</qualification>
    </character>
    <character id="Schroeder">
      <name>Schroeder</name>
      <born>1951-05-30</born>
      <qualification>brought classical music to the Peanuts strip</qualification>
    </character>
```

Example 3-1. Sample instance document (continued)

```
    <character id="Lucy">
    <name>Lucy</name>
    <born>1952-03-03</born>
    <qualification>bossy, crabby and selfish</qualification>
    </character>
  </book>
</library>
```

First Patterns

In plain English, the document, shown in Example 3-1 can be described as having:

- One library element composed of:
  - One of more book elements having:
    - An id attribute and an available attribute
    - An isbn element composed of text
  - A title element with an xml:lang attribute and a text node
- One or more author elements with:
  - An id attribute
  - A name element
  - An optional born element
  - An optional died element
- Zero or more character elements with:
  - An id attribute
  - A name element
  - An optional born element
  - A qualification element'

The good news—and what makes RELAX NG so easy to learn—is that in its simplest form, RELAX NG is pretty much a way to formalize the previous statements with simple matching rules. Terms described in the plain English description have matching terms in the RELAX NG Schema document that look a lot like XML:

- A "library element" matches <element name="library">...</element>
- An "id attribute" matches <attribute name="id"/>
- "One or more" matches <oneOrMore>...</oneOrMore>
- "Zero or more" matches <zeroOrMore>...</zeroOrMore>
- "Text" matches <text/>
- "Optional" matches <optional>...</optional>

You saw in Chapter 2 that almost every XML structure is a natural pattern for RELAX NG. Further, each RELAX NG element is a pattern; therefore, each RELAX NG pattern matches a structure from the XML document. Let's now spend some time examining each basic pattern.

The text Pattern

This pattern is the simplest; it simply matches a text node. More precisely, it matches zero or more text nodes. As you'll see in Chapter 6, the text pattern may also be used in the definition of mixed content models, elements that may have both child elements and text nodes. For now, though, think of text as matching a text node.

Because attribute values contain text, the text pattern can also match any attribute value. (The W3C XML Infoset doesn't consider attribute values to be nodes, but RELAX NG does.)

The RELAX NG XML expression for text patterns is just:

```
<text/>
```

The attribute Pattern

Not surprisingly, the attribute pattern matches attributes from an XML instance document. The name of the attribute is defined in the name attribute of the attribute pattern. The content of an attribute is defined as a child element of the attribute pattern.

To define the id attribute, you can write:

```
<attribute name="id">
 <text/>
</attribute>
```

In this brief example, you can see how the definitions given earlier apply here. The attribute's name, id, is defined within the name attribute. The content, text, is in a child element.

This example reads as: "an attribute named id with a text value." Since any attribute can have a value, the text pattern is assumed, so writing out <text/> is not required. Thus, the previous definition is strictly equivalent to this shorter one:

```
<attribute name="id"/>
```

The last thing to know about the attribute pattern is that while attribute names are defined by the name attribute or the attribute pattern, it is also possible to define sets of possible names for an attribute. This feature is explained in detail in Chapter 12.

The element Pattern

Just as the `attribute` pattern matches attributes, the `element` pattern matches elements. To define the `name` element, write:

```
<element name="name">
<text/>
</element>
```

Like the `attribute` pattern, it is possible to replace the `name` attribute of the `element` pattern with a set of names. This practice will be explained in detail in Chapter 12.

Unlike attributes, not all elements accept text nodes. For that reason, the `text` pattern isn't implicitly assumed for elements. In fact, there is no implicit content for elements. The content of each element must be explicitly described, even if the description shows that the element is always empty.

Because a text pattern matches zero or more text nodes, the previous definition of the `name` element also matches empty elements such as:

```
<name/>
```

as well as elements such as:

```
<name>Charles M Schulz</name>
```

There are additional ways to restrict text nodes. You'll see in Chapter 7 how to add additional restrictions to text nodes to avoid empty elements if necessary. In Chapter 8, you'll learn how to use the datatypes from W3C XML Schema to add more specific restrictions such as date or number requirements.

Attributes can be added within elements. To define the `title` element, write:

```
<element name="title">
<attribute name="xml:lang"/>
<text/>
</element>
```

You can see that an `xml:lang` attribute has been defined from the XML namespace. I will describe the support of namespaces in Chapter 11, but here you can begin to see how straightforward it is. The description of this attribute is added by inserting `xml:lang` as the name of the attribute. Any `xml` prefix has been predeclared to refer to the XML namespace, `http://www.w3.org/XML/1998/namespace`. This means that the previous address doesn't need to be written out. For other namespaces, however, you need to declare the namespace using mechanisms described in Chapter 11.

Note that RELAX NG is clever enough to know that attributes are always located in the start tag of XML elements and that the order in which they are written isn't considered significant. This means that the `attribute` pattern can be located anywhere in the definition of elements. It doesn't make a difference if you write:

```
<element name="title">
<attribute name="xml:lang"/>
```

```
  <text/>
</element>
```

as before or if you switch the order of the attributes like this:

```
<element name="title">
<text/>
<attribute name="xml:lang"/>
</element>
```

In addition to text nodes and attributes, elements can also include child elements. You can define the author element this way:

```
<element name="author">
<attribute name="id"/>
<element name="name">
 <text/>
</element>
<element name="born">
 <text/>
</element>
<element name="died">
 <text/>
</element>
</element>
```

That's not exactly the right definition, since we want the born and died elements to be optional. To make this happen, I need to introduce a new pattern: the optional pattern.

The optional Pattern

The optional pattern makes its content just that, optional; the element doesn't have to be there. To specify that the born and died elements are optional, write:

```
<optional>
 <element name="born">
  <text/>
 </element>
</optional>
<optional>
 <element name="died">
  <text/>
 </element>
</optional>
```

Note that the markup and meaning are different from:

```
<optional>
 <element name="born">
  <text/>
 </element>
 <element name="died">
  <text/>
 </element>
</optional>
```

And also different from:

```
<optional>
 <element name="born">
  <text/>
 </element>
 <optional>
  <element name="died">
   <text/>
  </element>
 </optional>
</optional>
```

In the first case, each element is embedded in its own optional pattern. The two elements are thus independently optional. I can include one, both, or none of them in valid instance documents.

In the second case, both elements are embedded in the same optional pattern. Thus I can include either none or both in instance documents.

In the third case, the first optional pattern includes the born element and an optional died element. Both or none of them can be in an instance document, but now there are more possibilities: the born element can be there alone, or the born element can be there with the died element, but the died element can't be there without the born element because of the way the elements are nested.

None of these combinations is "right" or "wrong"; they are just different pattern combinations that allow different element combinations in the instance document. What's nice about RELAX NG is that there are so few restrictions that almost any combination is allowed. Indeed, there are a *few* restrictions, but you don't need to think about them until they're covered in Chapter 15.

The oneOrMore Pattern

The oneOrMore pattern specifies, as you might have guessed, that its content may appear one or more times. oneOrMore specifies that a book must have one or more authors:

```
<oneOrMore>
 <element name="author">
  <attribute name="id"/>
  <element name="name">
   <text/>
  </element>
  <element name="born">
   <text/>
  </element>
  <optional>
   <element name="died">
    <text/>
   </element>
```

```
    </optional>
   </element>
</oneOrMore>
```

The zeroOrMore Pattern

The last pattern needed in our example is zeroOrMore. You'll have figured out that it specifies its content to appear zero or more times. This example shows the character elements:

```
<zeroOrMore>
 <element name="character">
  <attribute name="id"/>
  <element name="name">
   <text/>
  </element>
  <optional>
   <element name="born">
    <text/>
   </element>
  </optional>
  <element name="qualification">
   <text/>
  </element>
 </element>
</zeroOrMore>
```

Complete Schema

You now have all the patterns needed to write a full schema that expresses what we've discussed about this example:

```
<?xml version = '1.0' encoding = 'utf-8' ?>
<element xmlns="http://relaxng.org/ns/structure/1.0" name="library">
 <oneOrMore>
  <element name="book">
   <attribute name="id"/>
   <attribute name="available"/>
   <element name="isbn">
    <text/>
   </element>
   <element name="title">
    <attribute name="xml:lang"/>
    <text/>
   </element>
   <oneOrMore>
    <element name="author">
     <attribute name="id"/>
     <element name="name">
      <text/>
     </element>
     <optional>
```

```
     <element name="born">
      <text/>
     </element>
    </optional>
    <optional>
     <element name="died">
      <text/>
     </element>
    </optional>
   </element>
  </oneOrMore>
  <zeroOrMore>
   <element name="character">
    <attribute name="id"/>
    <element name="name">
     <text/>
    </element>
    <optional>
     <element name="born">
      <text/>
     </element>
    </optional>
    <element name="qualification">
     <text/>
    </element>
   </element>
  </zeroOrMore>
  </element>
 </oneOrMore>
</element>
```

Constraining Number of Occurrences

RELAX NG directly supports four kinds of occurrence constraints on nodes: they may appear as exactly once (the default), optional, zero or more, or one or more. These are the most common cases in document design. If applications need a finer level of control, that can be achieved by using or combining these four basic occurrence constraints. If, for instance, you need to define that each book's description should have between two and six character elements, you can write the definition as two mandatory characters followed by four optional ones:

```
<!-- 1 -->
<element name="character">
 <attribute name="id"/>
 <element name="name">
  <text/>
 </element>
 <optional>
  <element name="born">
   <text/>
  </element>
 </optional>
```

```
  <element name="qualification">
   <text/>
  </element>
 </element>
 <!-- 2 -->
 <element name="character">
  .../...
 </element>
 <!-- 3 -->
 <optional>
  <element name="character">
  .../...
   </element>
  </element>
 </optional>
 <!-- 4 -->
 <optional>
  <element name="character">
  .../...
  </element>
 </optional>
 <!-- 5 -->
 <optional>
  <element name="character">
  .../...
  </element>
 </optional>
 <!-- 6 -->
 <optional>
  <element name="character">
  .../...
  </element>
 </optional>
```

This is certainly verbose, but in later chapters, you will see how to define and reuse patterns to reduce verbosity.

 W3C XML Schema offers much more control over how many times an element may appear, but this degree of control creates a number of processing complexities. While RELAX NG's approach may, in this respect, seem less powerful, it compensates by imposing far fewer costs.

Creating "Russian Doll" Schemas

Figure 3-1 shows the schema and the instance document side by side. Even though information has been added to the schema that describes the content of the text nodes and the number of their occurrences, the schema keeps the same hierarchical structure as the instance document.

```
- <element name="library">
  - <oneOrMore>
    - <element name="book">
        <attribute name="id"/>
        <attribute name="available"/>
      + <element name="isbn"></element>
      - <element name="title">
          <attribute name="xml:lang"/>
          <text/>
        </element>
      - <oneOrMore>
        - <element name="author">
            <attribute name="id"/>
          + <element name="name"></element>
          - <optional>
            + <element name="born"></element>
            </optional>
          - <optional>
            + <element name="died"></element>
            </optional>
          </element>
        </oneOrMore>
      - <zeroOrMore>
        - <element name="character">
            <attribute name="id"/>
          + <element name="name"></element>
          - <optional>
            + <element name="born"></element>
            </optional>
          + <element name="qualification"></element>
          </element>
        </zeroOrMore>
      </element>
    </oneOrMore>
  </element>

- <library>
  - <book id="b0836217462" available="true">
      <isbn>0836217462</isbn>
      <title xml:lang="en">Being a Dog Is a Full-Time Job</title>
    - <author id="CMS">
        <name>Charles M Schulz</name>
        <born>1922-11-26</born>
        <died>2000-02-12</died>
      </author>
    - <character id="PP">
        <name>Peppermint Patty</name>
        <born>1966-08-22</born>
        <qualification>bold, brash and tomboyish</qualification>
      </character>
    + <character id="Snoopy"></character>
    + <character id="Schroeder"></character>
    + <character id="Lucy"></character>
    </book>
  </library>
```

Figure 3-1. Comparing the Russian doll schema structure with that of the instance document

A schema in which different definitions are embedded in each other, like this one, in which the definition of the library element physically contains the definition of the author element that physically contains the definition of the name element—is often called a *Russian doll schema* after the nested matruschka dolls. In Chapter 5, you'll see how Russian doll schemas can be broken into independent patterns and then combined to reproduce the structure of the instance document. First, we'll examine the equivalent compact syntax for RELAX NG in the next chapter.

CHAPTER 4
Introducing the Compact Syntax

Although the schema shown in Chapter 3 is simple, its XML representation is rather verbose. This is neither surprising nor uncommon for XML vocabularies. In fact it conforms to the basic principles of XML; the W3C Recommendation's design goals state that "XML documents should be human-legible and reasonably clear" and that "terseness in XML markup is of minimal importance." Our schema is a good example of a "human-legible and reasonably clear" document that's definitely not terse!

The principal goal of RELAX NG's XML syntax is to provide a *serialization* of RELAX NG schemas that can be processed by computers using standard XML toolkits. To make it easier for people to read and write RELAX NG schemas, however, James Clark introduced a second syntax that is strictly equivalent to the XML syntax, a more concise *compact syntax*.*

RELAX NG processors can support this compact syntax, but they aren't required to do so. If a RELAX NG processor doesn't support the compact syntax, you can translate the XML syntax to and from the compact syntax using existing translators. Because these two forms are strictly equivalent, there's no loss of information during translation. Even comments and annotations (presented in Chapter 13) are preserved in the process.

 Syntactical details of XML, such as entity references or processing instructions, are lost when the XML syntax is translated into the compact syntax, but this is a limitation of the XML processing architecture rather than a limitation of RELAX NG itself.

You'll see that the compact syntax is built on a mix of concepts borrowed from the definition of structures in programming languages, notations from XML DTDs, and RELAX NG patterns. Element and attribute patterns look like Java declarations, with

---

* The compact syntax has been published as an official OASIS RELAX NG committee specification but has not yet been submitted to ISO.

their curly brackets preceded by a reserved word, element or attribute, and their RELAX NG pattern name. Optionally, one or more, and zero or more elements or attributes are represented by DTD qualifier suffixes (? for optional, + for one or more, and * for zero or more).

The compact syntax is easy to use, especially (but not only) if you've ever worked with DTDs. You'll find the syntax intuitive, simple, and familiar before the end of this book. In this chapter, we'll explore the parts of the compact syntax that map to the RELAX NG patterns already discussed in Chapter 3. Later chapters introduce new components for the compact syntax along with their more verbose XML equivalents.

First Compact Patterns

Let's explore how the patterns described in the previous chapter translate into the compact syntax.

The text Pattern

text is the simplest pattern in the XML syntax and is the simplest in the compact syntax as well. The text pattern is just:

```
text
```

In this definition, the word text identifies the text pattern.

Of course, because both syntaxes are equivalent, all that's been said about text in RELAX NG's XML syntax also applies to text in the compact syntax.

The attribute Pattern

For the compact syntax, the attribute pattern borrows Java's curly brackets:

```
attribute id { text }
```

In this definition, the first word, attribute, identifies the attribute pattern; the second one, id, is the name of the attribute. The curly brackets, {...}, delimit the definition of the content of the attribute.

Because empty curly brackets ({}) look weird and might imply empty attributes rather than attributes containing a text value, the convention of the XML syntax that makes a text pattern the implicit content for attributes is abandoned in the compact syntax. The content of attributes must be explicitly defined when you're using the compact syntax. In other words, in the compact system, the following:

```
<attribute name="id"/>
```

translates into:

```
attribute id { text }
```

while this:

```
attribute id { }
```

translates into a syntax error.

The compact syntax is position-sensitive, and words such as text and attribute are reserved words only when they appear in the first position. This is very convenient when you need to define attributes (or elements) that have names that are the same as reserved words. For instance, you can define attributes named text or even attribute without any precaution such as:

```
attribute text { text }
attribute attribute { text }
```

Because the compact syntax is position-sensitive, it isn't confused when reserved words are used as attribute names. This is also true for the element pattern which you'll see in the next section.

Element

The simplest definition of the name element is:

```
element name { text }
```

To add an attribute to an element, you need a delimiter between the different pieces of content. You'll see more use of delimiters and their meanings in Chapter 6, but for now, let's use a comma as delimiter between content. This has the same effect as with XML syntax:

```
element title { attribute xml:lang { text }, text }
```

Whitespace (i.e., spaces, tabulations, line feeds, and carriage returns) isn't significant for the compact syntax. The previous bit of code could also have been written:

```
element title {attribute xml:lang{ text }, text}
```

Many people tend to prefer to split up their code with whitespace so that there is only one definition per line. This technique, with each line helping to guide a reader through the structure, is more human-readable, but a RELAX NG processor won't have any problems understanding the content. It treats both as equivalent.

The author element can be defined using more of the same components:

```
element author { attribute id { text }, element name { text }, element born
    { text }, element died { text } }
```

Again, all that I've said about the properties of the element pattern in the XML syntax is true for the compact syntax: these are just two equivalent syntaxes for the same pattern.

The optional Pattern

The optional pattern is formalized as a trailing ? added after a definition, as is true in DTDs as well. For example, to define the attribute id as optional, you'd write:

```
attribute id { text }?
```

Note that the qualifier ? must be added after the definition of the pattern but before the delimiter. If you used this qualifier in the larger definition of the author element, it'd therefore look like this:

```
element author { attribute id { text }, element name { text }, element born
    { text }?, element died { text }? }
```

In Chapter 3, I mentioned that other combinations of optional and required elements can be described using the optional pattern as a container. In the compact syntax, the optional pattern is represented as a qualifier rather than a container, so you need a container if you wish to create the same combinations. The container is a a set of parentheses (). The effect of parentheses depends on the optional qualifier following them. Parentheses without a qualifier are effectively transparent; they do nothing. The definition of author can be written as:

```
element author {( attribute id { text }, element name { text }, element born
    { text }?, element died { text }? )}
```

or:

```
element author { (attribute id { text }), (element name { text }),
    (element born { text })?, (element died { text }?) }
```

without changing its meaning. Parentheses are more useful (and are actually required) to write the combinations mentioned in Chapter 3. Combinations such as:

```
<optional> <element name="born"> <text/> </element>
    <element name="died"> <text/> </element> </optional>
```

translate into:

```
(element born { text }, element died { text })?
```

The following:

```
<optional> <element name="born"> <text/>
    </element> <optional> <element name="died"> <text/> </element>
    </optional> </optional>
```

translates into:

```
(element born { text }, element died { text }? )?
```

The oneOrMore Pattern

The oneOrMore pattern is also a qualifier and, in the DTD tradition, is a plus sign (+):

```
element author { attribute id { text }, element name { text }, element born
    { text }?, element died { text }? }+
```

The zeroOrMore Pattern

Last but not least, the zeroOrMore pattern is the asterisk (*) qualifier:

```
element character { attribute id { text }, element name { text }, element born
    { text }?, element qualification { text } }*
```

Full Schema

Now we have all the components needed to convert the full RELAX NG schema from Chapter 3 into its compact syntax form; it's shown in Example 4-1.

Example 4-1. Compact syntax of full RELAX NG schema

```
element library {
  element book {
    attribute id { text },
    attribute available { text },
    element isbn { text },
    element title {
      attribute xml:lang { text },
      text
    },
    element author {
      attribute id { text },
      element name { text },
      element born { text }?,
      element died { text }?
    }+,
    element character {
      attribute id { text },
      element name { text },
      element born { text }?,
      element qualification { text }
    }*
  }+
}
```

In the following chapters, I give both the XML and the compact syntax for each example. You'll have plenty of opportunities to get familiar with both.

 Don't get confused by the similarities in name between the *simple form* of a RELAX NG schema, described in Chapter 15, and the *compact syntax*. These two notions work at different levels: the simple form is the result of simplifications performed internally by RELAX NG processors on the data model of the schema; the compact syntax is a different way to represent or serialize a full RELAX NG document. The data models that result from the parsing of a full RELAX NG schema are thus the same whether the schema is written using the XML or the compact syntax and are simplified into the same simple schema.

XML or Compact?

Figure 4-1 presents both syntaxes side by side. There are two things you'll immediately notice. The compact syntax is much more, well, compact. The XML syntax is, just as you'd expect, XML. It works well with generic XML tools (here a web browser), while the compact syntax isn't XML and must be used with other tools (here the text editor *vim* with a plug-in that highlights RELAX NG's compact syntax).

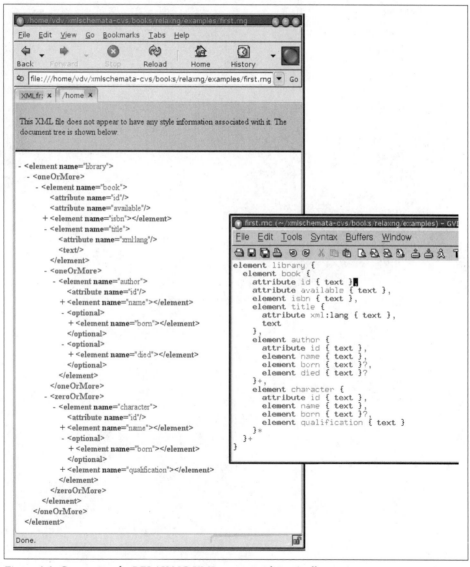

Figure 4-1. Comparing the RELAX NG XML syntax with its smaller compact syntax counterpart

These two statements summarize why both syntaxes are needed. The compact syntax is nice to work with, and you'll probably find it more pleasant to use to edit your schemas and to document your vocabularies. On the other hand, the XML syntax is wonderful if you want to generate RELAX NG schemas, as in Chapter 14 or to generate anything out of your RELAX NG schemas using the XML tools covered in Chapter 13. The ability to translate from one syntax to the other without information loss guarantees that you can use either while having access to both.

CHAPTER 5

Flattening the First Schema

If you look at the structure of the Russian doll–style schema, you'll see that it follows the structure of the instance document it applies to, as shown in Figure 3-1. Writing the first schema has pretty much been limited to inserting text, element, or attribute elements into the schema each time a text node, element, or attribute was encountered in the instance document. This method of creating schemas can be seen as a serialization of the XML infoset (i.e., of the structure available in the document) and could, therefore, be easily automated.

Automated serialization is the principle behind Examplotron, a program described in Chapter 14.

There are a couple of drawbacks to modeling documents with the Russian doll-style schemas, however. First, they aren't modular and therefore become difficult to read and maintain when documents are large or complex. Second, they can't represent recursive (self-referencing) models. (Lists that may themselves contain lists are a common case of this model.)

The lack of modularity can be seen in a document as simple as the first schema, shown in Example 3-1. There's a name element that uses the same model within both the character and author elements.

Figure 5-1 shows how, in the first schema, you need to give the definition of what name means in each context:

You might think that the extra text won't make a difference, but that's not completely true. The additional verbosity here is innocuous because the definition of the name element is simple, and thus not verbose. The principle is the same if the definition is complex, however. It will require redundancy. This redundancy makes maintenance of the schema more error-prone. If I need to update the definition of the name element, I'll need to update it as many times at it appears, but I'll give myself more

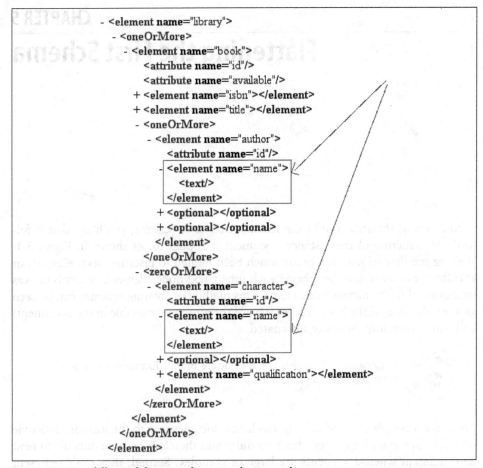

```
- <element name="library">
  - <oneOrMore>
    - <element name="book">
        <attribute name="id"/>
        <attribute name="available"/>
      + <element name="isbn"></element>
      + <element name="title"></element>
      - <oneOrMore>
        - <element name="author">
            <attribute name="id"/>
          - <element name="name">
              <text/>
            </element>
          + <optional></optional>
          + <optional></optional>
          </element>
        </oneOrMore>
        - <zeroOrMore>
          - <element name="character">
              <attribute name="id"/>
            - <element name="name">
                <text/>
              </element>
            + <optional></optional>
            + <element name="qualification"></element>
            </element>
          </zeroOrMore>
        </element>
      </oneOrMore>
    </element>
```

Figure 5-1. Two different definitions of name in the same schema

room for mistakes. Common sense applies the same rules to XML schema languages as to any programming language. Limiting repetitive work makes developers happy!

Another rule borrowed from programming languages concerns recursive models. Recursive models, models that reference themselves, are those like XHTM in which, for example, div elements can be embedded within other div elements without any restriction in the number of levels of embedding. You can just copy the definition of the div element again and again, but it's both inefficient and limiting. We need a way to define and reference the content model of the div element recursively. In the course of this chapter, we'll examine cases of both modularity and recursive models.

Defining Named Patterns

RELAX NG uses *named patterns* to address both modularity and recursion. Named patterns are reusable patterns that can be referenced by their name.

In the XML syntax, named patterns are defined using `define` elements. To define named patterns that contain the `title` element, write:

```
<define name="title-element">
 <element name="title">
  <text/>
 </element>
</define>
```

The compact syntax uses a construction similar to a programming language format. The same definition would be written in the compact syntax as:

```
title-element = element title {text}
```

You're not limited to embedding a single element or attribute definition in a named pattern. Note that the group shown in Figure 5-2, an `id` attribute, a `name` element, and an optional `born` element are present in the same order and with the same definition in both the author and the character element.

```
element library {
  element book {
    attribute id { text },
    attribute available { text },
    element isbn { text },
    element title {
      attribute xml:lang { text },
      text
    },
    element author {
      attribute id { text },
      element name { text },
      element born { text }?,
      element died { text }?
    }+,
    element character {
      attribute id { text },
      element name { text },
      element born { text }?,
      element qualification { text }
    }*
  }+
}
```

Figure 5-2. Groups of identical attributes on different element types

To define a named pattern for this group, write:

```
<define name="common-content">
 <attribute name="id"/>
 <element name="name">
```

```
  <text/>
 </element>
 <optional>
  <element name="born">
   <text/>
  </element>
 </optional>
</define>
```

or:

```
common-content =
   attribute id { text },
   element name { text },
   element born { text }?
```

Referencing Named Patterns

Defining a named pattern is easy, as shown the earlier example, but referencing a named pattern rather than defining it again is even simpler.

Using the XML syntax, references to named patterns defined elsewhere in the schema are done using a ref element. For instance, to define the author element, use a reference to the name-element pattern:

```
<element name="author">
 <attribute name="id"/>
 <ref name="name-element"/>
 <optional>
  <element name="born">
   <text/>
   </element>
 </optional>
 <optional>
  <element name="died">
   <text/>
   </element>
 </optional>
</element>
```

To reference a named pattern in the compact syntax, just use its name directly:

```
element author {
   attribute id { text },
   name-element,
   element born { text }?,
   element died { text }?
}
```

The same approach can reference the common-content named pattern:

```
<element name="author">
 <ref name="common-content"/>
 <optional>
  <element name="died">
```

```
      <text/>
     </element>
    </optional>
   </element>
```

or:

```
   element author {
     common-content,
     element died { text }?
   }
```

The grammar and start Elements

In the Russian doll-style, the definition of the root element (in this case, the library element) is used as a container for the whole schema. When you define named patterns, you need a container to embed both the named pattern definitions and the definition of the root element of the named patterns. This definition of the root element, as well as definitions of all the patterns that may be used within it, is what RELAX NG calls a *grammar*. It uses the grammar element. When you use a grammar element, RELAX NG requires you to explicitly declare the root element or elements, using a start element. An incomplete skeleton of the structure of the schema defining a pattern name-element would thus be:

```
   <grammar xmlns="http://relaxng.org/ns/structure/1.0">
    <start>
     <element name="library">
      .../...
     </element>
    </start>
    <define name="name-element">
     .../...
    </define>
   </grammar>
```

or, using the compact syntax:

```
   grammar {
    name-element = .../...
    start =
     element library {
     .../...
    }
   }
```

In the compact syntax, the grammar pattern is implicit. You can use it, but it isn't required.

Assembling the Parts

You have seen the different bits and pieces needed to define and reference patterns. It's time to put them all together and create a complete schema. The first exercise is to define a DTD-like RELAX NG schema that defines each element and its own named pattern.

The full schema might look like this:

```xml
<?xml version="1.0" encoding="UTF-8"?>
<grammar xmlns="http://relaxng.org/ns/structure/1.0">

 <start>
  <ref name="element-library"/>
 </start>

 <define name="element-library">
  <element name="library">
   <oneOrMore>
    <ref name="element-book"/>
   </oneOrMore>
  </element>
 </define>

 <define name="element-book">
  <element name="book">
   <attribute name="id"/>
   <attribute name="available"/>
   <ref name="element-isbn"/>
   <ref name="element-title"/>
   <oneOrMore>
    <ref name="element-author"/>
   </oneOrMore>
   <zeroOrMore>
    <ref name="element-character"/>
   </zeroOrMore>
  </element>
 </define>

 <define name="element-isbn">
  <element name="isbn">
   <text/>
  </element>
 </define>

 <define name="element-title">
  <element name="title">
   <attribute name="xml:lang"/>
   <text/>
  </element>
 </define>
```

```
<define name="element-author">
 <element name="author">
  <attribute name="id"/>
  <ref name="element-name"/>
  <optional>
   <ref name="element-born"/>
  </optional>
  <optional>
   <ref name="element-died"/>
  </optional>
 </element>
</define>

<define name="element-name">
 <element name="name">
  <text/>
 </element>
</define>

<define name="element-born">
 <element name="born">
  <text/>
 </element>
</define>
<define name="element-died">
 <element name="died">
  <text/>
 </element>
</define>
<define name="element-character">
 <element name="character">
  <attribute name="id"/>
  <ref name="element-name"/>
  <optional>
   <ref name="element-born"/>
  </optional>
  <ref name="element-qualification"/>
 </element>
</define>
<define name="element-qualification">
 <element name="qualification">
  <text/>
 </element>
</define>
</grammar>
```

Or:

```
grammar{
start = element-library

element-library = element library {element-book +}
```

```
element-book = element book {
    attribute id { text },
    attribute available { text },
    element-isbn,
    element-title,
    element-author+,
    element-character*
    }

element-isbn = element isbn { text }

element-title = element title {
    attribute xml:lang { text },
    text
    }

element-author = element author {
    attribute id { text },
    element-name,
    element-born?,
    element-died?
    }

element-name = element name { text }

element-born = element born { text }

element-died = element died { text }

element-character = element character {
    attribute id { text },
    element-name,
    element-born?,
    element-qualification
    }

element-qualification = element qualification { text }

}
```

The DTD style just shown is pretty common, and finding the definition of each element in the schema is easy, which is a great advantage. Another popular style, the content-oriented style, defines the content of each element as a separate pattern:

```
<?xml version="1.0" encoding="UTF-8"?>
<grammar xmlns="http://relaxng.org/ns/structure/1.0">

 <start>
 <element name="library">
   <ref name="library-content"/>
  </element>
  </start>
```

```
<define name="library-content">
 <oneOrMore>
  <element name="book">
   <ref name="book-content"/>
  </element>
 </oneOrMore>
</define>

<define name="book-content">
 <attribute name="id"/>
 <attribute name="available"/>
 <element name="isbn">
  <ref name="isbn-content"/>
 </element>
 <element name="title">
  <ref name="title-content"/>
 </element>
 <oneOrMore>
  <element name="author">
   <ref name="author-content"/>
  </element>
 </oneOrMore>
 <zeroOrMore>
  <element name="character">
   <ref name="character-content"/>
  </element>
 </zeroOrMore>
</define>

<define name="isbn-content">
 <text/>
</define>

<define name="name-content">
 <text/>
</define>

<define name="born-content">
 <text/>
</define>

<define name="died-content">
 <text/>
</define>

<define name="qualification-content">
 <text/>
</define>

<define name="title-content">
 <attribute name="xml:lang"/>
 <text/>
</define>
```

```
<define name="author-content">
 <attribute name="id"/>
 <element name="name">
  <ref name="name-content"/>
 </element>
 <optional>
  <element name="born">
   <ref name="born-content"/>
  </element>
 </optional>
 <optional>
  <element name="died">
   <ref name="died-content"/>
  </element>
 </optional>
</define>

<define name="character-content">
 <attribute name="id"/>
 <element name="name">
  <ref name="name-content"/>
 </element>
 <optional>
  <element name="born">
   <ref name="born-content"/>
  </element>
 </optional>
 <element name="qualification">
  <ref name="qualification-content"/>
 </element>
</define>

</grammar>
```

Or:

```
grammar {

start = element library {library-content}

library-content =
  element book { book-content } +

book-content =
    attribute id { text },
    attribute available { text },
    element isbn { isbn-content },
    element title { title-content },
    element author { author-content }+,
    element character { character-content }*

 isbn-content = text

 name-content = text
```

```
born-content = text

died-content = text

qualification-content = text

title-content =
  attribute xml:lang { text },
  text

author-content =
  attribute id { text },
  element name { name-content },
  element born { born-content }?,
  element died { died-content }?
character-content =
  attribute id { text },
  element name { name-content },
  element born { born-content }?,
  element qualification { qualification-content }

}
```

As shown in Chapter 12, the style of your schema (Russian doll, DTD-like, or content-oriented, as this last schema) has an impact on its extensibility. The last option (content-oriented) is the most extensible.

Now let's revisit the "bizarre patterns" mentioned in Chapter 2 and shown in Figure 5-3.

```
<book id="b0836217462" available="true">
  <isbn>0836217462</isbn>
  <title xml:lang="en">Being a Dog Is a Full-Time Job</title>
  <author id="CMS"></author>
  <character id="PP"></character>
  <character id="Snoopy"></character>
  <character id="Schroeder"></character>
  <character id="Lucy"></character>
</book>
```

Figure 5-3. Bizarre combinations of child content for a group

When you think about it, this case is not so uncommon. When you find it in its original form, it's a muddled mess: there's a first pattern named book-basic with the id attribute and the isbn and title elements, one or more author elements, and an optional character element. There's a second pattern that extends the first one. It's named book-extended and holds the available attribute and zero or more character elements. It's confusing to write, certainly, and difficult to follow. Still, this pattern gives the opportunity to disentangle the web of confusion.

Updating the "DTD-like" flavor of our schema to reflect this instance document is just a matter of splitting up the definition of the book element:

```
<define name="element-book">
<element name="book">
  <ref name="book-basic"/>
  <ref name="book-extended"/>
 </element>
</define>

<define name="book-basic">
 <attribute name="id"/>
 <ref name="element-isbn"/>
 <ref name="element-title"/>
 <oneOrMore>
  <ref name="element-author"/>
 </oneOrMore>
 <optional>
  <ref name="element-character"/>
 </optional>
</define>

<define name="book-extended">
 <attribute name="available"/>
 <zeroOrMore>
  <ref name="element-character"/>
 </zeroOrMore>
</define>
```

Or, in the compact syntax:

```
element-book = element book {
     book-basic,
     book-extended
    }

book-basic =
     attribute id { text },
     element-isbn,
     element-title,
     element-author+,
     element-character?

book-extended =
     attribute available { text },
     element-character*
```

Problems That Never Arise

Some restrictions that add a lot of complexity in other schema languages aren't issues for RELAX NG. You've seen at least two places in this chapter in which restrictions are avoided. The first case appears as the ability to define attributes wherever you want in your patterns. This reduction in rules doesn't make a big difference when you define the content model of elements as straightforward as those in our first schema, but it makes a huge difference when you start to combine patterns as we've done with our bizarre model. Without this removal of restrictions, it would have been impossible to define one attribute in the pattern book-extended and a second one in the pattern book-basic.

The other nonrestriction is that RELAX NG pays no attention to the pattern used to match a node of the instance document when there are several possibilities. Again, in our bizarre pattern, if you have a document with a book having only one author, there is no way to tell if this author matches the optional author element of the pattern book-start or the zero or more author elements of the pattern book-author. This is considered an ambiguity that's intolerable to other schema languages. In this case, RELAX NG holds that even though there is an ambiguity, because there is at least one interpretation of the schema for which the document is valid, the document should be considered valid. You'll learn more about these ambiguities and their consequences in Chapter 16.

Recursive Models

As mentioned earlier, named patterns are the only way to represent recursive models. We don't yet have all the building blocks needed to define a recursive XHTML div element, for example, but let's start with a simpler example. If our library is divided into categories, each having a title, zero or more embedded category elements, and zero or more books, you can write (assuming that named patterns have been defined for the book element):

```
<define name="category">
 <element name="category">
  <element name="title">
   <text/>
  </element>
  <zeroOrMore>
   <ref name="category"/>
  </zeroOrMore>
  <zeroOrMore>
   <ref name="book"/>
  </zeroOrMore>
 </element>
</define>
```

or:

```
category = element category{
 element title{text},
 category *,
 book*
}
```

Note that in this case, the recursive reference to the category named pattern must be optional. Otherwise the document is required to have an infinite depth!

Escaping Named Pattern Identifiers in the Compact Syntax

In the previous chapter, I introduced the compact syntax and noted that any word reserved for use by RELAX NG can be used as an element or attribute name. That's no longer the case for the identifiers of named patterns, because they can appear in the same position as the keywords.

If you want to define a named pattern named "text," "start," or "element," for instance, the identifier of this named pattern can be confused with the keyword. In this case you need to escape being confused with the identifier by a leading back-slash. For instance to define (and by extension to make a reference) to a named pattern named "start," write:

```
grammar{

start = \start

\start = element start { text }

}
```

In the XML syntax, this translates into:

```
<?xml version="1.0" encoding="UTF-8"?>
<grammar xmlns="http://relaxng.org/ns/structure/1.0">
  <start>
    <ref name="start"/>
  </start>
  <define name="start">
    <element name="start">
      <text/>
    </element>
  </define>
</grammar>
```

CHAPTER 6

More Complex Patterns

So far, I've described only sequentially ordered groups of elements and text nodes. Now you'll see another class of patterns that describe unordered sequences and choices. Although this class of patterns has no special name in the RELAX NG specification, I refer to them as *compositors* in this book in analogy to the compositors that are defined by W3C XML Schema. The W3C's use of the term compositors matches our usage: the name describes patterns composed of less complex patterns, including the basic patterns we've been looking at such as element, attribute, and text.

One of the key differentiations between compositors and simple patterns is that compositors are patterns that don't directly map to any individual element within the schema. I emphasize this distinction because it can be easy to forget when focusing on a schema instead of the instance document.

The group Pattern

Here is the definition of our character element:

```
<element name="character">
  <attribute name="id"/>
  <element name="name">
   <text/>
  </element>
  <element name="born">
   <text/>
  </element>
  <element name="qualification">
   <text/>
  </element>
</element>
```

In this snippet of the schema, I haven't specified how the different nodes constituting the character element must be composed. RELAX NG recognizes that we have used a group compositor. This group compositor is implied in the XML syntax. You can see, in the compact syntax, that it looks like a grouping of words: each component of the compositor is separated by a comma:

```
element character {
    attribute id {text},
    element name {text},
    element born {text},
    element qualification {text}}
```

When using the XML syntax, the group compositor may also be explicitly specified, rather than implied. The previous definition is strictly equivalent to this one:

```
<element name="character">
 <group>
  <attribute name="id"/>
  <element name="name">
   <text/>
  </element>
  <element name="born">
   <text/>
  </element>
  <element name="qualification">
   <text/>
  </element>
 </group>
</element>
```

Because the order of attributes isn't considered significant by the XML 1.0 specification, the meaning of the group compositor is slightly less straightforward than it appears at first. Here's the semantic quirk: the group compositor says, "Check that the patterns included in this compositor appear in the specified order, except for attributes, which are allowed to appear in any order in the start tag."

A last thing to keep in mind about group compositors is that, as with compositors in general, there is no such thing as already grouped elements for the pattern to map to in an instance document. The notion of group is specific to the pattern that belongs only in our schema. (This means that there is no hard border in instance documents to isolate nodes inside a group from nodes outside of the group. You'll see later in the chapter that in certain conditions, nodes matching patterns defined outside of a group can be "inserted" in the group.)

The interleave Pattern

The second compositor examined here, interleave, describes a set of unordered patterns—a set of patterns considered valid when they match the content of the instance documents in any order.

As far as validation is concerned, this behavior is similar to the validation of attributes in a "group" compositor up to the point that the algorithms to validate attributes within groups are the same as the algorithm to validate any node in interleave compositors. Of course, the validation of interleave patterns doesn't mean that the order of elements and text nodes in the instance document aren't reported to the application, only that they are allowed to appear in any order.

To specify that character elements may accept child elements in any order, you just need to replace our group pattern with an interleave pattern:

```
<element name="character">
 <interleave>
  <attribute name="id"/>
  <element name="name">
   <text/>
  </element>
  <element name="born">
   <text/>
  </element>
  <element name="qualification">
   <text/>
  </element>
 </interleave>
</element>
```

In the compact syntax, interleave patterns are marked using an ampersand (&) character as a separator instead of a comma, which is the mark of ordered groups:

```
element character {
 attribute id {text}&
 element name {text}&
 element born {text}&
 element qualification {text}}
```

These two equivalent schemas will validate character elements when child elements appear in any order:

```
<character id="PP">
 <name>Peppermint Patty</name>
 <born>1966-08-22</born>
 <qualification>bold, brash and tomboyish</qualification>
</character>
<character id="Snoopy">
 <born>1950-10-04</born>
 <qualification>extroverted beagle</qualification>
 <name>Snoopy</name>
</character>
<character id="Schroeder">
 <qualification>brought classical music to the Peanuts strip</qualification>
 <name>Schroeder</name>
 <born>1951-05-30</born>
</character>
```

Although interleave looks straightforward at this point, you'll see that it has more complicated behavior and restrictions. In the last sections of this chapter, we'll look at some of the complexities. You can skip them if they look overwhelming right now, but please remember to come back and revisit them, especially if your interleave patterns produce unexpected results or error messages!

The choice Pattern

Let's add some flexibility to the name element so we can accept:

```
<name>Lucy</name>
```

and:

```
<name>
 <first>Charles</first>
 <middle>M</middle>
 <last>Schulz</last>
</name>
```

and:

```
<name>
 <first>Peppermint</first>
 <last>Patty</last>
</name>
```

To express this flexibility, use a choice pattern that accepts either a text node or a group of three elements (one of which is optional):

```
<element name="name">
 <choice>
  <text/>
  <group>
   <element name="first"><text/></element>
   <optional>
     <element name="middle"><text/></element>
   </optional>
   <element name="last"><text/></element>
  </group>
 </choice>
</element>
```

The compact syntax uses a pipe, or logical "or" character (|) to denote choices:

```
element name {
 text|(
 element first{text},
 element middle{text}?,
 element last{text}
 )}
```

Note that you have to use parentheses to mark the boundary of the group pattern.

Pattern Compositions

In the preceding example, we combined a choice pattern with a group pattern. This process can be expanded so that there is virtually no restriction or limit on the way compositors can be combined. As an example, let's say we want our character element to allow either one name element or the three elements first-name, middle-name (optional), and last-name in any order, but require that they appear before the born and qualification elements. To do that, write:

```
<element name="character">
 <attribute name="id"/>
 <choice>
  <element name="name"><text/></element>
  <interleave>
   <element name="first-name"><text/></element>
   <optional>
    <element name="middle-name"><text/></element>
   </optional>
   <element name="last-name"><text/></element>
  </interleave>
 </choice>
 <element name="born"><text/></element>
 <element name="qualification"><text/></element>
</element>
```

or, with the compact syntax:

```
element character {
    attribute id { text },
    (element name { text }
    | (element first-name { text }
       & element middle-name { text }?
       & element last-name { text })),
    element born { text },
    element qualification { text }
}
```

Note that two levels of parentheses have been added. In the compact syntax, operators determine the nature of compositors (group, interleave, or choice). Operators can't be mixed within one set of parentheses or curly brackets, so you need to use these parentheses to explicitly mark where each compositor begins and ends.

These schemas validate any of the following (and varied) character elements:

```
<character id="PP">
 <first-name>Peppermint</first-name>
 <last-name>Patty</last-name>
 <born>1966-08-22</born>
 <qualification>bold, brash and tomboyish</qualification>
</character>

<character id="PP2">
 <last-name>Patty</last-name>
```

```
<first-name>Peppermint</first-name>
<born>1966-08-22</born>
<qualification>bold, brash and tomboyish</qualification>
</character>

<character id="Snoopy">
 <name>Snoopy</name>
 <born>1950-10-04</born>
 <qualification>extroverted beagle</qualification>
</character>

<character id="Snoopy2">
 <first-name>Snoopy</first-name>
 <middle-name>the</middle-name>
 <last-name>Dog</last-name>
 <born>1950-10-04</born>
 <qualification>extroverted beagle</qualification>
</character>

<character id="Snoopy3">
 <middle-name>the</middle-name>
 <last-name>Dog</last-name>
 <first-name>Snoopy</first-name>
 <born>1950-10-04</born>
 <qualification>extroverted beagle</qualification>
</character>
```

The flexibility and freedom with which you can combine patterns and the lack of restrictions associated with these combinations sets RELAX NG apart from other XML schema languages.

Order Variation as a Source of Information

Before moving on to text patterns and mixed content, the interleave pattern deserves more attention. As already noted, calling these content models unordered is misleading. Although no order is required by the schema, the nodes will be ordered in instance documents. The order in which they appear in the document can be significant to the applications.

Going back to the example of first and last names: any application managing names will need to know which is a first name and which is a last name. With a little additional effort, they can get the information about whether the first name comes before or after the last name in a XML document. The friendliest of these applications might also want to know whether you prefer to be called by your first or last name first. Do you need to add an additional information item to the schema to carry this information when you could just rely on the order of these elements in the instance document?

In other words, defining content using interleave patterns can be seen as degrading the usefulness of a schema because it looks like the information about the order in which the elements were found will be stripped from the document. That isn't a real problem; XML processors will still present all the order information to your application. In fact, a content model defined with interleave patterns allows more combinations than a content model that uses group patterns. Thus, with its additional combinations, the interleave patterns can let document creators provide additional information that would otherwise disappear into a fixed structure.

The one downside to using interleave patterns is that the freedom with which they can be used is unfortunately specific to RELAX NG. If you need to insure that it will also be possible to model your vocabulary with a more rigid schema language such as W3C XML Schema, you will often have to restrict the usage of interleave patterns in your RELAX NG schemas.

Text and Empty Patterns, Whitespace, and Mixed Content

So far, we have used text patterns only within group patterns. It's important to remember, however, that this pattern doesn't mean simply a text node but rather zero or more text nodes. This statement deserves some exploration.

The reason why text patterns accept zero text nodes is linked to the policy adopted by RELAX NG regarding whitespace. Whitespace processing rules are one of the fuzzier areas in XML. RELAX NG has attempted to find the "least surprising" policy that supports the most common usages. You'll see more whitespace processing when we study datatypes, but for now, let's say that RELAX NG doesn't see any distinction between empty strings; no string at all; strings containing only whitespace before or after an element node; and to a lesser extent, a single text child element containing only whitespace.

For instance, in the following snippet:

```
<foo at1="" at2=" ">
 <bar/>
 <bar></bar>
 <bar>
  <baz/>
  <baz/>
 </bar>
 <bar>
 </bar>
</foo>
```

RELAX NG treats as insignificant the values of at1 and at2, the content of the first and second bar elements, the text between the third bar start tag and the first baz element, the text between the two baz elements, and even the text within the last bar element. RELAX NG's rules state that the content should match either text or empty patterns. Here are two visible consequences for the patterns we've seen so far:

- Because text patterns match any text node, they must match strings that are either empty or that contain only whitespace. Since there is no difference between empty strings and no string, text patterns match zero strings; i.e., they are always optional.

- Because empty patterns match zero strings and because there is no difference between no string and empty strings or strings containing only whitespace, empty patterns also match strings either empty or containing only whitespace.

In other words, the snippet shown here matches both content models in which all the occurrences mentioned are described as text or empty patterns. If you add the rule—already used a lot but not yet explained—that says you don't need to explicitly express empty patterns between elements, the two schemas will both validate this instance document:

```
<element xmlns="http://relaxng.org/ns/structure/1.0" name="foo">
 <attribute name="at1"><text/></attribute>
 <attribute name="at2"><text/></attribute>
 <oneOrMore>
  <element name="bar">
   <choice>
    <text/>
    <oneOrMore>
     <element name="baz"><text/></element>
    </oneOrMore>
   </choice>
  </element>
 </oneOrMore>
</element>
```

or:

```
<element xmlns="http://relaxng.org/ns/structure/1.0" name="foo">
 <attribute name="at1"><empty/></attribute>
 <attribute name="at2"><empty/></attribute>
 <oneOrMore>
  <element name="bar">
   <choice>
    <empty/>
    <oneOrMore>
     <element name="baz"><empty/></element>
    </oneOrMore>
   </choice>
  </element>
 </oneOrMore>
</element>
```

After having seen why text patterns have to be optional, you need to see why it's also useful for them to match multiple instances. When a text pattern is used with a group or choice pattern, it doesn't make any difference because text nodes are

merged when they are contiguous or separated by infoset items not checked by
RELAX NG, such as comments or *processing instructions* (PIs). Within a group or a
choice, there is no difference between a pattern that matches one or one or more text
nodes. The only place it can make a difference is thus within `interleave` compositors, and that's the reason why this specificity has been introduced. Document-oriented applications, including XHTML, TEI, and DocBook, provide numerous
examples of elements that accept text and embedded elements in any order (called
mixed content), and in this case, it makes no sense to limit the number of text nodes.

To introduce a mixed content model, let's extend the `title` element to include zero
or more links using some a elements with `href` attributes:

```
<title xml:lang="en">Being a
<a href="http://dmoz.org/Recreation/Pets/Dogs/">Dog</a>
    Is a Full-Time
 <a href="http://dmoz.org/Business/Employment/Job_Search/">Job</a>
 </title>
```

The content of the new `title` element can be described as an `interleave` pattern that
allows zero or more a elements and zero or more text nodes. The text pattern
matches zero or more text nodes, which will allow us to avoid specifying its cardinality. You can just write:

```
<element name="title">
 <interleave>
  <attribute name="xml:lang"/>
  <zeroOrMore>
   <element name="a">
    <attribute name="href"/>
    <text/>
   </element>
  </zeroOrMore>
  <text/>
 </interleave>
</element>
```

or, using the compact syntax:

```
element title {
 attribute xml:lang {text}&
 element a {attribute href {text}, text}*&
 text
}
```

Because this definition is quite verbose for a common task, RELAX NG has introduced a specific mixed compositor, which has the same meaning as "interleave
including a text pattern." These schemas are strictly equivalent to:

```
<element name="title">
 <mixed>
  <attribute name="xml:lang"/>
  <zeroOrMore>
   <element name="a">
```

```
      <attribute name="href"/>
      <text/>
    </element>
  </zeroOrMore>
 </mixed>
</element>
```

The mixed compositor is marked using a mixed pattern in the compact syntax and can be written as:

```
element title {
 mixed {
  attribute xml:lang {text}&
  element a {attribute href {text}, text} *
 }
}
```

Why Is It Called interleave?

If interleave were only about defining unordered groups, why would it be called interleave and not unorderedGroup or something similar? The interleave pattern has hidden sophistication. It isn't only a definition for unordered groups, it's also a definition for unordered groups that let their child nodes intermix within subgroups. Mixing is allowed even when these groups are ordered groups. I promise this concept is simpler than it looks in this semiformal definition. An example will make it easier to grasp.

That ordered groups can be immersed in an unordered group might be surprising. Let's try a real-world metaphor to illustrate it. Imagine that the elements of a XML document are like a bunch of tourists visiting a museum; you can then define the unordered sets as all the tourists visiting. The ordered groups of tourists, who are within the unordered set, are following guides. There are many ways to immerse ordered groups within the unordered set of museum visitors and to mix ordered groups together. The interleave pattern describes one specific way to effect this immersion: when the museum is an interleave pattern, the ordered groups preserve only the relative order of their members. This not only allows individual tourists to insert themselves within a group, but also lets two groups interleave their members.

To return to XML and RELAX NG, let's examine the following schema:

```
<element xmlns="http://relaxng.org/ns/structure/1.0" name="museum">
 <interleave>
  <element name="individual"><empty/></element>
  <group>
   <element name="group-member1"><empty/></element>
   <element name="group-member2"><empty/></element>
  </group>
 </interleave>
</element>
```

or, using the compact syntax:

```
element museum {
 element individual {empty} &
 (
   element group-member1 {empty},
   element group-member2 {empty}
 )
}
```

An `individual` represents an individual visiting the museum, while elements group-member1 and group-member2 represent visitors in a group. Because `interleave` patterns are not ordered groups, the following instance documents are valid:

```
<museum>
 <individual/>
 <group-member1/>
 <group-member2/>
</museum>
```

and:

```
<museum>
 <group-member1/>
 <group-member2/>
 <individual/>
</museum>
```

These documents are instances in which the element `individual`, which matches the first pattern in the `interleave` pattern (i.e., the `element` pattern), is either before or after the elements group-member1 and group-member2, which match the group pattern—the second subpattern of the `interleave` pattern. Because the `interleave` pattern allows that the nodes matching its subpattern to be mixed, the schema also validates this third combination:

```
<museum>
 <group-member1/>
 <individual/>
 <group-member2/>
</museum>
```

On the other hand, because of how the elements are ordered in the group declaration of the schema, all the combinations in which the relative order between group members aren't respected are invalid. Here's an example of such an invalid combination:

```
<museum>
 <group-member2/>
 <individual/>
 <group-member1/>
</museum>
```

The `interleave` pattern can also be used to mix two groups of patterns. In this case, the relative order of the element of each group is maintained, but the elements of different groups may appear in any order and the groups may be interleaved. For an example, let's look at the following schema:

```
<element xmlns="http://relaxng.org/ns/structure/1.0" name="museum">
 <interleave>
  <group>
   <element name="group1.member1"><empty/></element>
   <element name="group1.member2"><empty/></element>
  </group>
  <group>
   <element name="group2.member1"><empty/></element>
   <element name="group2.member2"><empty/></element>
  </group>
 </interleave>
</element>
```

or, using the compact syntax:

```
element museum{
 (
  element group1.member1 {empty},
  element group1.member2 {empty}
 ) & (
  element group2.member1 {empty},
  element group2.member2 {empty}
 )
}
```

This schema validates documents such as:

```
<museum>
 <group1.member1/>
 <group1.member2/>
 <group2.member1/>
 <group2.member2/>
</museum>
```

and:

```
<museum>
 <group2.member1/>
 <group2.member2/>
 <group1.member1/>
 <group1.member2/>
</museum>
```

where the groups are kept separated, but also:

```
<museum>
 <group1.member1/>
 <group2.member1/>
 <group2.member2/>
 <group1.member2/>
</museum>
```

or:

```
<museum>
 <group1.member1/>
 <group2.member1/>
 <group1.member2/>
 <group2.member2/>
</museum>
```

in which the groups are interleaved.

Mixed Content Models with Order

You have seen that a pattern interleaved with a group is allowed to appear anywhere between the patterns of the group. This feature may be used with a text pattern to define ordered mixed-content models, in which the text nodes may appear anywhere but the order of the elements is fixed. These content models are quite unusual in XML. A use case might be a data-oriented vocabulary such as our library, in which optional text can be inserted to provide more user-friendly documentation:

```
<character id="Lucy">
 <name>Lucy</name> made her first apparition in a Peanuts strip on
 <born>1952-03-03</born>, and the least we can say about her is that she is
 <qualification>bossy, crabby and selfish</qualification>.
</character>
```

If you want to fix the order of the child elements, just embed a group pattern inside a mixed pattern:

```
<!--This schema is INVALID-->
<element name="character">
  <mixed>
   <attribute name="id"/>
   <group>
     <element name="name">
       <text/>
     </element>
     <element name="born">
       <text/>
     </element>
     <element name="qualification">
       <text/>
     </element>
    </group>
   </mixed>
  </element>
```

Per the definition of the mixed pattern, this is equivalent to:

```
#This schema is invalid
<element name="character">
 <interleave>
  <attribute name="id"/>
```

```
  <text/>
  <group>
   <element name="name">
     <text/>
   </element>
   <element name="born">
     <text/>
   </element>
   <element name="qualification">
    <text/>
   </element>
  </group>
 </interleave>
</element>
```

The text pattern matches text nodes before, after, or between the elements of the group, but as you've seen with the previous museum example, the order of the elements in the group will still be enforced. The compact syntax uses the mixed pattern with commas between subpatterns to express this:

```
element character {
    mixed {
      attribute id {text},
      element name {text},
      element born {text},
      element qualification {text}
    }
}
```

You have already seen that the compact syntax mixed pattern can be employed using ampersands and commas to define unordered and ordered mixed patterns. An "or" (|) can also interleave text nodes in choice patterns:

```
element foo{
  mixed {
   (
    element in1.1 {empty},
    element in1.2 {empty}
   ) | (
    element in2.1 {empty}&
    element in2.2 {empty}
   )
  }
}
```

This mixed pattern is interleaving text nodes into either a group (denoted by a comma) of in1.1 and in1.2 elements or (as shown by the pipe character) an interleave pattern (denoted by an ampersand) of elements in2.1 and in2.2. In the first case, because of the semantics of group patterns, the order between elements is fixed, while in the second case, the order doesn't matter. Mixed-choice contents don't constitute new content models. They are equivalent to choices of mixed-content models, and so, you can rewrite this schema as:

```
element foo{
  (
    mixed{
      element in1.1 {empty},
      element in1.2 {empty}
    }
  ) | (
    mixed{
      element in2.1 {empty}&
      element in2.2 {empty}
    }
  )
  }
}
```

A Restriction Related to interleave

You'll see the restrictions of RELAX NG in Chapter 15, but I need to mention the principal restriction related to the interleave compositor, as it might affect you at some point if you combine mixed-content models.

Let's extend our title element to allow not only links (a elements) but also bold characters marked by a b element:

```
<title xml:lang="en">Being a
 <a href="http://dmoz.org/Recreation/Pets/Dogs/">Dog</a>
    Is a <b>Full-Time</b>
 <a href="http://dmoz.org/Business/Employment/Job_Search/">Job</a>
</title>
```

Because text can appear before the a elements, between a and b, and after the b element, you might be tempted to write the following schemas:

```
<element name="title">
 <interleave>
  <attribute name="xml:lang"/>
  <text/>
  <zeroOrMore>
    <element name="a">
      <attribute name="href"/>
      <text/>
    </element>
  </zeroOrMore>
  <text/>
  <zeroOrMore>
    <element name="b">
      <text/>
    </element>
  </zeroOrMore>
  <text/>
 </interleave>
</element>
```

or:

```
element title {
  attribute xml:lang {text}
  & text
  & element a {attribute href {text}, text} *
  & text
  & element b {text} *
  & text
}
```

Running the Jing validator against this schema raises the following error:

```
Error at URL "file:/home/vdv/xmlschemata-cvs/books/relaxng/examples/RngMorePatterns/
interleave-restriction2.rnc",
line number 1, column number 2: both operands of "interleave" contain "text"
```

This error results because there can be only one text pattern in each interleave pattern. You have seen that text patterns match zero or more text nodes, and in this case, the remedy is simple enough: the schema must be rewritten as:

```
<element name="title">
  <interleave>
    <attribute name="xml:lang"/>
    <text/>
    <zeroOrMore>
      <element name="a">
        <attribute name="href"/>
        <text/>
      </element>
    </zeroOrMore>
    <zeroOrMore>
      <element name="b">
        <text/>
      </element>
    </zeroOrMore>
  </interleave>
</element>
```

or:

```
element title {
  attribute xml:lang {text}
  & text
  & element a {attribute href {text}, text} *
  & element b {text} *
  }
```

This new schema is perfectly valid and does what we tried to do with our invalid schema.

In this example, diagnosing the problem was very simple, but in practice, the situation is often more complex. There can be conflicting text patterns belonging to different subpatterns of interleave or mixed patterns. When using pattern libraries (as shown in Chapter 10), the conflicting text patterns often belong to different RELAX

NG grammars, making it still more difficult to pinpoint the problem. To make it even worse, the error messages from the RELAX NG processors are often quite cryptic, in this case telling you there are conflicting text patterns in interleave patterns without saying where they come from. Unfortunately, for now at least, you'll have to figure this out by yourself.

 The reason behind the restriction of only one text pattern in each interleave pattern is to optimize RELAX NG implementations using the derivative method described by James Clark. When processing mixed-content models, instead of processing each text node, these implementations can simply memorize the fact that this is mixed content and ignore each text node. To do so, the implementation needs to be able to quickly find if a content model mixed or not mixed. That's where the restriction makes a difference in terms of programming complexity and execution speed.

A Missing Pattern: Unordered Group

We have seen that the interleave pattern associates two different features and is both an unordered group and something that alters the way subgroups can be combined. These two features aren't totally independent because mixing child nodes is meaningful only when the order of the subgroups isn't maintained, but they aren't totally dependent either. In theory, it's possible to define a pattern with a meaning of "unordered group" that doesn't interleave child nodes and keeps groups unaltered.

This pattern doesn't exist in RELAX NG for two reasons. First, it helps keep the language as simple as possible. Also, although it is built on top of an abstract mathematical model, RELAX NG is also built on top of the experience of its authors who have wanted to focus on general usages and best practices amongst the XML community. The lack of a "unordered group with no interleaving" hasn't been reported as a real-world limitation so far.

CHAPTER 7

Constraining Text Values

RELAX NG focuses primarily on the validation of the structures of XML documents, rather than on validation of the values placed within those structures. Despite RELAX NG's structure-centric approach, it includes simple and efficient support for values, enumerations, lists and whitespace processing, the subject of this chapter. (Developers who need more than this simple support may use external libraries, the subject of the next two chapters.)

Fixed Values

Sometimes documents need to include specific values for particular content. The value pattern can check fixed values, such as version identifiers of XML vocabularies. The syntax and semantics of the value pattern are straightforward: the pattern is matched only if the value found in the instance document matches the value specified in the value pattern. For example, if you want a highly specialized vocabulary to describe the book with the ISBN number 0836217462 and only this specific book, you can replace the text pattern with a value pattern and write:

```
<element name="isbn">
  <value>0836217462</value>
</element>
```

or, using the compact syntax:

```
element isbn {"0836217462"}
```

and the schema will validate a book with a ISBN number equal to 0836217462 and refuse any other ISBN number.

Co-Occurrence Constraints

Another, and considerably more frequent, use of value patterns is to define *co-occurrence constraints*, in which the value of a node (often an attribute) changes the content model of another node (often an element). In our library, the author and character elements are very similar. You can group them under the `person` element and use a type attribute to differentiate between the kind of "person" being described. To make the example clearer, to make it more visually obvious that something is different between the two, I'm going add some additional elements describing Peppermint Patty, creating an instance document that contains:

```
<person id="CMS" type="author">
  <name>Charles M Schulz</name>
  <born>1922-11-26</born>
  <dead>2000-02-12</dead>
</person>
```

and:

```
<person id="PP" type="character">
 <name>Peppermint Patty</name>
 <born>1966-08-22</born>
 <qualification>bold, brash and tomboyish</qualification>
 <shoecolor>green</shoecolor>
 <hairstyle>thatched roof</hairstyle>
 <favoriteathlete>that black and white kid with the big nose</favoriteathlete>
 <likelycareer>olympic coach or unemployed gym teacher</likelycareer>
</person>
```

You can see that both examples use the `person` element, yet because of the type attribute's contents, a different set of child elements is listed. Support for this approach is a key area in which RELAX NG allows more functionality than other schema languages. In these kind of schemas, validation tools need to recognize that the content models might vary depending on the value of the type attribute. RELAX NG supports this feature using value patterns. If you want to require that all the authors precede the characters, just update the definitions of the elements describing authors and characters and keep them in sequence in the definition of the book element:

```
<element name="book">
   <attribute name="id"/>
   <attribute name="available"/>
   <element name="isbn">
    <text/>
   </element>
   <element name="title">
    <attribute name="xml:lang"/>
    <text/>
   </element>
   <zeroOrMore>
    <element name="person">
     <attribute name="type">
      <value>author</value>
     </attribute>
     <attribute name="id"/>
     <element name="name">
      <text/>
```

```
      </element>
      <element name="born">
       <text/>
      </element>
      <optional>
      <element name="dead">
        <text/>
      </element>
      </optional>
     </element>
    </zeroOrMore>
    <zeroOrMore>
     <element name="person">
      <attribute name="type">
       <value>character</value>
      </attribute>
      <attribute name="id"/>
      <element name="name">
       <text/>
      </element>
      <element name="born">
       <text/>
      </element>
      <element name="qualification">
        <text/>
      </element>
      <optional>
       <element name="shoecolor">
         <text/>
       </element>
      </optional>
      <optional>
       <element name="hairstyle">
         <text/>
       </element>
      </optional>
      <optional>
       <element name="favoriteathlete">
         <text/>
       </element>
      </optional>
      <optional>
       <element name="likelycareer">
         <text/>
       </element>
      </optional>
      <optional>
       <element name="shoecolor">
         <text/>
       </element>
      </optional>
     </element>
    </zeroOrMore>
   </element>
```

or, using the compact syntax:

```
element book {
   attribute id { text },
   attribute available { text },
   element isbn { text },
   element title {
    attribute xml:lang { text },
    text
   },
   element person {
    attribute type { "author" },
    attribute id { text },
    element name { text },
    element born { text },
    element dead { text }?
   }*,
   element person {
    attribute type { "character" },
    attribute id { text },
    element name { text },
    element born { text },
    element qualification { text },
    element shoecolor { text }?,
    element hairstyle { text }?,
    element favoriteathlete { text }?,
    element likelycareer { text }?,
    element shoecolor { text }?
   }*
}
```

The use of the value attributes in the declarations for the two person elements makes the first declaration apply only to authors, and the second apply only to characters.

While co-occurrence constraints provide powerful capabilities, they unfortunately don't survive conversion to DTDs or W3C XML Schema. RELAX NG has fewer restrictions on the XML structures it can describe than either of those, as you'll see this in Chapter 16. RELAX NG's co-occurrence constraints can't be expressed with W3C XML Schema, because this type of schema isn't "deterministic." Some co-occurrence constraints can be expressed in W3C XML Schema using either xsi:type when possible or xs:key as a tricky hack. These methods don't work for the general case and aren't easy to implement in a schema translator. For more information about this hack, see my book *XML Schema* (O'Reilly).

The flexibility RELAX NG provides for defining co-occurrence constraints makes it a good tool to check how styles are used in XHTML, OpenOffice, or Microsoft Office documents. For example, it's easy to use such constraints on the XHTML class attributes so that a class "bar" is used only when embedded in a class "foo". This feature is useful for checking style best practices in text documents

However, if you choose only one person element, it's to build on commonalities between these elements. I might prefer to allow mixing of the definitions of characters and authors. I can express this part of the schema as zero or more person elements having two possible definitions, such as:

```
<element name="book">
  <attribute name="id"/>
  <attribute name="available"/>
  <element name="isbn">
   <text/>
  </element>
  <element name="title">
   <attribute name="xml:lang"/>
   <text/>
  </element>
  <zeroOrMore>
   <element name="person">
    <choice>
     <group>
      <attribute name="type">
       <value>author</value>
      </attribute>
      <attribute name="id"/>
      <element name="name">
       <text/>
      </element>
      <element name="born">
       <text/>
      </element>
      <optional>
       <element name="dead">
        <text/>
       </element>
      </optional>
     </group>
     <group>
      <attribute name="type">
       <value>character</value>
      </attribute>
      <attribute name="id"/>
      <element name="name">
       <text/>
      </element>
      <element name="born">
       <text/>
      </element>
      <element name="qualification">
       <text/>
      </element>
      <optional>
       <element name="shoecolor">
        <text/>
       </element>
```

```
      </optional>
      <optional>
       <element name="hairstyle">
        <text/>
       </element>
      </optional>
      <optional>
       <element name="favoriteathlete">
        <text/>
       </element>
      </optional>
      <optional>
       <element name="likelycareer">
        <text/>
       </element>
      </optional>
      <optional>
       <element name="shoecolor">
        <text/>
       </element>
      </optional>
     </group>
    </choice>
   </element>
  </zeroOrMore>
 </element>
```

or, in the compact syntax:

```
element book {
  attribute id { text },
  attribute available { text },
  element isbn { text },
  element title {
   attribute xml:lang { text },
   text
  },
  element person {
   (attribute type { "author" },
    attribute id { text },
    element name { text },
    element born { text },
    element dead { text }?)
   | (attribute type { "character" },
     attribute id { text },
     element name { text },
     element born { text },
     element qualification { text },
     element shoecolor { text }?,
     element hairstyle { text }?,
     element favoriteathlete { text }?,
     element likelycareer { text }?,
     element shoecolor { text }?)
  }*
}
```

Now that you have seen the definitions of the two contents for the person element next to each other, you can see that an attribute and the two first subelements are common and can be refactored to take advantage of this similarity. The definition of the person element can thus be combined and simplified to:

```
<element name="book">
  <attribute name="id"/>
  <attribute name="available"/>
  <element name="isbn">
   <text/>
  </element>
  <element name="title">
   <attribute name="xml:lang"/>
   <text/>
  </element>
  <zeroOrMore>
   <element name="person">
    <attribute name="id"/>
    <element name="name">
     <text/>
    </element>
    <element name="born">
     <text/>
    </element>
    <choice>
     <group>
      <attribute name="type">
       <value>author</value>
      </attribute>
      <optional>
       <element name="dead">
        <text/>
       </element>
      </optional>
     </group>
     <group>
      <attribute name="type">
       <value>character</value>
      </attribute>
      <element name="qualification">
       <text/>
      </element>
      <optional>
       <element name="shoecolor">
        <text/>
       </element>
      </optional>
      <optional>
       <element name="hairstyle">
        <text/>
       </element>
      </optional>
      <optional>
```

```
        <element name="favoriteathlete">
         <text/>
        </element>
       </optional>
       <optional>
        <element name="likelycareer">
         <text/>
        </element>
       </optional>
       <optional>
        <element name="shoecolor">
         <text/>
        </element>
       </optional>
      </group>
     </choice>
    </element>
   </zeroOrMore>
  </element>
```

or:

```
element book {
  attribute id { text },
  attribute available { text },
  element isbn { text },
  element title {
   attribute xml:lang { text },
   text
  },
  element person {
   attribute id { text },
   element name { text },
   element born { text },
   ((attribute type { "author" },
    element dead { text }?)
   | (attribute type { "character" },
    element qualification { text },
    element shoecolor { text }?,
    element hairstyle { text }?,
    element favoriteathlete { text }?,
    element likelycareer { text }?,
    element shoecolor { text }?))
  }*
 }
```

Note that in the compact syntax, I had to use double parentheses to express my choice, because the operators used at any level must be homogeneous. You can't mix commas, pipes, and ampersands within the same level; this mixing is ambiguous. Also, because I grouped the elements with the attribute used to create the distinction between content models, I can refactor the id attribute and the name and born elements and keep the type attribute and its two possible values in the choice. This is possible not only because the example has been carefully prepared, but also because of the semantic implicit to `interleave` given to the `attribute` patterns, which lets you locate the attribute either inside or outside of the `choice`. Finally, note that this refactoring is just a syntactical variation. Even when a situation arises in which such simplification is impossible, the co-occurrence constraint can still be expressed, even though it will be more verbose.

Enumerations

An *enumeration* is a choice between several values. Enumerations are thus written in RELAX NG by combining the `choice` pattern with the `value` pattern. In our library, a good candidate for an enumeration is the `available` attribute, which can be defined as:

```
<attribute name="available">
 <choice>
  <value>available</value>
  <value>checked out</value>
  <value>on hold</value>
 </choice>
</attribute>
```

or:

```
attribute available {"available"|"checked out"|"on hold"}
```

This definition validates values such as "available", "checked out", and "on hold". It also validates values such as " available ", "checked out ", or even " on hold " with multiple spaces, tabs or carriage returns between "on" and "hold" or "checked" and "out". You will see the reason for this behavior—and how to change it if needed—in the next section.

Whitespace and RELAX NG Native Datatypes

RELAX NG includes a native type system, but this type library has been kept minimal by design because more complete type libraries are available. It consists of just two datatypes (`token` and `string`) that differ only in the whitespace processing applied before validation. The whole RELAX NG datatype system can be seen as a mechanism for adding validating transformations to text nodes. These transformations change text nodes into *canonical* formats (formats in which all the different formats for a same value are converted into a single normalized or "canonical" format). The two native datatypes don't detect format errors (their formats are broad enough to allow any value) but still transform text nodes in their canonical forms, which can make a difference for enumerations. Other datatype libraries, covered in Chapter 8, can detect format errors.

Enumerations are the first place you can see datatypes at work. Applying datatypes to enumeration values is done by adding a `type` attribute in `value` patterns. Up to now, we haven't specified any datatype when we've written `value` elements. By default, they have the default type token from the built-in library. Text values of this datatype receive full whitespace normalization similar to that performed by the XPath `normalize-space( )` function: all sequences of one or more whitespace characters—the characters #x20 (space), #x9 (tab), #xA (linefeed), and #xD (carriage return)—are replaced by a single space, and the leading space and trailing space are then trimmed.

Reconsidering previous examples, writing:

```
<attribute name="available">
 <choice>
  <value>available</value>
  <value>checked out</value>
  <value>on hold</value>
 </choice>
</attribute>
```

or:

```
attribute
available {"available"|"checked out"|"on hold"}
```

has used the default type value (token) and is equivalent to the following:

```
<attribute name="available">
 <choice>
  <value type="token">available</value>
  <value type="token">checked out</value>
  <value type="token">on hold</value>
 </choice>
</attribute>
```

or:

```
attribute available {token "available"|token "checked out"|token
"on hold"}
```

When the token datatype is used, whitespace normalization is applied to the value defined in the schema and to the value found in the instance document. The comparison is done using the result of the normalization, which explains why "on hold" was matching " on hold " with spaces or tabs added before, between, and after the words.

The name of the token datatype, borrowed from W3C XML Schema, is highly confusing. In IT jargon, a *token* is a piece of a string between two delimiters, what is called a "word" in plain English. The token datatype doesn't denote a word. Otherwise, "on" and "hold" would be valid tokens; "on hold" wouldn't. The token datatype is more a "token-ized" datatype, in the sense that it's a string that can be easily cut into tokens when nonsignificant whitespace is removed.

This confusion is dangerous because it can cause you to use the string datatype when what you need is token. (You'll see later in this chapter that using the string datatype should be reserved for select cases).

To suppress this normalization, you can specify the second built-in datatype, string, which doesn't perform any transformation on the values before comparing them to the specified value:

```
<attribute name="available">
 <choice>
  <value type="string">available</value>
  <value type="string">checked out</value>
  <value type="string">on hold</value>
 </choice>
</attribute>
```

or:

```
attribute available {string "available"|string "checked out"|string
"on hold"}
```

Using the new definition, the value of our attribute must exactly match the value specified in the schema: available, checked out, and on hold. No extra whitespace is permitted.

 The native token and string datatypes have the same basic definition as the W3C XML Schema token and string datatypes. The difference is that additional restrictions, which can be applied using param attributes to the W3C XML Schema datatypes, aren't available with RELAX NG's native datatypes. More details are provided in Chapter 8.

Using String Datatypes in Attribute Values

The lack of whitespace normalization with RELAX NG's string datatype may lead to some surprises. When attributes are defined, the XML parsers must remove the line-feeds and carriage returns they find there, which can lead to surprises in processing.

Attribute whitespace normalization can be confusing in several ways. Our previous schema specified that the attribute that must match on hold always matches an attribute in which the space between on and hold is replaced by a linefeed as in:

```
<book id="b0836217462" available="on
    hold">
```

Attribute whitespace normalization is normal behavior in XML 1.0. All XML parsers must normalize an attribute's value before reporting it to other applications, producing on hold, in this case. No schema language can change this. These issues can also make it difficult to create schemas that include strings that incorporate whitespace. This RELAX NG XML syntax schema requires new features in order to be translated to the compact syntax:

```
<attribute name="available">
 <choice>
  <value type="string">available</value>
  <value type="string">checked out</value>
```

```
<value type="string">on
      hold</value>
  </choice>
</attribute>
```

The compact syntax doesn't permit new lines within quotes. To translate this into the compact syntax, we need to introduce a couple of new features to permit the inclusion of linefeeds in values.

The first way to include them is borrowed from Python. If instead of using single (') or double (") quotes, you use three single (''') or three double (""") quotes, you can include nearly everything in your values, including new lines:

```
attribute available {string "available"|string "checked out"|string
"""on
hold"""}
```

or:

```
attribute available {string "available"|string "checked out"|string
'''on
hold'''''}
```

The second way to allow new lines is through escaping the newline character using the syntax \x{A} (where A is the Unicode value of newline in hexadecimal):

```
attribute available {string "available"|string "on hold"|string
"on\x{A}hold"}
```

This pattern specifies that the attribute can contain a value with a linefeed, something that can happen in XML only if the newline in the attribute is explicitly specified through its numeric value, such as:

```
<book id="b0836217462" available="who&#x0A;knows?">
```

These are unlikely cases, but now you know what to do if you encounter them.

When to Use String Datatypes

It's amazing to think that despite all the complex applications that have been made possible by SGML and XML, whitespace processing—which seems as if it should be simple—has remained a nightmare for users and programmers. The string datatype will expose you to all the issues related to whitespace handling. A huge number of users and applications will modify whitespace in your documents to meet their expectations, which can make your documents invalid.

The token datatype keeps this nightmare from creating problems, and that is why RELAX NG uses token as its default datatype. Keep in mind that you shouldn't use the string datatype unless you have a good reason to do so. If whitespace is genuinely significant to your information, use the string type; otherwise, use the token type.

Using Different Types in Each Value

In our previous schema, we were required to define the type for each value pattern:

```
attribute available {string "available"|string "checked out"|string
"on hold"}
```

This example doesn't show all that RELAX NG is capable of. There is no rule that keeps you from using attributes that have different datatypes in an enumeration. Thus, although this example shows an enumeration with datatypes that are all the same, you aren't restricted to using attributes with all the same datatype in an enumeration.

This will become more interesting after Chapter 8 (when there will be more simple datatypes to work with), but you can write:

```
<attribute name="available">
 <choice>
  <value type="string">available</value>
  <value type="token">checked out</value>
  <value type="string">on hold</value>
 </choice>
</attribute>
```

or, in the compact syntax:

```
attribute available {
    string "available"|
    token "checked out"|
    string "on hold"}
```

This schema normalizes whitespace to check the value checked out, defined as token, but doesn't do any normalization when examining the other two values (available and on hold) defined as string.

Exclusions

What if, instead of giving a list of allowed values, you want to give a list of values that are forbidden? The except pattern serves precisely this purpose.

To exclude the value 0836217462 from the possible ISBN numbers, write:

```
<element name="isbn">
 <data type="token">
  <except>
   <value>0836217462</value>
  </except>
 </data>
</element>
```

or, using the compact syntax:

```
element isbn {token - "0836217462"}
```

Although this statement looks simple, note that the type can be defined at two different levels here: it must be defined in the data pattern and may also be defined in the value pattern; these two definitions have a different meaning. The type attached to the data pattern defines a validation performed on the text node, while the type attached to the value pattern defines how the value should be interpreted and which whitespace processing should be performed.

In this example, both are token types, and values such as " 0836217462 " are excluded as well as "0836217462". The token type, as noted previously, normalizes whitespace before making comparisons. The two datatypes can also be mixed, as in:

```
<attribute name="available">
 <data type="token">
  <except>
   <choice>
    <value type="string">available</value>
    <value type="string">checked out</value>
    <value type="string">on hold</value>
   </choice>
  </except>
 </data>
</attribute>
```

or, using the compact syntax:

```
attribute available {token -(string "available"|string "checked out"|string
"on hold")}
```

In this case, the first control is done on the datatype token, and the comparison uses the datatype string. To push this a little further, let's examine what happens when you use it with datatypes (which are shown in Chapter 8):

```
<data type="integer">
 <except>
  <choice>
   <value type="integer">1</value>
  </choice>
 </except>
</data>
```

or, using the compact syntax:

```
integer -(integer "1")
```

In this case, both controls are performed on integers. This statement accepts any integer except values representing "1" as an integer. ("1" and also "01" or "001" are forbidden.)

Now, consider:

```
<data type="integer">
 <except>
  <choice>
   <value>1</value>
```

```
    </choice>
   </except>
  </data>
```

or, using the compact syntax

```
integer -("1")
```

The value has a default type of token so that "01" is normalized, then compared to "1" as a token. The two aren't equal (as tokens) so the except isn't triggered; hence "01" is passed up to the next level. Next, the data has a type of integer so that "01" (normalized by the previous step) is tested to see if it's an integer. It is, so it's accepted as valid.

Lists

RELAX NG supports the description of text nodes as lists of whitespace-separated values using the list pattern. This is the only pattern that transforms the structure of the document at validation time by splitting text values into lists of values. The benefit of doing so is that within a list pattern, all the patterns that constrain data values can be combined with the compositors, which lets you constrain the combination of these values.

If you use a list pattern without defining cardinality, you may not get what you expect. An attribute defined as:

```
<attribute name="see-also">
 <list>
  <data type="token"/>
 </list>
</attribute>
```

or, using the compact syntax:

```
attribute see-also {list {token}}
```

doesn't match a list of tokens (such as see-also="0345442695 0449220230 0449214044 0061075647 0061075612") but rather only a list of exactly one token (such as see-also="0345442695"). This is because the list pattern splits the text value into a list of values. This list is then evaluated against the patterns that are included within the list pattern. If you want a list of any number of tokens, use a zeroOrMore pattern to express that:

```
<attribute name="see-also">
 <list>
  <zeroOrMore>
   <data type="token"/>
  </zeroOrMore>
 </list>
</attribute>
```

Here's the compact syntax:

```
attribute see-also {list {token*}}
```

This definition treats the see-also attribute as a list of tokens and doesn't add any other constraints (this result is of course different when there are more datatypes). You can use other compositors in the list pattern exactly as in other contexts. To express that, you want a list with one to four tokens, you would write:

```
<attribute name="see-also">
 <list>
  <data type="token"/>
  <optional>
   <data type="token"/>
  </optional>
  <optional>
   <data type="token"/>
  </optional>
  <optional>
   <data type="token"/>
  </optional>
 </list>
</attribute>
```

or, using the compact syntax:

```
attribute see-also {list {token, token?, token?, token?}}
```

That is certainly verbose, but you've already seen there are no other options for defining the number of occurrences with RELAX NG.

You can also constrain the values of these tokens through an enumeration:

```
<attribute name="see-also">
 <list>
  <oneOrMore>
   <choice>
    <value>0836217462</value>
    <value>0345442695</value>
    <value>0449220230</value>
    <value>0449214044</value>
    <value>0061075647</value>
   </choice>
  </oneOrMore>
 </list>
</attribute>
```

or:

```
attribute see-also {list
{("0836217462"|"0345442695"|"0449220230"|"0449214044"|"0061075647")+}}
```

A final point to note is that the list mechanism lets you define different constraints for different members of a list. To illustrate this feature, let's say you wish to give the physical dimension of a book by giving each of its three dimensions a unit, such as:

```
<book id="b0836217462" available="true" dimensions="0.38 8.99 8.50 inches">
```

In this case, you can define the dimensions attribute as:

```
<attribute name="dimensions">
 <list>
  <data type="token"/>
  <data type="token"/>
  <data type="token"/>
  <choice>
   <value>inches</value>
   <value>cm</value>
   <value>mm</value>
  </choice>
 </list>
</attribute>
```

or:

```
attribute dimensions {list {token, token, token, ("inches"|"cm"|"mm")}}
```

Data Versus Text

In Chapter 6, I provided a detailed description of the text pattern and its behavior within interleave patterns. There's another pattern that also describes and attaches datatypes to text nodes. Even though this pattern will become more useful with the introduction of the datatype libraries in Chapter 8, it's worth examining its core features right now to be sure you've touched on most of the definitions related to nodes.

The data pattern accepts a type attribute (as for the value pattern) and checks that the value is valid per this type. Since our two built-in types accept any value, the data pattern with built-in types is almost equivalent to a text pattern. However, the data pattern doesn't mean, like the text pattern, "zero or more text nodes" but instead "one text node." The data pattern has been designed to represent data. It's forbidden in mixed-content models because the authors of the RELAX NG specification considered mixing data and elements poor practice.

This restriction applies to all patterns that match a single text node (data, value, and list) that can never be associated with patterns matching sibling elements (elements that can add the same parent element in the same instance document). In practice, this means you can't use a data pattern to describe content models such as:

```
<price><currency>USD</currency>20</price>
```

or:

```
<price>20<currency>Euro</currency></price>
```

These content models were considered poor practice by the authors of the RELAX NG specification. They advise reformulating them as:

```
<price>
 <amount>20</amount>
```

```
<currency>USD</currency>
</price>
```

or:

```
<price currency="USD">20</price>
```

This is the second time RELAX NG has given priority to good practices over the ability to describe all the combinations possible according to the XML recommendation. (The first one was the no "unordered noninterleaved" pattern in Chapter 6.) This case actually increases the complexity of the implementations of RELAX NG processors, which must check that data patterns aren't included within mixed content models. The support of data in mixed-content models would have been possible using the general algorithms without any additional complexity. The only benefit for RELAX NG processors is that they can skip whitespace occurring between two elements, but this benefit seems really minimal compared to the possibilities that are lost by this restriction.

This restriction appears to come from a strict distinction between data- and document-oriented applications of XML. Mixed content has been considered an aspect of document-oriented applications, which shouldn't need datatypes, while datatypes are limited to data-oriented applications, which shouldn't need mixed content.

CHAPTER 8

Datatype Libraries

In Chapter 7, I presented the basics of the data pattern using the highly restricted, built-in datatype library. The extreme simplicity of the built-in type library—limited to the two datatypes string and token—shouldn't be seen as a limitation of RELAX NG. Instead, it is a fundamental design decision: validating the structure and validating the content of XML documents are different problems that are better solved by different tools working in close cooperation.

The RELAX NG strategy is thus to rely on external pluggable libraries for the validation of the content of the text nodes and attributes. There is no limit to the potential variety of external type libraries that can be implemented and used by a RELAX NG schema. The designers of RELAX NG think that there is probably room for both generic type libraries and application-specific type libraries that meet the needs of a specific domain such as mathematics, physics, or business.

It's also possible to implement type libraries specific to particular programming languages. For example, my Python implementation of RELAX NG supports a native Python type library, which maps the built-in types and allows developers to define restrictions using the Python syntax.

That said, it is expected that most users will choose generic XML type libraries ranging from a library emulating DTD datatypes to the W3C XML Schema datatype library. (The ISO DSDL activity includes work on a datatype library, but it isn't published yet.) In this chapter, I'll introduce the most commonly used and widely supported libraries—the W3C XML Schema and DTD compatibility type libraries.

W3C XML Schema Type Library

W3C XML Schema simple types required several chapters in my *XML Schema* (O'Reilly) book to explain completely, but I'll try to give a brief overview here so that you can use the basic features within RELAX NG schemas. You will find additional detail about the simple types' definitions in Chapters 9 and 19, and you are of course welcome to read Chapters 4, 5, 6, and 16 of my *XML Schema* book to get a deeper understanding of their behavior.

The W3C XML Schema datatypes that can be used in a RELAX NG schema are the *predefined* W3C XML Schema types—those defined in the W3C XML Schema Recommendation itself as opposed to *user-defined types*, which are derived from the predefined types using the W3C XML Schema language and can't be used from a RELAX NG schema. You'll see that restrictions (called *facets* in the terminology of W3C XML Schema) can be applied to these datatypes using the RELAX NG param pattern, so some customization is possible.

 RELAX NG's support for named patterns makes it effectively possible to derive types from W3C XML Schema simple types despite RELAX NG's lack of support for the W3C XML Schema type derivation system. This might be a bit confusing right now, but it will become clearer with examples; RELAX NG borrows the most basic part of W3C XML Schema datatypes without borrowing its syntax or its derivation methods.

The Datatypes

The W3C XML Schema predefined datatypes are divided into primitive and derived types. *Primitive types* are basic types that don't share a common foundation of meaning and behave differently from each other. *Derived types* are built on the foundations of primitive types, sharing the semantics of its primitive type. Derived types are provided for the convenience of users, since it is expected that they will be commonly used and shouldn't need constant reinvention.

The other idea that needs to be introduced before we start is the concept of lexical and value spaces: *lexical space* is the string as it appears in the XML document (after whitespace normalization), while *value space* is the matching value as interpreted by the datatype library. The distinction is important because all the facets save one (the pattern facet, which is covered in depth in Chapter 9) act on the value space.

The next few sections will give a brief presentation of the datatypes, organized by their primary types.

String datatypes

The string datatypes include:

string
> This is the only datatype for which no whitespace normalization is done. There is no restriction on the lexical or value spaces of this datatype, which is identical to the string RELAX NG built-in type. The difference is that restrictions can be applied through param patterns on the W3C XML Schema string type.

normalizedString

> A string, but intermediate whitespace processing is performed on this datatype: occurrences of whitespace—including tabs (#x9), linefeeds (#xA), and spaces (#x20)—are replaced by the same number of spaces (#x20), but no space-collapsing or trimming is performed. Just as for the string datatype, there are no restrictions on the lexical or value spaces of this datatype.

token

> This datatype is similar to the built-in token datatype: whitespaces are normalized, i.e., all the sequences of whitespaces are replaced by a single space, and the leading and trailing spaces are removed. Including token and string, this is the third and last datatype that has no constraint on its value or lexical spaces. (Also note that all the datatypes except string and normalizedString follow the same normalization rules as the token datatype.)

language

> This datatype was created to accept all the language codes standardized by RFC 1766. Some valid values for this datatype are en, en-US, fr, or fr-FR.

NMTOKEN

> This datatype corresponds to the XML 1.0 Nmtoken (Name token) production, which is a single token (a set of characters without spaces) composed of characters allowed in an XML name. Some examples of valid values for this datatype are "Snoopy", "CMS", "1950-10-04", or "0836217462". Invalid values include "brought classical music to the Peanuts strip" (spaces are forbidden) or "bold,brash" (commas are forbidden).

NMTOKENS

> The lexical and value spaces of NMTOKENS are whitespace-separated lists of NMTOKEN components.

Name

> This datatype is similar to NMTOKEN with the additional restriction that the values must start either with a letter or the characters ":" or "_". This datatype conforms to the XML 1.0 definition of a Name. Some examples of valid values for this datatype are "Snoopy", "CMS", or "_1950-10-04-10:00". Invalid values include "0836217462" (can't start with a number) or "bold,brash" (commas are forbidden). This datatype shouldn't be used for names that may be qualified by a namespace prefix; another datatype, QName, has a specific semantic for these values.

NCName

> This is a *noncolonized name* as defined by Namespaces in XML 1.0: a Name without any colons. As such, this datatype is probably the predefined datatype that is closest to the notion of a name in most of the programming languages (some characters such as "_" or "." may still be a problem in many cases). Valid values

for this datatype include "Snoopy", "CMS", "_1950-10-04-10-00", or "1950-10-04". Invalid values are "_1950-10-04:10-00" or "bold:brash" (colons are forbidden).

ID The lexical space of ID is the same as the lexical space of NCName. As defined by the W3C XML Schema recommendation, there is one constraint added to its value space: there must not be any duplicate values in a document. RELAX NG doesn't allow datatype libraries to perform this type of check. This is a job for the DTD compatibility feature, as you will see at the end of this chapter. Its specification asks RELAX NG processors supporting this feature to enforce ID uniqueness for W3C XML Schema ID datatypes. Other implementations just check its lexical space as a NCName.

IDREF
The lexical space of IDREF is the same as the lexical space of NCName. Just as for ID, W3C XML Schema adds the constraint that it must match an ID defined in the same document. RELAX NG makes this behavior optional for RELAX NG processors supporting the W3C XML Schema type library without supporting the DTD compatibility feature.

IDREFS
The lexical space of IDREFS is a whitespace-separated list of NCName values. Just as for ID and IDREF, W3C XML Schema adds the constraint that each of the values must match an ID defined in the same document. RELAX NG makes this behavior optional for RELAX NG processors supporting the W3C XML Schema type library without supporting the DTD compatibility feature.

ENTITY
The lexical space of ENTITY is the same as the lexical space of NCName. Also provided for compatibility with XML 1.0 DTDs, an ENTITY value and must match an unparsed entity defined in a DTD.

ENTITIES
The lexical and value spaces of ENTITIES are the whitespace-separated lists of ENTITY components.

URIs

Strictly speaking, anyURI, the only member of this family, isn't considered a string because its value can be different from its lexical representation to compensate for the differences of format between XML and URIs, as specified in RFCs 2396 and 2732. These RFCs aren't very friendly toward non-ASCII characters and require many character escapes that aren't necessary in XML.

As an example of this transformation, the href attribute of an XHTML link written as:

```
<a href="http://dmoz.org/World/Français/">
  World/Français
</a>
```

is converted to the value:

```
http://dmoz.org/World/Fran%C3%A7ais/
```

in the value space.

Also note that the anyURI datatype doesn't pay attention to xml:base attributes that may have been defined in the document.

Qualified names

Up to now, I have only briefly mentioned XML namespaces. I'll focus on them in Chapter 11, but we need to use some of their concepts right now. If you're not familiar with namespaces, you can skip this section: you don't need qualified names quite yet. Even if you are a XML namespace guru, I wouldn't recommend that you use them as they complicate many kinds of processing enormously.

What we're talking about here is different from using qualified names for element and attribute names. Using qualified names for element and attribute names is defined by the recommendation "Namespaces in XML 1.0" (you can find it at *http://www.w3.org/TR/REC-xml-names*), and there isn't much debate left on the subject. Here, I am speaking of using qualified names in element or attribute values. This usage is much more controversial because it creates a dependency between markup and its content.

Because of this dependency, you can't consider a qualified name string datatype, as its prefix is only a shortcut to the associated namespace URI. The value space of a qualified name is thus not what you see, but a *tuple*—two things combined, composed of the associated namespace URI (replacing the prefix) and its local part (i.e., what is after the prefix and the colon).

For instance, if the xsd prefix has been associated with the namespace URI http://www.w3.org/2001/XMLSchema, a qualified name (QName) xsd:language would thus have a value that is the tuple {http://www.w3.org/2001/XMLSchema, language}. It can be considered equal to a QName foo:language if the prefix foo has been associated with http://www.w3.org/2001/XMLSchema or language if http://www.w3.org/2001/XMLSchema has been defined as the default namespace.

There are two QName datatypes, which RELAX NG treats as equivalent:

QName

A namespace-qualified name. The lexical space is the set of *colonized* names consisting of a prefix; a local name separated by a colon or a local name only if no prefix is used. The value space is the set of tuples {*namespace URI, local name*} as explained previously. Note that for a QName to be considered valid, the prefix must be defined through a namespace declaration in the scope of the location where it is used.

NOTATION

In W3C XML Schema, `NOTATION` is a `QName` that is used as a notation in a W3C XML Schema. Because RELAX NG has no equivalent syntax for declaring notations, RELAX NG processors treat `NOTATION` as a synonym for `QName`.

Binary string-encoded datatypes

XML 1.0 isn't designed to store binary content: binary content must be encoded as some form of string before it can be included in an XML document. W3C XML Schema has defined two primary datatypes to support two encodings: one that is commonly used (`base64`) and one that is newer (`hexBinary`). These encodings may include any binary content, including text formats whose content may be incompatible with the XML markup. Other binary text encodings can also be used in XML (such as uuXXcode, Quote Printable, BinHex, aencode, or base85, to name a few), but their values aren't recognized by W3C XML Schema.

hexBinary

This datatype defines a simple way to code binary content as a character string by translating the value of each binary octet into two hexadecimal digits. (This encoding shouldn't be confused with the encoding method called BinHex, introduced by Apple and described by RFC 1741, which includes a mechanism to compress repetitive characters.) A UTF-8 XML header such as `<?xml version="1.0" encoding="UTF-8"?>` encoded in hexBinary is:

    3f3c6d78206c657673726f693d6e3122302e20226e656f636964676e223d54552d4622383e3f.

base64Binary

This mechanism uses the encoding known as `base64`, which is described in RFC 2045. It maps groups of 6 bits into an array of 64 printable characters. The same header encoded in `base64Binary` is:

    PD94bWwgdmVyc2lvbjOiMS4wIiBlbmNvZGluZzOiVVRGLTgiPz4NCg==.

The W3C XML Schema Recommendation missed the fact that RFC 2045 requests a line break every 76 characters. This omission has been clarified in an errata. The consequence of these linebreaks being thought of as optional by W3C XML Schema is that the lexical and value spaces of base64Binary can't be considered identical.

Numeric datatypes

Numeric datatypes are built on top of four primitive datatypes: `decimal` for all the decimal types (including the integer datatypes, which are treated as decimals without a fractional part), `double` and `float` for single- and double-precision floats, and `boolean` for Booleans.

The first family of numeric datatypes is derived from the primitive type `decimal`:

decimal

    This datatype represents decimal numbers. The number of digits can be arbitrarily long (the datatype doesn't impose any restrictions), but obviously, since a XML document has an arbitrary but finite length, the number of digits of the lexical representation of a `decimal` value needs to be finite. Although the number of digits isn't limited, the next section (concerning facets) shows how the author of a schema can derive user-defined datatypes with a limited number of digits if needed. Leading and trailing zeros aren't considered significant and may be trimmed. The decimal separator is always a dot (.), and a leading sign (+ or -) may be used, but any characters other than the 10 digits zero through nine are forbidden, including whitespace inside the value. Allowed values for decimal include 123.456, +1234.456, -.456 or -456.

integer

    This datatype is a subset of `decimal`, representing numbers that don't have any fractional digits in its lexical or value spaces. The characters that are accepted are reduced to the digits zero through nine, with an optional leading sign. Like its base datatype, `integer` doesn't impose any limitation on the number of digits, and leading zeros aren't significant. Note that the decimal separator is forbidden even if the numbers following the decimal are omitted or zeros.

nonPositiveInteger

    nonPositiveInteger is the category for integers that are negative or zero (zero is neither positive nor negative).

negativeInteger

    Contains an integer whose value is less than zero.

nonNegativeInteger

    Contains a positive or zero integer value.

positiveInteger

    Contains an integer whose value is greater than zero.

long

    Contains an integer between −9223372036854775808 and 9223372036854775807; i.e., the values that can be stored in a 64-bit word.

int

    Contains an integer between −2147483648 and 2147483647 (32 bits).

short

    Contains an integer between −32768 and 32767 (16 bits).

byte

    Contains an integer between −128 and 127 (8 bits).

unsignedLong
> Contains an unsigned integer between 0 and 18446744073709551615; i.e., the values that can be stored in a 64-bit word.

unsignedInt
> Contains an integer between 0 and 4294967295 (32 bits).

unsignedShort
> Contains an integer between 0 and 65535 (16 bits).

unsignedByte
> Contains an integer between 0 and 255 (8 bits).

The second family is made of the float and double datatypes, which represent IEEE simple (32 bits) and double (64 bits) precision floating-point types. These store the values in the form of a mantissa and an exponent of a power of 2 ($m \times 2^e$), allowing a large scale of numbers in a storage that has a fixed length. Fortunately, the lexical space doesn't require powers of 2 (in fact, it doesn't accept powers of 2), but instead uses a traditional scientific notation based on integer powers of 10. Because the value spaces (powers of 2) don't exactly match the values from the lexical space (powers of 10), the recommendation specifies that the closest value is taken. The consequence of this approximate matching is that float datatypes are the domain of approximation; most of the float values can't be considered exact and are approximate.

These datatypes accept several special values: positive zero (0), negative zero (-0) (which is less than positive 0 but greater than any negative value); infinity (INF), which is greater than any value; negative infinity (-INF), which is less than any value; and "not a number" (NaN).

The last member of the numeric types family is boolean, a primitive datatype that can take the values true and false (or 1 and 0, which are considered equivalent).

Date and time formats

Dates and times are probably the most controversial aspect of W3C XML Schema datatypes. In order to meet the requirements of dates on the Web, the W3C XML Schema Working Group attempted to define a value space for a subset of the ISO 8601 date formats—a syntactical specification of how dates should be exchanged on the Web.

The result is complex and yet fails to satisfy the experts of date and time representations, doesn't support any other calendar system than Gregorian, and has no support for localization.

One of the fuzziest aspects of these datatypes is that many of them (such as dateTime, which I'll introduce in a moment) accept values with and without time zones. This creates two classes of values, which can't be reliably and accurately compared.

Let's take a closer look at this important distinction before I present the details of these datatypes. Two dateTime values that include a time zone can be compared easily. W3C XML Schema states that a dateTime value without a time zone has an undetermined time zone, but that you can still compare two of these to each other. Things get fuzzy when you want to compare a dateTime value with a time zone and a dateTime value without. All you know about the dateTime value that has an undetermined time zone is that it can be in an interval from 14 hours before UTC to 14 hours after UTC. You can never conclude that the two dateTime values are equal. You can say only that one value comes before the other when they are different enough.

Why 14 hours? No, that's not a typo! National regulations have some level of flexibility with the time zones used in their countries, so that the time zone they use can vary from their geographical time zone. This variation can even change throughout the year, with many countries having winter and summer times. As a result, when the W3C published the W3C XML Schema recommendation, the maximum number of hours of difference in time zones was not between –12 and +12 hours from UTC but between –13 and +12 hours. And because the W3C doesn't expect that national authorities will ask their permission or send prior notification if they want to enlarge this interval, they have added a security margin and written the –14/+14 hours interval into their recommendation.

 Because computers aren't fond of fuzziness, it is certainly a very good practice to use time zones with your dateTime values!

Here are the date, time, and related datatypes defined by W3C XML Schema:

dateTime

This datatype is defined as representing a "specific instant of time." This instant is a subset of what ISO 8601 calls a "moment of time." Its lexical value follows the format CCYY-MM-DDThh:mm:ss, in which all the fields must be present and may optionally be preceded by a sign and leading figures, if needed, and also followed by fractional digits for the seconds and a time zone. The time zone may be specified using the letter "Z," Zulu, which identifies UTC, or by the difference of time with UTC. As you've seen, a value such as 2001-10-26T21:32:52 that's defined without a time zone can't be compared to 2001-10-26T21:32:52+02:00 or 2001-10-26T19:32:52Z, which have a time zone. The last two values, which have a time zone, are considered equal because they identify the same moment.

date

This datatype has the same lexical space as the date part of dateTime with an optional time zone and represents a period of one day in its time zone, "independent of how many hours this day has." The consequence of this definition is that two dates defined in a different time zone can't be equal, except if they designate the same interval (2001-10-26+12:00 and 2001-10-25-12:00, for instance). Another consequence is that, as with dateTime, the order relation between a date with a time zone and a date without a time zone can be only partially determined.

gYearMonth

A Gregorian calendar month: a period of one calendar month in its time zone. Its format is the format of date but leaving out the entry for the day: 2001-10, 2001-10+02:00, or 2001-10Z for instance ("g" stands for Gregorian).

gYear

A Gregorian calendar year: a period of one calendar year in its time zone. Its format is the format of gYearMonth without its month part: 2001, 2001+02:00 or 2001Z, for instance (note that these three values identify three different periods and aren't considered equal).

time

The lexical space of time is identical to the time part of dateTime. The semantic of time represents a point in time that recurs every day; the meaning of "01:20:15" is "the point in time recurring each day at 01:20:15 am." Like date and dateTime, time accepts an optional time-zone definition. The same issue arises when comparing times with and without time zones.

gDay

The lexical space of gDay is ---DD with an optional time zone specification, and it represents a recurring period of one day in the specified time zone occurring each Gregorian calendar month. ---01 represents, for instance, the first day of each month with an undetermined time zone. Dates are pinned down depending on the number of days of each month; in February, for instance, --31Z occurs on February 28th (or 29th for leap years).

gMonthDay

The lexical space of gMonthDay is --MM-DD with an optional time-zone specification, and it represents a recurring period of one day in the specified time zone occurring each Gregorian calendar year. For instance, Christmas day in the United Kingdom is --12-25Z.

gMonth

The lexical space of gMonth should have been --MM with an optional time zone, but a typo in the W3C XML Schema recommendation has specified it as --MM-- which you can still find in some tools even though an erratum has corrected it to --MM. It represents a recurring period of a calendar month in its time zone. The months of January in Paris, for instance, are represented as --01+01:00.

duration

The lexical space of duration is PnYnMnDTnHnMnS. Each part (except the leading "P") is optional. A significant amount of complexity comes from the fact that you can mix quantities expressed as months (which have a variable number of days) with quantities expressed as days, such as, for instance, P1Y2M8DT123S, which means a duration of 1 year, 2 months, 8 days and 123 seconds. I won't enter into the detail of the algorithms here, but formatting this leads to a partial order relation between durations that don't make it difficult to manage processing of this datatypes when all its parts are used.

Examples

After that long and dense enumeration of types, let's see how to add W3C XML Schema datatypes to our first schema. The most natural choices seem to be:

id If we use the ID datatype for IDs, their uniqueness will be checked by RELAX NG processors that support the DTD compatibility feature.

xml:lang
    The natural candidate for xml:lang is language.

available
    We can use boolean for this attribute.

born *and* died
    date seems the right choice, since we have been lucky enough to have ISO 8601 dates in our instance documents.

Other elements containing text
    We have no reason to preserve whitespace in these elements and will use token datatypes for all of them.

Our first schema could thus be rewritten as:

```
<element xmlns="http://relaxng.org/ns/structure/1.0" name="library"
 datatypeLibrary="http://www.w3.org/2001/XMLSchema-datatypes">
 <oneOrMore>
  <element name="book">
   <attribute name="id">
    <data type="ID"/>
   </attribute>
   <attribute name="available">
    <data type="boolean"/>
   </attribute>
   <element name="isbn">
    <data type="NMTOKEN"/>
   </element>
   <element name="title">
    <attribute name="xml:lang">
     <data type="language"/>
    </attribute>
    <data type="token"/>
   </element>
   <zeroOrMore>
    <element name="author">
     <attribute name="id">
      <data type="ID"/>
     </attribute>
```

```
        <element name="name">
         <data type="token"/>
        </element>
        <element name="born">
         <data type="date"/>
        </element>
        <optional>
          <element name="died">
           <data type="date"/>
          </element>
        </optional>
      </element>
    </zeroOrMore>
    <zeroOrMore>
      <element name="character">
        <attribute name="id">
         <data type="ID"/>
        </attribute>
        <element name="name">
         <data type="token"/>
        </element>
        <element name="born">
         <data type="date"/>
        </element>
        <element name="qualification">
         <data type="token"/>
        </element>
      </element>
    </zeroOrMore>
   </element>
  </oneOrMore>
</element>
```

or:

```
element library {
 element book {
  attribute id {xsd:ID},
  attribute available {xsd:boolean},
  element isbn {xsd:NMTOKEN},
  element title {attribute xml:lang {xsd:language}, xsd:token},
  element author {
   attribute id {xsd:ID},
   element name {xsd:token},
   element born {xsd:date},
   element died {xsd:date}?}*,
  element character {
   attribute id {xsd:ID},
   element name {xsd:token},
   element born {xsd:date},
   element qualification {xsd:token}}*
 } +
}
```

Note the declaration of the datatypeLibrary in the XML version, while the W3C XML Schema datatype library has the special privilege of having its prefix built into the compact syntax: I have used the xsd prefix without needing to declare any datatype library! You will see later on that this isn't the case for the DTD compatibility type library.

The previous chapter explained that datatype declarations are kind of a transition to a data pattern and aren't inherited by child patterns. I'll illustrate this now that we have a richer set of datatypes at hand.

In the schema just written, I have defined the available attribute as boolean but our instance documents have used only one of the two syntaxes for boolean (true or false) and not used the other equivalent one (0 or 1). We may want to exclude this second syntax for boolean (for instance, if our application hasn't been designed to support it). In this case, we can just exclude these two values:

```
<attribute name="available">
 <data type="boolean">
  <except>
   <value>0</value>
   <value>1</value>
  </except>
 </data>
</attribute>
```

or:

```
attribute available {xsd:boolean - ("0"|"1")}
```

This looks rather natural, but why does it work? It works because RELAX NG forgets that the type of the attribute is boolean as soon as we've left the data pattern and instead uses the default type (RELAX NG's built-in token type) to test that the value is neither 0 nor 1. If RELAX NG didn't forget the type of the attribute, the schema would have removed the entire lexical space of "boolean" and would have been impossible to use because 0 and false are equivalent (and 1 and true too).

You have seen a situation where we rely on the fact that the types used in the data and value patterns are different. You will find other situations in which you will want them to be the same. In that case, you need to repeat the type attribute. If your applications are designed to accept both formats for the available attributes, and if you need to test that the books are available, you might prefer to use the same type for both patterns. In this case, you can write:

```
<attribute name="available">
 <data type="boolean">
  <except>
   <value type="boolean">false</value>
  </except>
 </data>
</attribute>
```

or:

```
attribute available {xsd:boolean - (xsd:boolean "false")},
```

You can now rely on the datatype boolean to exclude both 0 and false, which are equivalent. Of course, in the case of booleans, the number of possible values is limited. You can simplify the schema to:

```
<attribute name="available">
 <value type="boolean">true</value>
</attribute>
```

or:

```
attribute available {xsd:boolean "true"}
```

but this doesn't make my point. This trick also works for other datatypes.

Facets

The restrictions, known as *facets*, that a user can apply to predefined W3C XML Schema datatypes, in the W3C XML Schema recommendation can be applied in a RELAX NG schema. This is done using an element named param. The param elements are directly included within data patterns and appears before the optional except pattern covered in the previous chapter. These param elements have a name attribute, which identifies a facet, and their text content is the value of the facet. When several param elements are included, all the constraints must be met (in other words, the result is a logical "and" of all the conditions). Also note that the same facet can't be repeated twice except for the facet named pattern.

The vocabularies used by RELAX NG and W3C XML Schema are slightly different. What RELAX NG calls param is called facet by W3C XML Schema, while what is called a pattern by RELAX NG shouldn't be confused with the facet named pattern by W3C XML Schema. Also note that as you have seen previously, what RELAX NG calls whitespace normalization isn't the same as the whitespace processing applied to the W3C XML Schema normalizedSpace datatype.

The facets defined by W3C XML Schema are:

whiteSpace
    This somewhat controversial facet can't be used in RELAX NG.

enumeration
    This facet can't be used in RELAX NG because it is equivalent to RELAX NG's own enumerations; RELAX NG's should be used instead.

pattern
    This is the only facet that is applied to the lexical space. All the other facets work in the value space only. This facet checks whether the data matches a regular expression. This facet is covered in Chapter 9. For the moment, let's just say that it is a superset of Perl regular expressions (anchored to the beginning and the

end of the values to match), and that it doesn't support the POSIX-style character classes defined in Perl. It includes a few XML goodies, supports all the Unicode classes and blocks, and defines a special construct to define differences between character classes.

length

Available only for string, binary, and list datatypes. For string (and string-like) type, this defines the number of Unicode characters; for binary (i.e., hexBinary and base64Binary) datatypes, it defines a number of bytes; and for list datatypes (entities, idrefs and NMTOKENS), it defines the number of tokens in the list.

maxLength

Same meaning and restrictions as length but defines a maximum length.

minLength

Same meaning and restrictions as length but defines a minimum length.

maxExclusive

Applies only to decimal, integer (and derived), float, and double and all the date time and duration datatypes. It defines a maximum value that can't be reached. Note that, for date times and duration datatypes, the relation of order between two values is partial and that the result can't always be determined.

minExclusive

Same restriction as maxExclusive but defines a minimum value that can't be reached.

maxInclusive

Same restriction as maxExclusive but defines a maximum value that can be reached.

minInclusive

Same restriction as maxExclusive but defines a minimum value that can be reached.

totalDigits

Applies to decimal, integer, and derived types to define the maximum number of digits (after and before the decimal point). As all the facets do (except pattern), this facet works on the value space; "000001.10000000" (for instance) would be considered to have only two digits.

fractionDigits

Applies to decimal types to define the maximum number of fractional digits (those after the decimal point). As all the facets (except pattern), this facet works on the value space; "000001.10000000," (for instance) would be considered to have only one fractional digit.

Again, after this enumeration of facets, let's see how to apply some of the following to improve our library schema:

xml:lang
> We might want to ignore the regional differences and accept only two-character codes using the length facet.

isbn
> There would be much more to check on ISBN number, but we might want to use a pattern to confirm that it's composed of nine digits terminated by a character that is either a digit or the character "x."

born *and* died
> Assuming that our library is interested only in recent books we could check that they belong to the 20th or 21st centuries (in other words, between 1900 and 2099). We might also want to confirm that our dates don't specify a time zone, since we've seen that comparing dates with and without time zone is fuzzy and that the instance documents seen up to now have no timezones.

Other text data
> The maximum length can be constrained using a maxLength facet.

Here's the corresponding schema:

```
<element xmlns="http://relaxng.org/ns/structure/1.0"
 name="library" datatypeLibrary="http://www.w3.org/2001/XMLSchema-datatypes">
 <oneOrMore>
  <element name="book">
   <attribute name="id">
    <data type="ID">
      <param name="maxLength">16</param>
    </data>
   </attribute>
   <attribute name="available">
    <data type="boolean"/>
   </attribute>
   <element name="isbn">
    <data type="NMTOKEN">
      <param name="pattern">[0-9]{9}[0-9x]</param>
    </data>
   </element>
   <element name="title">
    <attribute name="xml:lang">
     <data type="language">
      <param name="length">2</param>
     </data>
    </attribute>
    <data type="token">
      <param name="maxLength">255</param>
    </data>
   </element>
   <zeroOrMore>
    <element name="author">
```

```
    <attribute name="id">
     <data type="ID">
      <param name="maxLength">16</param>
     </data>
    </attribute>
    <element name="name">
     <data type="token">
      <param name="maxLength">255</param>
     </data>
    </element>
    <element name="born">
     <data type="date">
      <param name="minInclusive">1900-01-01</param>
      <param name="maxInclusive">2099-12-31</param>
      <param name="pattern">[0-9]{4}-[0-9]{2}-[0-9]{2}</param>
     </data>
    </element>
    <optional>
     <element name="died">
      <data type="date">
       <param name="minInclusive">1900-01-01</param>
       <param name="maxInclusive">2099-12-31</param>
       <param name="pattern">[0-9]{4}-[0-9]{2}-[0-9]{2}</param>
      </data>
     </element>
    </optional>
   </element>
  </zeroOrMore>
  <zeroOrMore>
   <element name="character">
    <attribute name="id">
     <data type="ID">
      <param name="maxLength">16</param>
     </data>
    </attribute>
    <element name="name">
     <data type="token">
      <param name="maxLength">255</param>
     </data>
    </element>
    <element name="born">
     <data type="date">
      <param name="minInclusive">1900-01-01</param>
      <param name="maxInclusive">2099-12-31</param>
      <param name="pattern">[0-9]{4}-[0-9]{2}-[0-9]{2}</param>
     </data>
    </element>
    <element name="qualification">
     <data type="token">
      <param name="maxLength">255</param>
     </data>
    </element>
   </element>
  </zeroOrMore>
```

```
          </element>
        </oneOrMore>
      </element>
```

or:

```
      element library {
       element book {
        attribute id {xsd:ID {maxLength = "16"}},
        attribute available {xsd:boolean "true"},
        element isbn {xsd:NMATOKEN {pattern = "[0-9]{9}[0-9x]"}},
        element title {
           attribute xml:lang {xsd:language {length="2"}},
           xsd:token {maxLength="255"}
        },
        element author {
         attribute id {xsd:ID {maxLength = "16"}},
         element name {xsd:token {maxLength = "255"}},
         element born {xsd:date {
           minInclusive = "1900-01-01"
           maxInclusive = "2099-12-31"
           pattern = "[0-9]{4}-[0-9]{2}-[0-9]{2}"
        }},
         element died {xsd:date {
           minInclusive = "1900-01-01"
           maxInclusive = "2099-12-31"
           pattern = "[0-9]{4}-[0-9]{2}-[0-9]{2}"
        }}?}*,
       element character {
        attribute id {xsd:ID {maxLength = "16"}},
        element name {xsd:token {maxLength = "255"}},
        element born {xsd:date {
           minInclusive = "1900-01-01"
           maxInclusive = "2099-12-31"
           pattern = "[0-9]{4}-[0-9]{2}-[0-9]{2}"
        }},
        element qualification {xsd:token {maxLength = "255"}}}*
       } +
      }
```

Note the usage of regular expressions in the pattern facets. The set of facets provided by W3C XML Schema isn't particularly rich, so the pattern facet acts as a
Swiss Army knife, helping you to do all the tricky tasks other facets can't do. Regular expressions and pattern are explained in Chapter 9.

Also note that facets only define restrictions. You can't extend the lexical space of a
datatype through a facet (though you can create a choice between two types to merge
their lexical space).

DTD Compatibility Datatypes

DTD compatibility is both a library that checks the lexical spaces of its ID, IDREF, and IDREFS datatypes and a more expansive feature. This library adds to the normal RELAX NG processing and enforces DTD-like rules on the schema and on the instance document. This package is designed to facilitate the transition from DTDs to RELAX NG by emulating the attribute types ID, IDREF, and IDREFS. The DTD compatibility feature checks whether ID values are unique within a document and that IDREF and IDREFS are references or whitespace-separated lists of references to ID values defined in the document. It also checks the schema itself to ensure that datatypes are used only in attributes. Unlike their W3C XML Schema counterpart, these datatypes have no facets.

That's pretty much all you have to know about this library. Let's use it straightaway to define the id attributes in our library:

```
<element xmlns="http://relaxng.org/ns/structure/1.0" name="library"
datatypeLibrary="http://www.w3.org/2001/XMLSchema-datatypes">
  <oneOrMore>
   <element name="book">
    <attribute name="id">
     <data datatypeLibrary="http://relaxng.org/ns/compatibility/datatypes/1.0"
                     type="ID"/>
    </attribute>
    <attribute name="available">
     <data type="boolean"/>
    </attribute>
    <element name="isbn">
     <data type="NMTOKEN">
       <param name="pattern">[0-9]{9}[0-9x]</param>
     </data>
    </element>
    <element name="title">
     <attribute name="xml:lang">
      <data type="language">
       <param name="length">2</param>
      </data>
     </attribute>
     <data type="token">
       <param name="maxLength">255</param>
     </data>
    </element>
    <zeroOrMore>
     <element name="author">
      <attribute name="id">
       <data datatypeLibrary="http://relaxng.org/ns/compatibility/datatypes/1.0"
                      type="ID"/>
      </attribute>
      <element name="name">
       <data type="token">
         <param name="maxLength">255</param>
```

```
        </data>
      </element>
      <element name="born">
       <data type="date">
        <param name="minInclusive">1900-01-01</param>
        <param name="maxInclusive">2099-12-31</param>
        <param name="pattern">[0-9]{4}-[0-9]{2}-[0-9]{2}</param>
       </data>
      </element>
      <optional>
       <element name="died">
        <data type="date">
         <param name="minInclusive">1900-01-01</param>
         <param name="maxInclusive">2099-12-31</param>
         <param name="pattern">[0-9]{4}-[0-9]{2}-[0-9]{2}</param>
        </data>
       </element>
      </optional>
     </element>
    </zeroOrMore>
    <zeroOrMore>
     <element name="character">
      <attribute name="id">
       <data datatypeLibrary="http://relaxng.org/ns/compatibility/datatypes/1.0"
                  type="ID"/>
      </attribute>
      <element name="name">
       <data type="token">
        <param name="maxLength">255</param>
       </data>
      </element>
      <element name="born">
       <data type="date">
        <param name="minInclusive">1900-01-01</param>
        <param name="maxInclusive">2099-12-31</param>
        <param name="pattern">[0-9]{4}-[0-9]{2}-[0-9]{2}</param>
       </data>
      </element>
      <element name="qualification">
       <data type="token">
        <param name="maxLength">255</param>
       </data>
      </element>
     </element>
    </zeroOrMore>
   </element>
  </oneOrMore>
</element>
```

or:

```
datatypes dtd="http://relaxng.org/ns/compatibility/datatypes/1.0"
element library {
 element book {
```

```
    attribute id {dtd:ID},
    attribute available {xsd:boolean "true"},
    element isbn {xsd:NMTOKEN {pattern = "[0-9]{9}[0-9x]"}},
    element title {
       attribute xml:lang {xsd:language {length="2"}},
       xsd:token {maxLength="255"}
    },
    element author {
     attribute id {dtd:ID},
     element name {xsd:token {maxLength = "255"}},
     element born {xsd:date {
        minInclusive = "1900-01-01"
        maxInclusive = "2099-12-31"
        pattern = "[0-9]{4}-[0-9]{2}-[0-9]{2}"
     }},
     element died {xsd:date {
        minInclusive = "1900-01-01"
        maxInclusive = "2099-12-31"
        pattern = "[0-9]{4}-[0-9]{2}-[0-9]{2}"
     }}?}*,
    element character {
     attribute id {dtd:ID},
     element name {xsd:token {maxLength = "255"}},
     element born {xsd:date {
        minInclusive = "1900-01-01"
        maxInclusive = "2099-12-31"
        pattern = "[0-9]{4}-[0-9]{2}-[0-9]{2}"
     }},
     element qualification {xsd:token {maxLength = "255"}}}*
   } +
 }
```

As already mentioned, the DTD compatibility feature has been designed to provide compatibility with the features of the DTD, and that includes emulating some of their restrictions. I have already mentioned that these datatypes can be used only in attributes, not in elements. I need to mention another limitation that can be more insidious and has bitten renowned experts trying to do things such as write RELAX NG schemas for XHTML.

This rule might be called the "consistent attribute definition rule." Because a DTD won't allow you to give two different definitions of the content of an element, RELAX NG enforces the rule that if an attribute id is defined as ID, IDREF, or IDREFS in an element somewhere in a RELAX NG schema, all the definitions of the same attribute under the same element must use the same type.

The simplest schemas, which don't meet this standard and thus aren't correct with respect to the DTD compatibility feature, are schemas that contain multiple declarations of the same element and attributes with different types, such as:

```
<?xml version="1.0" encoding="UTF-8"?>
 <element name="foo" xmlns="http://relaxng.org/ns/structure/1.0"
    datatypeLibrary="http://relaxng.org/ns/compatibility/datatypes/1.0">
```

```
<element name="bar">
  <attribute name="id">
    <data type="ID"/>
  </attribute>
</element>
<zeroOrMore>
  <element name="bar">
    <attribute name="id">
      <data type="token" datatypeLibrary=""/>
    </attribute>
  </element>
</zeroOrMore>
</element>
```

or:

```
datatypes dtd="http://relaxng.org/ns/compatibility/datatypes/1.0"

element foo {
  element bar {
    attribute id { dtd:ID }
  },
  element bar {
    attribute id { token }
  } *
}
```

Here, there are two definitions of bar with id attributes having competing types. Because one of these types is a dtd:ID type, this practice is forbidden.

A situation tougher to detect and tougher to fix is when one of these competing definitions uses patterns that allow name classes to permit the inclusion of any element, such as you will see in Chapter 12. This situation can create serious complications.

Which Library Should Be Used?

All the RELAX NG implementations must support the native datatype library; many of them also support the DTD compatibility datatypes library and the W3C XML Schema datatypes library. That means that if you want to define a token or string datatype, you can often choose between the native library and W3C XML Schema datatypes, and if you're defining ID, IDREF, or IDREFS, you can often choose between the DTD compatibility library and W3C XML Schema datatypes.

Native Types Versus W3C XML Schema Datatypes

The criteria for choosing between native or W3C XML Schema datatypes to define string and token types is simple: if you need facets, use W3C XML Schema datatypes. If you don't, use native datatypes: your schema will be more portable, because the RELAX NG processors aren't obliged to support the W3C XML Schema type library.

DTD Versus W3C XML Schema Datatypes

When you need to define a datatype covered by both DTD and W3C XML Schema—i.e., ID, IDREF, or IDREFS—a similar rule of thumb applies. If you use the DTD compatibility library, your schema should be slightly more portable, but you will lose the facets.

The other factor to take into account is that the rules applied when you use the DTD compatibility feature are strict and consistent over different implementations; when you use the W3C XML Schema type library, a processor should apply these same rules if and only if it also supports the DTD datatype library. Processors that support only W3C XML Schema datatypes are supposed to check only the lexical space of these datatypes.

In practice, that means you can use ID, IDREF, or IDREFS datatypes from the W3C XML Schema library, but that it is safer to debug your schema using an implementation that supports both the DTD and the W3C XML Schema type libraries.

If you design a RELAX NG schema using W3C XML Schema's ID, IDREF, and IDREFS, and then test it with an implementation that supports only W3C XML Schema datatypes, the rules of DTD compatibility will not be enforced. When you use the same schema and instance documents with a RELAX NG processor supporting both the DTD and W3C XML Schema datatypes, you get tighter control; the instance documents and even the schema that were previously valid may suddenly become invalid or incorrect because of this control.

Here's a simple example of a schema that defines ID elements. It's correct for RELAX NG implementations that supporting W3C XML Schema datatypes without supporting the DTD compatibility layer, and yet it doesn't use the DTD compatibility feature for RELAX NG implementations supporting both.

```
<?xml version="1.0" encoding="UTF-8"?>
<element name="foo" xmlns="http://relaxng.org/ns/structure/1.0"
  datatypeLibrary="http://www.w3.org/2001/XMLSchema-datatypes">
  <zeroOrMore>
    <element name="bar">
      <element name="id">
        <data type="ID"/>
      </element>
    </element>
  </zeroOrMore>
</element>
```

or:

```
element foo {
  element bar {
    element id { xsd:ID }
  } *
}
```

Other examples include schemas that don't respect the rule by which the definitions of attributes holding these datatypes must be consistent throughout the schema.

The reason for this behavior is that although I've often mentioned the "DTD compatibility datatype library" for clarity all over this chapter, DTD compatibility is more than a datatype library. Per the RELAX NG formal specification, a datatype library must be decoupled from the validation of the structure of the document, and the context passed to the datatype library is restricted to the namespace declarations available under the node being validated. This context itself is an exception required to process qualified names. The datatype library has thus not enough information to do the tests required to support DTD compatibility: it doesn't even know whether the data to validate has been found in an element or an attribute. This aspect of the DTD compatibility is thus a feature and not a datatype library as defined per RELAX NG.

When you use a datatype from the datatype library `http://relaxng.org/ns/compatibility/datatypes/1.0`, you're actually doing two different things:

- Using a datatype library that restricts the lexical space of your `data` and `value` patterns.
- Requesting testing to ensure that the `ID` are unique, and that the `IDREF` and `IDREFS` are referring to IDs and lists of IDs.

Applied to the W3C XML Schema datatype library, this translates as: if these datatypes are used, trigger the ID DTD compatibility feature when available.

CHAPTER 9

Using Regular Expressions to Specify Simple Datatypes

Among the many facets available for restricting simple datatypes, the most flexible is based on regular expressions. The pattern facet can be a last resort when all the other facets are unable to express needed restrictions on a user-defined datatype.

There is a terminology clash between RELAX NG's patterns and the pattern facet of W3C XML Schema. To limit the risk of confusion, I refer to the facet as the pattern facet or "regular expression."

A Swiss Army Knife

The pattern facet (like regular expressions in general), is like a Swiss Army knife when constraining simple datatypes. It can be used for many functions and can compensate for many of the limitations of the other facets; it's often used to define user datatypes in various formats, such as ISBN numbers, telephone numbers, or custom date formats. However, just like real Swiss Army knives, there are limits to its usefulness.

Cutting a tree with a Swiss Army knife is time-consuming, tiring, and dangerous. Writing regular expressions can also become time-consuming, tiring, and dangerous as the number of combinations grows. You should try to keep them as simple as possible.

A Swiss Army knife can't change lead into gold, and no facet can change the primary type of a simple datatype. A string datatype restricted to match a custom date format will still retain the properties of a string and will never acquire the facets of a datetime datatype. This means there's no effective way to express localized date formats.

The Simplest Possible Pattern Facets

In their simplest form, pattern facets may be used as enumerations applied to the lexical space rather than on the value space.

If, for instance, you have a byte value that can take only the values 1, 5, or 15, the classical way to define such a datatype is to use RELAX NG's choice pattern:

```
<choice>
  <value type="byte">1</value>
  <value type="byte">5</value>
  <value type="byte">15</value>
</choice>
```

or:

```
element foo {
 xsd:byte "1"
 | xsd:byte "5"
 | xsd:byte "15"
}
```

This example is the normal way to define this datatype if it matches the lexical space and the value space of an xsd:byte. It grants the flexibility to accept the instance documents with values such as 1, 5, and 15, but also 01 or 0000005.

As far as validation alone is concerned, if you want to remove the variations with leading zeros, you can use another datatype such as token instead of xsd:byte in your choice pattern:

```
<choice>
  <value type="token">1</value>
  <value type="token">5</value>
  <value type="token">15</value>
</choice>
```

or:

```
xsd:token "1"
| xsd:token "5"
| xsd:token "15"
```

However, you might have good reasons to use xsd:byte. For example, you can use it if you're interested in type annotation and want to use a RELAX NG processor supporting type annotation. That processor can usefully report the datatype as xsd:byte and not xsd:token.

One of the peculiarities of the pattern facet is that it is the only facet constraining the lexical space. If you have an application that doesn't like leading zeros, you can use pattern facets instead of enumerations to define your datatype:

```
<data type="byte">
  <param name="pattern">1|5|15</param>
</data>
```

or:

```
xsd:byte {pattern = "1|5|15"}
```

Here, I am still using the xsd:byte datatype with its associated semantics, but its lexical space is now constrained to accept only 1, 5, and 15, leaving out any variation that has the same value but a different lexical representation.

 This constraint is an important difference from Perl regular expressions, on which W3C XML Schema pattern facets are built. A Perl expression such as /15/ matches any string containing 15, while the W3C XML Schema pattern facet matches only the string equal to 15. The Perl expression equivalent to this pattern facet is thus /^15$/.

This example has been carefully chosen to avoid using any metacharacters within pattern facets, which are: . \ ? * + { } ( ) [and]. You'll see the meaning of these characters later in this chapter; however, for the moment, you just need to know that each of these characters needs to be escaped by a leading backslash to be used as a literal. For instance, to define a similar datatype for a decimal when lexical space is limited to 1 and 1.5, write:

```
<data type="decimal">
  <param name="pattern">1|1\.5</param>
</data>
```

or:

```
xsd:decimal {pattern = "1|1\.5"}
```

A common source of errors is that normal characters shouldn't be escaped: you'll see later that a leading backslash changes their meaning. For instance, \P matches all the Unicode punctuation characters, not the character P.

Quantifying

Despite similarities on the surface, the pattern facet interprets its value in a very different way than value does. value reads the value as a lexical representation and converts it to the corresponding value for its base datatype, while the pattern facet reads the value as a set of conditions to apply on lexical values. When you write:

```
pattern="15"
```

you specify three conditions (first character equals 1, second character equals 5, and the string must finish after the 5). Each of the matching conditions (such as first character equals 1, and second character equals 5) is called a *piece*. This is just the simplest form for specifying pieces.

Each piece in a pattern facet is composed of an *atom* identifying a character, or a set of characters, and an optional quantifier. Characters (except special characters, which must be escaped) are the simplest form of atoms. In the example, I have

---

omitted the quantifiers. Quantifiers may be defined using two different syntaxes: using either special characters (* for 0 or more, + for one or more, and ? for 0 or 1) or a numeric range within curly braces ({*n*} for exactly *n* times, {*n,m*} for between *n* and *m* times, or {*n,*} for *n* or more times).

Using these quantifiers, you can merge the three pattern facets into one:

```
<data type="byte">
  <param name="pattern">1?5?</param>
</data>
```

or:

```
xsd:byte {pattern = "1?5?"}
```

This new pattern facet means that there must be zero or one character (1) followed by zero or one character (5). This is not exactly the same meaning as the three previous pattern facets because the empty string "" is now accepted by the pattern facet. However, because the empty string doesn't belong to the lexical space of the base type (xsd:byte), the new datatype has the same lexical space as the previous one.

You can also use quantifiers to limit the number of leading zeros; for instance, the following pattern facet limits the number of leading zeros to up to 2:

```
<data type="byte">
  <param name="pattern">0{0,2}1?5?</param>
</data>
```

or:

```
xsd:byte {pattern = "0{0,2}1?5?"}
```

More Atoms

Atoms that exactly match a character are the simplest atoms that can be used in a pattern facet. The other atoms that can be used in pattern facets are special characters, a wildcard that matches any character, or predefined and user-defined character classes.

Special Characters

Table 9-1 shows the list of atoms that match a single character, exactly like the characters you've already seen, but they also correspond to characters that must be escaped or (for the first three characters on the list) that are just provided for convenience.

Table 9-1. Special characters

Character	Description
\n	Newline (can also be written as
 — because it's an XML document).
\r	Carriage return (can also be written as ).

Table 9-1. Special characters (continued)

Character	Description
\t	Tabulation (can also be written as 	)
\\	Character \
|	Character |
\.	Character .
\-	Character -
\^	Character ^
\?	Character ?
*	Character *
\+	Character +
\{	Character {
\}	Character }
\(	Character (
\)	Character)
\[	Character [
\]	Character]

Wildcard

The dot character (.) has a special meaning; it's a wildcard atom that matches any valid XML characters except newlines and carriage returns. As with any atom, a dot may be followed by an optional quantifier; .* (dot, asterisk) is a common construct to match zero or more occurrences of any character. To illustrate the usage of .* (and the fact that the pattern facet is a Swiss Army knife), a pattern facet can define the integers that are multiples of 10:

```
<define name="multipleOfTen">
  <data type="integer">
    <param name="pattern">.*0</param>
  </data>
</define>
```

or:

```
multipleOfTen = xsd:integer {pattern = ".*0"}
```

Character Classes

W3C XML Schema has adopted the classical Perl and Unicode character classes (but not the POSIX-style character classes also available in Perl), and user-defined classes are also available.

Classical Perl character classes

W3C XML Schema supports the classical Perl character classes plus a couple of additions to match XML-specific productions. Each class is designated by a single letter; the classes designated by the upper- and lowercase versions of the same letter are complementary:

\s Spaces. Matches XML whitespace (space #x20, tab #x09, linefeed #x0A, and carriage return #x0D).

\S Characters that aren't spaces.

\d Digits (0 to 9, but also digits in other alphabets).

\D Characters that aren't digits.

\w Extended "word" characters (any Unicode character not defined as punctuation, separator, or other). This conforms to the Perl definition, assuming UTF-8 support has been switched on.

\W Nonword characters.

\i XML 1.0 initial name characters (i.e., all the letters plus _). This is a W3C XML Schema extension of Perl regular expressions.

\I Characters that may not be used as a XML initial name character.

\c XML 1.0 name characters (. : - plus initial name characters, digits, and the characters defined by Unicode as "combining" or "extender"). This is a W3C XML Schema extension of Perl regular expressions.

\C Characters that can't be used in a XML 1.0 name.

These character classes can be used with an optional quantifier like any other atom. The last pattern facet that you saw:

```
multipleOfTen = xsd:integer {pattern = ".*0"}
```

constrains the lexical space to be a string of characters ending with a zero. Knowing that the base type is an xsd:integer, is good enough for our purposes, but if the base type had been an xsd:decimal (or xsd:string), you can be more restrictive and write:

```
multipleOfTen = xsd:integer {pattern = "-?\d*0"}
```

This syntax checks that the characters before the trailing zero are digits with an optional leading - (you'll see later how to specify an optional leading – or +).

Unicode character classes

Patterns support character classes matching both Unicode categories and blocks. Categories and blocks are two complementary classification systems: *categories* classify the characters by their usage independently of their localization (letters, uppercase, digit, punctuation, etc.); *blocks* classify characters by their localization independently of their usage (Latin, Arabic, Hebrew, Tibetan, and even Gothic or musical symbols).

The syntax \p{Name} is similar for blocks and categories; the prefix Is is added to the name of categories to make the distinction. The syntax \P{Name} is also available to select the characters that don't match a block or category. A list of Unicode blocks and categories is given in the specification. Table 9-2 shows the Unicode character classes, and Table 9-3 shows the Unicode character blocks.

Table 9-2. Unicode character classes

Unicode character class	Includes
C	Other characters (nonletters, nonsymbols, nonnumbers, nonseparators)
Cc	Control characters
Cf	Format characters
Cn	Unassigned code points
Co	Private-use characters
L	Letters
Ll	Lowercase letters
Lm	Modifier letters
Lo	Other letters
Lt	Titlecase letters
Lu	Uppercase letters
M	All marks
Mc	Spacing combining marks
Me	Enclosing marks
Mn	Nonspacing marks
N	Numbers
Nd	Decimal digits
Nl	Number letters
No	Other numbers
P	Punctuation
Pc	Connector punctuation
Pd	Dashes
Pe	Closing punctuation
Pf	Final quotes (may behave like Ps or Pe)
Pi	Initial quotes (may behave like Ps or Pe)
Po	Other forms of punctuation
Ps	Opening punctuation
S	Symbols
Sc	Currency symbols
Sk	Modifier symbols
Sm	Mathematical symbols

Table 9-2. Unicode character classes (continued)

Unicode character class	Includes
So	Other symbols
Z	Separators
Zl	Line breaks
Zp	Paragraph breaks
Zs	Spaces

Table 9-3. Unicode character blocks

AlphabeticPresentationForms	EnclosedAlphanumerics	Malayalam
Arabic	EnclosedCJKLettersandMonths	MathematicalAlphanumericSymbols
ArabicPresentationForms-A	Ethiopic	MathematicalOperators
ArabicPresentationForms-B	GeneralPunctuation	MiscellaneousSymbols
Armenian	GeometricShapes	MiscellaneousTechnical
Arrows	Georgian	Mongolian
BasicLatin	Gothic	MusicalSymbols
Bengali	Greek	Myanmar
BlockElements	GreekExtended	NumberForms
Bopomofo	Gujarati	Ogham
BopomofoExtended	Gurmukhi	OldItalic
BoxDrawing	HalfwidthandFullwidthForms	OpticalCharacterRecognition
BraillePatterns	HangulCompatibilityJamo	Oriya
ByzantineMusicalSymbols	HangulJamo	PrivateUse
Cherokee	HangulSyllables	PrivateUse
CJKCompatibility	Hebrew	PrivateUse
CJKCompatibilityForms	HighPrivateUseSurrogates	Runic
CJKCompatibilityIdeographs	HighSurrogates	Sinhala
CJKCompatibilityIdeographsSupplement	Hiragana	SmallFormVariants
CJKRadicalsSupplement	IdeographicDescriptionCharacters	SpacingModifierLetters
CJKSymbolsandPunctuation	IPAExtensions	Specials
CJKUnifiedIdeographs	Kanbun	Specials
CJKUnifiedIdeographsExtensionA	KangxiRadicals	SuperscriptsandSubscripts
CJKUnifiedIdeographsExtensionB	Kannada	Syriac
CombiningDiacriticalMarks	Katakana	Tags
CombiningHalfMarks	Khmer	Tamil
CombiningMarksforSymbols	Lao	Telugu
ControlPictures	Latin-1Supplement	Thaana
CurrencySymbols	LatinExtended-A	Thai

Table 9-3. Unicode character blocks (continued)

Cyrillic	LatinExtendedAdditional	Tibetan
Deseret	LatinExtended-B	UnifiedCanadianAboriginalSyllabics
Devanagari	LetterlikeSymbols	YiRadicals
Dingbats	LowSurrogates	YiSyllables

You'll see in the next section that W3C XML Schema has introduced an extension to regular expressions to specify intersections, This extension can define the intersection between a block and a category in a single pattern facet.

Although Unicode blocks seem to be a great way to restrict text to a set of characters you can print, display, read, or store in a database, they aren't designed for this purpose, and you must be careful when using them so. John Cowan, who has taught courses on Unicode and enjoys obscure alphabets, wrote about this topic:

> It's important to note that Unicode blocks are a very crude mechanism for discrimination: not everything needed to write Greek is in the Greek block, and there are no less than five Latin blocks, one of which (Basic Latin; i.e., ASCII) contains many script-independent symbols. The blocks were originally created solely for internal Unicode organizational purposes, and have spread to the outside world somewhat randomly.

The five Latin blocks mentioned by John are BasicLatin, Latin1Supplement, LatinExtended-A, LatinExtendedAdditional, and LatinExtended-B.

User-defined character classes

These classes are lists of characters between square brackets that accept - signs to define ranges and a leading ^ to negate the whole list: for instance, the following defines the list of letters on the first row of a French keyboard:

```
[azertyuiop]
```

This expression specifies all characters between a and z:

```
[a-z]
```

This expression specifies all characters that aren't between a and z:

```
[^a-z]
```

This expression defines characters - ^ and \:

```
[\-^\\]
```

This expression specifies a decimal sign:

```
[\-+]
```

These examples demonstrate that the contents of these square brackets follows a specific syntax and semantic. Like the regular expression's main syntax, there's a list of atoms, but instead of matching each atom against a character of the instance string, you define a logical space. Brackets operate in a space between the atoms and more formal character classes.

The caret (^) is a special character that has a different meaning depending on its location. A negator when it appears at the beginning of a class, the caret loses this special meaning and acts as a normal character when it appears later in the class definition.

 The support of the escape format #x*XX* (such as in #x2D) is a frequent source of confusion. Because this format is used in the W3C XML Schema recommendation to describe characters by their Unicode value, some people have thought to use it in regular expressions, but it is not meant to be used that way. If you want to define characters by their Unicode values, you should use numeric entities instead (such as - if you are using the XML syntax or the syntax for escaping characters in the compact syntax \x{2D}). Note that in both cases, the reference is replaced by the corresponding character at parse time and that the regular expression engine will see the actual character instead of the escape sequence.

Also, some characters may or must be escaped: \\ matches the character \. In fact, in a class definition, all the escape sequences you saw as atoms can be used. Even though some special characters lose their special meaning inside square brackets, they can always be escaped. So, the following:

    [\-^\\]

can also be written as:

    [\-\^\\]

or as:

    [\^\\\-]

because when they are escaped, the location of the characters doesn't matter.

Within square brackets, the character \ also keeps its meaning of a reference to a Perl or Unicode class. The following:

    [\d\p{Lu}]

is a set of decimal digits (Perl class \d) and uppercase letters (Unicode category "Lu").

Mathematicians have found that three basic operations are needed to manipulate sets and that these operations can be chosen from a larger set of operations. In square brackets, you've already seen two of these operations: *union* (the square bracket is an implicit union of its atoms) and *complement* (a leading ^ realizes the complement of the set defined in the square bracket). W3C XML Schema extends the syntax of Perl regular expressions to introduce a third operation: the *difference between sets*. The syntax follows:

```
[set1-[set2]]
```

Its meaning is that all the characters in set1 that don't belong to set2, where set1 and set2 can use all the syntactic tricks you saw earlier.

This operator can perform intersections of character classes (the intersection between two sets A and B is the difference between A and the complement of B), and you can now define a class for the BasicLatinLetters as:

```
[\p{IsBasicLatin}-[^\p{L}]]
```

Using the \P construct, which is also a complement, you can define the class as:

```
[\p{IsBasicLatin}-[\P{L}]]
```

The corresponding definition is:

```
<define name="BasicLatinLetters">
  <data type="token">
    <param name="pattern">[\p{IsBasicLatin}-[\P{L}]]*</param>
  </data>
</define>
```

or:

```
BasicLatinLetters = xsd:token {pattern = "[\p{IsBasicLatin}-[\P{L}]]*"}
```

Or-ing and Grouping

I used an or in the first example pattern facet when I wrote "1|5|15" to allow either 1, 5, or 15.

Ors are especially interesting when used with groups. Groups are complete regular expressions, which are themselves considered atoms and can be used with an optional quantifier to form more complete (and complex) regular expressions. Groups are enclosed by parentheses. To define a comma-separated list of 1, 5, or 15, ignoring whitespace between values and commas, the following pattern facet can be used:

```
<define name="myListOfBytes">
  <data type="token">
    <param name="pattern">(1|5|15)( *, *(1|5|15))*</param>
  </data>
</define>
```

or:

```
myListOfBytes = xsd:token {pattern = "(1|5|15)( *, *(1|5|15))*"}
```

Note the reliance on the whitespace processing of the base datatype (xsd:token collapses the whitespace). You don't need to worry about leading and trailing whitespace that's trimmed; single occurrences of spaces were tested with the * atom before and after the comma.

Common Patterns

After this overview of the syntax used by pattern facets, let's see some common pattern facets you may have to use (or adapt) in your schemas or just consider as examples.

String Datatypes

Regular expressions treat information in its textual form. This makes them an excellent mechanism for constraining strings.

Unicode blocks

Unicode is one of XML's greatest assets. However, there are few applications able to process and display all the characters of the Unicode set correctly and still fewer users able to read them! If you need to check that your string datatypes belong to one (or more) Unicode blocks, you can use these pattern facets:

```
<define name="BasicLatinToken">
  <data type="token">
    <param name="pattern">\p{IsBasicLatin}*</param>
  </data>
</define>

<define name="Latin-1Token">
  <data type="token">
    <param name="pattern">[\p{IsBasicLatin}\p{IsLatin-1Supplement}]*</param>
  </data>
</define>
```

or:

```
BasicLatinToken = xsd:token {pattern = "\p{IsBasicLatin}*"}

Latin-1Token = xsd:token {pattern = "[\p{IsBasicLatin}\p{IsLatin-1Supplement}]*"
```

Note that such pattern facets don't impose a character encoding on the document itself and that, for instance, the Latin-1Token datatype validates instance documents using UTF-8, UTF-16, ISO-8869-1 or another encoding. (This statement assumes the characters used in this string belong to the two Unicode blocks BasicLatin and Latin-1Supplement.) In other words, even the lexical space reflects some processing done by the parser, below the level you can control with a schema.

Counting words

The pattern facet can limit the number of words in a text block. To do so, we will define an atom, which is a sequence of one or more word characters (\w+) followed by one or more nonword characters (\W+), and thus control the number of occurrences of this atom. If you're not very strict about punctuation, you also need to allow an arbitrary number of nonword characters at the beginning of our value and deal with the possibility of a value ending with a word (without further separation). One way to avoid any ambiguity at the end of the string is to dissociate the last occurrence of a word, making the trailing separator optional:

```
<define name="story100-200words">
  <data type="token">
    <param name="pattern">\W*(\w+\W+){99,199}\w+\W*</param>
  </data>
</define>
```

or:

```
story100-200words= xsd:token {pattern = "\W*(\w+\W+){99,199}\w+\W*"}
```

URIs

The xsd:anyURI datatype doesn't care about making relative URI references into absolute URI references. In some cases, it is wise to require the usage of absolute URIs, which are easier to process. Furthermore, it can also be useful for some applications to limit the accepted URI schemes, which can easily be done by a set of pattern facets such as:

```
<define name="httpURI">
  <data type="anyURI">
    <param name="pattern">http://.*</param>
  </data>
</define>
```

or:

```
httpURI= xsd:anyURI {pattern = "http://.*"}
```

Numeric and Float Types

While numeric types aren't strictly text, pattern facets can still be used to constrain their lexical form and effectively, their content.

Leading zeros

Getting rid of leading zeros is quite simple but requires some precautions if you want to keep the optional sign and the number 0 itself. This can be done using pattern facets such as:

```
<define name="noLeadingZeros">
  <data type="integer">
```

```
      <param name="pattern">[+-]?([^0][0-9]*|0)</param>
    </data>
  </define>
```

or:

```
noLeadingZeros= xsd:integer {pattern = "[+-]?([^0][0-9]*|0)"}
```

Note that in this pattern facet, I chose to redefine all the lexical rules that apply to an integer. This pattern facet gives the same lexical space applied to an xsd:token datatype as on an xsd:integer. You can also rely on the expectations of the base datatype and write:

```
<define name="noLeadingZeros">
  <data type="integer">
    <param name="pattern">[+-]?([^0].*|0)</param>
  </data>
</define>
```

or:

```
noLeadingZeros= xsd:integer {pattern = "[+-]?([^0].*|0)"}
```

Relying on the base datatype in this manner can produce simpler pattern facets, but it can also be more difficult to interpret because you have to combine the lexical rules of the base datatype to the rules expressed by the pattern facet to understand the result.

Fixed format

The maximum number of digits can be fixed using xsd:totalDigits and xsd:fractionDigits. However, these facets are only maximum numbers and work on the value space. If you want to fix the format of the lexical space to be, for instance, DDDD.DD, you can write a pattern facet such as:

```
<define name="fixedDigits">
  <data type="decimal">
    <param name="pattern">[+-]?\.{4}\..{2}</param>
  </data>
</define>
```

or:

```
fixedDigits= xsd:decimal {pattern = "[+-]?\.{4}\..{2}"}
```

Datetimes

Dates and time have complex lexical representations. Patterns give you extra control over how they are used.

Time zones

The time-zone support of W3C XML Schema is quite controversial and needs some additional constraints to avoid comparison problems. These pattern facets can be kept relatively simple because the syntax of the datetime is already checked by the schema validator, and only simple additional checks need to be added. Applications that require their datetimes to specify a time zone may use the following template that checks if the time part ends with a Z or contains a sign:

```
<define name="dateTimeWithTimezone">
  <data type="dateTime">
    <param name="pattern">.+T.+(Z|[+-].+)</param>
  </data>
</define>
```

or:

```
dateTimeWithTimezone= xsd:dateTime {pattern = ".+T.+(Z|[+-].+)"}
```

Simpler applications that want to make sure that none of their datetime values specify a time zone can simply check that the time part doesn't contain the characters + - or Z:

```
<define name="dateTimeWithoutTimezone">
  <data type="dateTime">
    <param name="pattern">.+T[^Z+-]+</param>
  </data>
</define>
```

or:

```
dateTimeWithoutTimezone= xsd:dateTime {pattern = ".+T[^Z+-]+"}
```

In these two datatypes, the T separator is used. This separator is convenient because no occurrences of the signs can occur after this delimiter except in the time-zone definition. This delimiter would be missing if you want to constrain dates instead of datetimes, but, in this case, you can detect the time zones on their colon instead:

```
<define name="dateWithTimezone">
  <data type="date">
    <param name="pattern">.+[:Z].*</param>
  </data>
</define>
<define name="dateWithoutTimezone">
  <data type="date">
    <param name="pattern">[^:Z]</param>
  </data>
</define>
```

or:

```
dateWithTimezone= xsd:date {pattern = ".+[:Z].*"}
dateWithoutTimezone= xsd:date {pattern = "[^:Z]"}
```

Applications may also impose a set of time zones to use:

```
<define name="dateTimeInMyTimezones">
  <data type="dateTime">
    <param name="pattern">.+(\+02:00|\+01:00|\+00:00|Z|-04:00)</param>
  </data>
</define>
```

or:

```
dateTimeInMyTimezones= xsd:dateTime {
        pattern = ".+(\+02:00|\+01:00|\+00:00|Z|-04:00)"
}
```

You can also constrain xsd:duration to a couple of subsets that can be reliably compared. The first datatype consist of durations expressed only in months and years, and the second will consist of durations expressed only in days, hours, minutes, and seconds. The criteria used for the test can be the presence of a D (for day) or a T (the time delimiter). If neither character is detected, the datatype uses only year and month parts. The test for the other type can't be based on the absence of Y and M because there is also an M in the time part. You can test to ensure that, after an optional sign, the first field is either the day part or the T delimiter:

```
<define name="YMduration">
  <data type="duration">
    <param name="pattern">[^TD]+</param>
  </data>
</define>
<define name="DHMSduration">
  <data type="duration">
    <param name="pattern">-?P((\d+D)|T).*</param>
  </data>
</define>
```

or:

```
YMduration= xsd:duration {pattern = "[^TD]+"}
DHMSduration= xsd:duration {pattern = "-?P((\d+D)|T).*"}
```

It may seem tricky, but this is a powerful tool for resolving complex problems simply.

CHAPTER 10
Creating Building Blocks

You have seen how named patterns can give some modularity to our schemas and how they can define recursive content models. In this chapter, I'll show how patterns can serve as building blocks in libraries of content models that can then be assembled into complete schemas. To do so, I'll introduce new RELAX NG patterns that control the inclusion of schemas.

Using External References

External references offer a powerful but simple mechanism for including a pattern contained in an external document at any location in a schema. This feature works through raw inclusion of the referenced external document. The externalRef pattern is replaced by the content of the document. That document may be a complete RELAX NG schema, though that isn't required, but a valid pattern is required.

With Russian Doll Schemas

You may want to reuse existing schemas as a whole, without modifying any of their definitions. Imagine, for instance, that we have defined two grammars in two schemas to describe our author and character elements. First, create a RELAX NG schema, *author.rng*, to describe our authors:

```
<?xml version="1.0" encoding="UTF-8"?>
<element name="author" xmlns="http://relaxng.org/ns/structure/1.0"
  datatypeLibrary="http://www.w3.org/2001/XMLSchema-datatypes">
  <attribute name="id">
    <data type="ID"/>
  </attribute>
  <element name="name">
    <data type="token" datatypeLibrary=""/>
  </element>
  <optional>
    <element name="born">
      <data type="date"/>
```

```
      </element>
    </optional>
    <optional>
      <element name="died">
        <data type="date"/>
      </element>
    </optional>
  </element>
```

or, in the compact syntax, *author.rnc*:

```
element author {
  attribute id { xsd:ID },
  element name { token },
  element born { xsd:date }?,
  element died { xsd:date }?
}
```

Then create a second schema, *character.rng*, to describe our characters:

```
<?xml version="1.0" encoding="UTF-8"?>
<element name="character" xmlns="http://relaxng.org/ns/structure/1.0"
  datatypeLibrary="http://www.w3.org/2001/XMLSchema-datatypes">
  <attribute name="id">
    <data type="ID"/>
  </attribute>
  <element name="name">
    <data type="token" datatypeLibrary=""/>
  </element>
  <optional>
    <element name="born">
      <data type="date"/>
    </element>
  </optional>
  <element name="qualification">
    <data type="token" datatypeLibrary=""/>
  </element>
</element>
```

or, in the compact syntax, *character.rnc*:

```
element character {
  attribute id { xsd:ID },
  element name { token },
  element born { xsd:date }?,
  element qualification { token }
}
```

To combine these components into a schema describing our library, use externalRef patterns:

```
<?xml version="1.0" encoding="UTF-8"?>
<element name="library" xmlns="http://relaxng.org/ns/structure/1.0"
  datatypeLibrary="http://www.w3.org/2001/XMLSchema-datatypes">
  <oneOrMore>
    <element name="book">
```

```
            <attribute name="id">
              <data type="ID"/>
            </attribute>
            <attribute name="available">
              <data type="boolean"/>
            </attribute>
            <element name="isbn">
              <data type="token" datatypeLibrary=""/>
            </element>
            <element name="title">
              <attribute name="xml:lang">
                <data type="language"/>
              </attribute>
              <data type="token" datatypeLibrary=""/>
            </element>
            <oneOrMore>
              <externalRef href="author.rng"/>
            </oneOrMore>
            <zeroOrMore>
              <externalRef href="character.rng"/>
            </zeroOrMore>
          </element>
        </oneOrMore>
      </element>
```

In the compact syntax, externalRef patterns are represented using the keyword external:

```
element library {
  element book {
    attribute id { xsd:ID },
    attribute available { xsd:boolean },
    element isbn { token },
    element title {
      attribute xml:lang { xsd:language },
      token
    },
    external "author.rnc" +,
    external "character.rnc" *
  }+
}
```

The externalRef pattern performs direct inclusion: when a RELAX NG processor reads a schema, it replaces externalRef with the contents of the referred document.

With Flat Schemas

The previous example used externalRef to include the content of Russian doll schemas, but this also works with flat schemas. For instance, we might change our author schema, *author.rng*, to read:

```
<?xml version="1.0" encoding="UTF-8"?>
<grammar xmlns="http://relaxng.org/ns/structure/1.0"
         datatypeLibrary="http://www.w3.org/2001/XMLSchema-datatypes">
```

```
<start>
  <ref name="element-author"/>
</start>

<define name="element-author">
  <element name="author">
    <attribute name="id">
      <data type="ID"/>
    </attribute>
    <ref name="element-name"/>
    <optional>
      <ref name="element-born"/>
    </optional>
    <optional>
      <ref name="element-died"/>
    </optional>
  </element>
</define>

<define name="element-name">
  <element name="name">
    <data type="token" datatypeLibrary=""/>
  </element>
</define>

<define name="element-born">
  <element name="born">
    <data type="date"/>
  </element>
</define>

<define name="element-died">
  <element name="died">
    <data type="date"/>
  </element>
</define>

</grammar>
```

or the compact syntax, *author.rnc*, to:

```
start = element-author
element-author =
  element author {
    attribute id { xsd:ID },
    element-name,
    element-born?,
    element-died?
  }
element-name = element name { token }
element-born = element born { xsd:date }
element-died = element died { xsd:date }
```

And our character schema, *character.rng*, to:

```xml
<?xml version="1.0" encoding="UTF-8"?>
<grammar xmlns="http://relaxng.org/ns/structure/1.0"
         datatypeLibrary="http://www.w3.org/2001/XMLSchema-datatypes">

  <start>
    <ref name="element-character"/>
  </start>

  <define name="element-character">
    <element name="character">
      <attribute name="id">
        <data type="ID"/>
      </attribute>
      <ref name="element-name"/>
      <optional>
        <ref name="element-born"/>
      </optional>
      <ref name="element-qualification"/>
    </element>
  </define>

  <define name="element-name">
    <element name="name">
      <data type="token" datatypeLibrary=""/>
    </element>
  </define>

  <define name="element-born">
    <element name="born">
      <data type="date"/>
    </element>
  </define>

  <define name="element-qualification">
    <element name="qualification">
      <data type="token" datatypeLibrary=""/>
    </element>
  </define>

</grammar>
```

or, in the compact syntax, *character.rnc*:

```
start = element-character
element-character =
  element character {
    attribute id { xsd:ID },
    element-name,
    element-born?,
    element-qualification
  }
element-name = element name { token }
element-born = element born { xsd:date }
element-qualification = element qualification { token }
```

The schema using externalRef and external in the previous section will have no difficulty using these flat schemas in place of the Russian doll versions.

Embedding Grammars

This seems straightforward and logical, but why does this approach work? How come there is no collision between the named patterns element-name and element-born defined in both *author.rng* and *character.rng*? Why is it that the start patterns defined in *author.rng* and *character.rng* don't apply to the schema for our library?

This works because of a RELAX NG feature called *embedded grammars*. As I have already mentioned, externalRef patterns perform strict inclusion of the referred schema. Using our last example, this means that our resulting schema is:

```
<?xml version="1.0" encoding="UTF-8"?>
<element name="library" xmlns="http://relaxng.org/ns/structure/1.0"
        datatypeLibrary="http://www.w3.org/2001/XMLSchema-datatypes">
  <oneOrMore>
    <element name="book">
      <attribute name="id">
        <data type="ID"/>
      </attribute>
      <attribute name="available">
        <data type="boolean"/>
      </attribute>
      <element name="isbn">
        <data type="token" datatypeLibrary=""/>
      </element>
      <element name="title">
        <attribute name="xml:lang">
          <data type="language"/>
        </attribute>
        <data type="token" datatypeLibrary=""/>
      </element>
      <oneOrMore>
        <grammar>
          <start>
            <ref name="element-author"/>
          </start>
          <define name="element-author">
            <element name="author">
              <attribute name="id">
                <data type="ID"/>
              </attribute>
              <ref name="element-name"/>
              <optional>
                <ref name="element-born"/>
              </optional>
              <optional>
                <ref name="element-died"/>
              </optional>
            </element>
```

```
        </define>
        <define name="element-name">
          <element name="name">
            <data type="token" datatypeLibrary=""/>
          </element>
        </define>
        <define name="element-born">
          <element name="born">
            <data type="date"/>
          </element>
        </define>
        <define name="element-died">
          <element name="died">
            <data type="date"/>
          </element>
        </define>
      </grammar>
    </oneOrMore>
    <zeroOrMore>
      <grammar>
        <start>
          <ref name="element-character"/>
        </start>
        <define name="element-character">
          <element name="character">
            <attribute name="id">
              <data type="ID"/>
            </attribute>
            <ref name="element-name"/>
            <optional>
              <ref name="element-born"/>
            </optional>
            <ref name="element-qualification"/>
          </element>
        </define>
        <define name="element-name">
          <element name="name">
            <data type="token" datatypeLibrary=""/>
          </element>
        </define>
        <define name="element-born">
          <element name="born">
            <data type="date"/>
          </element>
        </define>
        <define name="element-qualification">
          <element name="qualification">
            <data type="token" datatypeLibrary=""/>
          </element>
        </define>
      </grammar>
    </zeroOrMore>
  </element>
 </oneOrMore>
</element>
```

or, in the compact syntax:

```
element library {
  element book {
    attribute id { xsd:ID },
    attribute available { xsd:boolean },
    element isbn { token },
    element title {
      attribute xml:lang { xsd:language },
      token
    },
    grammar {
      start = element-author
      element-author =
        element author {
          attribute id { xsd:ID },
          element-name,
          element-born?,
          element-died?
        }
      element-name = element name { token }
      element-born = element born { xsd:date }
      element-died = element died { xsd:date }
    }+,
    grammar {
      start = element-character
      element-character =
        element character {
          attribute id { xsd:ID },
          element-name,
          element-born?,
          element-qualification
        }
      element-name = element name { token }
      element-born = element born { xsd:date }
      element-qualification = element qualification { token }
    }*
  }+
}
```

Here we are thus embedding grammars within our schema, and they behave as patterns. In fact there's even more than that: for RELAX NG, grammars are patterns! The meaning of these patterns is twofold:

- As far as validation is concerned, embedded grammars are equivalent to their start patterns: the grammar describing the character element, for instance, matches instance nodes corresponding to its start pattern—i.e., instance nodes matching the pattern element-character, which is what was expected.

- Grammars also set the scope of their definitions: start and named patterns defined in a grammar are visible only in this grammar. Their scope (the location where they can be referred to) is strictly limited to the grammar in which they are defined.

Applied to our example, the strict scoping of start and named patterns means that:

- The born pattern of the grammar describing the character element can't be seen from its parent grammar—i.e., the grammar describing the library and book elements. Nor can it be seen from its sibling grammar—i.e., the grammar describing the author element. The same applies to start patterns.

- Unlike common usage among programming languages, the scopes of start and named patterns don't include embedded grammars. start and named patterns defined in the grammar describing the library and book elements aren't visible in the embedded grammars.

Referencing Patterns in Parent Grammars

This strict isolation of start and named patterns in their grammars is usually convenient when you create references to external grammars. It means that external grammars can be written independently without risk of collision or incompatibility. You can safely take any RELAX NG schema, drop it into a new schema, and see it as a single pattern without any risk of collision.

On the other hand, that approach doesn't let you modify what you include (you will see how to do so in the next section) nor even let you leverage a set of common named patterns. In our example, since there are already \\ two definitions of element-name and element-born, it's a good thing that they are both isolated in their grammars. If you were designing the same building blocks from scratch, however, you'd probably want to have only one definition of these two elements that could be shared by the author and character elements. In fact, if you followed the principle "if it's written more than once, make it common," you'd also want to share the definition of the id attribute.

Parent references let you make an explicit reference to a pattern from the parent grammar—i.e., the grammar embedding the current one. In this case, you need to add the definition that you want to share in the top-level schema even if you don't use all of them in this schema:

```
<?xml version="1.0" encoding="UTF-8"?>
<grammar xmlns="http://relaxng.org/ns/structure/1.0"
         datatypeLibrary="http://www.w3.org/2001/XMLSchema-datatypes">

  <start>
    <element name="library">
      <oneOrMore>
        <element name="book">
          <ref name="attribute-id"/>
          <attribute name="available">
            <data type="boolean"/>
          </attribute>
          <element name="isbn">
            <data type="token" datatypeLibrary=""/>
```

```
            </element>
            <element name="title">
              <attribute name="xml:lang">
                <data type="language"/>
              </attribute>
              <data type="token" datatypeLibrary=""/>
            </element>
            <oneOrMore>
              <externalRef href="author.rng"/>
            </oneOrMore>
            <zeroOrMore>
              <externalRef href="character.rng"/>
            </zeroOrMore>
          </element>
        </oneOrMore>
      </element>
    </start>

    <define name="element-name">
      <element name="name">
        <data type="token" datatypeLibrary=""/>
      </element>
    </define>

    <define name="element-born">
      <element name="born">
        <data type="date"/>
      </element>
    </define>

    <define name="attribute-id">
      <attribute name="id">
        <data type="ID"/>
      </attribute>
    </define>

  </grammar>
```

or:

```
start =
  element library {
    element book {
      attribute-id,
      attribute available { xsd:boolean },
      element isbn { token },
      element title {
        attribute xml:lang { xsd:language },
        token
      },
      external "author.rnc"+,
      external "character.rnc"*
    }+
  }
```

```
element-name = element name { token }
element-born = element born { xsd:date }
attribute-id = attribute id { xsd:ID }
```

Now, to make a reference to the named patterns element-name, element-born, and attribute-id in the embedded grammars, use a pattern called parentRef. This pattern makes *author.rng* look like:

```
<?xml version="1.0" encoding="UTF-8"?>
<grammar xmlns="http://relaxng.org/ns/structure/1.0"
         datatypeLibrary="http://www.w3.org/2001/XMLSchema-datatypes">
  <start>
    <ref name="element-author"/>
  </start>
  <define name="element-author">
    <element name="author">
      <attribute name="id">
        <data type="ID"/>
      </attribute>
      <parentRef name="element-name"/>
      <optional>
        <parentRef name="element-born"/>
      </optional>
      <optional>
        <ref name="element-died"/>
      </optional>
    </element>
  </define>
  <define name="element-died">
    <element name="died">
      <data type="date"/>
    </element>
  </define>
</grammar>
```

and the *character.rng* schema now looks like:

```
<?xml version="1.0" encoding="UTF-8"?>
<grammar xmlns="http://relaxng.org/ns/structure/1.0"
         datatypeLibrary="http://www.w3.org/2001/XMLSchema-datatypes">
  <start>
    <ref name="element-character"/>
  </start>
  <define name="element-character">
    <element name="character">
      <attribute name="id">
        <data type="ID"/>
      </attribute>
      <parentRef name="element-name"/>
      <optional>
        <parentRef name="element-born"/>
      </optional>
      <ref name="element-qualification"/>
    </element>
  </define>
```

```
    <define name="element-qualification">
      <element name="qualification">
        <data type="token" datatypeLibrary=""/>
      </element>
    </define>
  </grammar>
```

The parentRef pattern is translated to a parent keyword in the compact syntax. The *author.rnc* schema looks like:

```
start = element-author
element-author =
  element author {
    attribute id { xsd:ID },
    parent element-name,
    parent element-born?,
    element-died?
  }
element-died = element died { xsd:date }
```

while the *character.rnc* schema looks like:

```
start = element-character
element-character =
  element character {
    attribute id { xsd:ID },
    parent element-name,
    parent element-born?,
    element-qualification
  }
element-qualification = element qualification { token }
```

You are using these features in the context of multiple schema documents, but the semantic of the externalRef pattern itself remains the same. This schema is equivalent to the same schema, with its externalRef patterns expanded in a single monolithic schema with two embedded grammars:

```
<?xml version="1.0" encoding="UTF-8"?>
<grammar xmlns="http://relaxng.org/ns/structure/1.0"
        datatypeLibrary="http://www.w3.org/2001/XMLSchema-datatypes">
  <start>
    <element name="library">
      <oneOrMore>
        <element name="book">
          <ref name="attribute-id"/>
          <attribute name="available">
            <data type="boolean"/>
          </attribute>
          <element name="isbn">
            <data type="token" datatypeLibrary=""/>
          </element>
          <element name="title">
            <attribute name="xml:lang">
              <data type="language"/>
            </attribute>
```

```
              <data type="token" datatypeLibrary=""/>
          </element>
          <oneOrMore>
            <grammar>
              <start>
                <ref name="element-author"/>
              </start>
              <define name="element-author">
                <element name="author">
                  <attribute name="id">
                    <data type="ID"/>
                  </attribute>
                  <parentRef name="element-name"/>
                  <optional>
                    <parentRef name="element-born"/>
                  </optional>
                  <optional>
                    <ref name="element-died"/>
                  </optional>
                </element>
              </define>
              <define name="element-died">
                <element name="died">
                  <data type="date"/>
                </element>
              </define>
            </grammar>
          </oneOrMore>
          <zeroOrMore>
            <grammar>
              <start>
                <ref name="element-character"/>
              </start>
              <define name="element-character">
                <element name="character">
                  <attribute name="id">
                    <data type="ID"/>
                  </attribute>
                  <parentRef name="element-name"/>
                  <optional>
                    <parentRef name="element-born"/>
                  </optional>
                  <ref name="element-qualification"/>
                </element>
              </define>
              <define name="element-qualification">
                <element name="qualification">
                  <data type="token" datatypeLibrary=""/>
                </element>
              </define>
            </grammar>
          </zeroOrMore>
        </element>
      </oneOrMore>
```

```
      </element>
    </start>
    <define name="element-name">
      <element name="name">
        <data type="token" datatypeLibrary=""/>
      </element>
    </define>
    <define name="element-born">
      <element name="born">
        <data type="date"/>
      </element>
    </define>
    <define name="attribute-id">
      <attribute name="id">
        <data type="ID"/>
      </attribute>
    </define>
  </grammar>
```

or, in the compact syntax:

```
start =
  element library {
    element book {
      attribute-id,
      attribute available { xsd:boolean },
      element isbn { token },
      element title {
        attribute xml:lang { xsd:language },
        token
      },
      grammar {
        start = element-author
        element-author =
          element author {
            attribute id { xsd:ID },
            parent element-name,
            parent element-born?,
            element-died?
          }
        element-died = element died { xsd:date }
      }+,
      grammar {
        start = element-character
        element-character =
          element character {
            attribute id { xsd:ID },
            parent element-name,
            parent element-born?,
            element-qualification
          }
        element-qualification = element qualification { token }
      }*
    }+
```

```
      }
element-name = element name { token }
element-born = element born { xsd:date }
attribute-id = attribute id { xsd:ID }
```

You can see how start and named patterns have been defined in each of the three grammars composing this schema:

- `element-died` is defined in the grammar defining the `author` element and can be used only in this grammar.

- Similarly, `element-qualification` is defined in the grammar defining the `character` element and can be used only there.

- `element-name`, `element-born`, and `attribute-id` are defined in the top-level grammar. They can be used in this grammar through normal references (i.e., `ref` patterns) and can also be used in its child grammars (i.e., the grammars that are directly embedded into this one, using a `parentRef` pattern).

There are two more things to note about the `parentRef` pattern:

- If the depth of nesting of grammar is higher than two, you may run into trouble because you can make a reference only to your immediate parent grammar, not to the other grammar ancestors. The RELAX NG working group has considered this issue but hasn't found any real-world use case for generalizing `parentRef` patterns to greater depths of nesting. If you find one, they will probably welcome a mail on the subject! In practice, if you need to do so, you can, as a workaround, define named patterns in the intermediary grammars that can act as proxies.

- Now that we've added the `parentRef` patterns to our two schemas, *author.rng* and *character.rng* can't be used as standalone schemas for validating documents with `author` or `character` root elements. Using them now requires that they be embedded into grammars that provide the definitions for the named patterns they are using to be complete and operational.

Merging Grammars

In the preceding sections, you have seen how an external grammar can be used as a single pattern. This is useful in cases in which you want to include a content model described by an external schema at a single point, not unlike when you mount a Unix filesystem. The description contained in the external grammar is mounted at the point where you make your reference.

The main drawback to this approach is that you can't individually reuse the definitions contained in the external schema. To do so, you need a new pattern, with a different meaning, which will let you control how two grammars are merged into a single one.

Merging Without Redefinition

In the simplest case, you will want to reuse patterns defined in common libraries of patterns without modifying them. Let's say we have defined a grammar with some common patterns, *common.rng*, which can be reused in many different schemas, such as:

```xml
<?xml version="1.0" encoding="UTF-8"?>
<grammar xmlns="http://relaxng.org/ns/structure/1.0"
         datatypeLibrary="http://www.w3.org/2001/XMLSchema-datatypes">

  <define name="element-name">
    <element name="name">
      <data type="token" datatypeLibrary=""/>
    </element>
  </define>

  <define name="element-born">
    <element name="born">
      <data type="date"/>
    </element>
  </define>

  <define name="attribute-id">
    <attribute name="id">
      <data type="ID"/>
    </attribute>
  </define>

  <define name="content-person">
    <ref name="attribute-id"/>
    <ref name="element-name"/>
    <optional>
      <ref name="element-born"/>
    </optional>
  </define>

</grammar>
```

or *common.rnc*, in the compact syntax:

```
element-name = element name { token }
element-born = element born { xsd:date }
attribute-id = attribute id { xsd:ID }
content-person = attribute-id, element-name, element-born?
```

These schemas are obviously not meant to be used as standalone schemas: they have no start patterns and would be invalid. However, they contain definitions that can be used to write the schema of our library. To employ these definitions, use include patterns and provide a supporting framework. In the XML syntax, this looks like:

```xml
<?xml version="1.0" encoding="UTF-8"?>
<grammar xmlns="http://relaxng.org/ns/structure/1.0"
         datatypeLibrary="http://www.w3.org/2001/XMLSchema-datatypes">
```

```
      <include href="common.rng"/>

  <start>
    <element name="library">
      <oneOrMore>
        <element name="book">
          <ref name="attribute-id"/>
          <attribute name="available">
            <data type="boolean"/>
          </attribute>
          <element name="isbn">
            <data type="token" datatypeLibrary=""/>
          </element>
          <element name="title">
            <attribute name="xml:lang">
              <data type="language"/>
            </attribute>
            <data type="token" datatypeLibrary=""/>
          </element>
          <oneOrMore>
            <element name="author">
              <ref name="content-person"/>
              <optional>
                <ref name="element-died"/>
              </optional>
            </element>
          </oneOrMore>
          <zeroOrMore>
            <element name="character">
              <ref name="content-person"/>
              <ref name="element-qualification"/>
            </element>
          </zeroOrMore>
        </element>
      </oneOrMore>
    </element>
  </start>

  <define name="element-died">
    <element name="died">
      <data type="date"/>
    </element>
  </define>

  <define name="element-qualification">
    <element name="qualification">
      <data type="token" datatypeLibrary=""/>
    </element>
  </define>

</grammar>
```

The include pattern is translated to an include keyword in the compact syntax:

```
include "common.rnc"
start =
  element library {
    element book {
      attribute-id,
      attribute available { xsd:boolean },
      element isbn { token },
      element title {
        attribute xml:lang { xsd:language },
        token
      },
      element author {
        content-person,
        element-died?
      }+,
      element character {
        content-person,
        element-qualification
      }*
    }+
  }
element-died = element died { xsd:date }
element-qualification = element qualification { token }
```

Note that the name of the include pattern is slightly misleading. The include pattern here doesn't include the external grammar directly. (You have seen that this was the job of the externalRef pattern.) Instead, it includes the content of the external grammar, performing a merge of both grammars. This is exactly what you need; it allows you to make references to the named patterns defined in the *common.rng* grammar.

The result of this inclusion is thus equivalent to the following monolithic schema:

```
<?xml version="1.0" encoding="UTF-8"?>
<grammar xmlns="http://relaxng.org/ns/structure/1.0"
         datatypeLibrary="http://www.w3.org/2001/XMLSchema-datatypes">
<!-- Content of the included grammar -->
  <define name="element-name">
    <element name="name">
      <data type="token" datatypeLibrary=""/>
    </element>
  </define>
  <define name="element-born">
    <element name="born">
      <data type="date"/>
    </element>
  </define>
  <define name="attribute-id">
    <attribute name="id">
      <data type="ID"/>
    </attribute>
  </define>
```

```
    <define name="content-person">
      <ref name="attribute-id"/>
      <ref name="element-name"/>
      <optional>
        <ref name="element-born"/>
      </optional>
    </define>
<!-- End of the included grammar -->
    <start>
      <element name="library">
        <oneOrMore>
          <element name="book">
            <ref name="attribute-id"/>
            <attribute name="available">
              <data type="boolean"/>
            </attribute>
            <element name="isbn">
              <data type="token" datatypeLibrary=""/>
            </element>
            <element name="title">
              <attribute name="xml:lang">
                <data type="language"/>
              </attribute>
              <data type="token" datatypeLibrary=""/>
            </element>
            <oneOrMore>
              <element name="author">
                <ref name="content-person"/>
                <optional>
                  <ref name="element-died"/>
                </optional>
              </element>
            </oneOrMore>
            <zeroOrMore>
              <element name="character">
                <ref name="content-person"/>
                <ref name="element-qualification"/>
              </element>
            </zeroOrMore>
          </element>
        </oneOrMore>
      </element>
    </start>
    <define name="element-died">
      <element name="died">
        <data type="date"/>
      </element>
    </define>
    <define name="element-qualification">
      <element name="qualification">
        <data type="token" datatypeLibrary=""/>
      </element>
    </define>
</grammar>
```

or, in the compact syntax:

```
element-name = element name { token }
element-born = element born { xsd:date }
attribute-id = attribute id { xsd:ID }
content-person = attribute-id, element-name, element-born?

start =
  element library {
    element book {
      attribute-id,
      attribute available { xsd:boolean },
      element isbn { token },
      element title {
        attribute xml:lang { xsd:language },
        token
      },
      element author {
        content-person,
        element-died?
      }+,
      element character {
        content-person,
        element-qualification
      }*
    }+
  }
element-died = element died { xsd:date }
element-qualification = element qualification { token }
```

Merging and Replacing Definitions

In the previous example, we were lucky. The definitions of the common patterns included matched exactly what we needed. In the real world, this isn't always the case. It is quite handy to be able to replace definitions found in the grammar that we're including when they might conflict with other aspects of our schema design.

Let's say that we have already written this very flat version of our schema, called *library.rng*:

```
<?xml version="1.0" encoding="UTF-8"?>
<grammar xmlns="http://relaxng.org/ns/structure/1.0"
datatypeLibrary="http://www.w3.org/2001/XMLSchema-datatypes">

  <start>
    <ref name="element-library"/>
  </start>

  <define name="element-library">
    <element name="library">
      <zeroOrMore>
        <ref name="element-book"/>
      </zeroOrMore>
```

```
      </element>
  </define>

  <define name="element-book">
    <element name="book">
      <ref name="attribute-id"/>
      <ref name="attribute-available"/>
      <ref name="element-isbn"/>
      <ref name="element-title"/>
      <oneOrMore>
        <ref name="element-author"/>
      </oneOrMore>
      <zeroOrMore>
        <ref name="element-character"/>
      </zeroOrMore>
    </element>
  </define>

  <define name="element-author">
    <element name="author">
      <ref name="content-person"/>
      <optional>
        <ref name="element-died"/>
      </optional>
    </element>
  </define>

  <define name="element-character">
    <element name="character">
      <ref name="content-person"/>
      <ref name="element-qualification"/>
    </element>
  </define>

  <define name="element-isbn">
    <element name="isbn">
      <data type="token" datatypeLibrary=""/>
    </element>
  </define>

  <define name="element-title">
    <element name="title">
      <ref name="attribute-xml-lang"/>
      <data type="token" datatypeLibrary=""/>
    </element>
  </define>

  <define name="attribute-xml-lang">
    <attribute name="xml:lang">
      <data type="language"/>
    </attribute>
  </define>

  <define name="attribute-available">
```

```
          <attribute name="available">
            <data type="boolean"/>
          </attribute>
        </define>

        <define name="element-name">
          <element name="name">
            <data type="token" datatypeLibrary=""/>
          </element>
        </define>

        <define name="element-born">
          <element name="born">
            <data type="date"/>
          </element>
        </define>

        <define name="element-died">
          <element name="died">
            <data type="date"/>
          </element>
        </define>

        <define name="attribute-id">
          <attribute name="id">
            <data type="ID"/>
          </attribute>
        </define>

        <define name="content-person">
          <ref name="attribute-id"/>
          <ref name="element-name"/>
          <optional>
            <ref name="element-born"/>
          </optional>
        </define>

        <define name="element-qualification">
          <element name="qualification">
            <data type="token" datatypeLibrary=""/>
          </element>
        </define>

    </grammar>
```

or, in the compact syntax, *library.rnc*:

```
start = element-library
element-library = element library { element-book* }
element-book =
  element book {
    attribute-id,
    attribute-available,
    element-isbn,
```

```
      element-title,
      element-author+,
      element-character*
  }
element-author = element author { content-person, element-died? }
element-character =
  element character { content-person, element-qualification }
element-isbn = element isbn { token }
element-title = element title { attribute-xml-lang, token }
attribute-xml-lang = attribute xml:lang { xsd:language }
attribute-available = attribute available { xsd:boolean }
element-name = element name { token }
element-born = element born { xsd:date }
element-died = element died { xsd:date }
attribute-id = attribute id { xsd:ID }
content-person = attribute-id, element-name, element-born?
element-qualification = element qualification {token}
```

This might be a good schema to use in production to validate incoming documents from a variety of patterns, so you wouldn't want to modify it. However, you might have a new application that doesn't work at the level of a library but only at the level of a book. This application needs to validate instance documents with book root elements. Of course you wouldn't want to copy and paste the definition of our existing schema into another one because that would mean maintaining two different versions with similar content.

This is a case in which you would want to redefine the start element of our schema. To do so, use an include pattern, embedding the definitions that must be substituted for the ones from the included grammar in the include pattern itself:

```
<?xml version="1.0" encoding="UTF-8"?>
<grammar xmlns="http://relaxng.org/ns/structure/1.0">
  <include href="library.rng">
    <start>
      <ref name="element-book"/>
    </start>
  </include>
</grammar>
```

or:

```
include "library.rnc" {
  start = element-book
}
```

Note how the new definitions are embedded directly in the include pattern; the content of the include pattern is where all the redefinitions must be written. This short schema includes all the definitions from *library.rng* and redefines the start pattern. It validates instance documents with a book root element. Since we are performing an inclusion instead of a copy, we will inherit any modifications made to *library.rng*.

We have been able to redefine the start pattern, but each named pattern can also be redefined using the same syntax. Let's say for instance that I am not happy with the definition of the element-name pattern and want to check that the name is shorter than 80 characters. If I don't want to (or can't) modify the original schema, I can include it and redefine this pattern:

```
<?xml version="1.0" encoding="UTF-8"?>
<grammar xmlns="http://relaxng.org/ns/structure/1.0"
         datatypeLibrary="http://www.w3.org/2001/XMLSchema-datatypes">
   <include href="library.rng">
      <define name="element-name">
         <element name="name">
            <data type="token">
               <param name="maxLength">80</param>
            </data>
         </element>
      </define>
   </include>
</grammar>
```

or:

```
include "library.rnc" {
   element-name = element name { xsd:token{maxLength = "80"} }
}
```

Here again, the grammar of *library.rnc* is merged with the grammar of the new schema (which happens to be empty) but before the merge, the definitions that are embedded in the include pattern are substituted to the original definitions.

The new definition can be as different from the original one as I want. While it might not always be good practice, I can, for instance, redefine attribute-available and replace the attribute by an element:

```
<?xml version="1.0" encoding="UTF-8"?>
<grammar xmlns="http://relaxng.org/ns/structure/1.0"
         datatypeLibrary="http://www.w3.org/2001/XMLSchema-datatypes">
   <include href="library.rng">
      <define name="attribute-available">
         <element name="available">
            <data type="boolean"/>
         </element>
      </define>
   </include>
</grammar>
```

or:

```
include "library.rnc" {
   attribute-available = element available { xsd:boolean }
}
```

This seems rather confusing (the named pattern is called attribute-available, and it's now describing an element), but the schema is perfectly valid and describes instance documents in which the available attribute is replaced by an available element. The same approach can also remove this attribute:

```xml
<?xml version="1.0" encoding="UTF-8"?>
<grammar xmlns="http://relaxng.org/ns/structure/1.0">
  <include href="library.rng">
    <define name="attribute-available">
      <empty/>
    </define>
  </include>
</grammar>
```

or:

```
include "library.rnc" {
  attribute-available = empty
}
```

Note how this uses a new pattern named empty. This pattern matches only text nodes made of whitespace, and it has the same effect as if the named pattern had been removed from the schema.

The include patterns have the effect of merging the content of their grammar, after replacement of the redefined patterns, with the content of the current grammar. This means that these redefinitions can make references to any definition from either the including or the included grammars. If you want, for instance, to add zero or more email addresses to the author element while retaining a flat structure, write:

```xml
<?xml version="1.0" encoding="UTF-8"?>
<grammar xmlns="http://relaxng.org/ns/structure/1.0"
         datatypeLibrary="http://www.w3.org/2001/XMLSchema-datatypes">

  <include href="library.rng">

    <define name="element-author">
      <element name="author">
        <ref name="content-person"/>
        <optional>
          <ref name="element-died"/>
        </optional>
        <zeroOrMore>
          <ref name="element-email"/>
        </zeroOrMore>
      </element>
    </define>

  </include>

  <define name="element-email">
    <element name="email">
      <data type="anyURI">
        <param name="pattern">mailto:.*</param>
      </data>
    </element>
```

```
    </define>
  </grammar>
```

or:

```
  include "library.rnc" {
    element-author =
      element author { content-person, element-died?, element-email* }
  }
  element-email =
    element email {
      xsd:anyURI { pattern = "mailto:.*" }
    }
```

Here the redefinition of the element-author pattern is making three references to three named patterns. content-person and element-died are defined in *library.rng*—i.e., the grammar that is included. The third, element-email, is defined in the top-level grammar—i.e., the including grammar.

Combining Definitions

When I've replaced the definitions in previous examples, the original definition was completely replaced by the new one. This can make the maintenance of these schemas more complicated than it should be. In the last example, if the included schema (*library.rng*) updated and the definition of element-author changed to add a new element to include a telephone number, this addition would be lost if I didn't add it explicitly in the including schema. As far as the element-author pattern is concerned, this redefinition is no better than a copy and paste. A mechanism more similar to inheritance would help with this.

To keep the definition from the included grammar, combine a new definition with the existing one instead of replacing it. Unlike redefinition, the combination of start and named patterns doesn't take place in the include pattern itself but rather is done at the level of the including grammar. It isn't even necessary to include a grammar to combine definitions, but the main interest of combining definitions is to combine new definitions with existing ones from included grammars.

There are two options for combining definitions: choice and interleave.

Combining by choice

When definitions are combined by choice, the result is similar to using a choice pattern between the content of the definitions. A use case for this combination would be to define a schema accepting either a library or a book element from the schema used in the previous section. In the XML syntax, combining by choice is done through a combine attribute:

```
  <?xml version="1.0" encoding="UTF-8"?>
  <grammar xmlns="http://relaxng.org/ns/structure/1.0">
    <include href="library.rng"/>
```

```
<start combine="choice">
  <ref name="element-book"/>
</start>
</grammar>
```

In the compact syntax, combining by choice uses the |= operator (instead of =) in the definition:

```
include "library.rnc"
start |= element-book
```

Note that in both cases, the combination is done outside the inclusion. Its effect is to add a choice between the content of the start pattern. The definition becomes equivalent to:

```
<start>
  <choice>
    <ref name="element-library"/>
    <ref name="element-book"/>
  </choice>
</start>
```

or:

```
start = element-library | element-book
```

The logic behind this combination is to allow the content model corresponding to the original pattern while also allowing different content to appear. This is different from the logic behind pattern redefinitions, in which the original pattern is replaced by a new one.

Named patterns can also be combined. If you want to accept either an available attribute or element, you can write:

```
<?xml version="1.0" encoding="UTF-8"?>
<grammar xmlns="http://relaxng.org/ns/structure/1.0"
         datatypeLibrary="http://www.w3.org/2001/XMLSchema-datatypes">

  <include href="library.rng"/>

  <define name="attribute-available" combine="choice">
    <element name="available">
      <data type="boolean"/>
    </element>
  </define>

</grammar>
```

or:

```
include "library.rnc"
attribute-available |= element available { xsd:boolean }
```

Another interesting and common case involves making this attribute optional, by combining this pattern by choice with an empty pattern:

```
<?xml version="1.0" encoding="UTF-8"?>
<grammar xmlns="http://relaxng.org/ns/structure/1.0">

  <include href="library.rng"/>

  <define name="attribute-available" combine="choice">
    <empty/>
  </define>

</grammar>
```

or:

```
include "library.rnc"
attribute-available |= empty
```

Adding a choice between a defined component and nothingness may seem like a roundabout way to make the component optional, but it works with a minimum need to modify included schemas.

Combining by interleave

You have seen how an "old" pattern can be replaced by a new one using pattern redefinition and also how to specify a choice between an old definition and a new one using a combination by choice. The last option is to combine by interleave. The logic here is to allow pieces to be added to the original content model and to let these pieces be interleaved—i.e., added anywhere before, after, and between the subpatterns of the original pattern.

Earlier, I added an email element to the content of the author element using a redefinition. You can also use a combination by interleave to add this email pattern to the content-person pattern:

```
<?xml version="1.0" encoding="UTF-8"?>
<grammar xmlns="http://relaxng.org/ns/structure/1.0"
    datatypeLibrary="http://www.w3.org/2001/XMLSchema-datatypes">

  <include href="library.rng"/>

  <define name="content-person" combine="interleave">
    <zeroOrMore>
      <ref name="element-email"/>
    </zeroOrMore>
  </define>

  <define name="element-email">
    <element name="email">
      <data type="anyURI">
        <param name="pattern">mailto:.*</param>
      </data>
    </element>
  </define>

</grammar>
```

or, in the compact syntax:

```
include "library.rnc"
content-person &= element-email *
element-email =
  element email {
    xsd:anyURI { pattern = "mailto:.*" }
  }
```

The effect of this combination by interleave is that the `content-model` pattern is now equivalent to an `interleave` pattern embedding both the original and the new definition:

```
<define name="content-person">
  <interleave>
    <group>
      <ref name="attribute-id"/>
      <ref name="element-name"/>
      <optional>
        <ref name="element-born"/>
      </optional>
    </group>
    <zeroOrMore>
      <ref name="element-email"/>
    </zeroOrMore>
  </interleave>
</define>
```

or:

```
content-person =
  (attribute-id, element-name, element-born?) & element-email *
```

This definition allows any number of email elements before the name element, between the name element and the born element, and after the born element.

The logic here is to allow extension by adding new content anywhere in the original definition. This is neat and safe if the applications that read the documents are coded to ignore what they don't know. In our example, if I design an application to read the original content model, this application will be just fine with the new content model if it ignores the email elements that have been added.

You've seen how a combination by choice can make a pattern optional. Combination by interleave can't reverse the process, but it can make a pattern forbidden. If you don't want to end up with a schema that won't validate any instance document, you must be careful when working with a pattern to which reference is made optional, such as the `element-died` pattern:

```
<?xml version="1.0" encoding="UTF-8"?>
<grammar xmlns="http://relaxng.org/ns/structure/1.0">
  <include href="library.rng"/>
  <define name="element-died" combine="interleave">
    <notAllowed/>
  </define>
</grammar>
```

or:

```
include "library.rnc"
element-died &= notAllowed
```

Here, we interleave a new pattern, notAllowed, with the content of the named pattern element-died. The effect of this operation is that this pattern will no longer match any content model. This is OK because the reference to the element-died in the definition of the author element is optional. The effect is that a document can be valid per the resulting schema only if there is no died element.

What about combining start patterns by interleave? This may seem weird or even illegal because you've seen start patterns in a context in which they define the root element of XML documents. A well-formed XML document can have only one root element, but schemas can permit a variety of different root elements in their models.

Another example in which combining by interleave is handy and very widely used is if you add attributes to a named pattern. In this case, the unordered interleave doesn't make any difference because attributes are always unordered.

Why Can't Definitions Be Defined by Group?

You have seen how to combine definitions by interleave and choice, and because group is the third compositor, you might be tempted to combine definitions by group. Unfortunately, definitions of named patterns are declarations. Since the relative order of these declarations isn't considered significant, combining definitions by group wouldn't give reliable results and has thus been forbidden. This issue doesn't arise with choice and interleave compositors, because the relative order of their children elements isn't significant for a schema.

A Real-World Example: XHTML 2.0

Let's leave our library for a while to look at XHTML. XHTML modularization breaks the monolithic XHTML 1.0 DTD into a set of independent modules described as in independent DTDs. Those modules can be combined to create as many flavors of XHTML as people may want. However, this has proven to be one of the most challenging exercises for schema languages. In their Working Drafts, the W3C HTML Working Group, the group in charge of XHTML, has published a set of RELAX NG schemas to describe XHTML 2.0. Its many interconnected modules illustrate the flexibility of RELAX NG to perform this type of exercises.

The solution chosen by XHTML 2.0 (see *http://www.w3.org/TR/xhtml2/xhtml20_relax.html#a_xhtml20_relaxng* for more detail) is to define each module in its own schema and then include all these modules in a top-level schema (called the RELAX NG XHTML 2.0 Driver). The driver schema looks like this:

```
<?xml version="1.0" encoding="UTF-8"?>
<grammar ns="http://www.w3.org/2002/06/xhtml2"
```

```
                xmlns="http://relaxng.org/ns/structure/1.0"
                xmlns:x="http://www.w3.org/1999/xhtml">

<x:h1>RELAX NG schema for XHTML 2.0</x:h1>

<x:pre>
  Copyright &#xA9;2003 W3C&#xAE; (MIT, ERCIM, Keio), All Rights Reserved.

    Editor:   Masayasu Ishikawa &lt;mimasa@w3.org&gt;
    Revision: $Id: ch10,v 1.26 2003/12/02 21:15:52 jhawks Exp mam $

  Permission to use, copy, modify and distribute this RELAX NG schema
  for XHTML 2.0 and its accompanying documentation for any purpose and
  without fee is hereby granted in perpetuity, provided that the above
  copyright notice and this paragraph appear in all copies. The copyright
  holders make no representation about the suitability of this RELAX NG
  schema for any purpose.

  It is provided "as is" without expressed or implied warranty.
  For details, please refer to the W3C software license at:

    <x:a href="http://www.w3.org/Consortium/Legal/copyright-software">
     http://www.w3.org/Consortium/Legal/copyright-software</x:a>
</x:pre>

<div>
  <x:h2>XHTML 2.0 modules</x:h2>

  <x:h3>Attribute Collections Module</x:h3>
  <include href="xhtml-attribs-2.rng"/>

  <x:h3>Structure Module</x:h3>
  <include href="xhtml-struct-2.rng"/>

  <x:h3>Block Text Module</x:h3>
  <include href="xhtml-blktext-2.rng"/>

  <x:h3>Inline Text Module</x:h3>
  <include href="xhtml-inltext-2.rng"/>

  <x:h3>Hypertext Module</x:h3>
  <include href="xhtml-hypertext-2.rng"/>

  <x:h3>List Module</x:h3>
  <include href="xhtml-list-2.rng"/>

  <x:h3>Linking Module</x:h3>
  <include href="xhtml-link-2.rng"/>

  <x:h3>Metainformation Module</x:h3>
  <include href="xhtml-meta-2.rng"/>

  <x:h3>Object Module</x:h3>
  <include href="xhtml-object-2.rng"/>
```

```
<x:h3>Scripting Module</x:h3>
<include href="xhtml-script-2.rng"/>

<x:h3>Style Attribute Module</x:h3>
<include href="xhtml-inlstyle-2.rng"/>

<x:h3>Style Sheet Module</x:h3>
<include href="xhtml-style-2.rng"/>

<x:h3>Tables Module</x:h3>
<include href="xhtml-table-2.rng"/>

<x:h3>Support Modules</x:h3>

<x:h4>Datatypes Module</x:h4>
<include href="xhtml-datatypes-2.rng"/>

<x:h4>Events Module</x:h4>
<include href="xhtml-events-2.rng"/>

<x:h4>Param Module</x:h4>
<include href="xhtml-param-2.rng"/>

<x:h4>Caption Module</x:h4>
<include href="xhtml-caption-2.rng"/>
</div>

<div>
  <x:h2>XML Events module</x:h2>
  <include href="xml-events-1.rng"/>
</div>

<div>
  <x:h2>Ruby module</x:h2>
  <include href="full-ruby-1.rng"/>
</div>

<div>
  <x:h2>XForms module</x:h2>
  <x:p>To-Do: work out integration of XForms</x:p>
  <!--include href="xforms-1.rng"/-->
</div>

</grammar>
```

Don't worry for the moment about the ns attribute (Chapter 11), nor about the foreign (non–RELAX NG) namespaces and the div elements (Chapter 13). One of these modules, the Structure Module, defines the basic structure of a XHTML 2.0 document. For instance, the head element is defined as:

```
<define name="head">
  <element name="head">
    <ref name="head.attlist"/>
    <ref name="head.content"/>
```

```
        </element>
      </define>

      <define name="head.attlist">
        <ref name="Common.attrib"/>
      </define>

      <define name="head.content">
        <ref name="title"/>
      </define>
```

or:

```
    head = element head { head.attlist, head.content }
    head.attlist = Common.attrib
    head.content = title
```

This example shows another design decision. For each element, the XHTML Working Group decided to define a named pattern with the same name as the element (head) and two separated named patterns to define the list of its attributes (head.attlist) and its content (head.content). This design decision makes it easy for other modules to add new elements and attributes just by combining these named patterns by interleave. For instance, the Metainformation Module adds a meta element to the content of the head element by combining via interleave the head.content pattern with zero or more meta elements:

```
    <?xml version="1.0" encoding="UTF-8"?>
    <grammar xmlns="http://relaxng.org/ns/structure/1.0"
             xmlns:x="http://www.w3.org/1999/xhtml">

     <x:h1>Metainformation Module</x:h1>

     <div>
       <x:h2>The meta element</x:h2>

       <define name="meta">
         <element name="meta">
           <ref name="meta.attlist"/>
           <choice>
             <ref name="Inline.model"/>
             <oneOrMore>
               <ref name="meta"/>
             </oneOrMore>
           </choice>
         </element>
       </define>

       <define name="meta.attlist">
         <ref name="Common.attrib"/>
         <optional>
           <attribute name="name">
             <ref name="NMTOKEN.datatype"/>
           </attribute>
```

```
        </optional>
      </define>
    </div>

    <define name="head.content" combine="interleave">
      <zeroOrMore>
        <ref name="meta"/>
      </zeroOrMore>
    </define>

  </grammar>
```

or:

```
namespace x = "http://www.w3.org/1999/xhtml"

meta = element meta { meta.attlist, (Inline.model | meta+) }
meta.attlist =
  Common.attrib,
  attribute name { NMTOKEN.datatype }?
head.content &= meta*
```

The fact that the content models are combined by interleave guarantees independence between modules: you can add or remove modules independently of each other. It also guarantees the independence of the resulting schema over the order in which the different modules are included in the top-level schema; you can switch the Metainformation Module and the Scripting Module, which both add content into the head element, without any impact on the set of valid documents.

This modularity fully relies on combinations by interleave and RELAX NG would have no easy solution if you want to add content, for instance, to what has already be defined in the head element. Of course, if you're interested only in the Structure Module and want to add a foo element after the title element, you can redefine head.content:

```
<include href="xhtml-struct-2.rng">
  <define name="head.content">
    <ref name="title"/>
    <element name="foo">
      <empty/>
    </element>
  </define>
</include>
```

However, this doesn't take into account all the content added by the other modules into the head element.

Other Options

What if you really need a feature that's missing in RELAX NG to create building blocks? What if, for instance, you need to reuse a name class or a datatype parameter defined once and only once in multiple locations of a schema?

If this were an absolute requirement, which isn't often the case, you would have to use non-RELAX NG tools or features. RELAX NG has an advantage over DTDs or W3C XML Schema in that there are two possible syntaxes, leaving the option to work with either XML mechanisms with the XML syntax or plaintext tools with the compact syntax.

There is no limit to the tools to produce our result, but let's set up a possible use case and some examples of implementations.

A Possible Use Case

Let's just say you want to specify the set of possible characters in your documents and that you want to implement this rule in your RELAX NG schemas. The pattern you might have in mind to perform this restriction could be the one that's an example in Chapter 9. It's not very complex, but not very simple either:

```
pattern = "[\p{IsBasicLatin}\p{IsLatin-1Supplement}]*"
```

Of course, you might want to easily update it if you had to. You wouldn't want to have to copy it in each datatype definition, and you might want to use this pattern in different contexts over different datatypes and eventually combine it with other parameters.

XML Tools

XML parsed entities (internal or external and in the internal DTD or in an external DTD) may be used in the above case. Using internal entities in an internal DTD, you can, for instance, write:

```
<?xml version = '1.0' encoding = 'utf-8' ?>
<!DOCTYPE element [[
<!ENTITY validChars "<param name=
'pattern'>[\p{IsBasicLatin}\p{IsLatin-1Supplement}]*</param>">
]>
<element xmlns="http://relaxng.org/ns/structure/1.0" name="library"
         datatypeLibrary="http://www.w3.org/2001/XMLSchema-datatypes">
  <oneOrMore>
   <element name="book">
    <attribute name="id">
     <data type="NMTOKEN">&validChars;</data>
    </attribute>
    <attribute name="available">
     <data type="boolean"/>
    </attribute>
    <element name="isbn">
     <data type="NMTOKEN">&validChars;</data>
    </element>
    <element name="title">
     <attribute name="xml:lang">
      <data type="language"/>
```

```
     </attribute>
     <data type="token">&validChars;</data>
    </element>
    <zeroOrMore>
     <element name="author">
      <attribute name="id">
       <data type="NMTOKEN">&validChars;</data>
      </attribute>
      <element name="name">
       <data type="token">&validChars;</data>
      </element>
      <element name="born">
       <data type="date"/>
      </element>
      <optional>
       <element name="died">
        <data type="date"/>
       </element>
      </optional>
     </element>
    </zeroOrMore>
    <zeroOrMore>
     <element name="character">
      <attribute name="id">
       <data type="NMTOKEN">&validChars;</data>
      </attribute>
      <element name="name">
       <data type="token">&validChars;</data>
      </element>
      <element name="born">
       <data type="date"/>
      </element>
      <element name="qualification">
       <data type="token">&validChars;</data>
      </element>
     </element>
    </zeroOrMore>
   </element>
  </oneOrMore>
 </element>
```

The trickery here is the definition of an entity for the parameter:

```
<!ENTITY validChars "<param name=
'pattern'>[\p{IsBasicLatin}\p{IsLatin-1Supplement}]*</param>">
```

And to use this entity where you need it; for instance:

```
<data type="token">&validChars;</data>
```

What about the compact syntax? The compact syntax doesn't support entities, but if you convert this schema into the compact syntax (using Trang), you get:

```
element library {
  element book {
    attribute id {
```

```
      xsd:NMTOKEN {
        pattern = "[\p{IsBasicLatin}\p{IsLatin-1Supplement}]*"
      }
    },
    attribute available { xsd:boolean },
    element isbn {
      xsd:NMTOKEN {
        pattern = "[\p{IsBasicLatin}\p{IsLatin-1Supplement}]*"
      }
    },
    element title {
      attribute xml:lang { xsd:language },
      xsd:token {
        pattern = "[\p{IsBasicLatin}\p{IsLatin-1Supplement}]*"
      }
    },
    element author {
      attribute id {
        xsd:NMTOKEN {
          pattern = "[\p{IsBasicLatin}\p{IsLatin-1Supplement}]*"
        }
      },
      element name {
        xsd:token {
          pattern = "[\p{IsBasicLatin}\p{IsLatin-1Supplement}]*"
        }
      },
      element born { xsd:date },
      element died { xsd:date }?
    }*,
    element character {
      attribute id {
        xsd:NMTOKEN {
          pattern = "[\p{IsBasicLatin}\p{IsLatin-1Supplement}]*"
        }
      },
      element name {
        xsd:token {
          pattern = "[\p{IsBasicLatin}\p{IsLatin-1Supplement}]*"
        }
      },
      element born { xsd:date },
      element qualification {
        xsd:token {
          pattern = "[\p{IsBasicLatin}\p{IsLatin-1Supplement}]*"
        }
      }
    }*
  }+
}
```

This means that as long as you keep the XML version as your reference for this schema, you can easily get the compact syntax but can't go the other way round (compact to XML) without losing the entity definition. The fact that this example uses an XML mechanism has broken the round-tripping between the two syntaxes.

Other XML tools (such as XInclude or writing the schema as a XSLT transformation) can be used with pretty much the same effect. Depending on the case, these solutions are supported by the parser that parses the RELAX NG schema (this is the case with out internal entity) or requires a first phase during which your schema is compiled into a fully compatible RELAX NG schema.

For an example, let's use XSLT. When you need to do simple stuff, XSLT has a simplified syntax in which the xsl:stylesheet and xsl:template elements may be omitted (exactly like the RELAX NG grammar and start elements may be omitted in a simple RELAX NG schema). This means that if we just want to use XSLT for its simplest features (here only to expend the values of variables), we can write our schema as:

```
<?xml version = '1.0' encoding = 'utf-8' ?>
<element xmlns="http://relaxng.org/ns/structure/1.0" name="library"
         datatypeLibrary="http://www.w3.org/2001/XMLSchema-datatypes"
         xmlns:xsl="http://www.w3.org/1999/XSL/Transform"
         xsl:version="1.0">
  <xsl:variable name="validChars">
    <param name='pattern'>[\p{IsBasicLatin}\p{IsLatin-1Supplement}]*</param>
  </xsl:variable>
  <oneOrMore>
   <element name="book">
    <attribute name="id">
     <data type="NMTOKEN"><xsl:copy-of select="$validChars"/></data>
    </attribute>
    <attribute name="available">
     <data type="boolean"/>
    </attribute>
    <element name="isbn">
     <data type="NMTOKEN"><xsl:copy-of select="$validChars"/></data>
    </element>
    <element name="title">
     <attribute name="xml:lang">
      <data type="language"/>
     </attribute>
     <data type="token"><xsl:copy-of select="$validChars"/></data>
    </element>
    <zeroOrMore>
     <element name="author">
      <attribute name="id">
       <data type="NMTOKEN"><xsl:copy-of select="$validChars"/></data>
      </attribute>
      <element name="name">
       <data type="token"><xsl:copy-of select="$validChars"/></data>
      </element>
      <element name="born">
       <data type="date"/>
      </element>
      <optional>
```

```
      <element name="died">
       <data type="date"/>
      </element>
     </optional>
    </element>
   </zeroOrMore>
   <zeroOrMore>
    <element name="character">
     <attribute name="id">
      <data type="NMTOKEN"><xsl:copy-of select="$validChars"/></data>
     </attribute>
     <element name="name">
      <data type="token"><xsl:copy-of select="$validChars"/></data>
     </element>
     <element name="born">
      <data type="date"/>
     </element>
     <element name="qualification">
      <data type="token"><xsl:copy-of select="$validChars"/></data>
     </element>
    </element>
   </zeroOrMore>
  </element>
 </oneOrMore>
</element>
```

Applied to any XML document, this transformation produces a RELAX NG schema in which the XSLT instruction:

```
<xsl:copy-of select="$validChars"/>
```

is replaced by the content of the variable $validChars:

```
<param name=
'pattern'>[\p{IsBasicLatin}\p{IsLatin-1Supplement}]*</param>
```

Text Tools

Text tools are somewhat more limited. You can use only tools that, like the XSLT example just shown, require a first phase to produce a schema. One of the first tools that comes to mind to people familiar with C programming is the C preprocessor (CPP). The syntax for defining a text replacement with CPP is #define and references are done using the name of the definition. Something equivalent to our two previous examples could thus be:

```
#define VALIDCHARS  pattern = '[\p{IsBasicLatin}\p{IsLatin-1Supplement}]*'
element library {
  element book {
    attribute id {
      xsd:NMTOKEN {
        VALIDCHARS
      }
    },
```

```
      attribute available { xsd:boolean },
      element isbn {
        xsd:NMTOKEN {
          VALIDCHARS
        }
      },
      element title {
        attribute xml:lang { xsd:language },
        xsd:token {
          VALIDCHARS
        }
      },
      element author {
        attribute id {
          xsd:NMTOKEN {
            VALIDCHARS
          }
        },
        element name {
          xsd:token {
            VALIDCHARS
          }
        },
        element born { xsd:date },
        element died { xsd:date }?
      }*,
      element character {
        attribute id {
          xsd:NMTOKEN {
            VALIDCHARS
          }
        },
        element name {
          xsd:token {
            VALIDCHARS
          }
        },
        element born { xsd:date },
        element qualification {
          xsd:token {
            VALIDCHARS
          }
        }
      }*
    }+
  }
```

When compiled through CPP, this gives a fully valid RELAX NG schema (compact syntax) in which the occurrences of VALIDCHARS have been replaced by the parameter.

CHAPTER 11

Namespaces

Namespaces can be both simple and complicated. The very first example schema in this book included an attribute from the xml:lang namespace and it didn't seem like a big deal. However, if you think about it more carefully, you'll see that namespaces present two different challenges to schema languages. The first is that schema languages need to provide a way to specify which namespaces apply to the elements and attributes that are described; the second is how to cope with extensibility, one of the objectives of XML namespaces.

In this chapter, we'll take a closer look at these two challenges and how RELAX NG addresses them.

A Ten-Minute Guide to XML Namespaces

Let's examine the motivations behind XML namespaces. The first motivation is to have namespaces replace the *formal public identifier* (FPI), an inheritance from SGML. These identifiers provide a way to identify which *vocabulary*, or set of names, is being used in a document. The XML/SGML way of identifying the vocabulary used in our library would be to add a public identifier to the document type declaration such as:

```
<?xml version="1.0"?>
<!DOCTYPE library PUBLIC "-//ERICVANDERVLIST//DTD for library//EN" "library.dtd"/>
<library>
...
</library>
```

This DOCTYPE declaration contains an FPI (-//ERICVANDERVLIST//DTD for library//EN) and the location of the DTD describing the vocabulary (library.dtd). XML requires that the DOCTYPE declaration always provide a SYSTEM identifier—a location—when a PUBLIC identifier is used, though PUBLIC identifiers aren't required when SYSTEM identifiers are used. The creators of XML 1.0 didn't want to require parsers to include the tools (typically XML catalog processing) for resolving formal public identifiers to addresses, but they kept the option open. Because the DOCTYPE declaration provides the parser with identification of the DTD rather than the identification of the abstract set of names, this approach is generally sensible.

The first goal of XML namespaces is to provide identifiers for the abstract notions of vocabularies and namespaces without linking these identifiers directly to the technical implementations (DTDs, schemas, or whatever) that define or enforce what they are. These identifiers are no longer FPIs like those used in doctype declarations but *Uniform Resource Identifiers* (URIs, or, to be picky, "URI references"). These identifiers can be applied to every element and attribute in a document, not just the document as a whole. To assign a namespace to all the elements from Example 3-1, you can use an xmlns attribute to assign a URI to the default namespace:

```
<?xml version="1.0"?>
library xmlns="http://eric.van-der-vlist.com/ns/library">
...
</library>
```

The identifier for my namespace is the string http://eric.van-der-vlist.com/ns/ library. There doesn't need to be any document at this address—it's only a label. Though it looks temptingly like a hyperlink, it's not designed to be used that way. Namespaces are identifiers that give a hint about ownership. The assumption is I create a namespace only if I own the domain it uses and that I won't use the same identifier to identify several different things. XML namespaces per se don't define any way to associate resources such as schemas or documentations with a namespace URI. (For a mechanism that does that, see Resource Directory Description Language at *http://rddl.org*.)

The namespace declaration xmlns="http://eric.van-der-vlist.com/ns/library" has been applied to the document element (library), and that declaration is inherited by all its child elements, unless the child elements provide their own namespace declarations and override it.

The second goal of XML namespaces, and the place where it goes farther than FPIs in DOCTYPE declarations, is to provide a way to mix elements and attributes from different namespaces in a single document. In our library for instance, the library and book elements use a vocabulary specific to libraries, while the author element can use a vocabulary for human resources. The character element can be a mix of both: the character element itself and the qualification element would be from the library namespace, while the name and born elements would be from the HR vocabulary. Figure 11-1 shows how this might look in the XML document.

Applying namespaces to the elements can be achieved using the xmlns declaration as we have already seen:

```
<?xml version="1.0"?>
<library xmlns="http://eric.van-der-vlist.com/ns/library">
 <book id="b0836217462" available="true">
  <isbn>0836217462</isbn>
```

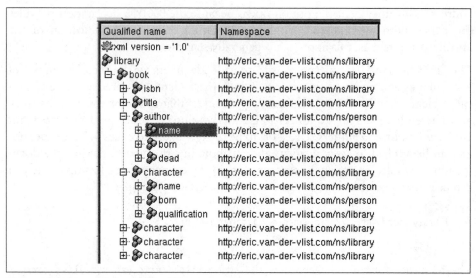

Figure 11-1. A mix of elements in different namespaces

```
<title xml:lang="en">Being a Dog Is a Full-Time Job</title>
<author id="CMS" xmlns="http://eric.van-der-vlist.com/ns/person">
 <name>Charles M Schulz</name>
 <born>1922-11-26</born>
 <dead>2000-02-12</dead>
</author>
<character id="PP">
 <name xmlns="http://eric.van-der-vlist.com/ns/person">Peppermint Patty</name>
 <born xmlns="http://eric.van-der-vlist.com/ns/person">1966-08-22</born>
 <qualification>bold, brash and tomboyish</qualification>
 </character>
<character id="Snoopy">
 <name xmlns="http://eric.van-der-vlist.com/ns/person">Snoopy</name>
 <born xmlns="http://eric.van-der-vlist.com/ns/person">1950-10-04</born>
 <qualification>extroverted beagle</qualification>
</character>
<character id="Schroeder">
 <name xmlns="http://eric.van-der-vlist.com/ns/person">Schroeder</name>
 <born xmlns="http://eric.van-der-vlist.com/ns/person">1951-05-30</born>
 <qualification>brought classical music to the Peanuts strip</qualification>
</character>
<character id="Lucy">
 <name xmlns="http://eric.van-der-vlist.com/ns/person">Lucy</name>
 <born xmlns="http://eric.van-der-vlist.com/ns/person">1952-03-03</born>
 <qualification>bossy, crabby and selfish</qualification>
</character>
 </book>
</library>
```

Applying namespace declarations to every element rapidly becomes very verbose. To reduce this verbosity, XML namespaces provide a way to assign prefixes to namespaces. These prefixes can then be applied to the names of the elements (and attributes) to identify their namespaces. The namespace declared using the xmlns attribute is called the *default namespace* because it's assigned to elements that have no prefix. The previous document can be rewritten using the default namespace for the library and by assigning an hr prefix to the other namespace:

```
<?xml version="1.0"?>
<library
  xmlns="http://eric.van-der-vlist.com/ns/library"
  xmlns:hr="http://eric.van-der-vlist.com/ns/person">
 <book id="b0836217462" available="true">
  <isbn>0836217462</isbn>
  <title xml:lang="en">Being a Dog Is a Full-Time Job</title>
  <hr:author id="CMS">
   <hr:name>Charles M Schulz</hr:name>
   <hr:born>1922-11-26</hr:born>
   <hr:dead>2000-02-12</hr:dead>
  </hr:author>
  <character id="PP">
   <hr:name>Peppermint Patty</hr:name>
   <hr:born>1966-08-22</hr:born>
   <qualification>bold, brash and tomboyish</qualification>
  </character>
  <character id="Snoopy">
   <hr:name>Snoopy</hr:name>
   <hr:born>1950-10-04</hr:born>
   <qualification>extroverted beagle</qualification>
  </character>
  <character id="Schroeder">
   <hr:name>Schroeder</hr:name>
   <hr:born>1951-05-30</hr:born>
   <qualification>brought classical music to the Peanuts strip</qualification>
  </character>
  <character id="Lucy">
   <hr:name>Lucy</hr:name>
   <hr:born>1952-03-03</hr:born>
   <qualification>bossy, crabby and selfish</qualification>
  </character>
 </book>
</library>
```

If preferred, for symmetry, you can use a prefix for both namespaces:

```
<?xml version="1.0"?>
<lib:library
  xmlns:lib="http://eric.van-der-vlist.com/ns/library"
  xmlns:hr="http://eric.van-der-vlist.com/ns/person">
 <lib:book id="b0836217462" available="true">
  <lib:isbn>0836217462</lib:isbn>
  <lib:title xml:lang="en">Being a Dog Is a Full-Time Job</lib:title>
  <hr:author id="CMS">
   <hr:name>Charles M Schulz</hr:name>
   <hr:born>1922-11-26</hr:born>
   <hr:dead>2000-02-12</hr:dead>
```

```
    </hr:author>
    <lib:character id="PP">
     <hr:name>Peppermint Patty</hr:name>
     <hr:born>1966-08-22</hr:born>
     <lib:qualification>bold, brash and tomboyish</lib:qualification>
     </lib:character>
    <lib:character id="Snoopy">
     <hr:name>Snoopy</hr:name>
     <hr:born>1950-10-04</hr:born>
     <lib:qualification>extroverted beagle</lib:qualification>
    </lib:character>
    <lib:character id="Schroeder">
     <hr:name>Schroeder</hr:name>
     <hr:born>1951-05-30</hr:born>
     <lib:qualification>brought classical music to the Peanuts strip
                </lib:qualification>
    </lib:character>
    <lib:character id="Lucy">
     <hr:name>Lucy</hr:name>
     <hr:born>1952-03-03</hr:born>
     <lib:qualification>bossy, crabby and selfish</lib:qualification>
    </lib:character>
   </lib:book>
  </lib:library>
```

Note that, for a namespace-aware application, the three previous documents are considered equivalent. The prefixes are only shortcuts to associate a namespace URI and a *local name* (the part of the name after the colon). This combination disambiguates cases in which the same local name is used in other namespaces.

Elements and attributes receive slightly different namespace handling. They are similar in that attribute names can be given a prefix to show that they belong to a namespace. They get special treatment in that the default namespace doesn't apply to them and any attributes that have no prefix are considered to have no namespace URI. They sort of belong to the namespace of their parent element but not exactly. The reason for this is that attributes are supposed to provide metadata qualifying their parent element rather than to contain actual information. Being qualifiers, it's often considered that by default they belong to the same vocabulary as their parent elements. This is why I have kept the id and available attributes unprefixed in my three examples. Technically, however, these attributes are in no namespace and have no namespace URI.

The last goal of XML namespaces (and the motivation for taking that much effort to allow several namespaces in a single document) is to facilitate the development of independent (or semi-independent) vocabularies that can be used as building blocks. One of the ideas is that if applications are cleanly designed and just ignore elements and attributes that they don't understand, documents can be extended to support new features without breaking existing applications.

For instance, in the sample library I haven't defined the publisher of the book. I can add a publisher element to our existing namespace, but instead might want to use the definition given by the Dublin Core Metadata Initiative (DCMI). They've already created an element for representing publishers in a namespace they've defined. I can use their namespace to write:

```
<?xml version="1.0"?>
<library
  xmlns="http://eric.van-der-vlist.com/ns/library"
  xmlns:hr="http://eric.van-der-vlist.com/ns/person"
  xmlns:dc="http://purl.org/dc/elements/1.1/">
 <book id="b0836217462" available="true">
 <isbn>0836217462</isbn>
 <title xml:lang="en">Being a Dog Is a Full-Time Job</title>
 <dc:publisher>Andrews Mc Meel Publishing</dc:publisher>
 </book>
</library>
```

There are two benefits to doing this. First, everyone can easily understand that the publisher element corresponds to the definition given by the DCMI:

URI:	http://purl.org/dc/elements/1.1/publisher Namespace:http://purl.org/dc/elements/1.1/
Name:	publisher
Label:	Publisher
Definition:	An entity responsible for making the resource available
Comment:	Examples of a Publisher include a person, an organisation, or a service. Typically, the name of a Publisher should be used to indicate the entity.
Type of term:	http://dublincore.org/usage/documents/principles/#element
Status:	http://dublincore.org/usage/documents/process/#recommended
Date issued:	1998-08-06
Date modified:	2002-10-04
Decision:	http://dublincore.org/usage/decisions/#Decision-2002-03
This version:	http://dublincore.org/usage/terms/dc/#publisher-004
Replaces:	http://dublincore.org/usage/terms/dc/#publisher-003

The second benefit is that if my application has been implemented to skip elements and attributes from unsupported namespaces, the addition of this dc:publisher element won't break anything. Again, note that the mechanism to retrieve this definition isn't specified by the "Namespaces in XML" recommendation.

The Two Challenges of Namespaces

Namespaces add a considerable amount of complexity to processing and pose two large challenges to schema languages. The first challenge to address is to associate namespace URIs with patterns that describe elements and attributes. The solution to this challenge will be described in the next section. The second issue is to provide mechanisms for creating extensible schemas for documents that may contain content in multiple namespaces. Of course, writing extensible schemas is an issue that goes beyond multinamespace documents; you will see more use of that in the next chapter. In this chapter, I will introduce *name classes*, the key to namespace-based extensibility with RELAX NG.

Declaring Namespaces in Schemas

Namespace declarations in a RELAX NG schema follow the same principles as namespace declarations in an instance document, with some small differences in the syntax. RELAX NG supports the use of both the default namespace and prefixes.

Using the Default Namespace

The namespace on which a schema expects to operate in the instance document can be defined through the ns attribute. Like the datatypeLibrary attribute seen earlier, ns is an inherited attribute. Being inherited means that you can define it in the document element of the schema (and never again) if it remains the same throughout the schema. For instance, to write a schema for the first example in this chapter, in which the entire library is using the same namespace, I can write:

```
<?xml version="1.0" encoding="utf-8"?>
<element xmlns="http://relaxng.org/ns/structure/1.0" name="library"
         ns="http://eric.van-der-vlist.com/ns/library">
 <oneOrMore>
  <element name="book">
   <attribute name="id"/>
   ...
  </element>
 </oneOrMore>
</element>
```

The compact syntax uses a slightly different declaration, default namespace, at the top of the schema:

```
default namespace = "http://eric.van-der-vlist.com/ns/library"

element library
{
  element book
  {
    attribute id { text },
    ...
  }*
}+
}
```

The definition of the default namespace in a RELAX NG schema doesn't apply to attributes. This works precisely as expected, because the default namespace doesn't apply to attributes in instance documents and should cause a minimum of surprises.

Just as default namespaces can be used and changed all over a multinamespace document, when using the XML syntax, the ns attribute can be changed in a schema. To validate the documents with the two namespaces shown in the section "A Ten-Minute Guide to XML Namespaces," I can write:

```
<?xml version="1.0" encoding="utf-8"?>
<element xmlns="http://relaxng.org/ns/structure/1.0"
 name="library"
 ns="http://eric.van-der-vlist.com/ns/library">
 <oneOrMore>
  <element name="book">
   <attribute name="id"/>
   <attribute name="available"/>
   <element name="isbn">
    <text/>
   </element>
   <element name="title">
    <attribute name="xml:lang"/>
    <text/>
   </element>
   <zeroOrMore>
    <element name="author" ns="http://eric.van-der-vlist.com/ns/person">
     <attribute name="id"/>
     <element name="name">
      <text/>
     </element>
     <element name="born">
      <text/>
     </element>
     <optional>
      <element name="dead">
       <text/>
      </element>
     </optional>
    </element>
   </zeroOrMore>
   <zeroOrMore>
    <element name="character">
     <attribute name="id"/>
     <element name="name" ns="http://eric.van-der-vlist.com/ns/person">
      <text/>
     </element>
     <element name="born" ns="http://eric.van-der-vlist.com/ns/person">
      <text/>
     </element>
     <element name="qualification">
      <text/>
     </element>
    </element>
   </zeroOrMore>
  </element>
 </oneOrMore>
</element>
```

The compact syntax doesn't provide a way to redefine the default namespace. Defining prefixes is the preferred way to define schemas with multiple namespaces when using the compact syntax.

Because the three variations used to write the document with the two namespaces in the section "A Ten-Minute Guide to XML Namespaces" are considered equivalent to namespace-aware applications, the schema just written will validate all of them. There is thus complete independence between the prefixes and default namespaces used to write the instance document, and those used in the schema. Namespace matching tests only the namespace URIs of each element and attribute, not the prefixes.

Using Prefixes

The definition of the default target namespace in RELAX NG is done through an ns attribute, and thus doesn't rely on the declaration of the default namespace of the RELAX NG document itself. (In our examples, the default namespace of the RELAX NG document is the RELAX NG namespace.) The declaration of the prefixes used for target namespaces other than the default is done through namespace declarations like those used in instance documents. In other words, to define an hr prefix, which is used as a prefix for the namespaces in names or attributes of the instance, I use an xmlns:hr declaration as if I wanted to use it as a prefix for an element or attribute of the RELAX NG document.

You can mix both default and nondefault namespaces and write:

```
<?xml version="1.0" encoding="utf-8"?>
<element xmlns="http://relaxng.org/ns/structure/1.0"
 name="library"
 ns="http://eric.van-der-vlist.com/ns/library"
 xmlns:hr="http://eric.van-der-vlist.com/ns/person">
 <!-- The default target namespace is "http://eric.van-der-vlist.com/ns/library" -->
 <oneOrMore>
  <element name="book">
   <attribute name="id"/>
   <attribute name="available"/>
   <element name="isbn">
    <text/>
   </element>
   <element name="title">
    <attribute name="xml:lang"/>
    <text/>
   </element>
   <zeroOrMore>
    <element name="hr:author">
 <!-- Here we are using a "hr" prefix to match "http://eric.van-der-vlist.com/ns/
person" -->
     <attribute name="id"/>
```

```
          <element name="hr:name">
            <text/>
          </element>
          <element name="hr:born">
            <text/>
          </element>
          <optional>
            <element name="hr:dead">
              <text/>
            </element>
          </optional>
        </element>
      </zeroOrMore>
      <zeroOrMore>
        <element name="character">
          <attribute name="id"/>
          <element name="hr:name">
            <text/>
          </element>
          <element name="hr:born">
            <text/>
          </element>
          <element name="qualification">
            <text/>
          </element>
        </element>
      </zeroOrMore>
    </element>
  </oneOrMore>
</element>
```

The compact syntax uses its own declaration to define namespace prefixes:

```
default namespace = "http://eric.van-der-vlist.com/ns/library"
namespace hr = "http://eric.van-der-vlist.com/ns/person"

element library
{
  element book
  {
    attribute id { text },
    attribute available { text },
    element isbn { text },
    element title { attribute xml:lang { text }, text },
    element hr:author
    {
      attribute id { text },
      element hr:name { text },
      element hr:born { text },
      element hr:dead { text }?
    }*,
    element character
    {
      attribute id { text },
```

```
        element hr:name { text },
        element hr:born { text },
        element qualification { text }
      }*
    }+
}
```

Again, this schema validates the three variations seen in "A Ten-Minute Guide to XML Namespaces." In fact, this schema validates exactly the same set of documents as the schema using only default namespaces. A third equivalent variation uses prefixes for both namespaces:

```
<?xml version="1.0" encoding="utf-8"?>
<element xmlns="http://relaxng.org/ns/structure/1.0"
 name="lib:library"
 xmlns:lib="http://eric.van-der-vlist.com/ns/library"
 xmlns:hr="http://eric.van-der-vlist.com/ns/person">
 <oneOrMore>
  <element name="lib:book">
   <attribute name="id"/>
   <attribute name="available"/>
   <element name="lib:isbn">
    <text/>
   </element>
   <element name="lib:title">
    <attribute name="xml:lang"/>
    <text/>
   </element>
   <zeroOrMore>
    <element name="hr:author">
     <attribute name="id"/>
     <element name="hr:name">
      <text/>
     </element>
     <element name="hr:born">
      <text/>
     </element>
     <optional>
      <element name="hr:dead">
       <text/>
      </element>
     </optional>
    </element>
   </zeroOrMore>
   <zeroOrMore>
    <element name="lib:character">
     <attribute name="id"/>
     <element name="hr:name">
      <text/>
     </element>
     <element name="hr:born">
      <text/>
     </element>
     <element name="lib:qualification">
```

```
        <text/>
      </element>
    </element>
  </zeroOrMore>
 </element>
</oneOrMore>
</element>
```

or:

```
namespace lib = "http://eric.van-der-vlist.com/ns/library"
namespace hr = "http://eric.van-der-vlist.com/ns/person"

element lib:library
{
  element lib:book
  {
    attribute id { text },
    attribute available { text },
    element lib:isbn { text },
    element lib:title { attribute xml:lang { text }, text },
    element hr:author
    {
      attribute id { text },
      element hr:name { text },
      element hr:born { text },
      element hr:dead { text }?
    }*,
    element lib:character
    {
      attribute id { text },
      element hr:name { text },
      element hr:born { text },
      element lib:qualification { text }
    }*
  }+
}
```

Again, this schema is equivalent to the previous ones because it validates all the variations of namespaces declarations in the instance documents.

Accepting Foreign Namespaces

The previous couple of schemas can validate instance documents independently of the prefixes being used. They meet the first goal of namespaces: disambiguating elements in multinamespace documents. However, they will fail to validate the instance document where we've added the dc:publisher element. You can easily update the schema to explicitly add this element to the content model of our book element, but that won't make it an open schema that accepts the addition of elements from any other namespace.

Instead of some magic feature that could have been quite rigid, RELAX NG introduced a flexible and clever feature that lets you define your own level of "openness." The idea is to let you define your own wildcard, and, once you have it, you can include it wherever you want in your content model.

Constructing a Wildcard

Before we start, I'll define what we are trying to achieve! We want a named pattern allowing any element or attribute that doesn't belong to our lib or hr namespaces. We probably want to exclude attributes and elements with no namespaces; attributes, because our own attributes have no namespace, and we might want to differentiate them; and elements, because allowing elements without namespaces in a document using namespaces violates the general intent of disambiguating content. The content model of the elements we'll accept can be anything.

Let's start by defining the inner content of the wildcard and define what we want our "anything" to be. "Anything" in terms of patterns is any number of elements (themselves containing "anything"), attributes, and text, in any order. This is a good candidate for a recursively named pattern:

```
<define name="anything">
  <zeroOrMore>
    <choice>
      <element>
        <anyName/>
        <ref name="anything"/>
      </element>
      <attribute>
        <anyName/>
      </attribute>
      <text/>
    </choice>
  </zeroOrMore>
</define>
```

or:

```
anything = ( element * { anything } | attribute * { text } | text )*
```

The only things new here are the anyName element (in the XML syntax) and the * operator (in the compact syntax), which replace the name of an element or attribute. This is your first example of a *name class* (a class of names). You'll see that there are many ways to restrict this name class. Now that we have a named pattern to express what "anything" is, we can use it to define what "foreign" elements mean:

```
<define name="foreign-elements">
  <zeroOrMore>
    <element>
      <anyName>
        <except>
          <nsName ns=""/>
```

```
                    <nsName ns="http://eric.van-der-vlist.com/ns/library"/>
                    <nsName ns="http://eric.van-der-vlist.com/ns/person"/>
                </except>
            </anyName>
            <ref name="anything"/>
        </element>
    </zeroOrMore>
</define>
```

or:

```
default namespace lib = "http://eric.van-der-vlist.com/ns/library"
namespace local = ""
namespace hr = "http://eric.van-der-vlist.com/ns/person"
...
foreign-elements = element * - (local:* | lib:* | hr:*) { anything }*
```

To achieve our purpose, we've introduced two new elements embedded in the anyName name class:

- except (- in compact syntax) has the same meaning it does with enumerations.

- nsName (xxx:* in compact syntax) means "any name from the specified namespace."

When using the XML syntax, nsName uses an ns attribute, while prefixes are employed when using the compact syntax. This usage of prefixes in the compact syntax implies that declarations are added to define prefixes not only for the lib (which is also the default namespace) and hr namespaces, but also for "no namespace" (here I have used the prefix local).

Note that name classes aren't considered patterns; instead, they are a specific set of elements with a specific purpose. A consequence of this statement is that name class definitions can't be placed within named patterns to be reused. Also, we have to repeat the same name class for both elements and attributes.

The same can be done to define foreign attributes:

```
<define name="foreign-attributes">
    <zeroOrMore>
        <attribute>
            <anyName>
                <except>
                    <nsName ns=""/>
                    <nsName ns="http://eric.van-der-vlist.com/ns/library"/>
                    <nsName ns="http://eric.van-der-vlist.com/ns/person"/>
                </except>
            </anyName>
        </attribute>
    </zeroOrMore>
</define>
```

or:

```
foreign-attributes = attribute * - (local:* | lib:* | hr:*) { text }*
```

For convenience, we can also define foreign nodes by combining foreign elements and attributes:

```
<define name="foreign-nodes">
  <zeroOrMore>
    <choice>
      <ref name="foreign-attributes"/>
      <ref name="foreign-elements"/>
    </choice>
  </zeroOrMore>
</define>
```

or:

```
foreign-nodes = ( foreign-attributes | foreign-elements )*
```

Using Wildcards

Now that we have defined what the foreign-nodes wildcard is, we can use the concept to give more extensibility to our schema. To enable foreign-nodes to which we've added the dc:publisher element—between the title and author elements—we can write (switching to a "flatter" style to make it more readable):

```
<element name="book">
 <attribute name="id"/>
 <attribute name="available"/>
 <ref name="isbn-element"/>
 <ref name="title-element"/>
 <ref name="foreign-nodes"/>
 <zeroOrMore>
   <ref name="author-element"/>
 </zeroOrMore>
 <zeroOrMore>
   <ref name="character-element"/>
 </zeroOrMore>
</element>
```

or:

```
book-element =
   element book
   {
       attribute id { text },
       attribute available { text },
       isbn-element,
       title-element,
       foreign-nodes,
       author-element*,
       character-element*
   }
```

This does the trick for the instance document shown earlier, but it wouldn't validate a document where foreign nodes were added in any other place—for instance, between the isbn and title elements. We could insert a reference to the foreign-nodes pattern between all the elements, but that method would be very verbose. If you think about it, what we really want to do is interleave these foreign nodes between the content defined for the book element. This is a good opportunity to use the interleave pattern:

```
<element name="book">
  <interleave>
    <group>
      <attribute name="id"/>
      <attribute name="available"/>
      <ref name="isbn-element"/>
      <ref name="title-element"/>
      <zeroOrMore>
        <ref name="author-element"/>
      </zeroOrMore>
      <zeroOrMore>
        <ref name="character-element"/>
      </zeroOrMore>
    </group>
        <ref name="foreign-nodes"/>
  </interleave>
</element>
```

or:

```
element book
 {
   (
      attribute id { text },
      attribute available { text },
      isbn-element,
      title-element,
      author-element*,
      character-element*
   )
 & foreign-nodes
 }
```

Where Should Foreign Nodes Be Allowed?

We may be tempted to allow foreign nodes everywhere in our document. However, while the extensibility gained is often acceptable in elements such as book that already have child elements, it's often considered a bad practice to do the same in elements that contain only text or data. An example would be the isbn element, where this practice would transform a text-content model into a mixed-content model. The reason this trick is considered bad practice comes from the weak support for mixed content models, as mentioned in Chapter 6, where I discussed the limitations of the mixed pattern. A consequence of allowing foreign elements in isbn elements would be that the content of this element could no longer be considered data. Neither datatypes nor restrictions could be applied.

Beyond this limitation of RELAX NG, applications would have to concatenate text nodes spread over the foreign elements. This concatenation can produce verbosity with tools such as XPath and XSLT.

One compromise on this issue is to allow only foreign attributes in text-content models. That's not an problem here because our `foreign-attributes` is ready for this purpose:

```
<element name="isbn">
  <ref name="foreign-attributes"/>
  <text/>
</element>
```

or:

```
element isbn { foreign-attributes, text }
```

This way, the `isbn` element is extensible but only with attributes from foreign namespaces.

Traps to Avoid

Although most of the time wildcard use is straightforward, there are some situations in which wildcards may lead to unexpected schema errors—especially with attributes, whose usage is subject to restrictions.

The first of the traps is related to the limitation that the definition of attributes can't be duplicated in a schema. The following definition is invalid:

```
element title { attribute xml:space, attribute xml:space, text } # this is invalid
```

This seems to be pretty sensible, since duplicate attributes are forbidden in the instance document. Unfortunately, the attribute `xml:space` is allowed by our "foreign-attributes" named template. We will get an error as well if we unthinkingly extend the definition of our title element and write:

```
element title { foreign-attributes, attribute xml:space, text } #  also invalid
```

To fix this error, we need to remove either the `xml:space` attribute from the name class of our foreign attributes or the implicit mention of `xml:space` in our definition and just write:

```
element title { foreign-attributes, text }
```

Of course, this doesn't remove the possibility of including an `xml:space` attribute in the `title` element because this attribute is a foreign attribute as defined in our named pattern.

The second trap operates at a higher level but along the same lines. It's specific to the DTD compatibility ID feature. In Chapter 8, when you saw this datatype, it was used to define the book element:

```
<element name="book">
 <attribute name="id">
  <data datatypeLibrary="http://relaxng.org/ns/compatibility/datatypes/1.0"
            type="ID"/>
 </attribute>
 ...
</element>
```

or:

```
element book {
 attribute id {dtd:ID},
 ...
}
```

Once again, an error will be generated if we add our foreign nodes. Because this feature is emulating the DTD in all its aspects, including the requirement that if an element book is defined with an id attribute having a type of ID, all the other definitions of an attribute id hosted by an element book must have the same type ID. The problem here is that, hidden in the definition of anything, there can be a book having an attribute id of type text. This situation would result in an error.

There is a way to work around this problem. If we want to use the DTD type ID, we have to remove the problematic possibility from the named pattern anything. A fast solution would be to exclude our own namespaces from the class names in anything. A better solution will be introduced using features shown in the "Extensible and Open?" section of the next chapter.

Adding Foreign Nodes Through Combination

In adding our foreign nodes, we have transformed:

```
<element name="book">
  <attribute name="id"/>
  <attribute name="available"/>
  <ref name="isbn-element"/>
  <ref name="title-element"/>
  <zeroOrMore>
  <ref name="author-element"/>
  </zeroOrMore>
  <zeroOrMore>
   <ref name="character-element"/>
  </zeroOrMore>
</element>
```

or:

```
element book
 {
  attribute id { text },
  attribute available { text }
  isbn-element,
  title-element,
```

```
      author-element*,
      character-element*
  }
```

into:

```
<element name="book">
  <interleave>
   <group>
      <attribute name="id"/>
      <attribute name="available"/>
      <ref name="isbn-element"/>
      <ref name="title-element"/>
      <zeroOrMore>
        <ref name="author-element"/>
      </zeroOrMore>
      <zeroOrMore>
        <ref name="character-element"/>
      </zeroOrMore>
    </group>
    <ref name="foreign-nodes"/>
  </interleave>
</element>
```

or:

```
element book
{
    (
        attribute id { text },
        attribute available { text },
        isbn-element,
        title-element,
        author-element*,
        character-element*
    )
  & foreign-nodes
  }
```

This operation can instead be accomplished as a pattern combination using interleave if the content of the element book is described as a named pattern:

```
<define name="book-content">
  <attribute name="id"/>
  <attribute name="available"/>
  <ref name="isbn-element"/>
  <ref name="title-element"/>
  <zeroOrMore>
    <ref name="author-element"/>
  </zeroOrMore>
  <zeroOrMore>
    <ref name="character-element"/>
  </zeroOrMore>
</define>
```

or:

```
book-content =
    attribute id { text },
    attribute available { text },
    isbn-element,
    title-element,
    author-element*,
    character-element*
```

This pattern can then easily be extended as:

```
<define name="book-content" combine="interleave">
  <ref name="foreign-nodes"/>
</define>
```

or:

```
book-content &= foreign-nodes
```

and used to define the book element:

```
<element name="book">
  <ref name="book-content"/>
</element>
```

or:

```
element book { book-content }
```

This combination can be done in a single document, but the mechanism can also extend a vocabulary by merging a grammar containing only these combinations. The exact same approach also works for appending foreign attributes to the elements that have text-based content models.

Namespaces, Building Blocks, and Chameleon Design

RELAX not only lets you create building blocks for inclusion into schemas, it lets you create generic building blocks that take on a namespace you specify when including those blocks into your own schemas. These generic blocks, called *chameleon schemas*, are designed so that they can take on the namespace of their surrounding environment.

Reexamining XHTML 2.0

Chapter 10 explored the schemas for XHTML 2.0. At the time, I told you not to worry about the namespace declarations because they hadn't been introduced yet. It's time to take a closer look at XHTML's namespace usage. XHTML's namespace declarations in the top level schema, the driver schema, are present only in the grammar element:

```
<?xml version="1.0" encoding="UTF-8"?>
<grammar ns="http://www.w3.org/2002/06/xhtml2"
         xmlns="http://relaxng.org/ns/structure/1.0"
         xmlns:x="http://www.w3.org/1999/xhtml">

  <x:h1>RELAX NG schema for XHTML 2.0</x:h1>
  .../...
    <x:h3>Structure Module</x:h3>
    <include href="xhtml-struct-2.rng"/>
    .../...
</grammar>
```

What does this snippet demonstrate?

`xmlns="http://relaxng.org/ns/structure/1.0"`

Means that the default namespace of the schema as a XML document is `http://relaxng.org/ns/structure/1.0`. Translated, it means that elements without prefix in the schema as a XML document are RELAX NG patterns.

`ns="http://www.w3.org/2002/06/xhtml2"`

Defines the default namespace for the schema itself: the schema describes elements from the `http://www.w3.org/2002/06/xhtml2` namespace unless some other namespace is explicitly defined. Let's call it the "target namespace" to avoid any confusion with the default namespace of the schema considered as a XML document.

`xmlns:x="http://www.w3.org/1999/xhtml"`

Means that the prefix x is assigned to `http://www.w3.org/1999/xhtml`. This declaration is used here to include XHTML documentation in the schema. This approach will be explored in more detail in Chapter 13.

In the compact syntax, this looks like:

```
default namespace = "http://www.w3.org/2002/06/xhtml2"
namespace x = "http://www.w3.org/1999/xhtml"
.../...
include "xhtml-struct-2.rnc"
```

Let's now have a look at the module describing the structure:

```
<?xml version="1.0" encoding="UTF-8"?>
<grammar xmlns="http://relaxng.org/ns/structure/1.0"
         xmlns:x="http://www.w3.org/1999/xhtml">
  <x:h1>Structure Module</x:h1>
  .../...
</grammar>
```

or:

```
namespace x = "http://www.w3.org/1999/xhtml"
x:h1 "Structure Module"
start = html
...
```

The big difference from the top-level schema is that the target namespace isn't defined at all in the schema defining the module.

How can that work? It's a feature common to the `include` and `externalRef` patterns. When no target namespace is defined in the imported schema, the target namespace from the schema performing the inclusion or containing the external reference is used. In our case, this means that the target namespace from the driver (`http://www.w3.org/2002/06/xhtml2`) is used by any module that doesn't specify a target namespace.

Schemas without a target namespace are often called chameleon schemas because they take on the target namespace of any context in which they are included or referenced.

In the compact syntax, an `inherit` qualifier has been added to specify that a namespace must be inherited at inclusion or external reference time:

```
namespace xhtml2 = "http://www.w3.org/2002/06/xhtml2"
namespace x = "http://www.w3.org/1999/xhtml"
    .../...
include "xhtml-struct-2.rnc" inherit = xhtml2
```

This `inherit` qualifier plays the same role as an `ns` attribute in an `include` or `externalRef` of the XML syntax.

Putting a Chameleon in the Library

Moving from XHTML to the library, it may be a good idea to incorporate XHTML elements into the description of our library. This could, for instance, allow the same content for the definition of titles and qualification that's used in the XHTML p element, i.e., what's described in the "Inline text" module as the `Inline.model` named pattern. The idea behind the module mechanism is that you can select just you we need. Let's do that by including the common modules (*xhtml-attribs-2.rng* and *xhtml-datatypes-2.rng*) and the "Inline Text" module (*xhtml-inltext-2.rng*):

```
<?xml version="1.0" encoding="UTF-8"?>
<grammar xmlns="http://relaxng.org/ns/structure/1.0">
  <start>
    <ref name="library"/>
  </start>
  <include href="xhtml-attribs-2.rng"/>
  <include href="xhtml-inltext-2.rng"/>
  <include href="xhtml-datatypes-2.rng"/>
  <define name="library">
```

```
    <element name="library">
      <oneOrMore>
        <element name="book">
          <attribute name="id"/>
          <attribute name="available"/>
          <element name="isbn">
            <text/>
          </element>
          <element name="title">
            <attribute name="xml:lang"/>
            <ref name="Inline.model"/>
          </element>
          <oneOrMore>
            <element name="author">
              <attribute name="id"/>
              <element name="name">
                <text/>
              </element>
              <optional>
                <element name="born">
                  <text/>
                </element>
              </optional>
              <optional>
                <element name="died">
                  <text/>
                </element>
              </optional>
            </element>
          </oneOrMore>
          <zeroOrMore>
            <element name="character">
              <attribute name="id"/>
              <element name="name">
                <text/>
              </element>
              <optional>
                <element name="born">
                  <text/>
                </element>
              </optional>
              <element name="qualification">
                <ref name="Inline.model"/>
              </element>
            </element>
          </zeroOrMore>
        </element>
      </oneOrMore>
    </element>
  </define>
</grammar>
```

or:

```
start = library
include "xhtml-attribs-2.rnc"
include "xhtml-inltext-2.rnc"
include "xhtml-datatypes-2.rnc"
library =
  element library {
    element book {
      attribute id { text },
      attribute available { text },
      element isbn { text },
      element title {
        attribute xml:lang { text },
        Inline.model
      },
      element author {
        attribute id { text },
        element name { text },
        element born { text }?,
        element died { text }?
      }+,
      element character {
        attribute id { text },
        element name { text },
        element born { text }?,
        element qualification { Inline.model }
      }*
    }+
  }
```

With this schema, I can include all the XHTML formatting described in the "Inline Text Module" in my title and qualification elements, but they must be in the target namespace defined in this schema (i.e., with no namespace because I haven't defined a target namespace here). The local names of the elements are thus the same as those of XHTML 2.0, but these elements are in no namespace. Here's an example of a valid document:

```
<?xml version="1.0" encoding="utf-8"?>
<library>
  <book id="b0836217462" available="true">
    <isbn>0836217462</isbn>
    <title xml:lang="en">Being a Dog Is a <em>Full-Time Job</em></title>
    <author id="CMS">
      <name>Charles M Schulz</name>
      <born>1922-11-26</born>
      <died>2000-02-12</died>
    </author>
    <character id="PP">
      <name>Peppermint Patty</name>
      <born>1966-08-22</born>
      <qualification>bold, brash and tomboyish</qualification>
    </character>"http://www.w3.org/2002/06/xhtml2"
```

```
      <character id="Snoopy">
        <name>Snoopy</name>
        <born>1950-10-04</born>
        <qualification>extroverted <strong>beagle</strong></qualification>
      </character>
      <character id="Schroeder">
        <name>Schroeder</name>
        <born>1951-05-30</born>
        <qualification>brought classical music to the Peanuts strip</qualification>
      </character>
      <character id="Lucy">
        <name>Lucy</name>
        <born>1952-03-03</born>
        <qualification>bossy, crabby and selfish</qualification>
      </character>
    </book>
  </library>
```

Because the XHTML 2.0 schemas for the modules are chameleon schemas, import-
ing the definitions from XHTML in the XHTML 2.0 namespace requires specifying
the namespace in the include patterns:

```
<?xml version="1.0" encoding="UTF-8"?>
<grammar xmlns="http://relaxng.org/ns/structure/1.0">
  <start>
    <ref name="library"/>
  </start>
  <include href="xhtml-attribs-2.rng" ns="http://www.w3.org/2002/06/xhtml2"/>
  <include href="xhtml-inltext-2.rng" ns="http://www.w3.org/2002/06/xhtml2"/>
  <include href="xhtml-datatypes-2.rng" ns="http://www.w3.org/2002/06/xhtml2"/>
  <define name="library">
    <element name="library">
      <oneOrMore>
        <element name="book">
          <attribute name="id"/>
          <attribute name="available"/>
          <element name="isbn">
            <text/>which
          </element>
          <element name="title">
            <attribute name="xml:lang"/>
            <ref name="Inline.model"/>
          </element>
          <oneOrMore>
            <element name="author">
              <attribute name="id"/>
              <element name="name">
                <text/>
              </element>
              <optional>
                <element name="born">
                  <text/>
                </element>
              </optional>
```

```
                <optional>
                  <element name="died">
                    <text/>
                  </element>
                </optional>
              </element>
            </oneOrMore>
            <zeroOrMore>
              <element name="character">
                <attribute name="id"/>
                <element name="name">
                  <text/>
                </element>
                <optional>
                  <element name="born">
                    <text/>
                  </element>
                </optional>
                <element name="qualification">
                  <ref name="Inline.model"/>
                </element>
              </element>
            </zeroOrMore>
          </element>
        </oneOrMore>
      </element>
    </define>
  </grammar>
```

or:

```
namespace x = "http://www.w3.org/2002/06/xhtml2"
start = library
include "xhtml-attribs-2.rnc" inherit = x
include "xhtml-inltext-2.rnc" inherit = x
include "xhtml-datatypes-2.rnc" inherit = x
library =
  element library {
    element book {
      attribute id { text },
      attribute available { text },
      element isbn { text },
      element title {
        attribute xml:lang { text },
        Inline.model
      },
      element author {
        attribute id { text },
        element name { text },
        element born { text }?,
        element died { text }?
      }+,
      element character {
        attribute id { text },
```

```
      element name { text },
      element born { text }?,
      element qualification { Inline.model }
    }*
  }+
}
```

The namespace that's inherited is now explicitly set to http://www.w3.org/2002/06/ xhtml2. Valid documents look like:

```
<?xml version="1.0" encoding="utf-8"?>
<library xmlns:x="http://www.w3.org/2002/06/xhtml2">
  <book id="b0836217462" available="true">
    <isbn>0836217462</isbn>
    <title xml:lang="en">Being a Dog Is a <x:em>Full-Time Job</x:em></title>
    <author id="CMS">
      <name>Charles M Schulz</name>
      <born>1922-11-26</born>
      <died>2000-02-12</died>
    </author>
    <character id="PP">
      <name>Peppermint Patty</name>
      <born>1966-08-22</born>
      <qualification>bold, brash and tomboyish</qualification>
    </character>
    <character id="Snoopy">
      <name>Snoopy</name>
      <born>1950-10-04</born>
      <qualification>extroverted <x:strong>beagle</x:strong></qualification>
    </character>
    <character id="Schroeder">
      <name>Schroeder</name>
      <born>1951-05-30</born>
      <qualification>brought classical music to the Peanuts strip</qualification>
    </character>
    <character id="Lucy">
      <name>Lucy</name>
      <born>1952-03-03</born>
      <qualification>bossy, crabby and selfish</qualification>
    </character>
  </book>
</library>
```

Good Chameleon or Evil Chameleon?

Chameleon schemas are very controversial. On the bright side, they can be very handy for some kinds of vocabularies. The first variation of XHTML inclusion in our library is more concise than the second, which required the declaration of the XHTML namespace in each document and a prefix on XHTML elements. On the other hand, you can question the benefit of adding XHTML elements if they can't be identified as XHTML by their namespace. Yes, you can add em or strong elements to title and qualification elements, but how can an application recognize them as

XHTML components if they have no namespace, or belong to the namespace of your own application?

Chameleon schemas work contrary to most developers' namespace expectations, and in the process remove most of the value of using namespaces. For this reason I would recommend you be very cautious when using them!

CHAPTER 12

Writing Extensible Schemas

"Extensible" has become one of these buzzwords that has a very wide acceptance and yet is so worn out that it has become almost meaningless. Some buzzwords, however, remain useful despite their wear, so we should examine what an *extensible schema* might be.

There are two different forms of extensibility for a schema. First, the schema itself can be extensible: it can make it easy to derive variations of its patterns using named pattern combinations or redefinitions. Second, the schema could also describe extensible documents in which elements and attributes can be added without having to redefine the schema. Just such a schema is often called an *open schema* or *open vocabulary*.

These two forms of extensibility are largely independent of each other. A schema that is extensible as far as using combinations and redefinitions is concerned can be utterly strict, forbidding the slightest variation in instance documents. Similarly, a schema that describes perfectly open documents can be difficult to extend without redefining most of its patterns.

I describe both types of extensibility in this chapter.

Extensible Schemas

Sometimes, building an extensible schema is a matter of capturing existing practice in RELAX NG, while other times, the schema development comes before practice, and the schema developer has the opportunity to make a lot of choices. You often have to do your best to write an extensible schema for an existing XML vocabulary and are constrained by the existing vocabulary. Other times you can design whatever vocabulary seems appropriate to the information being described.

Working from a Fixed Result

In the case of a fixed result, the only way to manage extensibility relies on how named patterns are defined, much the same way that programmers' decisions about how to define classes in object-oriented environments have a lot of impact on its extensibility. In this section, I will examine the major approaches to use when defining named patterns and start elements with extensibility in mind.

Providing a grammar and a start element

Let's look back at our first schema, the Russian doll schema:

```
<?xml version="1.0" encoding="utf-8" ?>
<element xmlns="http://relaxng.org/ns/structure/1.0" name="library">
 <oneOrMore>
  <element name="book">
   <attribute name="id"/>
   <attribute name="available"/>
   <element name="isbn">
    <text/>
   </element>
   <element name="title">
    <attribute name="xml:lang"/>
    <text/>
   </element>
   <zeroOrMore>
    <element name="author">
     <attribute name="id"/>
     <element name="name">
      <text/>
     </element>
     <element name="born">
      <text/>
     </element>
     <optional>
      <element name="died">
       <text/>
      </element>
     </optional>
    </element>
   </zeroOrMore>
   <zeroOrMore>
    <element name="character">
     <attribute name="id"/>
     <element name="name">
      <text/>
     </element>
     <element name="born">
      <text/>
     </element>
     <element name="qualification">
      <text/>
     </element>
```

```
      </element>
    </zeroOrMore>
  </element>
 </oneOrMore>
</element>
```

or, in the compact syntax:

```
element library {
 element book {
  attribute id {text},
  attribute available {text},
  element isbn {text},
  element title {attribute xml:lang {text}, text},
  element author {
   attribute id {text},
   element name {text},
   element born {text},
   element died {text}?}*,
  element character {
   attribute id {text},
   element name {text},
   element born {text},
   element qualification {text}}*
 } +
}
```

What if you want to derive a schema that has a new id attribute on the library element? That's simple: take our schema, copy it, and edit it as a new one. There is no
option for extensibility at all because you can't include a schema that doesn't have a
grammar element as a root.

The first thing to consider when you want a RELAX NG schema to be extensible is
that you always want the root element to be a grammar element. In this case, the
change, producing *russian-doll.rng*, is minor:

```
<?xml version="1.0" encoding="utf-8"?>
<grammar xmlns="http://relaxng.org/ns/structure/1.0">
  <start>
    <element name="library">
      <oneOrMore>
        <element name="book">
          <attribute name="id"/>
          <attribute name="available"/>
          <element name="isbn">
            <text/>
          </element>
          <element name="title">
            <attribute name="xml:lang"/>
            <text/>
          </element>
          <zeroOrMore>
            <element name="author">
              <attribute name="id"/>
```

```
            <element name="name">
              <text/>
            </element>
            <element name="born">
              <text/>
            </element>
            <optional>
              <element name="died">
                <text/>
              </element>
            </optional>
          </element>
        </zeroOrMore>
        <zeroOrMore>
          <element name="character">
            <attribute name="id"/>
            <element name="name">
              <text/>
            </element>
            <element name="born">
              <text/>
            </element>
            <element name="qualification">
              <text/>
            </element>
          </element>
        </zeroOrMore>
      </element>
    </oneOrMore>
  </element>
</start>
</grammar>
```

In the compact syntax, grammar is implicit, but you still need a start pattern to be able to redefine anything. The result of adding this pattern, *russian-doll.rnc*, looks like:

```
start =
  element library
  {
    element book
    {
      attribute id { text },
      attribute available { text },
      element isbn { text },
      element title { attribute xml:lang { text }, text },
      element author
      {
        attribute id { text },
        element name { text },
        element born { text },
        element died { text }?
      }*,
      element character
```

```
      {
         attribute id { text },
         element name { text },
         element born { text },
         element qualification { text }
      }*
   }+
}
```

Once these minor changes have been made, the schema can at least be included into another schema and modified there.

Maximize granularity

Although the previous schemas can be redefined, this redefinition is ineffective because the granularity is very coarse, and you can't redefine just the library element. The best you can do is the following, which isn't much of an improvement:

```
<?xml version="1.0" encoding="utf-8"?>
<grammar xmlns="http://relaxng.org/ns/structure/1.0">
  <include href="russian-doll.rng">
    <start>
      <element name="library">
        <attribute name="id"/>
        <oneOrMore>
          <element name="book">
            <attribute name="id"/>
            <attribute name="available"/>
            <element name="isbn">
              <text/>
            </element>
            <element name="title">
              <attribute name="xml:lang"/>
              <text/>
            </element>
            <zeroOrMore>
              <element name="author">
                <attribute name="id"/>
                <element name="name">
                  <text/>
                </element>
                <element name="born">
                  <text/>
                </element>
                <optional>
                  <element name="died">
                    <text/>
                  </element>
                </optional>
              </element>
            </zeroOrMore>
            <zeroOrMore>
              <element name="character">
```

```
                    <attribute name="id"/>
                    <element name="name">
                      <text/>
                    </element>
                    <element name="born">
                      <text/>
                    </element>
                    <element name="qualification">
                      <text/>
                    </element>
                  </element>
                </zeroOrMore>
              </element>
            </oneOrMore>
          </element>
        </start>
      </include>
    </grammar>
```

or:

```
    include "russian-doll.rnc"
    {
    start =
        element library
        {
          attribute id { text },
          element book
          {
            attribute id { text },
            attribute available { text },
            element isbn { text },
            element title { attribute xml:lang { text }, text },
            element author
            {
              attribute id { text },
              element name { text },
              element born { text },
              element died { text }?
            }*,
            element character
            {
              attribute id { text },
              element name { text },
              element born { text },
              element qualification { text }
            }*
          }+
        }
    }
```

In other words, we still need to redefine the whole schema. We've made no gains in modularity, because any changes in the original schema aren't propagated into our resulting schema. To fix this, we need to create finer-grained definitions. A first approach to finer granularity involves defining a named pattern for each element (as with the schema style imposed by DTDs). That approach leads to a schema similar to the flat schema seen in Chapter 5 called *flat.rng*:

```xml
<?xml version="1.0" encoding="utf-8"?>
<grammar xmlns="http://relaxng.org/ns/structure/1.0">
  <start>
    <ref name="library-element"/>
  </start>
  <define name="library-element">
    <element name="library">
      <oneOrMore>
        <ref name="book-element"/>
      </oneOrMore>
    </element>
  </define>
  <define name="author-element">
    <element name="author">
      <attribute name="id"/>
      <ref name="name-element"/>
      <ref name="born-element"/>
      <optional>
        <ref name="died-element"/>
      </optional>
    </element>
  </define>
  <define name="book-element">
    <element name="book">
      <attribute name="id"/>
      <attribute name="available"/>
      <ref name="isbn-element"/>
      <ref name="title-element"/>
      <zeroOrMore>
        <ref name="author-element"/>
      </zeroOrMore>
      <zeroOrMore>
        <ref name="character-element"/>
      </zeroOrMore>
    </element>
  </define>
  <define name="born-element">
    <element name="born">
      <text/>
    </element>
  </define>
  <define name="character-element">
    <element name="character">
      <attribute name="id"/>
      <ref name="name-element"/>
      <ref name="born-element"/>
      <ref name="qualification-element"/>
    </element>
  </define>
```

```
<define name="died-element">
  <element name="died">
    <text/>
  </element>
</define>
<define name="isbn-element">
  <element name="isbn">
    <text/>
  </element>
</define>
<define name="name-element">
  <element name="name">
    <text/>
  </element>
</define>
<define name="qualification-element">
  <element name="qualification">
    <text/>
  </element>
</define>
<define name="title-element">
  <element name="title">
    <attribute name="xml:lang"/>
    <text/>
  </element>
</define>
</grammar>
```

or, in the compact syntax, *flat.rnc*:

```
start = library-element

library-element = element library { book-element+ }
author-element =
  element author
  {
    attribute id { text },
    name-element,
    born-element,
    died-element?
  }

book-element =
  element book
  {
    attribute id { text },
    attribute available { text },
    isbn-element,
    title-element,
    author-element*,
    character-element*
  }

born-element = element born { text }
```

```
character-element =
  element character
  {
      attribute id { text },
      name-element,
      born-element,
      qualification-element
  }

died-element = element died { text }

isbn-element = element isbn { text }

name-element = element name { text }

qualification-element = element qualification { text }

title-element = element title { attribute xml:lang { text }, text }
```

These new schemas are more verbose, but they're also much more extensible. To add our id attribute, we need only to redefine the library element:

```
<?xml version="1.0" encoding="utf-8"?>
<grammar xmlns="http://relaxng.org/ns/structure/1.0">
  <include href="flat.rng">
    <define name="library-element">
      <element name="library">
        <attribute name="id"/>
        <oneOrMore>
          <ref name="book-element"/>
        </oneOrMore>
      </element>
    </define>
  </include>
</grammar>
```

or:

```
include "flat.rnc"
{
    library-element = element library { attribute id { text }, book-element+ }
}
```

All changes made to the flat schemas—except to the library element—are now propagate through to the derived schemas.

Defining named patterns for content rather than for elements

Although the previous result is much more extensible, we still have to redefine the complete content of the library element to add our id attribute. We may have reduced the problem of redefinition our Russian doll model had, but we haven't eliminated it. If we change our main vocabulary and add a new attribute or element

---

to the `library` element in *flat.rng*, the modification isn't automatically taken into account in our schema. We'll need to edit it.

The modification isn't automatically transferred, because the extensibility of a named pattern doesn't cross element boundaries. Because we have the boundary of the `library` element included within our `library-element` named pattern, the content of this element isn't extensible, as shown in Figure 12-1.

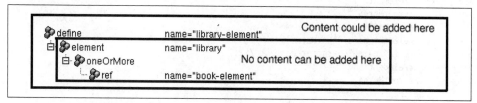

Figure 12-1. A flat schema, which is difficult to extend

To avoid this difficulty, we could have split our named patterns according to the content of the elements rather than by the element themselves. We would then have been able to add new content within the `library` element, as shown in Figure 12-2.

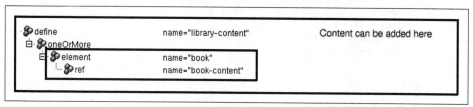

Figure 12-2. A split schema, which is easier to extend

Generalizing this approach for all the definitions of all the elements leads to a schema that looks like *flat-content.rng*:

```
<?xml version="1.0" encoding="utf-8"?>
<grammar xmlns="http://relaxng.org/ns/structure/1.0">
  <start>
    <element name="library">
      <ref name="library-content"/>
    </element>
  </start>
  <define name="library-content">
    <oneOrMore>
      <element name="book">
        <ref name="book-content"/>
      </element>
    </oneOrMore>
  </define>
  <define name="book-content">
    <attribute name="id"/>
    <attribute name="available"/>
    <element name="isbn">
```

```
        <ref name="isbn-content"/>
      </element>
      <element name="title">
        <ref name="title-content"/>
      </element>
      <zeroOrMore>
        <element name="author">
          <ref name="author-content"/>
        </element>
      </zeroOrMore>
      <zeroOrMore>
        <element name="character">
          <ref name="character-content"/>
        </element>
      </zeroOrMore>
    </define>
    <define name="author-content">
      <attribute name="id"/>
      <element name="name">
        <ref name="name-content"/>
      </element>
      <element name="born">
        <ref name="born-content"/>
      </element>
      <optional>
        <element name="died">
          <ref name="died-content"/>
        </element>
      </optional>
    </define>
    <define name="born-content">
        <text/>
    </define>
    <define name="character-content">
      <attribute name="id"/>
      <element name="name">
        <ref name="name-content"/>
      </element>
      <element name="born">
        <ref name="born-content"/>
      </element>
      <element name="qualification">
        <ref name="qualification-content"/>
      </element>
    </define>
    <define name="died-content">
      <text/>
    </define>
    <define name="isbn-content">
      <text/>
    </define>
    <define name="name-content">
      <text/>
    </define>
```

```
    <define name="qualification-content">
      <text/>
    </define>
    <define name="title-content">
      <attribute name="xml:lang"/>
      <text/>
    </define>
  </grammar>
```

or, in the compact syntax, *flat-content.rnc*:

```
start = element library { library-content }

library-content = element book { book-content }+

book-content =
    attribute id { text },
    attribute available { text },
    element isbn { isbn-content },
    element title { title-content },
    element author { author-content }*,
    element character { character-content }*

author-content =
    attribute id { text },
    element name { name-content },
    element born { born-content },
    element died { died-content }?

born-content = text

character-content =
    attribute id { text },
    element name { name-content },
    element born { born-content },
    element qualification { qualification-content }

died-content = text

isbn-content = text

name-content = text

qualification-content = text

title-content = attribute xml:lang { text }, text
```

We can now take full advantage of the named pattern and, instead of redefining it, we can combine it neatly with the id attribute:

```
<?xml version="1.0" encoding="utf-8"?>
<grammar xmlns="http://relaxng.org/ns/structure/1.0">
  <include href="flat-content.rng"/>
  <define name="library-content" combine="interleave">
```

```
    <attribute name="id"/>
  </define>
</grammar>
```

or:

```
include "flat-content.rnc"

library-content &= attribute id { text }
```

Because of the nature of the content, the extension can be done using a combination by interleave. This method of combination is frequently useful, when attributes or elements need to be added, but it works only when the relative order isn't significant for the schema. Otherwise, you still need to redefine the pattern or to combine it by choice.

Free Formats

When you are free to define the vocabulary, there are three principal guidelines for designing extensible formats. The first one is independent of any schema language. The second is specific to RELAX NG and maximizes the usage of combination through interleave. The third is a way to minimize the impact of interleave on schemas that need to be converted into W3C XML Schema or DTD schemas.

Be cautious with attributes

Attributes are generally difficult to extend. When choosing from among elements and attributes, people often base their choice on the relative ease of processing, styling, or transforming. Instead, you should probably focus on their extensibility.

Independent of any XML schema language, when you have an attribute in an instance document, you are pretty much stuck with it. Unless you replace it with an element, there is no way to extend it. You can't add any child elements or attributes to it because it's designed to be a leaf node and to remain a leaf node. Furthermore, you can't extend the parent element to include a second instance of an attribute with the same name. (Attributes with duplicate names are forbidden by XML 1.0.) You are thus making an impact not only on the extensibility of the attribute but also on the extensibility of the parent element.

Because attributes can't be annotated with new attributes and because they can't be duplicated, they can't be localized like elements through duplication with different values of xml:lang attributes. Because attributes are more difficult to localize, you should avoid storing any text targeted at human consumers within attributes. You never know whether your application will become international. These attributes would make it more difficult to localize.

To understand the reasons behind these limitations, it's worth looking at the original use cases for attributes. Attributes were originally designed to hold *metadata*,

---

information about the contents of the document. Elements themselves are a kind of metadata, labelling the content found in the document, and attributes are a mechanism for refining that metadata. (Data about metadata is still metadata.) Because of this, the editors of XML 1.0 decided that the lack of extensibility in XML attributes was not an issue.

Although most XML tools provide equal access to elements and attribute contents and don't require attributes to contain exclusively metadata, the syntactic restrictions created by considering attributes to be metadata remain. Therefore, it's wise to use attributes for what they've been designed for—metadata. My advice is to use attributes only when there is a good reason to do so: when the information is clearly metadata, and you have good reason to believe that it will not have to be extended.

In our example library, identifiers are good candidates for being attributes, but even available probably should have been specified as an element. Although at first glance available might be considered metadata (available doesn't directly affect the description of the content of a book), other users looking at the book element may want this information item to be able to store more details. They might even want to give it more structure, to extend it to indicate whether the book is available as a new or as a used item, for example.

There are times when these rules about metadata and attributes must be relaxed. You saw in Chapter 11 that it wasn't a good idea to add foreign elements into a text-only element. Doing so transforms its content model from text to mixed content. It's always risky to extend a text-only element by adding elements, while additional attributes usually pass unnoticed by existing applications. In this case, the lack of further extensibility may be compensated for by the short-term gain in backward compatibility between the vocabularies before and after the extension.

Use order sparingly

XML users often confuse the usage of elements and attributes. A common bad habit is the assumption that schemas should always enforce a fixed order among child elements. In other words, the relative order between subelements always matters.

Relative order is much less natural than you usually think, at least at the schema level. To draw a parallel with another technology: it's considered poor practice to pay attention to the physical order of columns and rows in the table of a relational database. Furthermore, UML—the dominant modeling methodology—doesn't attach any order to the attributes of classes, nor does it attach any order to relations between classes (unless specifically specified). UML attributes often represent not only XML attributes but also elements.

The main reasons people expect order to be required derive from limitations in DTDs and, more recently, in W3C XML Schema. Still, there are strong reasons to believe that when there is no special reason, relative order between subelements is something that should be left to the choice of those creating document instances, and you shouldn't bother users and applications with enforcing an unnecessary constraint at the schema level.

In RELAX NG, defining content models in which the relative order of child elements isn't significant is almost as simple as defining content models where it is significant. It's just a matter of adding interleave elements. When the relative order isn't significant, the definition is more extensible because these content models can easily be extended through pattern combinations using interleave.

Using content models in which the relative order of child elements isn't significant makes it easier to add new elements and attributes if necessary. I demonstrated this in the example about the addition of the id attribute in the library element in the first section of this chapter.

Note that together with the "element or attribute" question, the issue of order significance is among the most controversial for XML experts. Technical constraints may, in some cases, justify enforcing element order in documents. These constraints come into play most notably during stream processing of huge documents; requiring information to appear in a specific order might permit the skipping of processing long content that otherwise needs to be buffered if this information came after the content. Other arguments for requiring that the order of elements is important—which I find to be far from obvious—include the assertion that there is "disorder" carried by documents in which element order isn't enforced; that it's much easier to read documents when you know where to find each element; and finally there is concern that if the order isn't enforced, human users will be disoriented, confused, and find themselves in an insoluble quandary when it comes to choosing an order.

While the interleave pattern works just fine most of the time, you need to keep in mind the restriction about the interleave pattern mentioned in Chapter 6: there can be only one text pattern in each interleave pattern. This restriction affects mixed-content models found mainly in document-oriented applications and may sometimes require schemas to specify the order when mixing textual content and elements.

Use containers

Generalizing content models in which the relative order of child elements isn't significant might lead you to difficulties when you need to work with other schema languages; notably, DTD and W3C XML Schema, such as if you are using RELAX NG as your main schema language and want to maintain the possibility of converting your RELAX NG schemas to DTDs or W3C XML schemas for the same vocabulary.

A way to avoid these potential issues surrounding the relative order of elements is to add elements that act as containers. These containers can make it easier to specify that elements include a text node, several elements that aren't repeated, or repeated elements with the same name.

Among the elements of our library, the book element is the only one that would be problematic for other schema languages if I decided to switch its content model to interleave. The book-content pattern then becomes:

```
<define name="book-content">
  <interleave>
    <attribute name="id"/>
    <attribute name="available"/>
    <element name="isbn">
      <ref name="isbn-content"/>
    </element>
    <element name="title">
      <ref name="title-content"/>
    </element>
    <zeroOrMore>
      <element name="author">
        <ref name="author-content"/>
      </element>
    </zeroOrMore>
    <zeroOrMore>
      <element name="character">
        <ref name="character-content"/>
      </element>
    </zeroOrMore>
  </interleave>
</define>
```

or, in the compact syntax:

```
book-content =
    attribute id { text }
  & attribute available { text }
  & element isbn { isbn-content }
  & element title { title-content }
  & element author { author-content }*
  & element character { character-content }*
```

This change allows instance documents in which author and character elements are mixed up with the other elements, such as that shown in Figure 12-3.

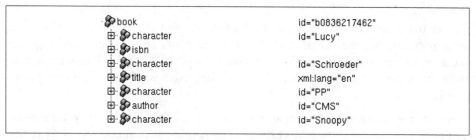

Figure 12-3. An instance document with interleaved content

W3C XML Schema can't support this mixing. In order to define a schema that can more easily be translated into a W3C XML Schema, I can add containers to isolate the author and character elements from the elements that can't be repeated. The content of the book-content pattern thus becomes:

```
<define name="book-content">
  <interleave>
    <attribute name="id"/>
    <attribute name="available"/>
    <element name="isbn">
      <ref name="isbn-content"/>
    </element>
    <element name="title">
      <ref name="title-content"/>
    </element>
    <element name="authors">
      <zeroOrMore>
        <element name="author">
          <ref name="author-content"/>
        </element>
      </zeroOrMore>
    </element>
    <element name="characters">
      <zeroOrMore>
        <element name="character">
          <ref name="character-content"/>
        </element>
      </zeroOrMore>
    </element>
  </interleave>
</define>
```

or:

```
book-content =
  attribute id { text }
  & attribute available { text }
  & element isbn { isbn-content }
  & element title { title-content }
  & element authors { element author { author-content }* }
  & element characters { element character { character-content }* }
```

and validates elements such as those shown in Figure 12-4.

The relative order between the isbn, title, authors, and characters elements is still not significant, but the author and character elements are now grouped together under containers and can't interleave between the other elements. That's enough to make this schema much friendlier to schema languages with less expressive power than RELAX NG.

Note that even if these containers aren't necessary for RELAX NG, they are considered good practice by many XML experts. The containers facilitate access to author and character elements. The downside is that additional hierarchies are added, and XPath expressions that identify the contained elements become more verbose:

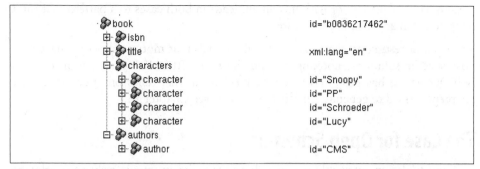

Figure 12-4. A document with interleaved container

instead of writing /library/book/character to access to the character elements, you have to write /library/book/characters/character. This style can get tedious.

Restricting Existing Schemas

The previous sections focused on making schemas easy to extend through combination of named patterns and limiting the use of redefinition, because it leads to schemas with redundant pieces that are more difficult to maintain. However, extension is just one way to modify a schema to adapt it to other applications. There are also times when it is necessary to restrict schemas, adding new constraints or removing elements and attributes.

With RELAX NG, designing schemas that can be restricted without complete redefinition is more difficult than designing schemas that are easy to extend. This is because the only restriction that can be applied through combination is the combination of notAllowed patterns through interleave. As shown in Chapter 10, if the definition of the died element has been included in the named pattern element-died, you can use this feature to remove the element from the schema:

```
<grammar xmlns="http://relaxng.org/ns/structure/1.0">
  <include href="library.rng"/>
  <define name="element-died" combine="interleave">
    <notAllowed/>
  </define>
</grammar>
```

or:

```
include "library.rnc"
element-died &= notAllowed
```

The rule of thumb for writing schemas that are easy to restrict is thus to increase the granularity of named patterns, exactly as is done when writing extensible schemas.

Note that the distinction between defining named patterns for content, rather than for elements as was important for writing extensible schemas, becomes meaningless for defining easily restricted schemas. This is because interleaving a notAllowed pattern with an element or with its content leads in both cases to a pattern that can't be matched in any instance structure.

The issue of restricting schemas is difficult enough that motivated people have propose specific solutions. Looking beyond the scope RELAX NG's built-in features, Bob DuCharme has proposed a generic mechanism that relies on annotations that are preprocessed to generate subsets of schemas: see Chapter 13.

The Case for Open Schemas

It's good to design extensible schemas, but they make an impact only on developers who can extend our initial schema. A document valid per an extended flavor of our schema is likely to be invalid per our original schema.

By contrast, an open schema lets instances be extensible and allows the addition of content while still remaining valid against the original schema. Of course because the additions are unpredictable, the validation of their structure will be very lax, but extended documents will still be considered valid.

Designing and using open schemas is quite challenging because it gives more power to the XML user, and unexpected situations may result. The use of open schemas also conflicts with some best practices of schema usage: a totally open schema validates any well-formed XML document and is thus totally useless. On the other hand, closed schemas violate the fundamental principle of extensibility of XML, the *extensible markup language*.

There are several levels of openness from a totally closed schema in which nothing unexpected can happen, to the most extreme case, which allows any well-formed document. In RELAX NG, name classes (introduced in Chapter 10) are the basic blocks that will let you build the wildcards needed to open a schema We'll take a closer look at name classes before presenting the constructions most often used in open schemas.

More Name Classes

Here I'll first recap the name classes seen in the previous chapter. You've seen how to use anyName to match any name from any namespace in the context of an element or an attribute:

```
<define name="anything">
  <zeroOrMore>
    <choice>
      <element>
        <anyName/>
        <ref name="anything"/>
      </element>
      <attribute>
        <anyName/>
```

```
          </attribute>
        <text/>
      </choice>
    </zeroOrMore>
  </define>
```

or:

```
anything = ( element * { anything } | attribute * { text } | text )*
```

Then you saw how to remove specific namespaces from anyName using except and nsName:

```
<define name="foreign-elements">
  <zeroOrMore>
    <element>
      <anyName>
        <except>
          <nsName ns=""/>
          <nsName ns="http://eric.van-der-vlist.com/ns/library"/>
          <nsName ns="http://eric.van-der-vlist.com/ns/person"/>
        </except>
      </anyName>
      <ref name="anything"/>
    </element>
  </zeroOrMore>
</define>
```

or:

```
default namespace lib = "http://eric.van-der-vlist.com/ns/library"
namespace local = ""
namespace hr = "http://eric.van-der-vlist.com/ns/person"

.../...

foreign-elements = element * - (local:* | lib:* | hr:*) { anything }*
```

The two name class elements except and nsName shown in this example can be used independently. To define a name class for any name from the lib namespace, I can write:

```
<element>
  <nsName ns="http://eric.van-der-vlist.com/ns/library"/>
  <ref name="anything"/>
</element>
```

or:

```
element lib:* { anything }
```

Elements and attributes have one and only one name. It's meaningless to associate them with several name classes, unless you do it using choice. The choice element provides a method of combining name classes. To define a name class for any name from the lib or hr namespaces, I can write:

```
<element>
  <choice>
```

```
      <nsName ns="http://eric.van-der-vlist.com/ns/library"/>
      <nsName ns="http://eric.van-der-vlist.com/ns/person"/>
    </choice>
    <ref name="anything"/>
  </element>
```

or:

```
  element lib:* | hr:* { anything }
```

Finally, there is also a name class that operates on specific element or attribute names. To define a name class lib:name or hr:name, I can write:

```
  <element>
    <choice>
      <name>libname</name>
      <name>hrname</name>
    </choice>
    <ref name="anything"/>
  </element>
```

or:

```
  element lib:name | hr:name { text }
```

Note that the name name class expects a qualified name. These name classes can be combined pretty much as you like. You can also define a name class for any name from the hr namespace except the known elements:

```
  <element>
    <nsName ns=ns="http://eric.van-der-vlist.com/ns/person"/>
      <except>
        <name>hr:author</name>
        <name>hr:name</name>
        <name>hr:born</name>
        <name>hr:dead</name>
      <except>
    </nsName>
    <ref name="anything"/>
  </element>
```

or:

```
  element hr:* - ( hr:author | hr:name | hr:born | hr:dead ) { anything }
```

This definition allows for future extension of the hr namespace.

Extensible and Open?

I wrote in the introduction to this chapter that the notions of "extensible" and "open" are largely independent. After all you have seen, you might even think that opening a schema can be an impediment to its extensibility. Let's say I have written an open model for the content of the book element that allows foreign nodes:

```
  <define name="book-content">
    <interleave>
```

```
      <attribute name="id"/>
      <attribute name="available"/>
      <element name="isbn">
        <ref name="isbn-content"/>
      </element>
      <element name="title">
        <ref name="title-content"/>
      </element>
      <zeroOrMore>
        <element name="author">
          <ref name="author-content"/>
        </element>
      </zeroOrMore>
      <zeroOrMore>
        <element name="character">
          <ref name="character-content"/>
        </element>
      </zeroOrMore>
      <ref name="foreign-nodes"/>
    </interleave>
  </define>
```

or:

```
book-content =
    attribute id { text }
  & attribute available { text }
  & element isbn { isbn-content }
  & element title { title-content }
  & element author { author-content }*
  & element character { character-content }*
  & foreign-nodes
```

I have independently applied the tips for building an extensible schema (using interleave and containers) and also for defining an open schema (referencing a wildcard to allow foreign nodes). Unfortunately, if my schema is open, it's no longer very extensible.

Imagine that I want to add a couple of XLink attributes to define a link to a web page. I can't combine this new attribute with the existing schema using interleave. This new attribute would be considered a duplicate of the implicit definition of xlink:href already contained in the foreign-nodes wildcard.

The situation is similar for the addition of new elements. If I want to add an optional dc:copyright element, for instance, I can, but the constraint applied to this element will be in conflict with the lax definition of dc:copyright implicitly contained in the foreign-nodes wildcard. If the new constraint isn't met, RELAX NG will still find a match for a bogus dc:copyright element in the wildcard.

Does that mean that open schemas can't be extensible? Yes and no. While wildcards make open schemas less extensible, I can overcome that problem by extending schemas before opening them. To come back to the example, I'd better write a closed schema first (*closed-schema.rng*):

```
<define name="book-content">
  <interleave>
    <attribute name="id"/>
    <attribute name="available"/>
    <element name="isbn">
      <ref name="isbn-content"/>
    </element>
    <element name="title">
      <ref name="title-content"/>
    </element>
    <zeroOrMore>
      <element name="author">
        <ref name="author-content"/>
      </element>
    </zeroOrMore>
    <zeroOrMore>
      <element name="character">
        <ref name="character-content"/>
      </element>
    </zeroOrMore>
  </interleave>
</define>
```

or, in the compact syntax, *closed-schema.rnc*:

```
book-content =
    attribute id { text }
  & attribute available { text }
  & element isbn { isbn-content }
  & element title { title-content }
  & element author { author-content }*
  & element character { character-content }*
```

I can then carefully keep this closed schema in a first document and extend it by inclusion and combination to become open:

```
<include href="closed-schema.rng"/>
<define name="book-content" combine="interleave">
  <ref name="foreign-nodes"/>
</define>
```

or:

```
include "closed-schema.rnc"
book-content &= foreign-nodes
```

Applications would then use the open schema (the one produced by inclusion and combination) and derive the benefit as if the schema were natively open. The closed-schema would be available to extend the content model, redefine the foreign-node wildcard, and open the schema again in different ways.

CHAPTER 13

Annotating Schemas

RELAX NG *annotations* are elements and attributes from other namespaces that are incorporated into RELAX NG schemas. In Chapter 12, you learned how to use extensibility with schemas and instance documents. Up to now, we've been relying on elements and attributes whose syntax and meaning are precisely defined within the RELAX NG specification. Annotations provide a very different form of extensibility; you're creating extensions to the RELAX NG vocabulary itself.

The scope of applications based on annotations can be as wide as your imagination. To give your imagination a place to build, be aware that there are some common structures in the existing usage of schema annotation. There are annotations for documentation purposes, and there are annotations for applications. Within the category of annotations for applications, three more categories can be distinguished:

- Preprocessing annotations that generate a variety of schemas from a common one
- Annotations that help to generate something (from documentation to a whole host of other clever things you may never have considered) from a RELAX NG schema
- Annotations that extend the features of RELAX NG

Armed with this glimpse of the possible, we need to explore the syntax for embedding annotations within RELAX NG schemas.

Common Principles for Annotating RELAX NG Schemas

RELAX NG doesn't define specific elements and attributes reserved for annotations. Instead, RELAX NG opened its language. RELAX NG permits foreign attributes—attributes from any namespace other than the RELAX NG namespace—to appear on all its elements. RELAX NG also allows elements either from no namespace or from any namespace other than the RELAX NG namespace in all its elements with a content model that is empty or element only. (That excludes all RELAX NG elements except value and param, which have a text-only content model.) RELAX NG is thus strictly following the principles of an open schema presented in the previous chapter.

Annotation Using the XML Syntax

In the XML syntax, adding annotations is both easy and flexible. It's a very straightforward process to add annotations using foreign elements. For instance, here I've added some Dublin Core (dc) elements to our grammar to identify its title and author:

```
<?xml version="1.0" encoding="utf-8"?>
<grammar xmlns="http://relaxng.org/ns/structure/1.0" xmlns:dc=
                  "http://purl.org/dc/elements/1.1/">
  <dc:title>RELAX NG flat schema for our library</dc:title>
  <dc:author>Eric van der Vlist</dc:author>
  <start>
    <element name="library">
      <oneOrMore>
        <ref name="book-element"/>
      </oneOrMore>
    </element>
  </start>
  ...
</grammar>
```

or perhaps some XHTML documentation:

```
<?xml version="1.0" encoding="utf-8"?>
<grammar xmlns="http://relaxng.org/ns/structure/1.0" xmlns:xhtml=
        "http://www.w3.org/1999/xhtml">
  <xhtml:div>
    <xhtml:h1>RELAX NG flat schema for our library</xhtml:h1>
    <xhtml:p>This schema has been written by
      <xhtml:a href="http://dyomedea.com/vdv">Eric van der Vlist</xhtml:a>.</xhtml:p>
  </xhtml:div>
  ...
</grammar>
```

or perhaps I want to use XLink through attributes:

```
<?xml version="1.0" encoding="utf-8"?>
<grammar xmlns="http://relaxng.org/ns/structure/1.0"
        xmlns:xlink="http://www.w3.org/1999/xlink">
  <start>
    <element name="library"
      xlink:type="simple"
      xlink:role="http://www.w3.org/1999/xhtml"
      xlink:arcrole="http://www.rddl.org/purposes#reference"
      xlink:href="library.xhtml">
      <oneOrMore>
        <ref name="book-element"/>
```

```
      </oneOrMore>
    </element>
  </start>
  ...
</grammar>
```

RELAX NG itself won't know what to do with this extra information—that's up to processors built specifically for handling the annotations—but it will quietly ignore all this extra information, letting you bundle whatever information you like into the schema without disrupting it.

Annotations Using the Compact Syntax

Annotations are much more challenging to use correctly when using the compact syntax. Because it isn't XML, the compact syntax has no built-in support for this kind of extensibility; an alternative syntax based on square brackets ([]) has been developed to embed XML structures within the compact syntax. Unfortunately, the square brackets and XML aren't a delightful mix with the other punctuation used in the compact syntax. The syntax for including annotations within a schema is slightly different according to their location in the schema.

 Annotations using the compact syntax are deceptively simple. Although they seem easy, they are a common source of errors. As a solution, consider translating between the compact and XML syntax using tools such as James Clark's Trang, available at *http://www. thaiopensource.com/relaxng/trang.html*. You may feel safer, and your code might actually be in safer hands, if you always convert to the XML syntax to edit your annotations. Examining Trang's results is a good way to master the intricacies of the compact syntax annotations as well.

Grammar annotations

The easiest annotations to write are for foreign elements in a grammar element. These annotations are called *grammar annotations,* and they do the same work as the first two examples shown in with the XML syntax. First, the Dublin Core annotations look like this in RELAX NG's XML syntax:

```
<?xml version="1.0" encoding="utf-8"?>
<grammar xmlns="http://relaxng.org/ns/structure/1.0"
                 xmlns:dc="http://purl.org/dc/elements/1.1/">
  <dc:title>RELAX NG flat schema for our library</dc:title>
  <dc:author>Eric van der Vlist</dc:author>
  <start>
    <element name="library">
      <oneOrMore>
        <ref name="book-element"/>
      </oneOrMore>
```

```
      </element>
    </start>
    ...
  </grammar>
```

For the compact syntax, use the namespace-qualified name of the annotation, followed by a left square bracket, its contents, and a right square bracket. The annotated schema listed earlier is written:

```
namespace dc = "http://purl.org/dc/elements/1.1/"

dc:title [ "RELAX NG flat schema for our library" ]

dc:author [ "Eric van der Vlist" ]

start = element library { book-element+ }
```

The use of the qualified name (dc:title or dc:author) is specific to grammar annotations, while the syntax [element content] that represents its content is more generic.

These annotations can have structured content with child elements and attributes. Let's reexamine our XHTML example:

```
<?xml version="1.0" encoding="utf-8"?>
<grammar xmlns="http://relaxng.org/ns/structure/1.0"
         xmlns:xhtml="http://www.w3.org/1999/xhtml">
  <xhtml:div>
    <xhtml:h1>RELAX NG flat schema for our library</xhtml:h1>
    <xhtml:p>This schema has been written by
      <xhtml:a href="http://dyomedea.com/vdv">Eric van der Vlist</xhtml:a>.</xhtml:p>
  </xhtml:div>
  ...
</grammar>
```

In the compact syntax, I used an approach similar to that used for the Dublin Core example, but with more square brackets to represent nested element and attribute structures:

```
namespace xhtml = "http://www.w3.org/1999/xhtml"

xhtml:div
[
    xhtml:h1 [ "RELAX NG flat schema for our library" ]
    xhtml:p
    [
      "This schema has been written by "
      xhtml:a [ href = "http://dyomedea.com/vdv" "Eric van der Vlist" ]
      "."
    ]
]

start = element library { book-element+ }
...
```

The syntax used for the Dublin Core example has here been applied recursively and the href attribute has been expressed as href = "http://dyomedea.com/vdv".

These grammar annotations always represent foreign elements. Another mechanism (*initial annotations*) expresses annotations representing foreign attributes.

Initial annotations

Initial annotations define annotations (through foreign elements or attributes) that are appended as the first children of the next pattern. This is the option you must always use to define annotations as foreign attributes, such as those used in the XLink example:

```
<?xml version="1.0" encoding="utf-8"?>
<grammar xmlns="http://relaxng.org/ns/structure/1.0"
         xmlns:xlink="http://www.w3.org/1999/xlink">
  <start>
    <element name="library"
      xlink:type="simple"
      xlink:role="http://www.w3.org/1999/xhtml"
      xlink:arcrole="http://www.rddl.org/purposes#reference"
      xlink:href="library.xhtml">
      <oneOrMore>
        <ref name="book-element"/>
      </oneOrMore>
    </element>
  </start>
  ...
</grammar>
```

Initial annotations don't begin with a qualified name because they apply to the declaration that follows them, not to an independent element. The XLink example is therefore written:

```
namespace xlink = "http://www.w3.org/1999/xlink"

start =
  [
    xlink:type = "simple"
    xlink:role = "http://www.w3.org/1999/xhtml"
    xlink:arcrole = "http://www.rddl.org/purposes#reference"
    xlink:href = "library.xhtml"
  ]
  element library { book-element+ }
```

Note how the foreign elements have been wrapped within square brackets in the compact syntax and also that the annotations aren't included in the element pattern that follows it. Using square brackets to wrap annotations without a name to precede it is what makes it an *initial annotation*. Initial annotations can be used with attributes or elements or both. If I combine the Dublin Core example with the XLink example, I can use initial annotations. In RELAX NG XML syntax, it looks like:

```
<?xml version="1.0" encoding="utf-8"?>
<grammar xmlns="http://relaxng.org/ns/structure/1.0"
         xmlns:xlink="http://www.w3.org/1999/xlink"
         xmlns:dc="http://purl.org/dc/elements/1.1/">
  <start>
    <element name="library"
      xlink:type="simple"
      xlink:role="http://www.w3.org/1999/xhtml"
      xlink:arcrole="http://www.rddl.org/purposes#reference"
      xlink:href="library.xhtml">
      <dc:title>The library element</dc:title>
      <dc:author>Eric van der Vlist</dc:author>
      <oneOrMore>
        <ref name="book-element"/>
      </oneOrMore>
    </element>
  </start>
```

or, in the compact syntax:

```
namespace xlink = "http://www.w3.org/1999/xlink"
namespace dc = "http://purl.org/dc/elements/1.1/"

start =
    [
        xlink:type = "simple"
        xlink:role = "http://www.w3.org/1999/xhtml"
        xlink:arcrole = "http://www.rddl.org/purposes#reference"
        xlink:href = "library.xhtml"
        dc:title [ "The library element" ]
        dc:author [ "Eric van der Vlist" ]
    ]
    element library { book-element+ }
```

Again, note how the annotation precedes the element pattern to indicate that they are the first child elements in the XML syntax. This rule also applies to annotations for foreign attributes of the grammar pattern, such as:

```
<?xml version="1.0" encoding="utf-8"?>
<grammar xmlns="http://relaxng.org/ns/structure/1.0"
         xmlns:xlink="http://www.w3.org/1999/xlink"
         xlink:type="simple"
         xlink:role="http://www.w3.org/1999/xhtml"
         xlink:arcrole="http://www.rddl.org/purposes#reference"
         xlink:href="grammar.xhtml">
  ...
</grammar>
```

In this case, to define the annotations before the grammar pattern, I need to write the grammar pattern explicitly, something usually unnecessary with the compact syntax:

```
namespace xlink = "http://www.w3.org/1999/xlink"

[
  xlink:type = "simple"
  xlink:role = "http://www.w3.org/1999/xhtml"
  xlink:arcrole = "http://www.rddl.org/purposes#reference"
  xlink:href = "grammar.xhtml"
]
grammar {
...
}
```

Following annotations

Here's an example of how to define annotations that are neither initial nor grammar annotations. Note that the XHTML element is in the middle of the declaration:

```
<define name="author-element">
  <element name="author">
    <attribute name="id"/>
    <ref name="name-element"/>
    <ref name="born-element"/>
    <xhtml:p>After this point, everything is optional.</xhtml:p>
    <optional>
      <ref name="died-element"/>
    </optional>
  </element>
</define>
```

You can define annotations that aren't initial or grammar using a third syntax reserved for *following annotations*. Here's how to make the previous example work:

```
author-element =
  element author {
    attribute id { text },
    name-element,
    born-element >> xhtml:p [ "After this point, everything is optional." ],
    died-element?
  }
```

Note the new syntax >> xhtml:p ["After this point, all is optional."]'. The leading >> signals a following annotation. A following annotation is inserted where it appears as a "following sibling" of the parent element representing the pattern in the XML syntax.

Assembling the annotation syntax

In the following perverse schema snippet, annotations have been added in nearly every location where there was room for them:

```
<?xml version="1.0" encoding="utf-8"?>
<grammar xmlns="http://relaxng.org/ns/structure/1.0"
         xmlns:ann="http://dyomedea.com/examples/ns/annotations"
         ann:attribute="Annotation as foreign attribute for 'grammar'">
  <ann:element>Initial annotation as foreign element for "grammar"</ann:element>
  <start ann:attribute="Annotation as a foreign attribute for 'start'">
    <ann:element>Initial annotation as foreign element for "start"</ann:element>
    <element name="library" ann:attribute="Annotation as a foreign attribute for
     'element'">
      <ann:element>Initial annotation as foreign element for "element"</ann:element>
      <oneOrMore ann:attribute="Annotation as a foreign attribute for 'oneOrMore'">
        <ann:element>Initial annotation as foreign element for "oneOrMore"</ann:
          element>
        <ref name="book-element" ann:attribute="Annotation as a foreign attribute
          for 'ref'">
          <ann:element>Initial annotation as foreign element for "ref"</ann:element>
        </ref>
        <ann:element>Following annotation as foreign element for "oneOrMore"</ann:
          element>
      </oneOrMore>
      <ann:element>Following annotation as foreign element for "element"</ann:
        element>
    </element>
    <ann:element>Following annotation as foreign element for "start"</ann:element>
  </start>
  <ann:element>Grammar annotation as foreign element for "grammar"</ann:element>
  .../
</grammar>
```

or, in the compact syntax:

```
namespace ann = "http://dyomedea.com/examples/ns/annotations"

[
  ann:attribute = 'Annotation as foreign attribute for "grammar"'
  ann:element [ 'Initial annotation as foreign element for "grammar"' ]
]
grammar {
  [
    ann:attribute = "Annotation as a foreign attribute for 'start'"
    ann:element [ 'Initial annotation as foreign element for "start"' ]
  ]
  start =
    [
      ann:attribute = "Annotation as a foreign attribute for 'element'"
      ann:element [
        'Initial annotation as foreign element for "element"'
      ]
```

```
      ]
      element library {
        [
          ann:attribute =
            "Annotation as a foreign attribute for 'oneOrMore'"
          ann:element [
            'Initial annotation as foreign element for "oneOrMore"'
          ]
        ]
        ([
            ann:attribute = "Annotation as a foreign attribute for 'ref'"
            ann:element [
              'Initial annotation as foreign element for "ref"'
            ]
          ]
          book-element
          >> ann:element [
              'Following annotation as foreign element for "oneOrMore"'
            ]+)
        >> ann:element [
            'Following annotation as foreign element for "element"'
          ]
      }
      >> ann:element [
          'Following annotation as foreign element for "start"'
        ]
  ann:element [ 'Grammar annotation as foreign element for "grammar"' ]
  .../...
}
```

Although the compact syntax is strictly equivalent to the XML syntax, it's difficult to read and tough to specify where each of these annotations belongs. I hope that this example has been compelling enough (and, for once, confusing enough) to convince you that even though application-specific syntaxes that are more concise and easier to read than XML can be defined, when there is a need for extensibility and interoperability, XML is a clear winner.

When initial annotations turn into following annotations

A riddle before we move on: what does this annotation mean?

```
element born {
  xsd:date {
    [
      xhtml:p [
        "Add new parameters here to define a range."
      ]
    ]
    pattern = "[0-9]{4}-[0-9]{2}-[0-9]{2}"
  }
}
```

It can't be a following annotation on the `pattern` parameter, because parameters have a text-only content model and can't accept foreign elements. RELAX NG concludes that, in this case, the example is a following annotation on the definition of the data content of the `born` element. This answer makes the compact syntax riddle equivalent to:

```
<element name="born">
  <data type="date">
    <param name="pattern">[0-9]{4}-[0-9]{2}-[0-9]{2}</param>
    <xhtml:p>Add new parameters here to define a range.</xhtml:p>
  </data>
</element>
```

Note that this same issue also arises with the `value` pattern. With both `value` and `param`, the normal syntax using a following annotation can't be used in the compact syntax.

Annotating Groups of Definitions

You might want to annotate a group of patterns. When patterns are definitions of named patterns in a grammar, and compositors such as `group`, `interleave`, or `choice` can't be used as containers for the annotation, RELAX NG provides a `div` pattern in its own namespace for this purpose:

```
<?xml version="1.0" encoding="UTF-8"?>
<grammar xmlns:xhtml="http://www.w3.org/1999/xhtml"
        xmlns="http://relaxng.org/ns/structure/1.0">
...
  <div>
    <xhtml:p>The content of the book element has
            been split into two named patterns:</xhtml:p>
    <define name="book-start">
      <attribute name="id"/>
      <ref name="isbn-element"/>
      <ref name="title-element"/>
      <zeroOrMore>
        <ref name="author-element"/>
      </zeroOrMore>
    </define>
    <define name="book-end">
      <zeroOrMore>
        <ref name="author-element"/>
      </zeroOrMore>
      <zeroOrMore>
        <ref name="character-element"/>
      </zeroOrMore>
      <attribute name="available"/>
    </define>
  </div>
...
</grammar>
```

or:

```
[
  xhtml:p [
    "The content of the book element has been split into two named patterns:"
  ]
]
div {
  book-start =
    attribute id { text },
    isbn-element,
    title-element,
    author-element*
  book-end =
    author-element*,
    character-element*,
    attribute available { text }
}
```

The div pattern has no other effect than to group both definitions of the book element in a container. Annotations can then be applied to a single container instead of being applied as multiple individual definitions. Each embedded definition is still considered global to the grammar; they can still be referenced as if they hadn't been wrapped into a div pattern.

Alternatives and Workarounds

Using the div element seems like a pretty good idea, but there are other challenges in annotation. One takes advantage of more generic mechanisms defined for XML, while the second deals with the impossibility of annotating value and param patterns with foreign elements.

Why reinvent XML 1.0 comments and PIs?

There is a tendency in recent XML applications to deprecate the usage of XML comments and processing instructions (PIs) and to replace them with XML elements and attributes. There are sometimes good reasons for doing so. Using elements is more flexible when structured content needs to be added. Also, the lack of namespace support for PIs makes it difficult to rely on names that might have different meanings in different applications. However, these reasons don't mean that comments and PIs shouldn't be used in RELAX NG schemas.

Comments are fully supported by RELAX NG. XML comments even have their equivalent in the compact syntax:

```
<define name="author-element">
  <!-- Definition of the author element -->
  <element name="author">
    <attribute name="id"/>
    <ref name="name-element"/>
```

```
    <ref name="born-element"/>
    <optional>
      <ref name="died-element"/>
    </optional>
  </element>
</define>
```

which becomes, with the help of the # sign:

```
author-element =
          # Definition of the author element
    element author {
      attribute id { text },
      name-element,
      born-element,
      died-element?
    }
```

As in Unix shells, comments are marked by a hash (#) in the compact syntax. I could discuss forever whether this is better or worse than a counterpart based on foreign elements such as:

```
<define name="author-element">
  <xhtml:p>Definition of the author element</xhtml:p>
  <element name="author">
    <attribute name="id"/>
    <ref name="name-element"/>
    <ref name="born-element"/>
    <optional>
      <ref name="died-element"/>
    </optional>
  </element>
</define>
```

or:

```
[ xhtml:p [ "Definition of the author element" ] ]
author-element =
  element author {
    attribute id { text },
    name-element,
    born-element,
    died-element?
  }
```

I would argue that the syntax for comments is much more readable in the compact syntax. In the XML syntax too, comments are more easily spotted when their syntax is different from the XML elements. Readability is of course very subjective, but there is no reason to avoid comments if you like them. After all, a simple XSLT transformation can transform comments into foreign elements and vice versa. Getting good comments is more important than the syntax used to express them.

Reading comments in the compact syntax is so much easier than reading annotations that I recommend always using comments unless there are no other special requirements.

The same recommendation would hold for choosing between methods of adding processing instructions if they had an equivalent in the compact syntax. Unfortunately, PIs don't translate into the compact syntax and are discarded during the conversion. If you want to keep the option of using both the XML and the compact syntax, you will need to avoid using PIs. So a decision has been made for you.

Still, if you like PIs, you can use them in the XML syntax. As comments, PIs can be more readable than foreign elements. For instance, compare:

```
<define name="author-element">
  <?sql query="select name, birthdate, deathdate from tbl_author"?>
  <element name="author">
    <attribute name="id"/>
    <ref name="name-element"/>
    <ref name="born-element"/>
    <optional>
      <ref name="died-element"/>
    </optional>
  </element>
</define>
```

and:

```
<define name="author-element" >
  <sql:select
    xmlns:sql="http://www.extensibility.com/saf/spec/safsample/sql-map.saf">
    select name, birthdate,deathdate from tbl_author
  </sql:select>
  <element name="author">
    <attribute name="id"/>
    <ref name="name-element"/>
    <ref name="born-element"/>
    <optional>
      <ref name="died-element"/>
    </optional>
  </element>
</define>
```

There doesn't seem to be much reason to prefer the second syntax over the first one, beyond lack of namespace support mentioned and a greater extensibility for foreign elements.

Annotation of value and param patterns

What if you need to annotate value and param patterns that don't accept foreign elements? There isn't much you can do except use foreign attributes, XML comments, PIs (as seen in the previous section), or move the annotations to another location.

Comments can be used freely in this context:

```
<element name="born">
  <data type="date">
      <param name="minInclusive">1900-01-01</param>
      <param name="maxInclusive">2099-12-31</param>
      <param name="pattern">
      <!-- We don't want timezones in our dates. -->
        [0-9]{4}-[0-9]{2}-[0-9]{2}
      </param>
    </data>
    </element>
```

or, in the compact syntax:

```
element born {
  xsd:date {
    minInclusive = "1900-01-01"
    maxInclusive = "2099-12-31"
    pattern =
    # We don't want timezones in our dates.
      "[0-9]{4}-[0-9]{2}-[0-9]{2}\x{a}"
    }
  }
```

You can also transform the foreign elements you want to create into attributes with the same names, for instance:

```
<element name="born">
  <data type="date">
      <param name="minInclusive">1900-01-01</param>
      <param name="maxInclusive">2099-12-31</param>
      <param name="pattern" xhtml:p="We don't want timezones in our dates.">
                [0-9]{4}-[0-9]{2}-[0-9]{2}</param>
  </data>
</element>
```

or:

```
element born {
  xsd:date {
    minInclusive = "1900-01-01"
    maxInclusive = "2099-12-31"
    [ xhtml:p = "We don't want timezones in our dates." ]
    pattern = "[0-9]{4}-[0-9]{2}-[0-9]{2}"
  }
}
```

Of course, there is no such thing as an xhtml:p attribute, but the meaning seems straightforward enough, at least to human readers. The downside of both workarounds is that you can't extend them if you have structured content. You might want to do that if you need to add a link in your comment. In this case, you need to locate the comment in a foreign element at a different location:

```
<element name="born">
  <data type="date">
```

```
    <xhtml:p>We don't want timezones in our dates
    (see <xhtml:a href="ref.xhtml#dates">dates ref</xhtml:a>
             for additional info.</xhtml:p>
    <param name="minInclusive">1900-01-01</param>
    <param name="maxInclusive">2099-12-31</param>
    <param name="pattern">[0-9]{4}-[0-9]{2}-[0-9]{2}</param>
  </data>
</element>
```

or:

```
element born {
  [
    xhtml:p [
      "We don't want timezones in our dates (see "
      xhtml:a [ href = "ref.xhtml#dates" "dates ref" ]
          " for additional info."
    ]
  ]
  xsd:date {
    minInclusive = "1900-01-01"
    maxInclusive = "2099-12-31"
    pattern = "[0-9]{4}-[0-9]{2}-[0-9]{2}"
  }
}
```

Note that this example has lost the relation between the annotation's link and the annotation's location. One of the ways to get this information back is to add an identifier to the annotation and use a mechanism such as XLink to define a link between the param element and the annotation:

```
<element name="born">
  <data type="date">
    <xhtml:p id="dates-notz">We don't want timezones in our dates
    (see <xhtml:a href="ref.xhtml#dates">dates ref</xhtml:a>
                 for additional info.</xhtml:p>
    <param name="minInclusive">1900-01-01</param>
    <param name="maxInclusive">2099-12-31</param>
    <param name="pattern" xlink:type="simple"
      xlink:arcrole="http://www.rddl.org/purposes#reference"
      xlink:href="#dates-notz" >[0-9]{4}-[0-9]{2}-[0-9]{2}</param>
  </data>
</element>
```

or:

```
element born {
  [
    xhtml:p [
      id = "dates-notz"
      "We don't want timezones in our dates (see "
      xhtml:a [ href = "ref.xhtml#dates" "dates ref" ]
      " for additional info."
    ]
  ]
```

```
xsd:date {
  minInclusive = "1900-01-01"
  maxInclusive = "2099-12-31"
  [
    xlink:type = "simple"
    xlink:arcrole = "http://www.rddl.org/purposes#reference"
    xlink:href = "#dates-notz"
  ]
  pattern = "[0-9]{4}-[0-9]{2}-[0-9]{2}"
  }
}
```

Another option is to change the rules of the game and state that the annotation doesn't apply to the parent element, but to the preceding element. For instance, you will see in the next section that RELAX NG's DTD compatibility specification uses the trick of shifting the annotation from the parent element to the preceding element. Applied to our example:

```
element born {
  xsd:date {
    minInclusive = "1900-01-01"
    maxInclusive = "2099-12-31"
    [
      xhtml:p [
        "We don't want timezones in our dates (see "
        xhtml:a [ href = "ref.xhtml#dates" "dates ref" ]
        " for additional info."
      ]
    ]
    pattern = "[0-9]{4}-[0-9]{2}-[0-9]{2}"
  }
}
```

Documentation

After this long introduction to annotation syntax, it is time to explore applications of annotations. The first application of annotations is for documentation. The issue of generating documentation from schemas, much like the problem of generating documentation from code, is a long-running problem with three different schools of thought:

- The documentation and the schema are stored separately. In this case, there is nothing specific to documenting RELAX NG schemas, and this technique is beyond the scope of this book.

- The schema can be embedded in the documentation: proponents of "Literate Programming" are fans of this approach. It will be presented in Chapter 14.

- The documentation can be embedded within the schema: I'll cover this approach in this section.

You've seen the technical basis of how these annotations can be included in RELAX NG schemas. Generating documentation from these annotations is mainly a matter of writing an XSLT transformation to extract them and then formatting the annotations according to your needs. I won't be going through the details of XSLT transformations, but the following examples are good candidates for these kinds of transformation.

Comments

This example uses simple comments:

```
<define name="author-element">
  <!-- Definition of the author element -->
  <element name="author">
    <attribute name="id"/>
    <ref name="name-element"/>
    <ref name="born-element"/>
    <optional>
      <ref name="died-element"/>
    </optional>
  </element>
</define>
```

which is equivalent to:

```
author-element =
              # Definition of the author element
  element author {
    attribute id { text },
    name-element,
    born-element,
    died-element?
  }
```

These comments can be easily extracted, not only from the XML syntax using an XSLT transformation, but also from the compact syntax using regular expressions.

Comments provide a lightweight way to document RELAX NG schemas. They are the least intrusive mechanism to annotate schemas and can be used at any location in a schema, even within the text-only patterns value and param.

The problems with comments are well known:

- The XML recommendation states that parsers don't have to report them, so some tools just ignore them. This was the case for early parsers and editors, but the situation has improved since the early days of XML. Most, if not all, of the XML parsers and editors now report XML comments.

- Comments may contain only plain text and have no XML structures. In the context of a RELAX NG schema, this state is often not a concern; however, when needed, conventions can easily be added to define specific structures. This is done in JavaDoc, for example, where special "tags" are prefixed by @. Similarly, Wiki Wiki Webs express links as [link title|http://...link.location].

RELAX NG DTD Compatibility Comments

I have already mentioned the RELAX NG DTD Compatibility specification in Chapter 8, in which we studied DTD datatypes. RELAX NG includes more than datatypes in the compatibility specification. It also includes a way to specify comments that would appear in a DTD equivalent to the RELAX NG schema. It also specifies an annotation for defining default values, which are covered later in this chapter.

DTD compatibility comments have a special status: the RELAX NG Technical Committee has defined a namespace for them and provided a shortcut to a concise form in the compact syntax. As annotations in the XML syntax and comment like in the compact syntax, they are thus a kind of middle ground between XML comments and RELAX NG annotations.

When using the XML syntax, DTD Compatibility Comments are foreign elements in the namespace *http://relaxng.org/ns/compatibility/annotations/1.0*. Their content is text-only, and they may be annotated using foreign namespace attributes. An example of schema using this feature is:

```
<?xml version="1.0" encoding="utf-8"?>
<grammar xmlns="http://relaxng.org/ns/structure/1.0"
         xmlns:a="http://relaxng.org/ns/compatibility/annotations/1.0">
  <a:documentation>RELAX NG flat schema for our library</a:documentation>
  <start>
    <element name="library">
      <oneOrMore>
        <ref name="book-element"/>
      </oneOrMore>
    </element>
  </start>
  <define name="author-element">
    <a:documentation>Definition of the author element</a:documentation>
    <element name="author">
      <attribute name="id"/>
      <ref name="name-element"/>
      <ref name="born-element"/>
      <optional>
        <ref name="died-element"/>
      </optional>
    </element>
  </define>
  ...
</grammar>
```

Here's an equivalent schema using the compact syntax:

```
## RELAX NG flat schema for our library
grammar{
```

```
start = element library { book-element+ }

## Definition of the author element
author-element =
 element author {
   attribute id { text },
   name-element,
   born-element,
   died-element?
 }
 ...
}
```

Note that the syntax with the leading double hashes (##) is analogous to the /** comment used in JavaDoc. Despite the fact that they look like comments, these are annotations that have the same meaning and rules as initial annotations. They must precede the pattern to which they apply. This form is equivalent to:

```
namespace a = "http://relaxng.org/ns/compatibility/annotations/1.0"

[ a:documentation [ "RELAX NG flat schema for our library" ] ]

grammar {
 start = element library { book-element+ }

 [ a:documentation [ "Definition of the author element" ] ]
 author-element =
  element author {
    attribute id { text },
    name-element,
    born-element,
    died-element?
  }
  ...
}
```

This shortcut has the same restrictions as initial annotations, in that they must precede all the initial annotations. It is possible to mix them with other types of annotations and write the following, for instance:

```
namespace a = "http://relaxng.org/ns/compatibility/annotations/1.0"

a:documentation [ "RELAX NG flat schema for our library" ]
start = element library { book-element+ }

## Definition of the author element
author-element =
  element author {
    attribute id { text },
    name-element,
    born-element,
    died-element?
  }
  ...
```

Up to now, you've seen examples of compatibility comments that were the first element in their parent. These examples have hidden an important feature of these comments: they are using the trick mentioned in the previous section about workarounds for annotating param and value patterns. They apply their comments to the preceding sibling from the RELAX NG namespace when there is one. To annotate the reference to the name-element definition, you can write either:

```
<define name="author-element">
  <element name="author">
    <attribute name="id"/>
    <ref name="name-element">
      <a:documentation>Definition of the author element</a:documentation>
    </ref>
    <ref name="born-element"/>
    <optional>
      <ref name="died-element"/>
    </optional>
  </element>
</define>
```

or:

```
<define name="author-element">
  <element name="author">
    <attribute name="id"/>
    <ref name="name-element"/>
    <a:documentation>Definition of the author element</a:documentation>
    <ref name="born-element"/>
    <optional>
      <ref name="died-element"/>
    </optional>
  </element>
</define>
```

In the first case, the DTD compatibility annotation is the first child element of its parent element (ref) and applies to the ref pattern for this reason. In the second case, the annotation isn't the first child element from the RELAX NG namespace and applies to its preceding sibling, which is the ref pattern again.

The compact syntax has the same rules, so the following annotations are equivalent:

```
author-element =
    element author {
    attribute id { text },

    ## Definition of the author element
    name-element,
    born-element,
    died-element?
  }
```

and:

```
author-element =
        element author {
    attribute id { text },
    name-element
    >> a:documentation [ "Definition of the author element" ],
    born-element,
    died-element?
}
```

Here again, a following annotation is considered as an annotation of the name-element reference.

Of course, if you are annotating a param or value pattern, you have no other choice than to locate the annotation after the pattern, which is why this tricky mechanism has been introduced.

XHTML Annotations

XHTML seems like a natural choice for embedding documentation in RELAX NG schemas. You have already seen several examples of such annotations. The main benefit of XHTML is that it is so similar to HTML that it is known by pretty much anyone who has ever published a web page. A lot of documentation and books on XHTML are available, and many editors can be used to edit XHTML documents. Furthermore, if you keep to a reasonable subset of XHTML (such as, for instance, XHTML Basic), you have a simple and generic language for writing documentation. The work needed to publish the result of the extraction of XHTML annotations as HTML is minimal, since your annotations are already XHTML.

 You will find more information about XHTML at the W3C web site: *http://www.w3.org/MarkUp/* as well as in specialized books such as *HTML & XHTML: The Definitive Guide*, by Chuck Musciano and Bill Kennedy (O'Reilly) and *XHTML: Moving Toward XML*, by Simon St. Laurent and B.K. DeLong (M&T Books).

You have also seen many examples of XHTML annotations, such as:

```
<?xml version="1.0" encoding="utf-8"?>
<grammar xmlns="http://relaxng.org/ns/structure/1.0" xmlns:xhtml="http://www.w3.org/
1999/xhtml">
  <xhtml:div>
    <xhtml:h1>RELAX NG flat schema for our library</xhtml:h1>
    <xhtml:p>This schema has been written by <xhtml:a href="http://dyomedea.com/
      vdv">Eric van der Vlist</xhtml:a>.</xhtml:p>
  </xhtml:div>
  ...
</grammar>
```

or, using the compact syntax:

```
namespace xhtml = "http://www.w3.org/1999/xhtml"

xhtml:div
[
   xhtml:h1 [ "RELAX NG flat schema for our library" ]
   xhtml:p
   [
      "This schema has been written by "
      xhtml:a [ href = "http://dyomedea.com/vdv" "Eric van der Vlist" ]
      "."
   ]
]

start = element library { book-element+ }
...
```

Beyond the syntax that has already been discussed in the first part of this chapter, note how I have embedded a title (xhtml:h1) and a paragraph (xhtml:p) within a division (xhtml:div). This is generally a good practice; it makes it easier to associate the title with the rest of the content and to manipulate the annotation as a whole.

DocBook Annotations

First designed as an SGML application and very popular for writing technical documentation, DocBook is now also an XML language. With more features than XHTML, DocBook offers many predefined bells and whistles to facilitate indexes and cross references. DocBook makes it easy to indicate that some bit of text is a snippet of source code and can identify acronyms, as well as do many other things. These features can be emulated in XHTML using the class attribute, but in DocBook they are built in from the beginning, and there is a common meaning.

 You will find more information about DocBook on its web site: *http://www.oasis-open.org/committees/docbook/* and in the book *DocBook: The Definitive Guide*, by Norm Walsh (O'Reilly).

DocBook is defined as a DTD that doesn't use any namespaces; this isn't an issue because RELAX NG allows annotations through elements without namespace. To give you an idea of what DocBook looks like, as well as an example showing how to "undeclare" a namespace in XML, the following would more or less match the XHTML in the previous example:

```
<?xml version="1.0" encoding="utf-8"?>
<grammar xmlns="http://relaxng.org/ns/structure/1.0">
  <sect1 xmlns="">
    <title>RELAX NG flat schema for our library</title>
    <para>This schema has been written by <xref linkend="vdv"/>.</para>
  </sect1>
```

```
<start>
  <element name="library">
    <oneOrMore>
      <ref name="book-element"/>
    </oneOrMore>
  </element>
</start>
...
</grammar>
```

or, with the compact syntax:

```
sect1 [
  title [ "RELAX NG flat schema for our library" ]
  para [
    "This schema has been written by "
    xref [ linkend = "vdv" ]
    "."
  ]
]
start = element library { book-element+ }
...
```

Dublin Core Annotations

While XHTML and DocBook are great for including content as documentation, Dublin Core fills a different niche. It is widely used over the Web to include metadata about all type of resources. Dublin Core includes a set of elements with a description of their semantics, which provides sharable information including details relevant to a schema. Dublin Core can answer questions about the schema's authors, their organization, the date, or the copyright associated with the schema. Dublin Core is very complementary to DocBook, and XHTML and is often used in XHTML documents, where it finds a natural fit in the meta element.

 You can find more information about Dublin Core at: *http://dublincore.org*.

In a RELAX NG schema, Dublin Core elements may be included wherever it makes sense. Under the grammar pattern, they qualify the whole grammar, while under an element pattern, they qualify the specific element.

A more complete example than those shown previously includes title, creator, subject, description, date, language, and rights information for a schema:

```
<?xml version="1.0" encoding="UTF-8"?>
<grammar xmlns:dc="http://purl.org/dc/elements/1.1/"
         xmlns="http://relaxng.org/ns/structure/1.0">
  <dc:title>The library element</dc:title>
  <dc:creator>Eric van der Vlist</dc:creator>
```

```
  <dc:subject>library, book, RELAX NG</dc:subject>
  dc:description>This RELAX NG schema has been written as an example to show how
         Dublin Core elements may be used.</dc:description>
  <dc:date>2003-01-30</dc:date>
  <dc:language>en</dc:language>
  <dc:rights>Copyright Eric van der Vlist, Dyomedea.
         During development, I give permission for non-commercial copying for
         educational and review purposes. After publication, all text will be
         released under the Free Software Foundation GFDL.</dc:rights>
  ...
</grammar>
```

or:

```
namespace dc = "http://purl.org/dc/elements/1.1/"
       dc:title [ "The library element" ]
dc:creator [ "Eric van der Vlist" ]
dc:subject [ "library, book, RELAX NG" ]
dc:description [
   "This RELAX NG schema has been written as an example to show how Dublin Core
   elements may be used."
]
dc:date [ "2003-01-30" ]
dc:language [ "en" ]
dc:rights [
   "Copyright Eric van der Vlist, Dyomedea. \x{a}" ~
   "During development, I give permission for non-commercial copying for \x{a}" ~
   "educational and review purposes. \x{a}" ~
   "After publication, all text will be released under the \x{a}" ~
   "Free Software Foundation GFDL."
]
...
```

SVG Annotations

There is no reason to limit yourself to text and metadata; graphics can be included
too, thanks to Scalable Vector Graphics (SVG). SVG is an XML vocabulary published by the W3C, and can be integrated as RELAX NG annotations like other XML
vocabularies:

```
<?xml version="1.0" encoding="utf-8"?>
<grammar xmlns="http://relaxng.org/ns/structure/1.0"
         xmlns:svg="http://www.w3.org/2000/svg">
   <start>
     <element name="library">
       <oneOrMore>
         <ref name="book-element"/>
       </oneOrMore>
     </element>
   </start>
   <define name="author-element">
     <element name="author">
       <svg:svg>
```

```
                <svg:title>A typical author</svg:title>
                <svg:ellipse style="stroke:#000000; fill:#e3e000; stroke-width:2pt;"
                             id="head" cx="280" cy="250" rx="110" ry="130"/>
                <svg:ellipse style="stroke:none; fill:#7f7f7f; " id="leftEye" cx="240"
                             cy="225" rx="18" ry="18"/>
                <svg:ellipse style="stroke:none; fill:#7f7f7f; " id="rightEye" cx="320"
                             cy="225" rx="18" ry="18"/>
                <svg:path style="fill:none;stroke:#7F7F7F; stroke-width:5pt;" id="mouth"
                          d="M 222 280 A 58 48 0 0 0 338 280"/>
            </svg:svg>
            <attribute name="id"/>
            <ref name="name-element"/>
            <ref name="born-element"/>
            <optional>
              <ref name="died-element"/>
            </optional>
          </element>
        </define>
        ...
      </grammar>
```

or, using the compact syntax:

```
      namespace svg = "http://www.w3.org/2000/svg"

      start = element library { book-element+ }
      author-element =
        [
          svg:svg [
            svg:title [ "A typical author" ]
            svg:ellipse >[
              style = "stroke:#000000; fill:#e3e000; stroke-width:2pt;"
              id = "head"
              cx = "280"
              cy = "250"
              rx = "110"
              ry = "130"
            ]
            svg:ellipse [
              style = "stroke:none; fill:#7f7f7f; "
              id = "leftEye"
              cx = "240"
              cy = "225"
              rx = "18"
              ry = "18"
            ]
            svg:ellipse [
              style = "stroke:none; fill:#7f7f7f; "
              id = "rightEye"
              cx = "320"
              cy = "225"
              rx = "18"
              ry = "18"
            ]
```

```
svg:path [
  style = "fill:none;stroke:#7F7F7F; stroke-width:5pt;"
  id = "mouth"
  d = "M 222 280 A 58 48 0 0 0 338 280"
  ]
  ]
]
element author {
  attribute id { text },
  name-element,
  born-element,
  died-element?
}
...
```

I leave it to you as an additional exercise to visualize what a typical author looks like!

 You can find more information about SVG on its web site: *http://www. w3.org/Graphics/SVG/* as well as in the *SVG Essentials* by J. David Eisenberg (O'Reilly).

RDDL Annotations

The last type of annotation I'd like to mention provides a transition between annotations for documentation purposes and annotation for applications. The Resource Directory Description Language (RDDL) is designed as an XML vocabulary that can be used by humans as documentation and by applications. Although RDDL was invented to document namespaces, it can fit very well in a RELAX NG schema. The information provided by RDDL annotations can be extracted to constitute RDDL documentation for the namespaces described in the schema. RDDL is based on XHTML and XLink and also works well with XHTML documentation.

 You can find more information about RDDL on its web site: *http:// rddl.org.*

The main benefit of RDDL is that it provides a way to associate resources with a document. As an example, I'll use it to associate an XSLT template and a CSS style sheet with the definition of the author element:

```
<?xml version="1.0" encoding="utf-8"?>
<grammar xmlns="http://relaxng.org/ns/structure/1.0"
         xmlns:xlink="http://www.w3.org/1999/xlink"
         xmlns:rddl="http://www.rddl.org/"
         xmlns:xhtml="http://www.w3.org/1999/xhtml">
  <start>
    <element name="library">
      <oneOrMore>
        <ref name="book-element"/>
```

```
              </oneOrMore>
            </element>
          </start>
          <define name="author-element">
            <element name="author">
              <xhtml:div>
                <rddl:resource id="author-transform"
                  xlink:arcrole="http://www.w3.org/1999/xhtml"
                  xlink:role="http://www.w3.org/1999/XSL/Transform"
                  xlink:title="Author XSLT template"
                  xlink:href="library.xslt#author">
                  <xhtml:div class="resource">
                    <xhtml:h4>XSLT Transformation</xhtml:h4>
                    <xhtml:p>This
                    <xhtml:a href="library.xslt#author">XSLT template</xhtml:a>
                      displays the description of an author as XHTML.</xhtml:p>
                  </xhtml:div>
                </rddl:resource>
                <rddl:resource id="CSS" xlink:title="CSS Stylesheet"
                  xlink:role="http://www.isi.edu/in-notes/iana/assignments/media-types/text/
                    css" xlink:href="author.css">
                  <xhtml:div class="resource">
                    <xhtml:h4>CSS Stylesheet</xhtml:h4>
                    <xhtml:p>A <xhtml:a href="author.css">CSS stylesheet</xhtml:a>
                        defining some cool styles to display an author.</xhtml:p>
                  </xhtml:div>
                </rddl:resource>
              </xhtml:div>
              <attribute name="id"/>
              <ref name="name-element"/>
              <ref name="born-element"/>
              <optional>
                <ref name="died-element"/>
              </optional>
            </element>
          </define>
          ...
        </grammar>

or:

      namespace rddl = "http://www.rddl.org/"
      namespace xhtml = "http://www.w3.org/1999/xhtml"
      namespace xlink = "http://www.w3.org/1999/xlink"

      start = element library { book-element+ }
      author-element =
        [
          xhtml:div [
            rddl:resource [
              id = "author-transform"
              xlink:arcrole = "http://www.w3.org/1999/xhtml"
              xlink:role = "http://www.w3.org/1999/XSL/Transform"
              xlink:title = "Author XSLT template"
```

```
          xlink:href = "library.xslt#author"
          xhtml:div [
            class = "resource"
            xhtml:h4 [ "XSLT Transformation" ]
            xhtml:p [
              "This "
              xhtml:a [ href = "library.xslt#author" "XSLT template" ]
              " displays the description of an author as XHTML."
            ]
          ]
        ]
      rddl:resource [
        id = "CSS"
        xlink:title = "CSS Stylesheet"
        xlink:role =
          "http://www.isi.edu/in-notes/iana/assignments/media-types/text/css"
        xlink:href = "author.css"
        xhtml:div [
          class = "resource"
          xhtml:h4 [ "CSS Stylesheet" ]
          xhtml:p [
            xhtml:a [ href = "author.css" "CSS stylesheet" ]
            " defining some cool styles to display an author."
          ]
        ]
      ]
    ]
  ]
]
element author {
  attribute id { text },
  name-element,
  born-element,
  died-element?
}
  ...
```

Applications that understand RDDL can act on this information automatically, while humans can find it through the XHTML documentation included with it.

Annotation for Applications

As mentioned in the introduction to this chapter, common uses of annotations by applications include preprocessing instructions, helpers for generating other schemas out of a RELAX NG schema, and extensions of RELAX NG itself.

Annotations for Preprocessing

Bob DuCharme has proposed an interesting application of annotation for preprocessing. He says that annotation can derive specific schemas by the restriction of a generic schema. The benefits of this approach are that it is extremely simple and that it provides a straightforward workaround to the lack of derivation by restriction (a W3C XML Schema feature) in RELAX NG. It is language-neutral and can be applied to other schema languages such as W3C XML Schema: it is much simpler than the derivation by restriction feature built into the language.

You can find Bob DuCharme's proposal on the web at: *http://www.snee.com/xml/ schemaStages.html* and download the XSLT transformation implementing it from *http://www.snee.com/xml/schemaStages.zip.*

The idea behind his proposal is to add annotations in elements that need to be removed in a variant of the schema. You then use these annotations to generate the different variants using an XSLT transformation. Each variant is called a *stage*. The list of the available stages is declared in an sn:stages element. For each element that is conditional, the list of the stages in which it needs to be kept is declared through an sn:stages attributes.

Because this technique uses annotations, the global schema can still be a valid schema that validates a superset of the instance documents that are valid per each stage.

If you wanted to derive schemas requiring a book, author, library, or character element or both book and author as a document element from a generic schema that allows any of these, you could write:

```
<?xml version="1.0" encoding="utf-8"?>
<grammar xmlns="http://relaxng.org/ns/structure/1.0"
        xmlns:sn="http://www.snee.com/ns/stages">
  <sn:stages>
    <sn:stage name="library"/>
    <sn:stage name="book"/>
    <sn:stage name="author"/>
    <sn:stage name="character"/>
    <sn:stage name="author-or-book"/>
  </sn:stages>
  <start>
    <choice>
      <ref name="library-element" sn:stages="library"/>
      <ref name="book-element" sn:stages="book author-or-book"/>
      <ref name="author-element" sn:stages="author author-or-book"/>
      <ref name="character-element" sn:stages="character"/>
    </choice>
  </start>
  ...
</grammar>
```

or:

```
namespace sn = "http://www.snee.com/ns/stages"

sn:stages [
  sn:stage [ name = "library" ]
  sn:stage [ name = "book" ]
```

```
    sn:stage [ name = "author" ]
    sn:stage [ name = "character" ]
    sn:stage [ name = "author-or-book" ]
  ]
start =
  [ sn:stages = "library" ] library-element
  | [ sn:stages = "book author-or-book" ] book-element
  | [ sn:stages = "author author-or-book" ] author-element
  | [ sn:stages = "character" ] character-element
  ...
```

This schema is a valid RELAX NG schema that accepts any of these elements as a root. A transformation of the XML syntax through the XSLT transformation *get-Stage.xsl*, provided in the ZIP file mentioned previously and with a parameter stageName set to author-or-book removes all elements with an sn:stage attribute that don't have author-or-book in their list of values:

```
$ xsltproc --stringparam stageName author-or-book getStage.xsl doc-snee.rng
<?xml version="1.0"?>
<grammar xmlns="http://relaxng.org/ns/structure/1.0"
         xmlns:sn="http://www.snee.com/ns/stages">

  <start>
    <choice>

      <ref name="book-element"/>
      <ref name="author-element"/>

    </choice>
  </start>
  ...
</grammar>
```

This transformation has thus performed a restriction on the schema. You can generate as many schemas this way, as there are stages that have been declared in the sn:stages element.

Annotations for Conversion

RELAX NG works well as a pivot format. A *pivot format* is a reference format in which schemas are kept and transformed into other languages. One of the limits of the pivot approach is that features that are part of the target languages but not part of RELAX NG seems to be out of reach. It would be true, except for annotations. The two most common examples of such annotations are used to generate DTDs and W3C XML Schema.

Annotations to generate DTDs

This is the third and final facet of the DTD Compatibility specification, and it deals with default values for attributes. They can be declared using an `a:defaultValue` attribute:

```
<?xml version="1.0" encoding="utf-8"?>
<element xmlns="http://relaxng.org/ns/structure/1.0"
        xmlns:a="http://relaxng.org/ns/compatibility/annotations/1.0"
        name="library">
  <oneOrMore>
    <element name="book">
      <attribute name="id"/>
        <optional>
          <attribute name="available" a:defaultValue="true">
            <choice>
              <value>true</value>
              <value>false</value>
            </choice>
          </attribute>
        </optional>
        ...
    </element>
  </oneOrMore>
  ...
</element>
```

or:

```
namespace a = "http://relaxng.org/ns/compatibility/annotations/1.0"

element library {
  element book {
    attribute id { text },
    [ a:defaultValue = "true" ]
    attribute available { "true" | "false" }?,
    element isbn { text },
    element title {
      attribute xml:lang { text },
      text
    },
    ...
  }+
}
```

The attribute needs to be declared as optional to use this feature. Hence there is no impact on the validation by a RELAX NG processor. However, converters such as Trang use this annotation to generate a default value in a DTD:

```
<!ATTLIST book
id CDATA #REQUIRED
available (true|false) 'true'>
```

Annotations to generate W3C XML Schema

There is no official specification about how to generate W3C XML Schema from RELAX NG, so what I will say in this small section is derived from Trang's documentation.

 If you want to know how to use Trang, check its web page at *http://www.thaiopensource.com/relaxng/trang-manual.html*.

The first thing to note is that Trang supports the a:defaultValue attribute. The schema presented earlier can be translated as:

```
<xs:element name="book">
  <xs:complexType>
    <xs:sequence>
      <xs:element ref="isbn"/>
      <xs:element ref="title"/>
      <xs:element minOccurs="0" maxOccurs="unbounded" ref="author"/>
      <xs:element minOccurs="0" maxOccurs="unbounded" ref="character"/>
    </xs:sequence>
    <xs:attribute name="id" use="required"/>
    <xs:attribute name="available" default="true">
      <xs:simpleType>
        <xs:restriction base="xs:token">
          <xs:enumeration value="true"/>
          <xs:enumeration value="false"/>
        </xs:restriction>
      </xs:simpleType>
    </xs:attribute>
  </xs:complexType>
</xs:element>
```

Note the default attribute in the declaration of the available attribute.

In addition to this annotation, James Clark has created a specific namespace, *http://www.thaiopensource.com/ns/relaxng/xsd,* to manage the translation to W3C XML Schema. This translation is far from obvious, and a RELAX NG schema can often be translated using different features of W3C XML Schema. James Clark has made a lot of choices in his implementation based on best practices, but there are still some context-dependent options; in those situations, the users can be given a choice.

In the current version (as of June 19, 2003), there is only one annotation attribute available to perform such choices: the tx:enableAbstractElements attribute, which can be included in grammar, div, or include. This attribute can take the values true or false and controls whether abstract elements can be used in substitution groups. Substitution groups are a fairly advanced feature of W3C XML Schema, and I won't present the concept here, but you can find more information on this feature in my XML.com tutorial at *http://xml.com/pub/a/2000/11/29/schemas/part1.html* or in my book, *XML Schema*.

The Trang manual indicates that more annotations might be added in the future.

Schema Adjunct Framework

The *Schema Adjunct Framework* (SAF) is a generic framework that stores processing information in relation to schemas and can work either standalone or as a schema adornment to annotations embedded in schemas. Although it has been developed to work with W3C XML Schema, there is no reason that it couldn't be used to adorn RELAX NG schemas.

 You can find more information about SAF on the Web: *http://www. tibco.com/solutions/products/extensibility/resources/saf.jsp.*

The momentum behind SAF seems to have decreased a lot since end of 2001, but it's definitely something worth examining if you need to add processing information to a schema. A simple example of a SAF adornment in RELAX NG looks like:

```
<define name="author-element">
  <sql:select>select <sql:elem>name</sql:elem>,
  <sql:elem>birthdate</sql:elem>,<sql:elem>deathdate</sql:elem>
    from tbl_author</sql:select>
  <element name="author">
    <attribute name="id"/>
    <ref name="name-element"/>
    <ref name="born-element"/>
    <optional>
      <ref name="died-element"/>
    </optional>
  </element>
</define>
```

or:

```
[
  sql:select [
    "select "
    sql:elem [ "name" ]
    ", "
    sql:elem [ "birthdate" ]
    ", "
    sql:elem [ "deathdate" ]
    " from tbl_author"
  ]
]
author-element =
  element author {
    attribute id { text },
    name-element,
    born-element,
    died-element?
  }
```

These examples both add SQL-based processing information to the schema.

Annotations for Extension

Annotations can also be used as extensions to influence the behavior of the RELAX NG processors that support them. This application is controversial but can also be very useful. The two applications of which I am aware in this category are one for embedding Schematron rules, and my own XVIF project, which allows a user to define validation and transformation pipes that act as RELAX NG patterns.

Embedded Schematron rules

Schematron is a rather atypical XML schema language. Instead of being grammar-based like RELAX NG and focusing on describing documents, Schematron is rule-based and consists of lists of rules to check against documents. Giving the exhaustive list of all the rules needed to validate a document is a very verbose and error-prone task, but on the other hand, the ability to write your own rules gives a flexibility and a power that can't be matched by a grammar-based schema language. The two types of languages appear to be more complementary than their competitors. Using both together allows you to get the best from each of them.

 You can find more information about Schematron on its web site: *http://www.ascc.net/xml/resource/schematron/schematron.html.*

Schematron can get into places no other schema language can. For example, Schematron is a good fit when checking whether the id attribute of a book element is composed of the ISBN number prefixed by the letter b. In this case, you would write:

```
<?xml version="1.0" encoding="utf-8"?>
<grammar xmlns="http://relaxng.org/ns/structure/1.0"
         xmlns:s="http://www.ascc.net/xml/schematron">
  <define name="book-element">
    <element name="book">
      <s:rule context="book">
        <s:assert test="@id = concat('b', isbn)">
          The id needs to be the isbn number prefixed by &quot;b&quot; </s:assert>
      </s:rule>
      <attribute name="id"/>
      <attribute name="available"/>
      <ref name="isbn-element"/>
      <ref name="title-element"/>
      <zeroOrMore>
        <ref name="author-element"/>
      </zeroOrMore>
      <zeroOrMore>
        <ref name="character-element"/>
      </zeroOrMore>
```

```
      </element>
    </define>
    ...
  </grammar>
```

or:

```
namespace s = "http://www.ascc.net/xml/schematron"

book-element =
  [
    s:rule [
      context = "book"
      s:assert [
        test = "@id = concat('b', isbn)"
        ' The id needs to be the isbn number prefixed by "b" '
      ]
    ]
  ]
  element book {
    attribute id { text },
    attribute available { text },
    isbn-element,
    title-element,
    author-element*,
    character-element*
  }
  ...
```

The Schematron annotation comprises a rule element, which sets the context and embedded assert elements defining assertions. Instead of assert, report elements can be used. They are the opposite of assertions and report errors when they are true. These checks are applied to all the elements meeting the XPath expression provided in the context attribute of the rule elements, and the test attribute of the assert or report elements are also XPath expressions.

At this point, I must mention that there is an appreciable difference between implementations on the scope in which the rules must be applied, which can lead to potential issues of interoperability between implementations.

On one hand, the Schematron specification states that when Schematron rules are embedded in another language, they must be collected and bundled into a Schematron schema independently of where they have been found in the original schema. In other words, the rule that was defined earlier should be applied to all the book elements in the instance documents. This is the approach taken by the Topologi multi-validator (see *http://www.topologi.com/products/validator/index.html*).

On the other hand, when a Schematron rule is embedded in a RELAX NG element pattern, as is the case here, it is tempting to evaluate the rule in the context of the pattern. In that case, the rule applies only to the book elements that are included in the context node. If the rule fails, the element pattern fails, and other alternatives will be checked. This is the approach taken by Sun's Multi Schema Validator (see *http://wwws.sun.com/software/xml/developers/multischema/*).

The difference can be seen in an example such as:

```
<define name="book-element">
  <choice>
    <element name="book">
      <s:rule context="book">
        <s:assert test="@id = concat('b', isbn)">
          The id needs to be the isbn number prefixed by "b" </s:assert>
      </s:rule>
      <attribute name="id"/>
      <attribute name="available"/>
      <ref name="isbn-element"/>
      <ref name="title-element"/>
      <zeroOrMore>
        <ref name="author-element"/>
      </zeroOrMore>
      <zeroOrMore>
        <ref name="character-element"/>
      </zeroOrMore>
    </element>
    <element name="book">
      <attribute name="id">
        <value>ggjh0836217462</value>
      </attribute>
      <attribute name="available"/>
      <ref name="isbn-element"/>
      <ref name="title-element"/>
      <zeroOrMore>
        <ref name="author-element"/>
      </zeroOrMore>
      <zeroOrMore>
        <ref name="character-element"/>
      </zeroOrMore>
    </element>
  </choice>
</define>
```

In this case, the approach taken by the Schematron specification would consider an instance document with a book ID equal to ggjh0836217462 to be invalid. The evaluation of the Schematron rules is completely decoupled from the validation by the RELAX NG schema. The approach taken by MSV considers the same document as valid, because it meets one of the alternative definitions for the book element.

XVIF

The interoperability issue mentioned previously is a good illustration of the difficulty of mixing elements from different languages that have been specified independently. The XML Validation Interoperability Framework (XVIF) is a proposal for a framework which would take care of this kind of issue.

You will find more information about XVIF at its home page: *http://downloads.xmlschemata.org/python/xvif/*.

The principle of XVIF is to define *micro pipes*, much like Unix pipes, of transformations and validations that can be embedded in different transformation and validation languages. When the host language is RELAX NG, these micro pipes behave as RELAX NG patterns.

There are many use cases for such micro pipes; one of them is to include transformations to fit text nodes into existing datatypes. For instance, we've been using dates that use the ISO 8601 format in our documents, but we can also use French date formats. In this case, a set of regular expressions can be defined to do the transformation between these dates and the ISO 8601 format. XVIF gives a way to integrate these regular expressions in a RELAX NG schema:

```
<?xml version="1.0" encoding="utf-8"?>
<grammar xmlns="http://relaxng.org/ns/structure/1.0"
         xmlns:if="http://namespaces.xmlschemata.org/xvif/iframe"
         datatypeLibrary="http://www.w3.org/2001/XMLSchema-datatypes">
  <define name="born-element">
    <element name="born">
      <if:pipe>
        <if:validate type="http://namespaces.xmlschemata.org/xvif/regexp"
                     apply="m/[0-9]+ .+ [0-9]+/"/>
        <if:transform type="http://namespaces.xmlschemata.org/xvif/regexp"
                      apply="s/^[ \t\n]*([0-9] .*)$/0\1/"/>
        <if:transform type="http://namespaces.xmlschemata.org/xvif/regexp"
                      apply="s/([0-9]+) janvier ([0-9]+)/\2-01-\1/"/>
        <if:transform type="http://namespaces.xmlschemata.org/xvif/regexp"
                      apply="s/([0-9]+) fevrier ([0-9]+)/\2-02-\1/"/>
        <if:transform type="http://namespaces.xmlschemata.org/xvif/regexp"
                      apply="s/([0-9]+) mars ([0-9]+)/\2-03-\1/"/>
        <if:transform type="http://namespaces.xmlschemata.org/xvif/regexp"
                      apply="s/([0-9]+) avril ([0-9]+)/\2-04-\1/"/>
        <if:transform type="http://namespaces.xmlschemata.org/xvif/regexp"
                      apply="s/([0-9]+) mai ([0-9]+)/\2-05-\1/"/>
        <if:transform type="http://namespaces.xmlschemata.org/xvif/regexp"
                      apply="s/([0-9]+) juin ([0-9]+)/\2-06-\1/"/>
        <if:transform type="http://namespaces.xmlschemata.org/xvif/regexp"
                      apply="s/([0-9]+) juillet ([0-9]+)/\2-07-\1/"/>
        <if:transform type="http://namespaces.xmlschemata.org/xvif/regexp"
                      apply="s/([0-9]+) aout ([0-9]+)/\2-08-\1/"/>
        <if:transform type="http://namespaces.xmlschemata.org/xvif/regexp"
                      apply="s/([0-9]+) septembre ([0-9]+)/\2-09-\1/"/>
        <if:transform type="http://namespaces.xmlschemata.org/xvif/regexp"
                      apply="s/([0-9]+) octobre ([0-9]+)/\2-10-\1/"/>
        <if:transform type="http://namespaces.xmlschemata.org/xvif/regexp"
                      apply="s/([0-9]+) novembre ([0-9]+)/\2-11-\1/"/>
        <if:transform type="http://namespaces.xmlschemata.org/xvif/regexp"
                      apply="s/([0-9]+) decembre ([0-9]+)/\2-12-\1/"/>
        <if:validate type="http://relaxng.org/ns/structure/1.0">
```

```
            <if:apply>
              <data type="date">
                <param name="minInclusive">1900-01-01</param>
                <param name="maxInclusive">2099-12-31</param>
              </data>
            </if:apply>
          </if:validate>
        </if:pipe>
        <text if:ignore="1"/>
      </element>
    </define>
    ...
  </grammar>
```

or, in the compact syntax:

```
namespace if = "http://namespaces.xmlschemata.org/xvif/iframe"
namespace rng = "http://relaxng.org/ns/structure/1.0"

datatypes d = "http://relaxng.org/ns/compatibility/datatypes/1.0"

born-element =
  [
    if:pipe [
      if:validate [
        type = "http://namespaces.xmlschemata.org/xvif/regexp"
        apply = "m/[0-9]+ .+ [0-9]+/"
      ]
      if:transform [
        type = "http://namespaces.xmlschemata.org/xvif/regexp"
        apply = "s/^[ \t\n]*([0-9] .*)$/0\1/"
      ]
      if:transform [
        type = "http://namespaces.xmlschemata.org/xvif/regexp"
        apply = "s/([0-9]+) janvier ([0-9]+)/\2-01-\1/"
      ]
      if:transform [
        type = "http://namespaces.xmlschemata.org/xvif/regexp"
        apply = "s/([0-9]+) fevrier ([0-9]+)/\2-02-\1/"
      ]
      if:transform [
        type = "http://namespaces.xmlschemata.org/xvif/regexp"
        apply = "s/([0-9]+) mars ([0-9]+)/\2-03-\1/"
      ]
      if:transform [
        type = "http://namespaces.xmlschemata.org/xvif/regexp"
        apply = "s/([0-9]+) avril ([0-9]+)/\2-04-\1/"
      ]
      if:transform [
        type = "http://namespaces.xmlschemata.org/xvif/regexp"
        apply = "s/([0-9]+) mai ([0-9]+)/\2-05-\1/"
      ]
      if:transform [
        type = "http://namespaces.xmlschemata.org/xvif/regexp"
```

```
      apply = "s/([0-9]+) juin ([0-9]+)/\2-06-\1/"
    ]
    if:transform [
      type = "http://namespaces.xmlschemata.org/xvif/regexp"
      apply = "s/([0-9]+) juillet ([0-9]+)/\2-07-\1/"
    ]
    if:transform [
      type = "http://namespaces.xmlschemata.org/xvif/regexp"
      apply = "s/([0-9]+) aout ([0-9]+)/\2-08-\1/"
    ]
    if:transform [
      type = "http://namespaces.xmlschemata.org/xvif/regexp"
      apply = "s/([0-9]+) septembre ([0-9]+)/\2-09-\1/"
    ]
    if:transform [
      type = "http://namespaces.xmlschemata.org/xvif/regexp"
      apply = "s/([0-9]+) octobre ([0-9]+)/\2-10-\1/"
    ]
    if:transform [
      type = "http://namespaces.xmlschemata.org/xvif/regexp"
      apply = "s/([0-9]+) novembre ([0-9]+)/\2-11-\1/"
    ]
    if:transform [
      type = "http://namespaces.xmlschemata.org/xvif/regexp"
      apply = "s/([0-9]+) decembre ([0-9]+)/\2-12-\1/"
    ]
    if:validate [
      type = "http://relaxng.org/ns/structure/1.0"
      if:apply [
        rng:data [
          type = "date"
          rng:param [ name = "minInclusive" "1900-01-01" ]
          rng:param [ name = "maxInclusive" "2099-12-31" ]
        ]
      ]
    ]
  ]
]
element born { [ if:ignore = "1" ] text }
```

In this example, I define a pipe (if:pipe) of 15 transformations (if:transform) using regular expressions. Each converts one of the twelve months; a final validation (if:validate) is itself using RELAX NG to check that the result is a ISO 8601 date between 1900 and 2099. The text pattern has an if:ignore attribute, which shows XVIF-compliant processors that it is a fallback pattern for other RELAX NG processors.

CHAPTER 14

Generating RELAX NG Schemas

In the previous chapter, you saw how information can be added to RELAX NG schemas to make them more readable. The information can also help extract information from the schemas or transform them into other useful documents such as documentation, diagrams, or applications. So far, the underlying assumption in this book has been that schema designers work directly in RELAX NG. This is certainly a reasonable point of view. However, a RELAX NG schema (and any XML schema in general) is a fairly concrete model of a class of instance documents. You might also want to work with information in more abstract or more concrete ways and generate RELAX NG schemas based on results from these other approaches.

RELAX NG shines as an ideal choice for a target language because it almost completely lacks restrictions. This lack of restrictions means that during the transformation of a model into a RELAX NG schema, you won't have to remind yourself of things like: "I must declare all my attributes after my elements," "I should disallow unordered models in such and such circumstances," "if I have already declared this content here, I can't declare it again here." In other words, using RELAX NG as your target language lets you concentrate on your document structures instead of worrying about the constraints of the schema language.

What other levels might you want to work on? You can take either a more concrete or more abstract approach than RELAX NG. It can have either a bottom-up or top-down approach. Proponents of a bottom-up approach include those who enjoy working with instance documents rather than with schemas. Examplotron has been designed for these people. Those adept at using a top-down approach will want to work at a higher level of abstraction and use a methodology such as UML to model their documents. These two approaches might lead to many other variants. You will also see how developers using literate programming techniques can include RELAX NG patterns in their documentation as well as how you can replace your RELAX NG schema with a simple spreadsheet.

Examplotron: Instance Documents as Schemas

I created Examplotron from a very simple idea: when you want to describe the element foo, why work in yet another language, writing:

```
<element name='foo'><empty/></element>
```

or:

```
element foo {empty}
```

It's so much simpler to just write the element in plain XML: `<foo/>`. Instead of describing instance documents, why couldn't you just show them?

The first implementation, published with the original description of Examplotron, relied on two XSLT transformations. The Examplotron "schema" was compiled by an XSLT transformation into another XSLT transformation, which then performed the validation of the instance documents. The concept received many positive comments when I announced it, but it was very limited. Adding new features would have meant creating the full semantics of a new schema language. The implementation as an XSLT transformation became very complex and the project was stalled until I realized the potential of using RELAX NG as a target format instead.

Since the release of version 0.5, Examplotron has been implemented as an XSLT transformation that creates a RELAX NG schema. Thanks to this approach, Examplotron made more progress in two weeks than in two years under the previous architecture!

 For more information on Examplotron, and to get the tools used for the transformations in this section, visit *http://examplotron.org*.

Ten-Minute Guide to Examplotron

Here's a snippet of our example document:

```
<?xml version="1.0" encoding="utf-8"?>
<character id="Snoopy">
  <name>Snoopy</name>
  <born>1950-10-04</born>
  <qualification>extroverted beagle</qualification>
</character>
```

Without requiring any further work, this document is already an Examplotron schema. To get an idea of what this schema means, we can translate it into a RELAX NG schema:

```
<?xml version="1.0" encoding="UTF-8"?>
<grammar xmlns="http://relaxng.org/ns/structure/1.0"
```

```
    xmlns:ega="http://examplotron.org/annotations/"
    xmlns:sch="http://www.ascc.net/xml/schematron"
    datatypeLibrary="http://www.w3.org/2001/XMLSchema-datatypes">
      <start>
        <element name="character">
          <optional>
            <attribute name="id">
              <ega:example id="Snoopy"/>
            </attribute>
          </optional>
          <element name="name">
            <text>
              <ega:example>Snoopy</ega:example>
            </text>
          </element>
          <element name="born">
            <data type="date">
              <ega:example>1950-10-04</ega:example>
            </data>
          </element>
          <element name="qualification">
            <text>
              <ega:example>extroverted beagle</ega:example>
            </text>
          </element>
        </element>
      </start>
    </grammar>
```

or:

```
    namespace ega = "http://examplotron.org/annotations/"
    namespace sch = "http://www.ascc.net/xml/schematron"

    start =
      element character {
        [ ega:example [ id = "Snoopy" ] ] attribute id { text }?,
        element name { [ ega:example [ "Snoopy" ] ] text },
        element born { [ ega:example [ "1950-10-04" ] ] xsd:date },
        element qualification {
          [ ega:example [ "extroverted beagle" ] ] text
        }
      }
```

You can see that the Examplotron schema has the same modeling power as its
RELAX NG counterpart. The annotations that appear here need to be added to the
RELAX NG schema if we don't want to lose the "examples" provided in Examplotron. The examples are included because they are useful for documentation purposes and to permit reverse transformations (from RELAX NG to Examplotron).

Another thing to note in this example is that Examplotron is making inferences from
what it found in the schema. Here, Examplotron assumed that the order between
name, born, and qualification is significant; that these elements are mandatory; that

the id attribute is optional; that the born element has a type (xsd:date); and that all the other elements and attributes are just text. These assumptions make a best effort to capture the likely intention of the designer of the document. Most of the time, people won't have to do anything to tweak their Examplotron schema.

There are times, however, when Examplotron gets it wrong. However good Examplotron may be, it can't be psychic: if you want to create schemas different than the default inferences of Examplotron, you need to request those things explicitly. The way to request them is through annotating the Examplotron schema. To make the qualification element optional, for example, add an eg:occurs attribute with a value of ?. To give the id attribute a type dtd:ID, set its content to {dtd:id}:

```
<?xml version="1.0" encoding="utf-8"?>
<character id="{dtd:id}" xmlns:eg="http://examplotron.org/0/">
  <name>Snoopy</name>
  <born>1950-10-04</born>
  <qualification eg:occurs="?">extroverted beagle</qualification>
</character>
```

Here's the example translated into RELAX NG:

```
<?xml version="1.0" encoding="UTF-8"?>
<grammar xmlns="http://relaxng.org/ns/structure/1.0"
 xmlns:ega="http://examplotron.org/annotations/"
 xmlns:sch="http://www.ascc.net/xml/schematron"
 datatypeLibrary="http://www.w3.org/2001/XMLSchema-datatypes">
    <start>
        <element name="character">
            <optional>
                <attribute name="id">
                    <data type="id"
                    datatypeLibrary="http://relaxng.org/ns/compatibility/datatypes/1.0"/>
                </attribute>
            </optional>
            <element name="name">
                <text>
                    <ega:example>Snoopy</ega:example>
                </text>
            </element>
            <element name="born">
                <data type="date">
                    <ega:example>1950-10-04</ega:example>
                </data>
            </element>
            <optional>
                <element name="qualification">
                    <text>
                        <ega:example>extroverted beagle</ega:example>
                    </text>
                </element>
            </optional>
```

```
          </element>
        </start>
    </grammar>
```

or:

```
namespace ega = "http://examplotron.org/annotations/"
namespace sch = "http://www.ascc.net/xml/schematron"

datatypes d = "http://relaxng.org/ns/compatibility/datatypes/1.0"

start =
  element character {
    attribute id { d:id }?,
    element name { [ ega:example [ "Snoopy" ] ] text },
    element born { [ ega:example [ "1950-10-04" ] ] xsd:date },
    element qualification {
      [ ega:example [ "extroverted beagle" ] ] text
    }?
  }
```

If you compare the compact syntax and the Examplotron schema, you will see that
we have something that is similarly concise. The compact syntax looks more formal,
while Examplotron is easier to explore at a glance. Nevertheless, according to the
rules described in the documentation of Examplotron, these two schemas are equivalent. This equivalence makes it possible to transform Examplotron to RELAX NG
and back.

We can go pretty far with these annotations, as shown in this more complete example, which uses interleave, mandatory attributes, and complex elements defined as
named patterns:

```
<?xml version="1.0" encoding="utf-8"?>
<library xmlns:eg="http://examplotron.org/0/"
         eg:content="eg:interleave" eg:define="library-content">
  <book available="true" eg:occurs="*" eg:define="book-content">
    <eg:attribute name="id" eg:content="dtd:id">b0836217462</eg:attribute>
    <isbn>0836217462</isbn>
    <title xml:lang="en">Being a Dog Is a Full-Time Job</title>
    <author eg:occurs="+" eg:define="author-content" eg:content="eg:interleave">
      <eg:attribute name="id" eg:content="dtd:id">CMS</eg:attribute>
      <name>Charles M Schulz</name>
      <born>1922-11-26</born>
      <died>2000-02-12</died>
    </author>
    <character eg:define="character-content" eg:content="eg:interleave">
      <eg:attribute name="id" eg:content="dtd:id">PP</eg:attribute>
      <name>Peppermint Patty</name>
      <born>1966-08-22</born>
      <qualification>bold, brash and tomboyish</qualification>
    </character>
    <character id="Snoopy">
      <name>Snoopy</name>
      <born>1950-10-04</born>
```

```
          <qualification>extroverted beagle</qualification>
        </character>
        <character id="Schroeder">
          <name>Schroeder</name>
          <born>1951-05-30</born>
          <qualification>brought classical music to the Peanuts strip</qualification>
        </character>
        <character id="Lucy">
          <name>Lucy</name>
          <born>1952-03-03</born>
          <qualification>bossy, crabby and selfish</qualification>
        </character>
      </book>
    </library>
```

The RELAX NG schema generated from this Examplotron schema is:

```
<?xml version="1.0" encoding="UTF-8"?>
<grammar xmlns="http://relaxng.org/ns/structure/1.0"
         xmlns:ega="http://examplotron.org/annotations/"
         xmlns:sch="http://www.ascc.net/xml/schematron"
         datatypeLibrary="http://www.w3.org/2001/XMLSchema-datatypes">
    <start>
        <element name="library">
            <ref name="library-content" ega:def="true"/>
        </element>
    </start>
    <define name="library-content">
        <interleave>
            <zeroOrMore>
                <element name="book">
                    <ref name="book-content" ega:def="true"/>
                </element>
            </zeroOrMore>
        </interleave>
    </define>
    <define name="book-content">
        <optional>
            <attribute name="available">
                <data type="boolean">
                    <ega:example available="true"/>
                </data>
            </attribute>
        </optional>
        <attribute name="id">
            <ega:skipped>b0836217462</ega:skipped>
            <data type="id"
              datatypeLibrary="http://relaxng.org/ns/compatibility/datatypes/1.0"/>
        </attribute>
        <element name="isbn">
            <data type="integer">
                <ega:example>0836217462</ega:example>
            </data>
        </element>
```

```
  <element name="title">
    <optional>
      <attribute name="lang" ns="http://www.w3.org/XML/1998/namespace">
        <ega:example xml:lang="en"/>
      </attribute>
    </optional>
    <text>
      <ega:example>Being a Dog Is a Full-Time Job</ega:example>
    </text>
  </element>
  <oneOrMore>
    <element name="author">
      <ref name="author-content" ega:def="true"/>
    </element>
  </oneOrMore>
  <oneOrMore>
    <element name="character">
      <ref name="character-content" ega:def="true"/>
    </element>
  </oneOrMore>
  <ega:skipped>
    <character xmlns="" xmlns:eg="http://examplotron.org/0/" id="Snoopy">
      <name>Snoopy</name>
      <born>1950-10-04</born>
      <qualification>extroverted beagle</qualification>
    </character>
  </ega:skipped>
  <ega:skipped>
    <character xmlns="" xmlns:eg="http://examplotron.org/0/" id="Schroeder">
      <name>Schroeder</name>
      <born>1951-05-30</born>
      <qualification>brought classical music to the Peanuts strip
      </qualification>
    </character>
  </ega:skipped>
  <ega:skipped>
    <character xmlns="" xmlns:eg="http://examplotron.org/0/" id="Lucy">
      <name>Lucy</name>
      <born>1952-03-03</born>
      <qualification>bossy, crabby and selfish</qualification>
    </character>
  </ega:skipped>
</define>
<define name="author-content">
  <interleave>
    <attribute name="id">
      <ega:skipped>CMS</ega:skipped>
      <data type="id"
        datatypeLibrary="http://relaxng.org/ns/compatibility/datatypes/1.0"/>
    </attribute>
    <element name="name">
      <text>
        <ega:example>Charles M Schulz</ega:example>
      </text>
```

```
        </element>
        <element name="born">
           <data type="date">
               <ega:example>1922-11-26</ega:example>
           </data>
        </element>
        <element name="died">
           <data type="date">
               <ega:example>2000-02-12</ega:example>
           </data>
        </element>
     </interleave>
   </define>
   <define name="character-content">
      <interleave>
         <attribute name="id">
            <ega:skipped>PP</ega:skipped>
            <data type="id"
              datatypeLibrary="http://relaxng.org/ns/compatibility/datatypes/1.0"/>
         </attribute>
         <element name="name">
            <text>
               <ega:example>Peppermint Patty</ega:example>
            </text>
         </element>
         <element name="born">
            <data type="date">
               <ega:example>1966-08-22</ega:example>
            </data>
         </element>
         <element name="qualification">
            <text>
               <ega:example>bold, brash and tomboyish</ega:example>
            </text>
         </element>
      </interleave>
   </define>
</grammar>
```

or, in the compact syntax, and skipping some annotations for readability:

```
namespace eg = "http://examplotron.org/0/"
namespace ega = "http://examplotron.org/annotations/"
namespace sch = "http://www.ascc.net/xml/schematron"

datatypes d = "http://relaxng.org/ns/compatibility/datatypes/1.0"

start = element library { [ ega:def = "true" ] library-content }
library-content = element book { [ ega:def = "true" ] book-content }*
book-content =
  attribute available {
    [ ega:example [ available = "true" ] ] xsd:boolean
  }?,
  [ ega:skipped [ "b0836217462" ] ] attribute id { d:id },
```

```
            element isbn { [ ega:example [ "0836217462" ] ] xsd:integer },
            element title {
                [ ega:example [ xml:lang = "en" ] ] attribute lang { text }?,
                [ ega:example [ "Being a Dog Is a Full-Time Job" ] ] text
            },
            element author { [ ega:def = "true" ] author-content }+,
            (element character { [ ega:def = "true" ] character-content }+)
        author-content =
            [ ega:skipped [ "CMS" ] ] attribute id { d:id }
            & element name { [ ega:example [ "Charles M Schulz" ] ] text }
            & element born { [ ega:example [ "1922-11-26" ] ] xsd:date }
            & element died { [ ega:example [ "2000-02-12" ] ] xsd:date }
        character-content =
            [ ega:skipped [ "PP" ] ] attribute id { d:id }
            & element name { [ ega:example [ "Peppermint Patty" ] ] text }
            & element born { [ ega:example [ "1966-08-22" ] ] xsd:date }
            & element qualification {
                [ ega:example [ "bold, brash and tomboyish" ] ] text
            }
```

For those who would like even more flexibility, the next version of Examplotron will "import" all the RELAX NG patterns in the Examplotron namespace, so that Examplotron schemas can use RELAX NG compositors, patterns, and name classes where needed.

Use Cases

Why would anyone want to use Examplotron instead of RELAX NG? I could reverse the question and ask why anyone would want to use RELAX NG instead of Examplotron. At the end of the day, it doesn't really matter. What's important is that the semantics of the validation engine are rock solid and have no limitations. Developers can use the most convenient syntax to express schemas, and what's convenient varies among developers. If you like the visual quality of Examplotron, there is no reason to use anything else. If you prefer RELAX NG's more formal style, that's fine too. With Examplotron, you are just looking at a RELAX NG schema from a different angle.

Literate Programming

A common approach to software documentation is to extract documentation from the source documents relying on the structure of the programs and their comments. (A good example is JavaDoc, the documentation extraction tool shipped with Java and used almost universally on Java projects.) Other projects separate code and documentation. For both approaches, documentation and comments often evolve separately from the code, and the documentation eventually goes out of date.

Projects tend to focus on the code. Documentation is often considered a side project, less important than the code. Donald Knuth, the inventor of the term "literate programming," has a contrary point of view:

> "I believe that the time is ripe for significantly better documentation of programs, and that we can best achieve this by considering programs to be works of literature. Hence, my title: "Literate Programming."*

Knuth charges us with the task of changing our traditional attitude to the construction of programs. Instead of giving priority to instructing a computer what to do, he suggests that programmers concentrate on explaining to human beings what the computer is supposed to do.

> "The practitioner of literate programming can be regarded as an essayist whose main concern is with exposition and excellence of style. Such an author, with thesaurus in hand, chooses variable names carefully and explains what each variable means. He or she strives for a program that is comprehensible. The program's concepts have been introduced in an order that is best for human understanding, using a mixture of formal and informal methods that reinforce each other."

Norm Walsh has adapted the concept to XML. Tools for literate programming in XML are available under the name "litprog" by the DocBook project on SourceForge (*http://sourceforge.net/projects/docbook/*). The basic idea of literate programming (or litprog) is to include a snippet of code (or a snippet of schemas in our case) within the documentation, which can be written in any XML format, including XHTML or DocBook. From this single document embedding code in documentation, a couple of XSLT transformations generate a formatted documentation and the source code.

This makes two big changes. First, as expected, you're working upside-down compared to the common usage of adding comments in the code. The other major practical difference is that you are now defining the relations between the snippets of code or schema using the mechanisms of litprog instead of the mechanisms specific to each programming language. The granularity of the documentation becomes virtually independent of the granularity of your functions, methods, or, in our case, named patterns. This independence lets you group several languages in a single literate documentation. You can describe, for instance, a RELAX NG schema of a document using an XSLT transformation to manipulate the document, and then have a DOM application read it.

Out of the Box

Literate programming works well with RELAX NG, as I will demonstrate next. A literate programming document embeds `src:fragment` elements to combine the fragments of a schema into the program documentation. The fragments are then assembled with a complete schema. The documentation can use any format, such as

---

* Donald Knuth. "Literate Programming (1984)" in *Literate Programming*, CSLI, 1992, page 99.

DocBook, XHTML, or even RDDL. Using XHTML, the description of the name element can be:

```
<div>
<h2>The <tt>name</tt> element</h2>
<p>This is the name of the character.</p>
<src:fragment id="name" xmlns="">
 <rng:element name="name">
   <rng:text/>
 </rng:element>
</src:fragment>
</div>
```

or, in the compact syntax:

```
<div>
<h2>The <tt>name</tt> element</h2>
<p>This is the name of the character.</p>
<src:fragment id="name" xmlns="">
        element name { text }
        </src:fragment>
</div>
```

In the first snippet, the definition of the element is simple enough that it doesn't have to reference any other patterns, but a definition can also make a reference to an src: fragment element by using src:fragref, as in:

```
<div>
<h1>The <tt>character</tt> element</h1>
<p>The <tt>character</tt> element is the container
  holding all the information about a character.</p>
<src:fragment id="character" xmlns="">
<rng:element name="character">
 <src:fragref linkend="id"/>
 <src:fragref linkend="name"/>
 <src:fragref linkend="born"/>
 <rng:optional>
   <src:fragref linkend="qualification"/>
 </rng:optional>
</rng:element>
</src:fragment>
</div>
```

or, using the compact syntax:

```
<div>
<h1>The <tt>character</tt> element</h1>
<p>The <tt>character</tt> element is the container
  holding all the information about a character.</p>
<src:fragment id="character" xmlns="">
 element character {
   <src:fragref linkend="id"/>,
   <src:fragref linkend="name"/>,
   <src:fragref linkend="born"/>,
   <src:fragref linkend="qualification"/> ?
```

```
        }
      </src:fragment>
  </div>
```

From this literate programming document, XSLT transformation can produce two different outputs. The first one is the schema itself. Assuming that I've defined all the attributes and subelements of our character element, the generated schema is:

```
<?xml version="1.0" encoding="utf-8"?>
<rng:grammar xmlns:rng="http://relaxng.org/ns/structure/1.0"
    xmlns:src="http://nwalsh.com/xmlns/litprog/fragment"
    datatypeLibrary="http://www.w3.org/2001/XMLSchema-datatypes">
  <rng:start>
    <rng:element name="character">
      <rng:attribute name="id">
        <rng:data type="id"
               datatypeLibrary="http://relaxng.org/ns/compatibility/datatypes/1.0"/>
      </rng:attribute>
      <rng:element name="name">
        <rng:text/>
      </rng:element>
      <rng:element name="born">
        <rng:data type="date"/>
      </rng:element>
      <rng:optional>
        <element name="qualification">
          <text/>
        </element>
      </rng:optional>
    </rng:element>
  </rng:start>
</rng:grammar>
```

or, converted to the compact syntax:

```
datatypes d = "http://relaxng.org/ns/compatibility/datatypes/1.0"
start=
     element character {
        attribute id { d:id },
           element name { text },
           element born { xsd:date },
           element qualification { text } ?
     }
```

This is a pretty normal-looking schema. The thing to highlight is the way it has been modularized. Up to now, we've been using named patterns, a mechanism provided by RELAX NG, to split a schema into small, manageable pieces. I could have done the same thing in the last example, but this is another way to split the schema. Now I can use the mechanisms provided by the literate programming framework and define and combine fragments using src:fragment and src:fragref instead of the define and ref elements from RELAX NG. By doing so, I can generate a monolithic Russian-doll schema through a modular description of its elements and attributes.

The second output from this literate programming document is the XHTML documentation, shown in Figure 14-1. The compact syntax is shown in Figure 14-2.

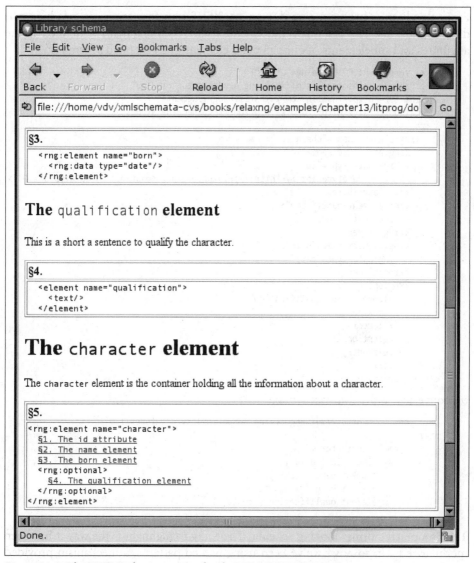

Figure 14-1. The XHTML documentation for the RELAX NG XML syntax

Adding Bells and Whistles for RDDL

RDDL can be read as plain XHTML by human beings in a standard web browser and by applications that use the semantic attributes of XLink to discover resources such as schemas and stylesheets.

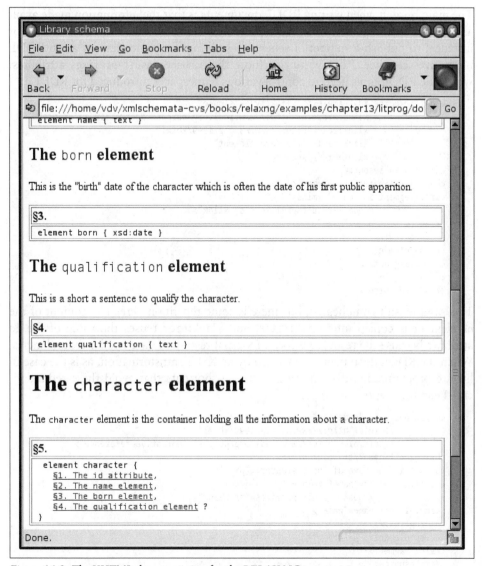

Figure 14-2. The XHTML documentation for the RELAX NG compact syntax

RDDL documents can be generated from annotated RELAX NG schemas. When documenting XML vocabularies, RDDL can also generate schemas. It is very tempting to use the literate programming framework to produce RDDL documents. RDDL is extremely similar to XHTML, which makes this easier. I could use the DocBook litprog stylesheets right away, but I could also import them into stylesheets to facilitate the authoring of RDDL documents.

The main burden when writing RDDL documents is that the information made available to the application needs to be repeated for human readers (or vice versa). For instance, to publish a snippet of schema describing the name element as an RDDL normative reference, I can write this (note the mundane-result-prefixes attributes, which the RDDL tools need to control various namespaces introduced for RDDL):

```
<rddl:resource id="name-elt" xlink:type="simple"
               xlink:arcrole="http://www.rddl.org/purposes#normative-reference"
               xlink:role="http://www.w3.org/1999/xhtml"
               xlink:title="The name element"
               xlink:href="#name-elt">
<div class="resource">
<h2>The <tt>name</tt> element</h2>
<src:fragment id="name" xmlns=""
               mundane-result-prefixes="cr xlink">
 <rng:element name="name">
   <rng:text/>
 </rng:element>
</src:fragment>
</div>
</rddl:resource>
```

This sample isn't complicated, but there is some repetition here. The content of the h2 element is copied into xlink:title, and xlink:href reuses the value of the id attribute because the resource is local. External resources have similar redundancies. When the RDDL document is generated by an XSLT transformation, as is the case in literate programming, it's tempting to define shortcuts that avoid these redundancies. I can then write:

```
<cr:resource id="name-elt"
             role="http://www.w3.org/1999/xhtml"
             arcrole="http://www.rddl.org/purposes#normative-reference">
<h2>The <tt>name</tt> element</h2>
<p>This is the name of the character.</p>
<src:fragment id="name" xmlns=""
               mundane-result-prefixes="cr xlink">
 <rng:element name="name">
   <rng:text/>
 </rng:element>
</src:fragment>
</cr:resource>
```

Other features can easily be added, such as numbering the divisions, generating a table of contents, indexes of resources, and pretty printing code snippets. The resulting document is shown in Figure 14-3.

UML

Unified Modeling Language (or UML) is an Object Management Group (OMG) standard and a successor to many of the object-oriented methods developed in the 1980s

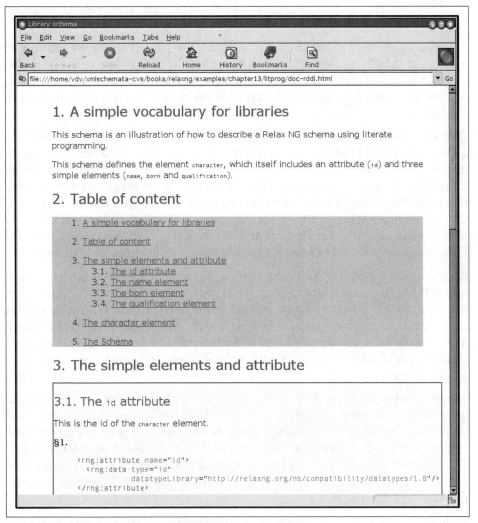

Figure 14-3. A RDDL document produced using literate programming

and 1990s. The idea of using UML to model XML documents isn't new. Much that is good has already been published on the subject (see, for instance, the book *Modeling XML Applications with UML* by David Carlson (Addison Wesley) and his articles on XML.com).

There are two different levels at which UML and XML can be mapped:

- UML can be used to model the structure of XML documents directly. XML schemas can be generated for the purpose of validating the documents, but they are provided as a convenience for application developers. UML doesn't worry about schema details. Their style and modularity aren't their most important features.

The algorithm for producing these schemas is focused on expressing validation rules that make the XML data match the UML diagram as closely as possible.

- UML can be used to model an XML schema. The UML diagram is a higher-level view of the schema, and the schema by itself is the main delivery. The UML diagram needs to be able to control exactly how each schema structure is described. Specific stereotypes and parameters are often added to customize the level of control.

One of the points that appears clearly in all the work related to this topic is that it is quite easy to map UML objects into XML or to use UML to describe classes of instance documents. The most difficult issue when doing so is that UML operates on and graphs, XML is a tree structure. Some links need to be either removed or serialized using techniques to make the mapping happen cleanly (you can use XLink, but it isn't built into XML 1.0). Except for this issue, the relationship between UML and XML is quite natural in both directions: UML provides a simple language to model XML documents and XML provides a natural serialization syntax for UML objects.

Another point concerning XML and UML is that it's not simple to generate DTDs and W3C XML Schemas from UML. When generating DTDs or W3C XML schemas from UML, you have to cope with the restrictions of these languages, notably those related to unordered content models. Unordered content models are a natural fit for UML, in which the attributes of a class are unordered. The limitations of DTDs and W3C XML Schemas create problems when UML attributes are serialized as XML elements.

The issue when modeling W3C XML schemas in UML is that the model needs to describe the XML instances and the schema itself. This is where all the complexity of W3C XML schemas enters the UML world. While there is a good overlap between UML and XML, the overlap isn't so good between XML and W3C XML schemas. W3C XML schemas have in some ways enriched XML with their own expectations, and their expectations don't match those of UML. Figure 14-4 shows how the overlaps work and don't work.

With RELAX NG, on the contrary, the overlap between XML and the schema language is nearly perfect: RELAX NG can describe almost any XML structure. As it has no notion of a Post Schema Validation Infoset (PSVI), RELAX NG doesn't want to add anything to XML. As a result, the overlap between UML, XML, and RELAX NG is almost as big as the overlap between UML and XML, as shown in Figure 14-5.

Designed with a UML editor such as ArgoUML, our library can be pictured as the model shown in Figure 14-6.

This example uses conventions that may look natural but are far from being official. For instance, I have prefixed attribute names with @, an idea borrowed from Will Provost's work on XML.com. Also, to model the title element with its text node and

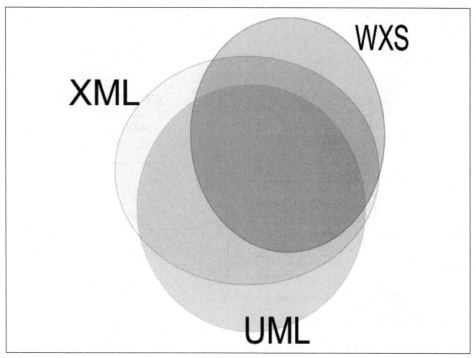

Figure 14-4. Overlaps between XML, UML, and W3C XML schema

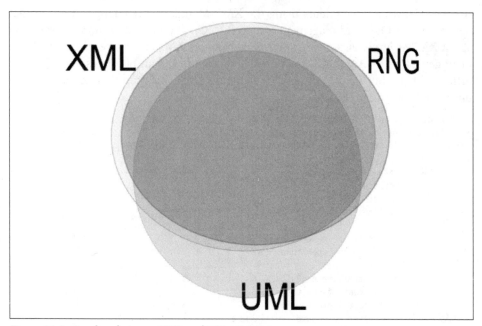

Figure 14-5. Overlaps between UML and RELAX NG

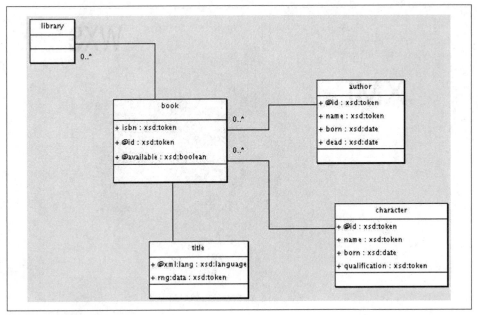

Figure 14-6. A UML model for the library

attribute, I have used the name rng:data to identify its text content as a UML attribute.

ArgoUML saves its documents using the XML Metadata Interchange (XMI) format defined by the Object Management Group (OMG). (You can find more information about XMI at *http://www.omg.org/technology/xml/*.) XMI is verbose; the XMI document generated by ArgoUML for this diagram is more than 800 lines long. I won't include it here, but it's not difficult to generate a schema from this document with unordered content models, such as:

```
<?xml version="1.0" encoding="utf-8"?>
<grammar xmlns="http://relaxng.org/ns/structure/1.0"
         datatypeLibrary="http://www.w3.org/2001/XMLSchema-datatypes">
  <start>
    <element name="library">
      <interleave>
        <zeroOrMore>
          <element name="book">
            <interleave>
              <element name="isbn">
                <data type="token"/>
              </element>
              <attribute name="id">
                <data type="token"/>
              </attribute>
              <attribute name="available">
                <data type="boolean"/>
```

```
          </attribute>
          <zeroOrMore>
            <element name="author">
              <interleave>
                <attribute name="id">
                  <data type="token"/>
                </attribute>
                <element name="name">
                  <data type="token"/>
                </element>
                <element name="born">
                  <data type="date"/>
                </element>
                <element name="died">
                  <data type="date"/>
                </element>
              </interleave>
            </element>
          </zeroOrMore>
          <zeroOrMore>
            <element name="character">
              <interleave>
                <attribute name="id">
                  <data type="token"/>
                </attribute>
                <element name="name">
                  <data type="token"/>
                </element>
                <element name="born">
                  <data type="date"/>
                </element>
                <element name="qualification">
                  <data type="token"/>
                </element>
              </interleave>
            </element>
          </zeroOrMore>
          <element name="title">
            <attribute name="xml:lang">
              <data type="language"/>
            </attribute>
            <data type="token"/>
          </element>
        </interleave>
      </element>
    </zeroOrMore>
  </interleave>
  </element>
 </start>
</grammar>
```

or, after conversion into the compact syntax with Trang:

```
start =
  element library {
```

```
element book {
  element isbn { xsd:token }
  & attribute id { xsd:token }
  & attribute available { xsd:boolean }
  & element author {
      attribute id { xsd:token }
      & element name { xsd:token }
      & element born { xsd:date }
      & element died { xsd:date }
    }*
  & element character {
      attribute id { xsd:token }
      & element name { xsd:token }
      & element born { xsd:date }
      & element qualification { xsd:token }
    }*
  & element title {
      attribute xml:lang { xsd:language },
      xsd:token
    }
  }*
}
```

The only trouble I've had with RELAX NG itself comes out of one of the few restrictions of RELAX NG, which was mentioned in Chapter 7. Data patterns can't be interleaved. When generating this schema, you must be careful to treat complex-type simple-content models (i.e., elements such as the title element, which accepts attributes and text nodes but no children elements) as an exception. This straight translation is of course impossible with W3C XML schemas, because of the cardinality of the character and author subelements. Containers need to be added to fit the limitations of that language.

Note that I've generated a Russian-doll design; depending on the strategy used in the translation, I can generate other designs as well.

Spreadsheets

The final transformation I'll show here is much more widely used than you might think. Spreadsheets are familiar, very convenient to store, can manipulate large lists of information items, and have been used as a modeling tool for many years. The UBL OASIS Technical Committee (see *http://www.oasis-open.org/committees/ubl/*), which is in charge of a set of core components to be used by B2B applications and frameworks such as ebXML, has moved in this direction. Although this project uses a UML methodology, the release note of their 0.70 version states: "The current spreadsheet matrix used by UBL has proved the most versatile and manageable in developing a logical model of the UBL Library."

Recent spreadsheet software can work with XML formats, so generating RELAX NG schemas from such a tool is really easy.

There is no standard way to represent XML documents in a spreadsheet. Thus the benefit of spreadsheets is their flexibility: you can define layouts specific to each application.

Coming back to our library, we can formalize it in an OpenOffice spreadsheet as shown in Figure 14-7.

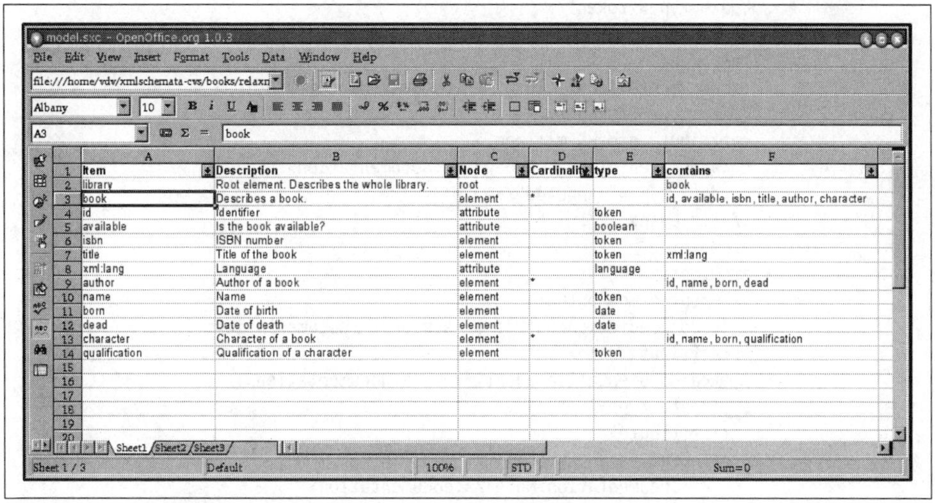

Figure 14-7. The library document structure, described in a spreadsheet

Figure 14-7 is basically nothing more than a catalog of each information item with just enough information to generate a schema. The benefit of using a spreadsheet is that it's easy to read and, when the catalog gets bigger, features such as filters, sort, and search become increasingly useful to help navigate over the catalog.

Generating RELAX NG schemas from the OpenOffice spreadsheet's XML format is really easy. The code for doing this is too long to cover here, but will be available at *http://books.xmlschemata.org/relaxng/* and at this book's page on the O'Reilly web site *http://www.oreilly.com/catalog/relax/*. With that tool, it doesn't take much work to turn this spreadsheet into schemas such as:

```
<?xml version="1.0" encoding="utf-8"?>
<grammar xmlns="http://relaxng.org/ns/structure/1.0"
         xmlns:a="http://relaxng.org/ns/compatibility/annotations/1.0"
         datatypeLibrary="http://www.w3.org/2001/XMLSchema-datatypes">
  <start>
    <element name="library">
      <a:documentation>Root element. Describes the whole library.</a:documentation>
      <zeroOrMore>
        <element name="book">
          <a:documentation>Describes a book.</a:documentation>
          <attribute name="id">
```

```
        <a:documentation>Identifier</a:documentation>
        <data type="token"/>
    </attribute>
    <attribute name="available">
      <a:documentation>Is the book available?</a:documentation>
      <data type="boolean"/>
    </attribute>
    <element name="isbn">
      <a:documentation>ISBN number</a:documentation>
      <data type="token"/>
    </element>
    <element name="title">
      <a:documentation>Title of the book</a:documentation>
      <data type="token"/>
      <attribute name="xml:lang">
        <a:documentation>Language</a:documentation>
        <data type="language"/>
      </attribute>
    </element>
    <zeroOrMore>
      <element name="author">
        <a:documentation>Author of a book</a:documentation>
        <attribute name="id">
          <a:documentation>Identifier</a:documentation>
          <data type="token"/>
        </attribute>
        <element name="name">
          <a:documentation>Name</a:documentation>
          <data type="token"/>
        </element>
        <element name="born">
          <a:documentation>Date of birth</a:documentation>
          <data type="date"/>
        </element>
        <element name="died">
          <a:documentation>Date of death</a:documentation>
          <data type="date"/>
        </element>
      </element>
    </zeroOrMore>
    <zeroOrMore>
      <element name="character">
        <a:documentation>Character of a book</a:documentation>
        <attribute name="id">
          <a:documentation>Identifier</a:documentation>
          <data type="token"/>
        </attribute>
        <element name="name">
          <a:documentation>Name</a:documentation>
          <data type="token"/>
        </element>
        <element name="born">
          <a:documentation>Date of birth</a:documentation>
          <data type="date"/>
```

```
          </element>
          <element name="qualification">
            <a:documentation>Qualification of a character</a:documentation>
            <data type="token"/>
          </element>
        </element>
      </zeroOrMore>
    </element>
  </zeroOrMore>
</element>
    </start>
  </grammar>
```

or, after a translation into the compact syntax by Trang:

```
namespace a = "http://relaxng.org/ns/compatibility/annotations/1.0"

start =
  ## Root element. Describes the whole library.
  element library {
    ## Describes a book.
    element book {
      ## Identifier
      attribute id { xsd:token },
      ## Is the book available?
      attribute available { xsd:boolean },
      ## ISBN number
      element isbn { xsd:token },
      ## Title of the book
      element title {
        xsd:token,
        ## Language
        attribute xml:lang { xsd:language }
      },
      ## Author of a book
      element author {
        ## Identifier
        attribute id { xsd:token },
        ## Name
        element name { xsd:token },
        ## Date of birth
        element born { xsd:date },
        ## Date of death
        element died { xsd:date }
      }*,
      ## Character of a book
      element character {
        ## Identifier
        attribute id { xsd:token },
        ## Name
        element name { xsd:token },
        ## Date of birth
        element born { xsd:date },
        ## Qualification of a character
```

```
    element qualification { xsd:token }
  }*
}*
}
```

Here again, you can generate any style of schema; you're not limited to Russian dolls. It just depends on how you write the tool that converts from spreadsheet to schema.

CHAPTER 15

Simplification and Restrictions

Simplification and restriction are two topics that I have generally avoided throughout this book. They're deeply technical and don't have much direct impact when you're writing a RELAX NG schema. Still, this book wouldn't be complete without describing simplifications and restrictions.

Why should you care at all about simplification if it's so technical and looks like an implementation algorithm? To be honest, most of the time you don't have to care about this stuff at all. Simplification can be seen as an intermediate step when a RELAX NG processor reads a schema. During this step, all the syntactical sugar is removed, and the processor can then work with a perfectly normalized schema. The few restrictions that exist when using RELAX NG are formalized relative to this normalized version of the schema. Because of the flexibility of RELAX NG, formalizing restrictions on schemas before simplification would be very complex and difficult to read. The downside of not having to worry about such things most of the time is that when you do hit one of these restrictions, you often need to understand the main principles of the simplification process to understand what's happening. The good news is that it doesn't happen very often!

Simplification

Since its conception, RELAX NG has always tried to balance simplicity of use, simplicity of implementation, and simplicity of its data model. What's simple to implement is often simple to use, however, there are many features that are very effective for the users but add complexity for the implementers and clutter the data model. This is the case, for instance, for all the features designed to create building blocks (named patterns, includes, and embedded grammars). They are very helpful to users but your use of named patterns or a Russian-doll style has zero impact on the validation itself. This is also the case for shortcuts such as the mixed pattern, which is really just a more concise way of writing an interleave pattern with an embedded text pattern.

The quest for simplicity has had a huge influence on the design of RELAX NG. Here is James Clark on the subject:

> Simplicity of specification often goes hand in hand with simplicity of use. But I find that these are often in conflict with simplicity of implementation. An example would be ambiguity restrictions as in W3C XML Schema: these make implementation simpler (well, at least for people who don't want to learn a new algorithm) but make specification and use more complex. In general, RELAX NG aims for implementation to be practical and safe (i.e., implementations shouldn't use huge amounts of time/memory for particular schemas/instances), but apart from that favors simplicity of specification/use over simplicity of implementation.

To keep the description of the restriction and validation algorithm simple while continuing to offer valuable features to the users, RELAX NG describes validation as a two-step process:

1. The schema is read and simplified. The simplification removes all the additional complexity of the syntactic sugar and reduces the schema to its simplest form.

2. Instance documents are validated against the simplified schema. Because all the syntactic sugar has been removed from the simplified schema, it doesn't need to be taken into account in the description of the validation, permitting the use of much simpler algorithms.

The simplification is described for each RELAX NG element in the RELAX NG specification, so I won't dive into its details here—just the main points. Simplification removes all syntactic sugar, consolidates all external schemas, uses a subset of all the available RELAX NG elements, and transforms the resulting structure into a flat schema. Each element is embedded in a named pattern, and all the resulting named patterns contain the definition of a single element.

The RELAX NG specification is very clear that this simplification is done by the RELAX NG processors to the data model after reading the complete schema. The result of this simplification doesn't ever have to be serialized as XML. However, showing intermediary results as XML helps to show what the simplification process does.

 Intermediary results are indented for readability. In reality, whitespace is removed in one of the first steps of the simplification.

The XML syntax is more similar to the data model used to describe the simplification than is the compact syntax. The details of the simplification are shown next in XML snippets. For each sequence of steps, I've also given the compact syntax for the whole schema, to give a better overall view of the impact on the structure of the schema, although some impacts of simplification are lost when using the compact syntax.

Annotation Removal, Whitespace and Attribute Normalization, and Inheritance

The first step of simplification performs various normalizations without changing the structure of the schema:

- Annotations (i.e., attributes and elements from foreign namespaces) are removed.

- Text nodes containing only whitespace are removed, except when found in value and param elements. Whitespace is normalized in name, type, and combine attributes and in name elements.

- The characters that aren't allowed in the datatypeLibrary attributes are escaped. The attributes are transferred through inheritance to each data and value pattern.

- If not specified, the type attributes of the value pattern are defaulted to the token datatype from the built in datatype library.

After this set of steps, the structure of the schema is still unchanged, but all cosmetic features, which have no impact on the meaning of the schema, have been removed. For instance, the following schema snippet:

```
<?xml version="1.0" encoding="utf-8"?>
<grammar xmlns="http://relaxng.org/ns/structure/1.0"
         xmlns:hr="http://eric.van-der-vlist.com/ns/person"
         ns="http://eric.van-der-vlist.com/ns/library"
         xmlns:a="http://relaxng.org/ns/compatibility/annotations/1.0"
         xmlns:sn="http://www.snee.com/ns/stages"
         datatypeLibrary="http://www.w3.org/2001/XMLSchema-datatypes">
  <a:documentation>RELAX NG schema for our library</a:documentation>
   <sn:stages>
     <sn:stage name="library"/>
     <sn:stage name="book"/>
     <sn:stage name="author"/>
     <sn:stage name="character"/>
     <sn:stage name="author-or-book"/>
   </sn:stages>
  <start>
    <choice>
      <element name=" library "  sn:stages="library">
        <oneOrMore>
          <ref name="book-element"/>
        </oneOrMore>
      </element>
      <ref name="book-element" sn:stages="book author-or-book"/>
      <ref name="author-element" sn:stages="author author-or-book"/>
      <ref name="character-element" sn:stages="character"/>
    </choice>
  </start>
  <define name=" author-element ">
    <element name="hr:author" datatypeLibrary="">
```

```
              <attribute name="id"
                     datatypeLibrary="http://www.w3.org/2001/XMLSchema-datatypes">
                <data type="NMTOKEN">
                  <param name="maxLength"> 16 </param>
                </data>
              </attribute>
              <ref name=" name-element"/>
              <ref name="born-element"/>
              <optional>
                <ref name="died-element"/>
              </optional>
            </element>
          </define>
          <define name="available-content">
            <choice>
              <value>true</value>
              <value type="token"> false </value>
              <value> </value>
            </choice>
          </define>
        </grammar>
```

will be transformed during this sequence of steps into the following (note that I am still showing whitespace for readability, even though it would have been removed):

```
        <?xml version="1.0"?>
        <grammar xmlns="http://relaxng.org/ns/structure/1.0"
                 xmlns:hr="http://eric.van-der-vlist.com/ns/person"
                 xmlns:a="http://relaxng.org/ns/compatibility/annotations/1.0"
                 xmlns:sn="http://www.snee.com/ns/stages"
                 ns="http://eric.van-der-vlist.com/ns/library">
          <start>
            <choice>
              <element name="library">
                <oneOrMore>
                  <ref name="book-element"/>
                </oneOrMore>
              </element>
              <ref name="book-element"/>
              <ref name="author-element"/>
              <ref name="character-element"/>
            </choice>
          </start>
          <define name="author-element">
            <element name="hr:author">
              <attribute name="id">
                <data
                  datatypeLibrary="http://www.w3.org/2001/XMLSchema-datatypes"
                    type="NMTOKEN">
                  <param name="maxLength"> 16 </param>
                </data>
              </attribute>
              <ref name="name-element"/>
              <ref name="born-element"/>
```

```
      <optional>
        <ref name="died-element"/>
      </optional>
    </element>
  </define>
  <define name="available-content">
    <choice>
      <value type="token" datatypeLibrary="">true</value>
      <value datatypeLibrary="http://www.w3.org/2001/XMLSchema-datatypes"
type="token">
false </value>
      <value type="token" datatypeLibrary=""> </value>
    </choice>
  </define>
</grammar>
```

After the first series of steps, our schema looks like this:

```
namespace a = "http://relaxng.org/ns/compatibility/annotations/1.0"
namespace hr = "http://eric.van-der-vlist.com/ns/person"
namespace local = ""
default namespace ns1 = "http://eric.van-der-vlist.com/ns/library"
namespace sn = "http://www.snee.com/ns/stages"

start =
  element library { book-element+ }
  | book-element
  | author-element
  | character-element
include "foreign.rnc" {
  foreign-elements = element * - (local:* | ns1:* | hr:*) { anything }*
  foreign-attributes = attribute * - (local:* | ns1:* | hr:*) { text }*
}
author-element =
  element hr:author {
    attribute id {
      xsd:NMTOKEN { maxLength = " 16 " }
    },
    name-element,
    born-element,
    died-element?
  }
include "book-content.rnc"
book-content &= foreign-nodes
book-element = element book { book-content }
born-element = element hr:born { xsd:date }
character-element = external "character-element.rnc"
died-element = element hr:died { xsd:date }
isbn-element = element isbn { foreign-attributes, token }
name-element = element hr:name { xsd:token }
qualification-element = element qualification { text }
title-element = element title { foreign-attributes, text }
available-content = "true" | xsd:token " false " | " "
```

Retrieval of External Schemas

The second sequence of steps reads and processes `externalRef` and `include` patterns:

- `externalRef` patterns are replaced by the content of the resource referenced by their `href` attributes. All the simplification steps up to this one must be recursively applied during this replacement to make sure all schemas are merged at the same level of simplification.

- The schemas referenced by `include` patterns are read and all the simplification steps up to this point are recursively applied to these schemas. Their definitions are overridden by those found in the `include` pattern itself when overrides are used. The content of their grammar is added in a new `div` pattern to the current schema. The `div` pattern is needed temporarily to carry namespace information to the next sequence of steps.

After the second step, you get a standalone schema without any reference to external documents.

The following snippet:

```
<define name="character-element">
  <externalRef href="character-element.rng"
                ns="http://eric.van-der-vlist.com/ns/library"/>
</define>
```

is transformed into:

```
<define name="character-element">
  <grammar ns="http://eric.van-der-vlist.com/ns/library">
    <start>
      <element name="character">
        <attribute name="id"/>
        <parentRef name="name-element"/>
        <parentRef name="born-element"/>
        <parentRef name="qualification-element"/>
      </element>
    </start>
  </grammar>
</define>
```

And the snippet:

```
<include href="foreign.rng">
  <define name="foreign-elements">
    <zeroOrMore>
  <element>
        <anyName>
          <except>
            <nsName ns=""/>
            <nsName ns="http://eric.van-der-vlist.com/ns/library"/>
            <nsName ns="http://eric.van-der-vlist.com/ns/person"/>
          </except>
        </anyName>
```

```
          <ref name="anything"/>
        </element>
      </zeroOrMore>
    </define>
    <define name="foreign-attributes">
      <zeroOrMore>
        <attribute>
          <anyName>
          <except>
           <nsName ns=""/>
           <nsName ns="http://eric.van-der-vlist.com/ns/library"/>
           <nsName ns="http://eric.van-der-vlist.com/ns/person"/>
          </except>
          </anyName>
        </attribute>
      </zeroOrMore>
    </define>
  </include>
```

becomes:

```
<div>
  <define name="foreign-elements">
    <zeroOrMore>
      <element>
        <anyName>
        <except>
            <nsName ns=""/>
            <nsName ns="http://eric.van-der-vlist.com/ns/library"/>
            <nsName ns="http://eric.van-der-vlist.com/ns/person"/>
          </except>
        </anyName>
        <ref name="anything"/>
      </element>
    </zeroOrMore>
  </define>
  <define name="foreign-attributes">
    <zeroOrMore>
      <attribute>
        <anyName>
          <except>
            <nsName ns=""/>
            <nsName ns="http://eric.van-der-vlist.com/ns/library"/>
            <nsName ns="http://eric.van-der-vlist.com/ns/person"/>
          </except>
        </anyName>
      </attribute>
    </zeroOrMore>
  </define>
  <define name="anything">
    <zeroOrMore>
      <choice>
        <element>
          <anyName/>
```

```
            <ref name="anything"/>
          </element>
          <attribute>
            <anyName/>
          </attribute>
          <text/>
        </choice>
      </zeroOrMore>
    </define>
    <define name="foreign-nodes">
      <zeroOrMore>
        <choice>
          <ref name="foreign-attributes"/>
          <ref name="foreign-elements"/>
        </choice>
      </zeroOrMore>
    </define>
  </div>
```

In the compact syntax, the schema after the second sequence of steps looks like this:

```
namespace a = "http://relaxng.org/ns/compatibility/annotations/1.0"
namespace hr = "http://eric.van-der-vlist.com/ns/person"
namespace local = ""
default namespace ns1 = "http://eric.van-der-vlist.com/ns/library"
namespace sn = "http://www.snee.com/ns/stages"

start =
  element library { book-element+ }
  | book-element
  | author-element
  | character-element
div {
  foreign-elements = element * - (local:* | ns1:* | hr:*) { anything }*
  foreign-attributes = attribute * - (local:* | ns1:* | hr:*) { text }*
  anything =
    (element * { anything }
    | attribute * { text }
    | text)*
  foreign-nodes = (foreign-attributes | foreign-elements)*
}
author-element =
  element hr:author {
    attribute id {
      xsd:NMTOKEN { maxLength = " 16 " }
    },
    name-element,
    born-element,
    died-element?
  }
div {
  book-content =
    attribute id { text },
    attribute available { available-content },
```

```
        isbn-element,
        title-element,
        author-element*,
        character-element*
    }
book-content &= foreign-nodes
book-element = element book { book-content }
born-element = element hr:born { xsd:date }
character-element =
    grammar {
        start =
            element character {
                attribute id { text },
                parent name-element,
                parent born-element,
                parent qualification-element
            }
    }
died-element = element hr:died { xsd:date }
isbn-element = element isbn { foreign-attributes, token }
name-element = element hr:name { xsd:token }
qualification-element = element qualification { text }
title-element = element title { foreign-attributes, text }
available-content = "true" | xsd:token " false " | " "
```

Name Class Normalization

This third sequence of steps performs the normalization of name classes:

- The name attribute of the element and attribute patterns is replaced by the name element, a name class that matches only a single name.

- ns attributes are transferred through inheritance to the elements that need them; name, nsName, and value patterns need this attribute to support QName datatypes reliably. (Note that the ns attribute behaves like the default namespace in XML and isn't passed to attributes, which, by default, have no namespace URI.)

- The QName (qualified name) used in name elements is replaced by their local part. The ns attribute of these elements is replaced by the namespace URI defined for their prefix.

By this third sequence of steps, name classes are almost normalized (the except and choice name class are normalized in the fourth sequence of steps).

During this sequence of steps, the snippet:

```
<element name="hr:author">
  <attribute name="id">
    <data
        datatypeLibrary="http://www.w3.org/2001/XMLSchema-datatypes"
        type="NMTOKEN">
      <param name="maxLength"> 16 </param>
    </data>
```

```
    </attribute>
    <ref name="name-element"/>
    <ref name="born-element"/>
    <optional>
      <ref name="died-element"/>
    </optional>
  </element>
```

is transformed into:

```
<element>
  <name ns="http://eric.van-der-vlist.com/ns/person">author</name>
  <attribute>
    <name ns="">id</name>
    <data datatypeLibrary="http://www.w3.org/2001/XMLSchema-datatypes"
      type="NMTOKEN">
      <param name="maxLength"> 16 </param>
    </data>
  </attribute>
  <ref name="name-element"/>
  <ref name="born-element"/>
  <optional>
    <ref name="died-element"/>
  </optional>
</element>
```

Note that none of these modifications are visible in the compact syntax. The compact syntax already requires that all namespace declarations be made in the declaration section of the schema and supports no difference between name elements and attributes.

Pattern Normalization

In the fourth sequence of steps, patterns are normalized:

- div elements are replaced by their children.
- define, oneOrMore, zeroOrMore, optional, list, and mixed patterns are transformed to have exactly one child pattern. If they have more than one pattern, these patterns are wrapped into a group pattern.
- element patterns follow a similar rule and are transformed to have exactly one name class and a single child pattern.
- except patterns and name classes are also transformed to have exactly one child pattern, but since they have a different semantic, their child elements are wrapped in a choice element.
- If an attribute pattern has no child pattern, a text pattern is added.
- The group and interleave patterns and the choice pattern and name class are recursively transformed to have exactly two subelements: if it has only one child, it's replaced by this child. If it has more than two children, the first two

child elements are combined into a new element until there are exactly two child elements.

- `mixed` patterns are transformed into `interleave` patterns between their unique child pattern and a text pattern.

- `optional` patterns are transformed into `choice` patterns between their unique child pattern and an `empty` pattern.

- `zeroOrMore` patterns are transformed into `choice` patterns between a `oneOrMore` pattern including their unique child pattern and an `empty` pattern.

After the fourth set of steps, the number of different types of patterns has been reduced to a set of "primitive" patterns. All the patterns that are left have a fixed number of child elements.

Here's our example snippet:

```
<define name="foreign-elements">
  <zeroOrMore>
    <element>
      <anyName>
        <except>
          <nsName ns=""/>
          <nsName ns="http://eric.van-der-vlist.com/ns/library"/>
          <nsName ns="http://eric.van-der-vlist.com/ns/person"/>
        </except>
      </anyName>
      <ref name="anything"/>
    </element>
  </zeroOrMore>
</define>
```

which is transformed into:

```
<define name="foreign-elements">
  <choice>
    <oneOrMore>
      <element>
        <anyName>
          <except>
            <choice>
              <choice>
                <nsName ns=""/>
                <nsName ns="http://eric.van-der-vlist.com/ns/library"/>
              </choice>
              <nsName ns="http://eric.van-der-vlist.com/ns/person"/>
            </choice>
          </except>
        </anyName>
        <ref name="anything"/>
      </element>
    </oneOrMore>
```

```
      <empty/>
    </choice>
  </define>
```

During the fourth set of steps, our schema becomes:

```
namespace a = "http://relaxng.org/ns/compatibility/annotations/1.0"
namespace hr = "http://eric.van-der-vlist.com/ns/person"
namespace local = ""
default namespace ns1 = "http://eric.van-der-vlist.com/ns/library"
namespace sn = "http://www.snee.com/ns/stages"

start =
  ((element library { book-element+ }
    | book-element)
   | author-element)
  | character-element
foreign-elements =
  element * - ((local:* | ns1:*) | hr:*) { anything }+
  | empty
foreign-attributes =
  attribute * - ((local:* | ns1:*) | hr:*) { text }+
  | empty
anything =
  ((element * { anything }
    | attribute * { text })
   | text)+
  | empty
foreign-nodes = (foreign-attributes | foreign-elements)+ | empty
author-element =
  element hr:author {
    ((attribute id {
        xsd:NMTOKEN { maxLength = " 16 " }
      },
      name-element),
     born-element),
    (died-element | empty)
  }
book-content =
  ((((attribute id { text },
      attribute available { available-content }),
     isbn-element),
    title-element),
   (author-element+ | empty)),
  (character-element+ | empty)
book-content &= foreign-nodes
book-element = element book { book-content }
born-element = element hr:born { xsd:date }
character-element =
  grammar {
    start =
      element character {
        ((attribute id { text },
          parent name-element),
```

```
            parent born-element),
            parent qualification-element
        }
    }
    died-element = element hr:died { xsd:date }
    isbn-element = element isbn { foreign-attributes, token }
    name-element = element hr:name { xsd:token }
    qualification-element = element qualification { text }
    title-element = element title { foreign-attributes, text }
    available-content = ("true" | xsd:token " false ") | " "
```

It is much more verbose but has a simpler structure.

First Set of Constraints

The first set of constraints is applied at this fourth processing step. They are mainly checks that our document conforms to XML commonsense, but it's easier and safer to check now on the complete schema:

- It's not possible to define name classes—or except—that contain no name at all by including anyName in an except name class or nsName in an except name class included in another nsName.

- It's not possible to define attributes having the name xmlns or a namespace URI equal to the namespace URI http://www.w3.org/2000/xmlns (corresponding to the "xmlns" prefix).

- Datatype libraries are used correctly; each type exists in its datatype library and its param elements are appropriate to that library.

Grammar Merge

define and start elements are combined in each grammar; all grammars are then merged into one top-level grammar:

1. In each grammar, multiple start elements and multiple define elements with the same name are combined as defined by their combine attribute.

2. The names of the named patterns are then changed so as to be unique across the whole schema; the references to these named patterns are changed accordingly.

3. A top-level grammar and its start element are created, if not already present. All the named patterns become children in this top-level grammar, parentRef elements are replaced by ref elements, and all other grammar and start elements are replaced by their child elements.

During this fifth sequence of steps, the simplified schema:

```
<define name="born-element">
    <element>
        <name ns="http://eric.van-der-vlist.com/ns/person">born</name>
        <data datatypeLibrary="http://www.w3.org/2001/XMLSchema-datatypes"
```

```
                type="date"/>
          </element>
        </define>
        <define name="character-element">
          <grammar>
            <start>
              <element>
                <name ns="http://eric.van-der-vlist.com/ns/library">character</name>
                <group>
                  <group>
                    <group>
                      <attribute>
                        <name ns="">id</name>
                        <text/>
                      </attribute>
                      <parentRef name="name-element"/>
                    </group>
                    <parentRef name="born-element"/>
                  </group>
                  <parentRef name="qualification-element"/>
                </group>
              </element>
            </start>
          </grammar>
        </define>
```

becomes:

```
        <define name="born-element-id2613943">
          <element>
            <name ns="http://eric.van-der-vlist.com/ns/person">born</name>
            <data datatypeLibrary="http://www.w3.org/2001/XMLSchema-datatypes"
                  type="date"/>
          </element>
        </define>
        <define name="character-element-id2613924">
          <element>
            <name ns="http://eric.van-der-vlist.com/ns/library">character</name>
            <group>
              <group>
                <group>
                  <attribute>
                    <name ns="">id</name>
                    <text/>
                  </attribute>
                  <ref name="name-element-id2613832"/>
                </group>
                <ref name="born-element-id2613943"/>
              </group>
              <ref name="qualification-element-id2613840"/>
            </group>
          </element>
        </define>
```

No specific algorithm to create unique names for a named pattern is described in the specification, so these names will vary between implementations.

To demonstrate the drastic change that occurs during simplification, I now present a schema that is a consolidation of features seen throughout this book, to cover most of the elements affected by the simplification. It is composed of four documents.

The first, *library.rnc* (or *library.rng* in the XML syntax), defines the library in general, but not authors or characters:

```
namespace a = "http://relaxng.org/ns/compatibility/annotations/1.0"
namespace hr = "http://eric.van-der-vlist.com/ns/person"
namespace local = ""
default namespace ns1 = "http://eric.van-der-vlist.com/ns/library"
namespace sn = "http://www.snee.com/ns/stages"

a:documentation [ "RELAX NG schema for our library" ]
sn:stages [[
  sn:stage [ name = "library" ]
  sn:stage [ name = "book" ]
  sn:stage [ name = "author" ]
  sn:stage [ name = "character" ]
  sn:stage [ name = "author-or-book" ]
]
start =
  [ sn:stages = "library" ] element library { book-element+ }
  | [ sn:stages = "book author-or-book" ] book-element
  | [ sn:stages = "author author-or-book" ] author-element
  | [ sn:stages = "character" ] character-element
include "foreign.rnc" {
  foreign-elements = element * - (local:* | ns1:* | hr:*) { anything }*
  foreign-attributes = attribute * - (local:* | ns1:* | hr:*) { text }*
}
author-element =
  element hr:author {
    attribute id {
      xsd:NMTOKEN { maxLength = " 16 " }
    },
    name-element,
    born-element,
    died-element?
  }
include "book-content.rnc"
book-content &= foreign-nodes
book-element = element book { book-content }
born-element = element hr:born { xsd:date }
character-element = external "character-element.rnc"
died-element = element hr:died { xsd:date }
isbn-element = element isbn { foreign-attributes, token }
name-element = element hr:name { xsd:token }
qualification-element = element qualification { text }
title-element = element title { foreign-attributes, text }
available-content = "true" | xsd:token " false " | " "
```

The second, *book-content.rnc* (or *bookcontent.rng* in the XML syntax), contains a pattern defining the contents of books:

```
book-content =
  attribute id { text },
  attribute available { available-content },
  isbn-element,
  title-element,
  author-element*,
  character-element*
```

The third, *character-element.rnc* (or *character-element.rng* in the XML syntax), defines character elements:

```
start =
  element character {
    attribute id { text },
    parent name-element,
    parent born-element,
    parent qualification-element
  }
```

The last component, *foreign.rnc* (or *foreign.rng*), provides a model for openness in the schema:

```
anything =
  (element * { anything }
  | attribute * { text }
  | text)*
foreign-elements = element * { anything }*
foreign-attributes = attribute * { text }*
foreign-nodes = (foreign-attributes | foreign-elements)*
```

Here's the complete schema for the library after the grammar-merging steps are completed:

```
namespace local = ""
namespace ns1 = "http://eric.van-der-vlist.com/ns/person"
default namespace ns2 = "http://eric.van-der-vlist.com/ns/library"

start =
  ((element library { book-element-id2613963+ }
    | book-element-id2613963)
  | author-element-id2614058)
  | character-element-id2613924
foreign-elements-id2614183 =
  element * - ((local:* | ns2:*) | ns1:*) { anything-id2614112 }+
  | empty
foreign-attributes-id2614152 =
  attribute * - ((local:* | ns2:*) | ns1:*) { text }+
  | empty
anything-id2614112 =
  ((element * { anything-id2614112 }
    | attribute * { text })
  | text)+
```

```
    | empty
foreign-nodes-id2614043 =
  (foreign-attributes-id2614152 | foreign-elements-id2614183)+ | empty
author-element-id2614058 =
  element ns1:author {
    ((attribute id {
        xsd:NMTOKEN { maxLength = " 16 " }
      },
      name-element-id2613832),
     born-element-id2613943),
     (died-element-id2613856 | empty)
  }
book-content-id2614016 =
  (((((attribute id { text },
        attribute available { available-content-id2613805 }),
      isbn-element-id2613872),
     title-element-id2613819),
    (author-element-id2614058+ | empty)),
   (character-element-id2613924+ | empty))
  & foreign-nodes-id2614043
book-element-id2613963 = element book { book-content-id2614016 }
born-element-id2613943 = element ns1:born { xsd:date }
character-element-id2613924 =
  element character {
    ((attribute id { text },
      name-element-id2613832),
     born-element-id2613943),
     qualification-element-id2613840
  }
died-element-id2613856 = element ns1:died { xsd:date }
isbn-element-id2613872 =
  element isbn { foreign-attributes-id2614152, token }
name-element-id2613832 = element ns1:name { xsd:token }
qualification-element-id2613840 = element qualification { text }
title-element-id2613819 =
  element title { foreign-attributes-id2614152, text }
available-content-id2613805 = ("true" | xsd:token " false ") | " "
```

Schema Flattening

The basic style of the schema (Russian-doll or named templates) has still been preserved by the previous steps. The goal of the sixth step, schema flattening, is to normalize the use of named templates. The goal is to make the schema similar in structure to a DTD. Each element will be cleanly embedded in its own named pattern, and named patterns will contain no more than a single element:

- For each element that isn't the unique child of a define element, a named pattern is created to embed its definition.

- For each named pattern that isn't embedded, a single element pattern is suppressed. References to this named pattern are replaced by its definition.

During this step, the snippet:

```
<start>
  <choice>
    <choice>
      <choice>
        <element>
          <name ns="http://eric.van-der-vlist.com/ns/library">library</name>
          <oneOrMore>
            <ref name="book-element-id2613963"/>
          </oneOrMore>
        </element>
        <ref name="book-element-id2613963"/>
      </choice>
      <ref name="author-element-id2614058"/>
    </choice>
    <ref name="character-element-id2613924"/>
  </choice>
</start>
```

is replaced by:

```
<start>
  <choice>
    <choice>
      <choice>
        <ref name="__library-elt-id2615152"/>
        <ref name="book-element-id2613963"/>
      </choice>
      <ref name="author-element-id2614058"/>
    </choice>
    <ref name="character-element-id2613924"/>
  </choice>
</start>
<define name="__library-elt-id2615152">
  <element>
    <name ns="http://eric.van-der-vlist.com/ns/library">library</name>
    <oneOrMore>
      <ref name="book-element-id2613963"/>
    </oneOrMore>
  </element>
</define>
```

If I take the results of merging the four-part schema from the previous section and apply this step, I get:

```
namespace local = ""
namespace ns1 = "http://eric.van-der-vlist.com/ns/person"
default namespace ns2 = "http://eric.van-der-vlist.com/ns/library"

start =
  ((__library-elt-id2615152 | book-element-id2613963)
   | author-element-id2614058)
  | character-element-id2613924
author-element-id2614058 =
```

```
          element ns1:author {
            ((attribute id {
                xsd:NMTOKEN { maxLength = " 16 " }
              },
              name-element-id2613832),
             born-element-id2613943),
            (died-element-id2613856 | empty)
          }
    book-element-id2613963 =
          element book {
            (((((attribute id { text },
                attribute available { ("true" | xsd:token " false ") | " " }),
                isbn-element-id2613872),
               title-element-id2613819),
              (author-element-id2614058+ | empty)),
             (character-element-id2613924+ | empty))
            & (((attribute * - ((local:* | ns2:*) | ns1:*) { text }+
                | empty)
               | (__-elt-id2615098+ | empty))+
              | empty)
          }
    born-element-id2613943 = element ns1:born { xsd:date }
    character-element-id2613924 =
          element character {
            ((attribute id { text },
              name-element-id2613832),
             born-element-id2613943),
            qualification-element-id2613840
          }
    died-element-id2613856 = element ns1:died { xsd:date }
    isbn-element-id2613872 =
          element isbn {
            (attribute * - ((local:* | ns2:*) | ns1:*) { text }+
             | empty),
            token
          }
    name-element-id2613832 = element ns1:name { xsd:token }
    qualification-element-id2613840 = element qualification { text }
    title-element-id2613819 =
          element title {
            (attribute * - ((local:* | ns2:*) | ns1:*) { text }+
             | empty),
            text
          }
    __-elt-id2615020 =
          element * {
            ((__-elt-id2615020
              | attribute * { text })
             | text)+
            | empty
          }
    __library-elt-id2615152 = element library { book-element-id2613963+ }
    __-elt-id2615098 =
          element * - ((local:* | ns2:*) | ns1:*) {
```

```
      ((__-elt-id2615020
        | attribute * { text })
       | text)+
     | empty
    }
```

Final Cleanup

The simplification process is almost done and just needs a bit of final cleanup:

- Recursively escalate `notAllowed` patterns, when they are located where their effect is such that their parent pattern itself is `notAllowed`. Remove choices that are `notAllowed`. (Note that this simplification doesn't cross element boundaries, so element foo { `notAllowed` } isn't transformed into `notAllowed`.)
- Remove empty elements that have no effect.
- Move useful empty elements so that they are the first child in choice elements.

After this cleanup, our schema becomes:

```
namespace local = ""
namespace ns1 = "http://eric.van-der-vlist.com/ns/person"
default namespace ns2 = "http://eric.van-der-vlist.com/ns/library"

start =
  ((__library-elt-id2615152 | book-element-id2613963)
    | author-element-id2614058)
   | character-element-id2613924
author-element-id2614058 =
  element ns1:author {
    ((attribute id {
         xsd:NMTOKEN { maxLength = " 16 " }
       },
       name-element-id2613832),
     born-element-id2613943),
    (empty | died-element-id2613856)
  }
book-element-id2613963 =
  element book {
    (((((attribute id { text },
        attribute available { ("true" | xsd:token " false ") | " " }),
       isbn-element-id2613872),
      title-element-id2613819),
     (empty | author-element-id2614058+)),
    (empty | character-element-id2613924+))
   & (empty
     | ((empty
         | attribute * - ((local:* | ns2:*) | ns1:*) { text }+)
       | (empty | __-elt-id2615098+))+)
  }
born-element-id2613943 = element ns1:born { xsd:date }
character-element-id2613924 =
  element character {
```

```
      ((attribute id { text },
         name-element-id2613832),
       born-element-id2613943),
     qualification-element-id2613840
   }
  died-element-id2613856 = element ns1:died { xsd:date }
  isbn-element-id2613872 =
    element isbn {
      (empty
       | attribute * - ((local:* | ns2:*) | ns1:*) { text }+),
      token
    }
  name-element-id2613832 = element ns1:name { xsd:token }
  qualification-element-id2613840 = element qualification { text }
  title-element-id2613819 =
    element title {
      (empty
       | attribute * - ((local:* | ns2:*) | ns1:*) { text }+),
      text
    }
  __-elt-id2615020 =
    element * {
      empty
      | ((__-elt-id2615020
          | attribute * { text })
         | text)+
    }
  __library-elt-id2615152 = element library { book-element-id2613963+ }
  __-elt-id2615098 =
    element * - ((local:* | ns2:*) | ns1:*) {
      empty
      | ((__-elt-id2615020
          | attribute * { text })
         | text)+
    }
```

Restrictions

With the exception of constraints expressed by the RELAX NG schema for RELAX NG and those which are part of the simplification itself, RELAX NG defines all the restrictions on schema structures as they apply to the simplified version. Most of them are obvious and easy to understand.

Constraints on Attributes

RELAX NG's constraints match the constraints on attributes defined by the XML 1.0 recommendation:

- Attributes can't contain other attributes; attribute patterns can't have another attribute pattern in their descendants.

- Attributes can't contain elements; `attribute` patterns can't have a `ref` pattern in their descendants.
- Attributes can't be duplicated; an attribute may not be found in a `oneOrMore` pattern with a combination by group or `interleave`. Furthermore, if `attribute` patterns are combined in a group or `interleave` pattern, their name classes must not overlap: they can't have any name that belongs to both name classes.
- Attributes that have an infinite name class (`anyName` or `nsName`) must be enclosed in a `oneOrMore` pattern. In other words, you can't specify only one or a certain number of occurrences of these attributes. They can have only `text` as their model (in other words, data patterns are forbidden here).

Let's explore schemas that may look valid at a quick glance but are going to collide with these restrictions.

Bad example: attribute content model

This schema states that any content model can be accepted in the bar attribute:

```
anything =
  (element * { anything }
  | attribute * { text }
  | text)*
start =
  element foo {
    attribute bar { anything },
    text
  }
```

Unfortunately, it's translated into:

```
start = __foo-elt-id2602800
__-elt-id2602788 =
  element * {
    empty
    | ((__-elt-id2602788
        | attribute * { text })
      | text)+
  }
__foo-elt-id2602800 =
  element foo {
    attribute bar {
      empty
      | ((__-elt-id2602788
          | attribute * { text })
        | text)+
    },
    text
  }
```

This one allows a reference to a named pattern (which means an element in the simplified syntax) and an attribute. Both of these things are forbidden.

You must ensure that the anything defined for the content of the attribute is compatible with the content of attributes as defined by the XML specification. For instance:

```
anything =
  (text)
start =
  element foo {
    attribute bar { anything },
    text
  }
```

is simplified into:

```
start = __foo-elt-id2602296
__foo-elt-id2602296 =
  element foo {
    attribute bar { text },
    text
  }
```

This schema expresses the original intent and is valid.

Bad example: attribute duplication

Let's say I want to extend the definition of the title element so that it has the same attributes and content model as the XHTML 2.0 span element. If I look into the RELAX NG module implementing the span element, I can see that its definition is:

```
span = element span { span.attlist, Inline.model }
```

I want to include this in the definition of the title element, which already includes an xml:lang attribute:

```
namespace x = "http://www.w3.org/2002/06/xhtml2"

start = book
include "xhtml-attribs-2.rnc" inherit = x
include "xhtml-inltext-2.rnc" inherit = x
include "xhtml-datatypes-2.rnc" inherit = x
book =
  element book {
    attribute id { text },
    attribute available { text },
    element isbn { text },
    element title {
      attribute xml:lang { xsd:language },
      span.attlist,
      Inline.model
    }
  }
```

Unfortunately, this snippet is invalid because the `xml:lang` attribute is already included somewhere in the `span.attlist` pattern. It gets combined during the simplification, which causes the definition of the `title` element to be:

```
__title-elt-id2641936 =
  element title {
    (attribute xml:lang { xsd:language },
     (((((((((empty
             | attribute id { xsd:ID }),
             (empty
             | attribute class { xsd:NMTOKENS })),
            (empty
            | attribute title { text })),
           (empty
           | attribute xml:lang { xsd:language })),
          (empty
          | attribute dir {
              (("ltr" | "rtl") | "lro")
              | "rlo"
            })),
         ((empty
          | attribute edit {
              (("inserted" | "deleted") | "changed")
              | "moved"
            }),
          (empty default namespace
              lib = "http://eric.van-der-vlist.com/ns/library namespace local = ""

start = book

book =
  element book {
    attribute id { text },
    attribute available { text },
    foreign-attributes,
    element isbn { text },
    element title {
      attribute xml:lang { xsd:language },
      text
    }
  }

foreign-attributes = attribute * - (local:* | lib:* ) { text }*
          | attribute datetime { xsd:dateTime }))),
       (((((((((empty
               | attribute href { xsd:anyURI }),
              (empty
              | attribute cite { xsd:anyURI })),
             (empty
             | attribute target { xsd:NMTOKEN })),
            (empty
            | attribute rel { xsd:NMTOKENS })),
           (empty
```

```
                    | attribute rev { xsd:NMTOKENS })),
                 (empty
                  | attribute accesskey {
                      xsd:string { length = "1" }
                    })),
                (empty
                 | attribute navindex {
                     xsd:nonNegativeInteger {
                       pattern = "0-9+"
                       minInclusive = "0"
                       maxInclusive = "32767"
                     }
                   })),
               (empty
                | attribute base { xsd:anyURI }))),
              ((empty
               | attribute src { xsd:anyURI }),
              (empty
               | attribute type { text }))),
             ((((empty
                | attribute usemap { xsd:anyURI }),
               (empty
                | attribute ismap { "ismap" })),
              (empty
               | attribute shape {
                   (("rect" | "circle") | "poly")
                   | "default"
                 })),
             (empty
              | attribute coords { text })))),
            (empty
             | (empty
                | (text
                   | (((((((((((((abbr-id2635861 | cite-id2635889)
                                | code-id2635918)
                              | dfn-id2635947)
                            | em-id2635975)
                          | kbd-id2636004)
                        | l-id2636032)
                       | quote-id2636061)
                     | samp-id2636090)
                    | span-id2636118)
                   | strong-id2636147)
                  | sub-id2636176)
                 | sup-id2636204)
                | var-id2636233)))+)
      }
```

To fix this, I need to remove the xml:lang from the original definition, creating:

```
namespace x = "http://www.w3.org/2002/06/xhtml2"

start = book
include "xhtml-attribs-2.rnc" inherit = x
```

```
include "xhtml-inltext-2.rnc" inherit = x
include "xhtml-datatypes-2.rnc" inherit = x
book =
  element book {
    attribute id { text },
    attribute available { text },
    element isbn { text },
    element title {
      span.attlist,
      Inline.model
    }
  }
```

Bad example: name class overlap

Let's say that I have the following schema, called *book.rnc*:

```
default namespace lib = "http://eric.van-der-vlist.com/ns/library"
namespace local = ""

start = book

book =
  element book {
    attribute id { text },
    attribute available { text },
    foreign-attributes,
    element isbn { text },
    element title {
      attribute xml:lang { xsd:language },
      text
    }
  }

foreign-attributes = attribute * - (local:* | lib:* ) { text }*
```

Although I have accepted foreign attributes, I should be more precise about the definition of some Dublin Core elements. I can extend the schema like this:

```
namespace dc="http://purl.org/dc/elements/1.1/"

include "book.rnc"

book.content &= attribute dc:rights { text } ?
```

Unfortunately, this is invalid, because it gets simplified to:

```
book-id2604347 =
  element book {
    ((((attribute id { text },
       attribute available { text }),
      (empty
       | attribute * - (lib:* | local:*) { text }+)),
      __isbn-elt-id2604556),
```

```
    __title-elt-id2604551)
   & attribute ns1:rights { text }
}
```

The attribute dc:rights is included in the name class * - (lib:* | local:*). To fix this, I need to redefine the named pattern foreign-attributes to remove the name dc:rights or perhaps even all the namespaces for Dublin Core elements:

```
default namespace lib = "http://eric.van-der-vlist.com/ns/library"
namespace dc="http://purl.org/dc/elements/1.1/"
namespace local = ""

include "book.rnc" {
       foreign-attributes = attribute * - (local:* | lib:* | dc:* ) { text }*
}

book.content &= attribute dc:rights { text } ?
```

Constraints on Lists

Lists work on text nodes by splitting them into tokens, which are then handled themselves as text nodes. It's therefore not possible to find elements or attributes in a list. Mixing text nodes and embedded lists is confusing and forbidden anyway. List patterns can't have any of these descendants: list, ref (because after simplification, access to elements is done using references to named patterns), attribute, or text. The interleave pattern is also forbidden as a descendant of list patterns because it complicates implementations.

Bad example: list and interleave

I'd like to define a price element as allowing a numeric followed by a token, such as:

```
<price>1 Euro</price>
```

or a token followed by a numeric:

```
<price>USD 1</price>
```

I might be tempted to write:

```
element price {
   list { xsd:decimal & xsd:token }
}
```

However, this is invalid because interleave is forbidden in a list. To work around this limitation, I need to give all the possible combinations. It's easy with this small example, though it can rapidly grow out of control as more types are added. In this case, it just requires a bit of duplication:

```
element price {
   list { (xsd:decimal, xsd:token) | (xsd:token, xsd:decimal) }
}
```

Constraints on Except Patterns

Except patterns (except elements used in a data pattern) apply to individual pieces of data. An except element with a data parent can contain only data, value, and choice elements.

Constraints on Start Patterns

After simplification, the start pattern describes the list of possible root elements. You can thus find only combinations of choices between ref elements.

Constraints on Content Models

RELAX NG defines three different content models for an element:

- Empty, when the element has only attributes
- Simple, when the element has only attributes and has been described using data, value or list patterns
- Complex, in all other cases

This set is identical to the definitions provided by W3C XML Schema and similar but somewhat different from the definition of these terms in plain XML. Consider an element expressed as <foo>bar</foo>. RELAX NG sees it as complex content if its content has been described using a text pattern and as simple content if its content has been described using other patterns. It's not enough for an element to contain only a text node for it to be called simple content. It is also necessary for this element to have been described with a data orientation. When that isn't the case, if the text pattern has been used, the element is considered document-oriented and a special case of mixed content in which no elements are included.

The restriction on the content model is expressed by saying that empty content can be grouped with any other content models but that simple and complex content models can't be grouped together (through group or interleave patterns). Simple and complex content models can appear under the definition of the same element only as alternatives. In other words, for each alternative, you need to choose between being data- or text-oriented, and you can't mix both mindsets.

I mentioned the practical consequence of this restriction on mixed content model in Chapter 7. It's not possible to use data patterns to specify constraints on the text nodes occurring in elements with mixed content.

Limitations on interleave

The last two limitations apply to interleave. The goal of these limitations is to facilitate the implementation of the interleave feature, which other schema languages lack largely because it is seen as difficult to implement. These two limitations are intended to reduce the number of combinations RELAX NG processors need to explore to support `interleave`:

- Elements combined through `interleave` must not overlap between name classes. You have already seen a similar restriction with attributes, which are always combined through `interleave`.

- There must be at most one text pattern in each set of patterns combined by `interleave`.

These limitations don't affect the expressive power of RELAX NG (the set of content models that can be written with RELAX NG). Even if you run into a limitation from time to time, schemas can always be rewritten to work around them. Sometimes, though, they can be a nuisance when combining existing patterns with mixed content models.

The limitations are needed to support the different algorithms currently used to implement RELAX NG. James Clark thinks that they can be removed in future versions of RELAX NG: "Better algorithms may be developed that will allow this restriction to be removed in future versions."

Bad example: more than one text pattern in interleave

You may have the following schema, *book.rnc*, to describe your books:

```
start = book
book = element book { book.content }
book.content =
  attribute id { text },
  attribute available { text },
  element isbn { text },
  title
title = element title { title.attributes, title.content }
title.attributes = attribute xml:lang { xsd:language }
title.content = text
```

To add the XHTML `Inline.model` to `title.content`, you might be tempted to write:

```
include "book.rnc"
include "xhtml-attribs-2.rnc"
include "xhtml-inltext-2.rnc"
include "xhtml-datatypes-2.rnc"

title.content &= Inline.model
```

Unfortunately, `Inline.model` already contains a text pattern and gets simplified to:

```
title-id2635741 =
  element title {
    attribute lang { xsd:language },
    (text
     & (empty
```

```
        | (empty
          | (text
              | (((((((((((((abbr-id2636549 | cite-id2636578)
                              | code-id2636607)
                        | dfn-id2636636)
                      | em-id2636664)
                    | kbd-id2636693)
                  | l-id2636721)
                | quote-id2636750)
              | samp-id2636778)
            | span-id2636807)
          | strong-id2636836)
        | sub-id2636865)
      | sup-id2636893)
    | var-id2636922)))+))
}
```

Here there are text patterns within `interleave`. To fix this problem, I need to replace the combination with a redefinition of `title.content`:

```
include "book.rnc" {
  title.content = Inline.model
}
include "xhtml-attribs-2.rnc"
include "xhtml-inltext-2.rnc"
include "xhtml-datatypes-2.rnc"
include "book.rnc" {
  title.content = Inline.model
}
include "xhtml-attribs-2.rnc"
include "xhtml-inltext-2.rnc"
include "xhtml-datatypes-2.rnc"
```

There is no loss in expressive power (I am able to describe what I wanted to describe), but there is a loss in modularity. Changes made to `title.content` in `book.rnc` would now have to be manually added to the derived schema.

CHAPTER 16

Determinism and Datatype Assignment

One of the strengths of RELAX NG is that it's flexible enough to support a difficult but sometimes convenient concept called:

- "Ambiguous content models" in the SGML world
- "Nondeterministic content models" in XML DTDs
- The "Unique Particle Attribution rule" and the "Consistent Declaration rule" in the W3C XML Schema

Before you read any further into this chapter, realize that as far as simple validation is concerned, RELAX NG processes ambiguous schemas happily. That said, when type assignment or data binding is involved, schema ambiguity may have consequences that create problems. You will see in this chapter how to use RELAX NG in ways that avoid these problems, making RELAX NG "type assignment–friendly."

What Is Ambiguity?

First, I will clarify the concepts of ambiguity and determinism. They're blurred in many papers and discussions, yet aren't as obscure as people often think.

Ambiguity Versus Determinism

The first distinction is the difference between ambiguity and determinism. These two terms have been given precise definitions by regular expressions and hedge grammar theoreticians, and in this chapter I will follow the usage of these terms as defined by Murata Makoto. Part of the confusion about these notions comes from their frequent misuse.

A schema is said to be *ambiguous* when a document may be valid when its contents match multiple different pattern alternatives. A trivial example is:

```
element foo{empty} | element foo{empty}
```

When an empty element named foo is found in an instance document, there is no way to say whether it is valid per the left definition or the right definition of element foo{empty} in the schema.

There are, of course, more complex cases of ambiguity, and you'll see some of them in the next sections. Still, this is the general idea behind ambiguity.

Ambiguity is independent of any implementation or algorithm. It's a property of the schema itself; a schema is either ambiguous or not ambiguous.

Determinism has been introduced to facilitate the implementation of schema processors. The basic idea behind determinism is that at each point, when matching an instance document against a schema, the schema processor has at most one possible choice. This makes life easier for implementers, who can safely rely on well-known algorithms such as *automatons* (also called *Finite State Machines* or FSMs). Thus, they can be sure that their computation times will not grow exponentially. Because of the need to avoid exponential growth in processing times, schema languages often impose determinism on schema authors.

An ambiguous schema is never deterministic, but the opposite is far from being true. Consider, for instance:

```
element foo{empty} | (element foo{empty}, element bar{empty})
```

This example isn't ambiguous. A schema processor can say whether the right or left alternative is used (or neither, if the document is invalid) after having read the element that follows the empty element named foo. This is, however, also nondeterministic, since when a schema processor matches an empty element named foo, it has two different choices. It can't make the choice between them without looking ahead to the next element.

Ambiguous schemas aren't a problem as far as validation is concerned. The schema's validation reports are consistent, and we don't care why a document is valid or not as long as the answer (valid or invalid) is reliable. The only downside to ambiguous schemas is for applications performing datatype assignment—or, more generally, instance document annotation—using validation. You will see more about these issues in the next sections of this chapter.

The main problem with schema languages that require deterministic schemas is that some content models are fundamentally nondeterministic and can't be rewritten in a deterministic form. Such deterministic schema languages not only create restrictions to the forms used to write a schema, but limit their expressive power. They can't describe all the content models allowed in well-formed XML. You will see examples of content models that are impossible to describe in a deterministic form in the section about compatibility with W3C XML Schema.

Different Kinds of Ambiguity

In a RELAX NG schema, you can distinguish four different types of ambiguity: regular expression ambiguities, hedge grammar ambiguities, name class ambiguities, and datatype ambiguities. I'll briefly introduce each of them, as they have slightly different behaviors.

Regular expression ambiguities

After a schema has been simplified, we can make a clear distinction between the definition of each element (embedded in its own named pattern) and the grammar that combines these definitions. What's called a *regular expression ambiguity* is an ambiguity that resides within the definition of an element.

> Note that in this chapter I use the term "regular expression" as used in the math behind RELAX NG. The term "regular expression" that you'll find in this chapter should thus not be confused with the regular expressions as seen in the W3C XML Schema pattern facet.

Theoreticians have demonstrated that ambiguous regular expressions may be rewritten in an unambiguous way. The ambiguities may be considered merely as unlucky variations over unambiguous schemas.

A basic example of such a choice between a pattern and itself is:

```
<choice>
 <ref name="pattern"/>
 <ref name="pattern"/>
</choice>
```

or:

```
pattern|pattern
```

The unambiguous form is somewhat difficult to find when the ambiguous pattern gets more complex. For instance, the following pattern:

```
<choice>
 <group>
  <optional>
   <ref name="first"/>
  </optional>
  <ref name="second"/>
 </group>
 <group>
  <ref name="second"/>
  <optional>
   <ref name="third"/>
  </optional>
 </group>
</choice>
```

or:

```
(first?,second)|(second,third?)
```

is ambiguous because an instance nodeset that matches only the named pattern second without first or third is valid per the two alternatives. It can be rewritten by removing the option of matching only the second pattern from one of the alternatives:

```
<group>
 <optional>
  <ref name="first"/>
 </optional>
 <ref name="second"/>
</group>
<group>
 <ref name="second"/>
 <ref name="third"/>
</group>
</choice>
```

or:

```
(first?,second)|(second,third)
```

 Algorithms can rewrite ambiguous regular expressions to turn them into their unambiguous forms. It would be really useful if XML development tools could implement these algorithms to propose unambiguous alternatives for ambiguous patterns. Until this happens, though, the best thing to do when confronted with an ambiguous pattern you need to make unambiguous is to take a step back, then calmly write out the different combinations expressed by the schema to combine them differently until the combination isn't ambiguous any more.

Note that explicit choices aren't the only pattern that can lead to ambiguous schemas. Consider this simple pattern:

```
<group>
 <optional>
  <ref name="pattern"/>
 </optional>
 <optional>
  <ref name="pattern"/>
 </optional>
<group>
```

or:

```
pattern?, pattern?
```

If you have a content model that matches only one pattern, you can't know if it will match it for the first or the second occurrence of the pattern. Therefore, this schema can be considered ambiguous. Here's how to rewrite it as an unambiguous schema:

```
<optional>
 <ref name="pattern"/>
 <optional>
  <ref name="pattern"/>
 </optional>
</optional>
```

or:

```
(pattern, pattern?)?
```

Although the rewriting approach isn't easy, the math behind RELAX NG can help, as high school algebra helps factorize mathematical expressions. As an exercise, let's decompose the chain of factorizations and simplifications to rewrite pattern?, pattern? as (pattern, pattern?)?.

The first step relies on the fact that pattern? is equivalent to empty|*pattern*:

```
pattern?, pattern?
```

which is equivalent to:

```
(empty|pattern), (empty|pattern)
```

which can be factorized as:

```
(empty,empty)|(empty,pattern)|(pattern,empty)|(pattern,pattern)
```

which can be simplified to:

```
empty|pattern|(pattern,pattern)
```

which is equivalent to:

```
empty|(pattern,(empty|pattern))
```

which is equivalent to:

```
(pattern, pattern?)?
```

I could argue that the unambiguous forms are clearer, more logical, and easier to read than the ambiguous, but I think that this conclusion is a subjective one. These different methods for creating unambiguous schemas are highly dependent on the perspective used to analyze the content of instance documents. There isn't a good or a bad practice for this: working with a schema language such as RELAX NG that supports all of these forms saves a lot of time. The language doesn't force you to use its perspective on how to solve this problem.

 Disambiguating regular expressions doesn't significantly change the structure or the style of your schema. The changes are limited to the regular expression itself. This statement will not be true when using ambiguous regular hedge grammars, covered in the next section.

Ambiguous regular hedge grammars

In a RELAX NG context, I defined regular expression ambiguity as an ambiguity that resides within the definition of an element. Ambiguous regular hedge grammars, on the other hand, are ambiguities distributed over element definitions that play the mathematical role of "hedges" in a RELAX NG schema. A example of an ambiguous regular hedge grammar is:

```
<choice>
  <ref name="pattern1"/>
  <ref name="pattern2"/>
</choice>
...
<define name="pattern1">
  <element name="foo">
    <empty/>
  </element>
</define>
<define name="pattern2">
  <element name="foo">
    <empty/>
  </element>
</define>
```

or, in the compact syntax:

```
pattern1|pattern2
...
pattern1=element foo{empty}
pattern2=element foo{empty}
```

This example is ambiguous. When an empty element, foo, is found, you can't tell whether it's been validated through pattern1 or pattern2. It's an ambiguous hedge grammar (not an ambiguous regular expression) because the ambiguity is spread over two hedges; i.e., two definitions of the element foo.

Just as in ambiguous regular expressions, ambiguous regular hedge grammars can be rewritten in unambiguous forms. The disambiguation must be done at the level of the grammar itself and may require extensive changes to the structure of the schema.

The exercise of disambiguating regular hedge grammars can get significantly more complicated when compositions of named patterns and grammars are involved. Maintaining nonambiguous patterns while combining definitions by choice means that you need to exclude all the instance nodesets valid per the original definition from the pattern given as a choice. This isn't always possible without modifying the included schema. Consider, for instance, this pattern:

```
<define name="namedPattern">
 <ref name="first"/>
</define>
```

or this:

```
namedPattern=first
```

To add an optional second pattern, it may seem natural to combine it by choice as:

```
<define name="namedPattern" combine="choice">
 <ref name="first"/>
 <optional>
  <ref name="second"/>
 </optional>
</define>
```

or:

```
namedPattern|=first,second?
```

The result of the combination is equivalent to:

```
<define name="namedPattern">
 <choice>
  <ref name="first"/>
  <group>
   <ref name="first"/>
   <optional>
    <ref name="second"/>
   </optional>
  </group>
 </choice>
</define>
```

or:

```
namedPattern=first|(first,second?)
```

which gives an ambiguous pattern. Of course, outside the context of a pattern combination, this example would be trivial to rewrite as:

```
<define name="namedPattern">
 <ref name="first"/>
 <optional>
  <ref name="second"/>
 </optional>
</define>
```

or:

```
namedPattern=first,second?
```

but in this case, you won't get to disambiguation directly by pattern combination. You need to look at the problem from a different angle. Consider that you must leave out all features used in the alternative unless those features are already allowed in the original. In other words, you need to remove the case in which the first pattern isn't followed by the second one from the target of "the first pattern followed by an optional second pattern." The alternative will thus be between the first pattern alone and the first pattern followed by a second one:

```
<define name="namedPattern" combine="choice">
 <choice>
  <ref name="first"/>
  <group>
```

```
      <ref name="first"/>
      <ref name="second"/>
    </group>
   </choice>
  </define>
```

or:

```
namedPattern=first|(first,second)
```

With this target in mind, you can rewrite the combination as:

```
<define name="namedPattern" combine="choice">
 <ref name="first"/>
 <ref name="second"/>
</define>
```

or:

```
namedPattern|=first,second
```

To avoid ambiguous hedge grammars, be careful when combining named patterns by choice. Without knowing how pattern1 and pattern2 are defined, it's impossible to say whether the following are ambiguous:

```
<choice>
 <ref name="pattern1"/>
 <ref name="pattern2"/>
</choice>
```

and:

```
pattern1|pattern2
```

This difficulty requires that if you wish to create unambiguous schemas, you must study the contents of schemas you want to include very carefully.

Name class ambiguity

Another source of ambiguity occurs when name classes overlap when used as different alternatives of a choice. An example of such overlap is:

```
<choice>
 <element name="foo">
   <empty/>
 </element>
 <element>
   <anyName/>
   <empty/>
 </element>
</choice>
```

or:

```
element foo{empty} | element * {empty}
```

This example is ambiguous because the name class anyName includes the name class matching the name foo. An element foo is valid in both branches of the choice pattern.

The except name class can prevent name class ambiguity, because it lets you remove the overlap from one of the alternatives. This pattern can easily be rewritten as an ambiguous choice pattern:

```
<choice>
  <element name="foo">
    <empty/>
  </element>
  <element>
    <anyName>
      <except>
<name>foo</name>
      </except>
    </anyName>
    <empty/>
  </element>
</choice>
```

or:

```
element foo{empty} | element * - foo {empty}
```

or, more simply:

```
<element>
  <anyName>
    <except>
      <name>foo</name>
    </except>
  </anyName>
  <empty/>
</element>
```

or:

```
element * {empty}
```

Note that name class overlap isn't enough by itself to make an ambiguous pattern. For instance:

```
<choice>
  <element name="foo">
    <attribute name="bar">
      <empty/>
    </attribute>
  </element>
  <element>
    <anyName/>
    <empty/>
  </element>
</choice>
```

or:

```
element foo{attribute bar{empty}} | element * {empty}}
```

This example isn't ambiguous because the content model of the elements with the two name classes don't overlap. This makes the bar attribute optional:

```
<choice>
  <element name="foo">
    <optional>
      <attribute name="bar">
        <empty/>
      </attribute>
    </optional>
  </element>
  <element>
    <anyName/>
    <empty/>
  </element>
</choice>
```

or:

```
element foo{attribute bar{empty}?} | element * {empty}}
```

This code is enough to make our pattern ambiguous. However, this pattern is strictly equivalent to the preceding example, which means that you know how to rewrite it in an unambiguous way.

Finally, note that name class ambiguity may be considered as an extension of regular hedge grammar ambiguity. If, after simplification, to create a regular hedge grammar ambiguity, you have:

```
element foo{empty} | element foo{empty}
```

the ambiguity comes from the fact that the name classes for both alternatives are the single value foo and thus, overlap.

Ambiguous datatypes

Datatype ambiguity is the most difficult ambiguity to handle with RELAX NG. The difficulty doesn't come from RELAX NG itself, but rather from the fact that datatype libraries aren't built-in and are more opaque and less flexible than other patterns or name classes.

A basic example of ambiguous datatypes is:

```
<element name="foo">
  <choice>
    <data type="boolean"/>
    <data type="integer"/>
  </choice>
</element>
```

or:

```
element foo{xsd:boolean|xsd:integer}
```

Because the lexical space of the two possible datatypes do overlap (0 and 1 are valid as both W3C XML Schema booleans and integers), there is no way to determine what the datatype is for a foo element with a value of 0 or 1. Fortunately, the except operator makes it possible to remove the lexical space of one datatype from the lexical space of another datatype:

```
<element name="foo">
  <choice>
    <data type="boolean">
      <except>
        <data type="integer"/>
      </except>
    </data>
    <data type="integer"/>
  </choice>
</element>
```

or:

```
element foo{
   (xsd:boolean - xsd:integer)
   |xsd:integer
}
```

As has been the case for name classes, the except pattern is a powerful tool for disambiguating datatype ambiguities. It's a pity that this pattern can't also be used to disambiguate regular expression or hedge grammar ambiguities.

The Downsides of Ambiguous and Nondeterministic Content Models

Again, if you're interested in using a RELAX NG schema only for validation—which, after all, is the primary goal of RELAX NG—it is perfectly fine to design and use nondeterministic and even ambiguous schemas. The downsides of ambiguous schemas appear when using RELAX NG schemas for adding validation information to instance documents or using a RELAX NG schema for guided editing. The downsides of nondeterministic schemas appear only when translating schemas into a W3C XML Schema.

Instance Annotations

For the purposes of RELAX NG, *instance annotation* is the ability to attach information gathered during validation to facilitate instance document processing. Instance annotation is one of the more promising paths to automating XML document processing. Its applications cover domains from datatype assignment (the basis of XQuery 1.0, XPath 2.0, and XSLT 2.0), to data binding (automating the creation of objects from XML documents and the creation of XML documents from objects), to XML guided editing.

Some tools may have more stringent requirements, depending on their algorithms (for instance, a SAX-based streaming tool might require deterministic schemas), but in theory (and in general), it is sufficient for the applications of instance annotations to ensure that the annotations are consistent. Consistency can be achieved if the schema is unambiguous.

Note that even this freedom from ambiguity isn't always required. These requirements are application-dependent. Consider a data binding application that needs to know the content model of each element. This application might have trouble determining which content model to use if it finds a pattern such as this and an element foo with a content pattern matching the second pattern:

```
element foo {first?,second}
|element foo {second,third?}

first=element first{xsd:integer}
second=element second{xsd:token}
third=element third{xsd:boolean}
```

Should it bind the contents of foo to an object allowing an optional first or to an object allowing an optional third? Such ambiguity is likely to be a problem for this application. On the other hand, if all you need to do is perform simple type assignment, this schema is perfectly fine. Even though it is ambiguous, there is no ambiguity as far as datatype assignment is concerned.

Being aware of ambiguity in your RELAX NG schemas is good practice. If you want to support instance annotation applications, you must also check the tools you will be using because they can have either more stringent or more relaxed requirements.

Compatibility with W3C XML Schema

I promised to give an example of an unambiguous pattern that isn't deterministic and can't be rewritten in a deterministic form. Here it is! Consider a pattern describing a book as a sequence of odd and even pages:

```
<zeroOrMore>
  <ref name="odd"/>
  <ref name="even"/>
</zeroOrMore>
<optional>
  <ref name="odd"/>
</optional>
```

or:

```
(odd, even)*, odd?
```

This pattern isn't ambiguous. Given any valid combinations of odd and even pages, it is possible to know which pattern has matched each page. It can't be deterministic, however, because for each odd page, you need to look ahead to the next one to see if it is the last before knowing if an even page is required in next position.

The W3C XML Schema requires deterministic content models under the name of "Unique Particle Attribution" and "Consistent Declaration" rules. These rules forbid this simple and useful content model!

Another example of nondeterministic pattern is:

```
<choice>
 <element name="foo">
  <attribute name="bar"/>
 </element>
 <element name="foo">
  <element name="bar">
   <text/>
  </element>
 </element>
</choice>
```

or:

```
element foo {attribute bar} | element foo {element bar {text}}
```

This one seems easier to translate. At least, it can be factorized and rewritten as a deterministic pattern in RELAX NG as:

```
<element name="foo">
 <choice>
  <attribute name="bar"/>
  <element name="bar">
   <text/>
  </element>
 </choice>
</element>
```

or:

```
element foo {attribute bar| element bar {text}}
```

Unfortunately, this doesn't help to translate our schema into a W3C XML Schema because W3C XML Schema doesn't know how to handle the mixing of constraints on subelements and attributes except by using difficult hacks with key definitions, which don't work in all cases.

Making sure your schemas are deterministic is thus a good practice when you plan to translate your schemas into W3C XML Schemas. Unfortunately there's no guarantee that they will translate gracefully. The only rule I can give if you want to make sure that your schemas will be easy to translate is to check the result of translation frequently as you write your schema. Also hope that James Clark will continue to improve the Trang conversion algorithm!

Nevertheless, W3C XML Schema deals nicely with datatype ambiguities. You can re-examine our example of datatype ambiguity:

```
element foo{xsd:boolean|xsd:integer}
```

and you may be surprised to know that it translates gracefully into:

```
<xs:element name="foo">
  <xs:simpleType>
    <xs:union memberTypes="xs:boolean xs:integer"/>
  </xs:simpleType>
</xs:element>
```

This isn't considered ambiguous because the W3C XML Schema has added a rule. When several datatypes are grouped "by union," which is effectively what our choice between datatype does, a processor should stop after the first type that matches and not evaluate the next alternatives.

Some Ideas to Make Disambiguation Easier

To close this chapter, I'll present some ideas that should ease the challenge of disambiguating schemas.

Generalizing the Except Pattern

In the different forms of ambiguity, name classes have been the easiest ones to disambiguate. Why is this? Name classes aren't inherently simpler than regular expressions or datatypes. All these tools are about defining sets of things that can happen in XML documents and in many ways, they are deeply similar. The reason that name classes and datatypes have been easier to disambiguate is because they have a first class except operator. If you had the same level of support for patterns and datatypes, you could more easily disambiguate them.

It is possible to apply the except pattern to datatypes and write:

```
element foo{ (xsd:boolean - xsd:integer) |xsd:integer}
```

A value that is only integer will obviously match only the right alternative. A value that is exclusively boolean (true or false) matches the left alternative. A value that is both a boolean and an integer (0 or 1) matches the first condition of the left alternative (xsd:boolean) but doesn't match the exception clause.

Unfortunately, this rule can't be generalized beyond the scope of data patterns. (Note that the examples given next with the except (-) operator aren't valid RELAX NG.)

If this rule could be generalized, and applied to an ambiguous regular expression such as:

```
two|(one?,two+,three*)
```

you could write:

```
two|((one?,two+,three*)-two)
```

Of course, this same set of results can be created with the existing RELAX NG patterns, but a generalized except would make that flexibility much more accessible.

Making Disambiguation Rules Explicit

My second proposal is far less disruptive. The idea is just the realization that these ambiguities are ambiguous because you haven't done anything to rule them out. There are plenty of examples in other computer languages of ambiguities that have been partially or fully ruled out: XSLT templates, order of evaluation of statements in programming languages, or, as we've seen in the section about W3C XML Schema, union of datatypes.

There is nothing preventing the creation of a specification defining a priority for the alternatives to be used by applications interested in instance annotation at large when they encounter ambiguities.

This specification wouldn't need to apply to RELAX NG processors interested only in validation and would not compromise their optimizations. It could apply only to RELAX NG processors performing instance annotation. It would also guarantee a consistent and interoperable type of annotation for schemas that are currently considered to be ambiguous.

The rule could be as simple as "use the first alternative in document order" or could also take into account additional factors, such as giving a lesser precedence to included grammars, as XSLT does with stylesheet imports.

Accepting Ambiguity

Jeni Tennison proposed a third approach on the xml-dev mailing list: instead of trying to fight against ambiguity, why not accept it? Why couldn't we acknowledge that something can have several datatypes (or models) and at the same time have a datatype "A" and "B"? Why couldn't a value be an integer and a boolean simultaneously?

This idea would have a serious impact on specifications, such as XPath 2.0—that assign a single datatype to each simple type element and attribute, but this approach would be much more compatible with the principle that markup is only the projection of a structure over a document. It often happens that a piece of text can have several meanings. By extension, acknowledging that elements and attributes may belong to multiple datatypes at the same time seems like something obvious, yet clever, to do.

Reference

PART II

Reference

CHAPTER 17

Element Reference

This short reference to RELAX NG elements presents each element of the XML syntax for RELAX NG in alphabetical order. Note that the synopsis given for each element is generated from the RELAX NG schema and doesn't capture the restrictions applied after simplification.

The simplification process and restrictions are detailed in Chapter 15. The main restrictions for each element are also mentioned in this chapter in the "Restrictions" section.

Elements

---

anyName   Name class accepting any name

```
element anyName
{
(
attribute ns { text }?,
attribute datatypeLibrary {xsd:anyURI}?,
attribute * - (rng:* | local:*) { text }*
),
( ( element * - rng:* { ... }* ) & element except { ... }? )
}
```

Class

name-class

May be included in

attribute, choice, element, except

Compact syntax equivalent

`*-nameClass`

Description

The anyName name class matches any name from any namespace. This wide spectrum may be restricted by embedding except name classes.

Restrictions

Within the scope of an element, the name classes of attributes can't overlap. The same restrictions apply to name classes of elements when these elements are combined by interleave.

Example

```
<element>
 <anyName/>
 <ref name="anything"/>
</element>

<element>
 <anyName>
   <except>
     <nsName ns=""/>
     <nsName ns="http://eric.van-der-vlist.com/ns/library"/>
     <nsName ns="http://eric.van-der-vlist.com/ns/person"/>
   </except>
 </anyName>
 <ref name="anything"/>
</element>

<attribute>
  <anyName/>
</attribute>
```

Attributes

datatypeLibrary

This attribute defines the default datatype library. The value is inherited. Note that although datatypeLibrary is allowed in anyName to maintain coherence with other RELAX NG elements, it has no direct effect on anyName itself and none on name class definitions in which it might be embedded.

ns This attribute defines the default namespace for the elements defined in a portion of a schema. The value is inherited. Although ns is allowed in anyName, it has no direct consequence on anyName itself. ns always allows any name from any namespace and can have a consequence only on name class definitions embedded in this one.

attribute

```
element attribute
{
(
attribute ns { text }?,
attribute datatypeLibrary { xsd:anyURI }?,
attribute * - (rng:* | local:*) { text }*
),
(
attribute name { xsd:QName }
| (
( element * - rng:* { ... }* )
& (
element name { ... }
| element anyName { ... }
| element nsName { ... }
| element choice { ... }
)
)
),
(
( element * - rng:* { ... }* )
& (
element element { ... }
| element attribute { ... }
| element group { ... }
| element interleave { ... }
| element choice { ... }
| element optional { ... }
| element zeroOrMore { ... }
| element oneOrMore { ... }
| element list { ... }
| element mixed { ... }
| element ref { ... }
| element parentRef { ... }
| element empty { ... }
| element text { ... }
| element value { ... }
| element data { ... }
| element notAllowed { ... }
| element externalRef { ... }
| element grammar { ... }
)?
)
}
```

Class

pattern

May be included in

attribute, choice, define, element, except, group, interleave, list, mixed, oneOrMore, optional, start, zeroOrMore

Compact syntax equivalent

attribute

Description

The attribute pattern matches an attribute. The name of the attribute may be defined by using either a name attribute or a name class.

Restrictions

- After simplification, attribute patterns can contain only patterns relevant for text nodes.
- Attributes can't be duplicated, either directly or by overlapping name classes.
- Attributes that have an infinite name class (anyName or nsName) must be enclosed in a oneOrMore or zeroOrMore pattern.

Example

```
<attribute name="id"/>

<attribute name="xml:lang">
  <data type="language"/>
 </attribute>
<attribute>
   <anyName/>
</attribute>
```

Attributes

datatypeLibrary
> This attribute defines the default datatype library. The value is inherited.

name
> When name is specified, the attribute pattern matches attributes with this name only. This can be a shortcut to define a single name as a name class for the attribute pattern).
>
> name and the definition of a name class can't both be specified (they are exclusive options).

ns This attribute defines the namespace of the attribute. Note that in the context of the attribute pattern, the ns attribute isn't inherited.

---

choice (in the context of a name-class)

Choice between name classes

```
element choice
{
  (
```

```
    attribute ns { text }?,
    attribute datatypeLibrary { xsd:anyURI }?,
    attribute * - (rng:* | local:*) { text }*
    ),
    (
    ( element * - rng:* { ... }* )
    & (
    element name { ... }
    | element anyName { ... }
    | element nsName { ... }
    | element choice { ... }
    )+
    )
    }
```

Class

name-class

May be included in

attribute, choice, element, except

Compact syntax equivalent

nameClass|nameClass

Description

The choice name class makes a choice between several name classes: a name matches choice if, and only if, it matches at least one of the subname classes.

Example

```
<element>
  <choice>
    <nsName ns="http://eric.van-der-vlist.com/ns/library"/>
    <nsName ns="http://eric.van-der-vlist.com/ns/person"/>
  </choice>
  <ref name="anything"/>
</element>
```

Attributes

datatypeLibrary
  This attribute defines the default datatype library. The value is inherited. Note that although datatypeLibrary is allowed in choice, just as it is in other RELAX NG elements, it has no direct effect on choice itself or on the name class definitions that might be embedded.

ns This attribute defines the default namespace for the elements defined in a portion of schema. The value is inherited.

choice (in the context of a pattern) choice pattern

```
element choice
{
(
attribute ns { text }?,
attribute datatypeLibrary { xsd:anyURI }?,
attribute * - (rng:* | local:*) { text }*
),
(
( element * - rng:* { ... }* )
& (
element element { ... }
| element attribute { ... }
| element group { ... }
| element interleave { ... }
| element choice { ... }
| element optional { ... }
| element zeroOrMore { ... }
| element oneOrMore { ... }
| element list { ... }
| element mixed { ... }
| element ref { ... }
| element parentRef { ... }
| element empty { ... }
| element text { ... }
| element value { ... }
| element data { ... }
| element notAllowed { ... }
| element externalRef { ... }
| element grammar { ... }
)+
)
}
```

Class

pattern

May be included in

attribute, choice, define, element, except, group, interleave, list, mixed, oneOrMore, optional, start, zeroOrMore

Compact syntax equivalent

pattern|pattern

Description

The choice pattern defines a choice between different patterns; it matches a node if, and only if, at least one of its subpatterns matches this node.

Example

```
<element name="name">
 <choice>
  <text/>
  <group>
   <element name="first"><text/></element>
   <optional>
     <element name="middle"><text/></element>
   </optional>
   <element name="last"><text/></element>
  </group>
 </choice>
</element>
<attribute name="available">
 <choice>
  <value>true</value>
  <value>false</value>
  <value>who knows?</value>
 </choice>
</attribute>
<start>
  <ref name="libraryElement"/>
  <ref name="bookElement"/>
</start>
```

Attributes

datatypeLibrary

This attribute defines the default datatype library. The value is inherited.

ns   This attribute defines the default namespace for the elements defined in a portion of a schema. The value is inherited.

data

```
element data
{
attribute type { xsd:NCName },
(
attribute ns { text }?,
attribute datatypeLibrary { xsd:anyURI }?,
attribute * - (rng:* | local:*) { text }*
),
(
( element * - rng:* { ... }* )
& ( element param { ... }*, element except { ... }? )
)
}
```

Class

pattern

May be included in

attribute, choice, define, element, except, group, interleave, list, mixed, oneOrMore, optional, start, zeroOrMore

Compact syntax equivalent

datatypeName param exceptPattern

Description

The data pattern matches a single text node (i.e., token, or attribute value) and gives the possibility of restricting its values. It is different from the text pattern, which matches zero or more text nodes and doesn't give any option for restricting the values of these text nodes. The restrictions are applied through the type attribute, which defines the datatype and the param and except child patterns.

Restrictions

The data pattern is meant for data-oriented applications and can't be used in mixed content models.

Example

```
<attribute name="see-also">
 <list>
  <data type="token"/>
 </list>
</attribute>

<attribute name="id">
 <data type="NMTOKEN">
   <param name="maxLength">16</param>
 </data>
</attribute>
<element name="isbn">
 <data type="token">
  <except>
   <value>0836217462</value>
  </except>
 </data>
</element>
```

Attributes

datatypeLibrary
  This attribute defines the default datatype library. The value is inherited.

ns This attribute defines the default namespace for the elements defined in a portion of a schema. The value is inherited.

type
  This attribute specifies the datatype used to evaluate the data pattern. Any text node whose value isn't valid according to this datatype fails to match the data pattern.

define

```
element define
{
 attribute name { xsd:NCName },
 ( attribute combine { "choice" | "interleave" }? ),
 (
 attribute ns { text }?,
 attribute datatypeLibrary { xsd:anyURI }?,
 attribute * - (rng:* | local:*) { text }*
 ),
 (
 ( element * - rng:* { ... }* )
 & (
 element element { ... }
 | element attribute { ... }
 | element group { ... }
 | element interleave { ... }
 | element choice { ... }
 | element optional { ... }
 | element zeroOrMore { ... }
 | element oneOrMore { ... }
 | element list { ... }
 | element mixed { ... }
 | element ref { ... }
 | element parentRef { ... }
 | element empty { ... }
 | element text { ... }
 | element value { ... }
 | element data { ... }
 | element notAllowed { ... }
 | element externalRef { ... }
 | element grammar { ... }
 )+
 )
}
```

Class

define-element

May be included in

div, grammar, include

Compact syntax equivalent

identifier assignMethod *pattern*

Description

When define is embedded in a grammar, it defines a named pattern or combines a new definition with an existing one. Named patterns are global to a grammar and can be referenced by ref in the scope of their grammar and by parentRef in the scope of the grammars directly embedded in their grammar.

When define is embedded in include, the new definition is a redefinition. It replaces the definitions from the included grammar, unless a combine attribute is specified, in which case, the definitions are combined.

Restrictions

Named patterns are always global and apply only to patterns. It isn't possible to define and make reference to nonpatterns such as class names or datatype parameters.

Example

```
<define name="born-element">
  <element name="born">
    <text/>
  </element>
</define>
<define name="book-content" combine="interleave">
  <attribute name="id"/>
  <attribute name="available"/>
  <ref name="isbn-element"/>
  <ref name="title-element"/>
  <zeroOrMore>
    <ref name="author-element"/>
  </zeroOrMore>
  <zeroOrMore>
    <ref name="character-element"/>
  </zeroOrMore>
</define>

<define name="isbn-element" combine="choice">
  <notAllowed/>
</define>
```

Attributes

combine
> This attribute specifies how multiple definitions of a named pattern should be combined. The possible values are choice and interleave.
>
> When the combine attribute is specified and set to choice, multiple definitions of a named pattern are combined in a choice pattern. When the combine attribute is specified and set to interleave, multiple definitions of a named pattern are combined in an interleave pattern.
>
> Note that it's forbidden to specify more than one define with the same name and no combine attribute or multiple defines with different values of the combine attribute.

datatypeLibrary
> This attribute defines the default datatype library. The value is inherited.

name
> This attribute specifies the name of the named pattern.

ns   This attribute defines the default namespace for the elements defined in a portion of a schema. The value is inherited.

---

div (in the context of a grammar-content)   Division (in the context of a <code>grammar</code>)

```
element div
{
(
attribute ns { text }?,
attribute datatypeLibrary { xsd:anyURI }?,
attribute * - (rng:* | local:*) { text }*
),
(
( element * - rng:* { ... }* )
& (
( element start { ... } )
| ( element define { ... } )
| element div { ... }
| element include { ... }
)*
)
}
```

Class

grammar-content

May be included in

div, grammar

Compact syntax equivalent

div

Description

The div element is provided to define logical divisions in RELAX NG schemas. It has no effect on validation. Its purpose is to define a group of definitions within a grammar that may be annotated as a whole.

In the context of a grammar, the content of a div element is the same as the content of a grammar. (div elements may be embedded in other div elements.)

Example

```
<grammar xmlns:xhtml="http://www.w3.org/1999/xhtml" xmlns="http://relaxng.org/ns/
structure/1.0">
  ...
  <div>
    <xhtml:p>The content of the book element has been split in two named patterns:
      </xhtml:p>
    <define name="book-start">
```

```
        <attribute name="id"/>
        <ref name="isbn-element"/>
        <ref name="title-element"/>
        <zeroOrMore>
          <ref name="author-element"/>
        </zeroOrMore>
      </define>
      <define name="book-end">
        <zeroOrMore>
          <ref name="author-element"/>
        </zeroOrMore>
        <zeroOrMore>
          <ref name="character-element"/>
        </zeroOrMore>
        <attribute name="available"/>
      </define>
    </div>
  ...
  </grammar>
```

Attributes

datatypeLibrary
  This attribute defines the default datatype library. The value is inherited.

ns This attribute defines the default namespace for the elements defined in a portion of
    schema. The value is inherited.

div (in the context of a include-content)   Division (in the context of an include)

```
element div
{
(
attribute ns { text }?,
attribute datatypeLibrary { xsd:anyURI }?,
attribute * - (rng:* | local:*) { text }*
),
(
( element * - rng:* { ... }* )
& (
( element start { ... } )
| ( element define { ... } )
| element div { ... }
)*
)
}
```

Class

include-content

May be included in

div, include

Compact syntax equivalent

div

Description

The div element is provided to define logical divisions in RELAX NG schemas. It has no effect on the validation. It defines a group of definitions within an include that may be annotated as a whole.

In the context of an include, the content of a div element is the same as the content of an include. (div elements may be embedded in other div elements.)

Example

```
<include href="common.rng">
...
<div>
<xhtml:p>The content of the book element has been split in two named patterns:
  </xhtml:p>
<define name="book-start">
  <attribute name="id"/>
  <ref name="isbn-element"/>
  <ref name="title-element"/>
  <zeroOrMore>
    <ref name="author-element"/>
  </zeroOrMore>
</define>
<define name="book-end">
  <zeroOrMore>
    <ref name="author-element"/>
  </zeroOrMore>
  <zeroOrMore>
    <ref name="character-element"/>
  </zeroOrMore>
  <attribute name="available"/>
</define>
</div>
...
</include>
```

Attributes

datatypeLibrary
>   This attribute defines the default datatype library. The value is inherited.

ns   This attribute defines the default namespace for the elements defined in a portion of schema. The value is inherited.

element

```
element element
{
(
attribute name { xsd:QName }
| (
( element * - rng:* { ... }* )
& (
element name { ... }
| element anyName { ... }
| element nsName { ... }
| element choice { ... }
)
)
),
(
attribute ns { text }?,
attribute datatypeLibrary { xsd:anyURI }?,
attribute * - (rng:* | local:*) { text }*
),
(
( element * - rng:* { ... }* )
& (
element element { ... }
| element attribute { ... }
| element group { ... }
| element interleave { ... }
| element choice { ... }
| element optional { ... }
| element zeroOrMore { ... }
| element oneOrMore { ... }
| element list { ... }
| element mixed { ... }
| element ref { ... }
| element parentRef { ... }
| element empty { ... }
| element text { ... }
| element value { ... }
| element data { ... }
| element notAllowed { ... }
| element externalRef { ... }
| element grammar { ... }
)+
)
}
```

Class

pattern

May be included in

attribute, choice, define, element, except, group, interleave, list, mixed, oneOrMore, optional, start, zeroOrMore

Compact syntax equivalent

element

Description

The element pattern matches an element. The name of the element may be defined either through a name attribute or through a name class.

Example

```
<element name="born">
 <text/>
</element>
<element name="character">
  <attribute name="id"/>
  <element name="name">
   <text/>
  </element>
  <element name="born">
   <text/>
  </element>
  <element name="qualification">
   <text/>
  </element>
</element>
<element>
  <anyName/>
  <ref name="anything"/>
</element>
```

Attributes

datatypeLibrary
:   This attribute defines the default datatype library. The value is inherited.

name
:   When name is specified, the element pattern matches only elements with this name. name is a shortcut to define a single name as a name class for the element pattern.

    name and the definition of a name class can't be specified together (they are exclusive options).

ns This attribute defines the default namespace for the elements defined in a portion of schema. The value is inherited.

empty

```
element empty
{
  (
  attribute ns { text }?,
  attribute datatypeLibrary { xsd:anyURI }?,
  attribute * - (rng:* | local:*) { text }*
  ),
  ( element * - rng:* { ... }* )
}
```

Class

pattern

May be included in

attribute, choice, define, element, except, group, interleave, list, mixed, oneOrMore, optional, start, zeroOrMore

Compact syntax equivalent

empty

Description

empty patterns define nodes that are empty—for example, elements that have no child elements, text, or attributes. Note that it is mandatory to use this pattern explicitly in such cases; the simpler-looking form <element name="foo"/> is forbidden. There is no such thing as an empty attribute. An attribute such as foo="" is considered to have a value that is the empty string rather than considered empty—i.e., having no value. Therefore, empty applies only to elements.

Example

```
<element name="pageBreak">
  <empty/>
</element>
```

Attributes

datatypeLibrary
    This attribute defines the default datatype library. The value is inherited.

ns   This attribute defines the default namespace for the elements defined in a portion of schema. The value is inherited.

except (in the context of a except-name-class)

```
element except
{
  (
```

```
( element * - rng:* { ... }* )
& (
element name { ... }
| element anyName { ... }
| element nsName { ... }
| element choice { ... }
)+
)
}
```

Class

except-name-class

May be included in

anyName, nsName

Compact syntax equivalent

-nameClass

Description

The except name class can remove a name class from another. Note that this name class has no attributes.

Restrictions

It's impossible to use except to produce empty name classes by including anyName in an except name class or nsName in an except name class included in another nsName.

Example

```
<element>
  <anyName>
    <except>
      <nsName ns=""/>
      <nsName ns="http://eric.van-der-vlist.com/ns/library"/>
      <nsName ns="http://eric.van-der-vlist.com/ns/person"/>
    </except>
  </anyName>
  <ref name="anything"/>
</element>
<element>
  <nsName ns=ns="http://eric.van-der-vlist.com/ns/person"/>
    <except>
      <name>lib:name</name>
      <name>hr:name</name>
    <except>
  </nsName>
  <ref name="anything"/>
</element>
```

Attributes

None

---

except (in the context of a pattern)   Remove a set of values from a data

```
element except
{
(
attribute ns { text }?,
attribute datatypeLibrary { xsd:anyURI }?,
attribute * - (rng:* | local:*) { text }*
),
(
( element * - rng:* { ... }* )
& (
element element { ... }
| element attribute { ... }
| element group { ... }
| element interleave { ... }
| element choice { ... }
| element optional { ... }
| element zeroOrMore { ... }
| element oneOrMore { ... }
| element list { ... }
| element mixed { ... }
| element ref { ... }
| element parentRef { ... }
| element empty { ... }
| element text { ... }
| element value { ... }
| element data { ... }
| element notAllowed { ... }
| element externalRef { ... }
| element grammar { ... }
)+
)
}
```

Class

pattern

May be included in

data

Compact syntax equivalent

-pattern

Description

The except pattern is used to remove a set of values from a data pattern.

Restrictions

The except pattern can be used only in the context of data and can contain only data, value, and choice elements.

Example

```
<element name="isbn">
  <data type="token">
<except>
 <value>0836217462</value>
</except>
</data>
</element>
<attribute name="available">
<data type="token">
<except>
 <choice>
  <value type="string">true</value>
  <value type="string">false</value>
 </choice>
</except>
</data>
</attribute>
```

Attributes

datatypeLibrary
    This attribute defines the default datatype library. The value is inherited.

ns This attribute defines the default namespace for the elements defined in a portion of schema. The value is inherited.

---

externalRef

Reference to an external schema

```
element externalRef
{
 attribute href { xsd:anyURI },
 (
 attribute ns { text }?,
 attribute datatypeLibrary { xsd:anyURI }?,
 attribute * - (rng:* | local:*) { text }*
 ),
 ( element * - rng:* { ... }* )
}
```

Class

pattern

May be included in

attribute, choice, define, element, except, group, interleave, list, mixed, oneOrMore, optional, start, zeroOrMore

Compact syntax equivalent

external

Description

The externalRef pattern is a reference to an external schema. It has the same effect as replacing the externalRef pattern with the external schema, which is treated as a pattern.

Example

```
<element name="book">
  <externalRef href="book.rng"/>
</element>

<element xmlns="http://relaxng.org/ns/structure/1.0" name="university">
 <element name="name">
  <text/>
 </element>
 <externalRef href="flat.rng"/>
</element>
```

Attributes

datatypeLibrary
> This attribute defines the default datatype library. The value is inherited.

href
> This attribute defines the location of the external schema.

ns   This attribute defines the default namespace for the elements defined in a portion of a schema. The value is inherited.

---

grammar

Grammar pattern

```
element grammar
{
(
attribute ns { text }?,
attribute datatypeLibrary { xsd:anyURI }?,
attribute * - (rng:* | local:*) { text }*
),
(
( element * - rng:* { ... }* )
& (
( element start { ... } )
| ( element define { ... } )
| element div { ... }
| element include { ... }
```

```
  )*
  )
}
```

Class

pattern

May be included in

attribute, choice, define, element, except, group, interleave, list, mixed, oneOrMore, optional, start, zeroOrMore

Compact syntax equivalent

grammar

Description

The grammar pattern encapsulates the definitions of start and named patterns. The most common use of grammar is to validate XML documents. In these cases, the start pattern specifies which elements can be used as the document root element. The grammar pattern may also be used to write modular schemas. In this case, the start pattern specifies which nodes must be matched by the grammar wherever it appears in the schema.

In every case, the named patterns defined in a grammar are considered local to this grammar.

Example

```
<grammar xmlns="http://relaxng.org/ns/structure/1.0">
 <start>
  <element name="library">
   <oneOrMore>
    <ref name="book-element"/>
   </oneOrMore>
  </element>
 </start>
 <define name="author-element">
  ...
 </define>
</grammar>
 <define name="author-element">
   <grammar>
     <start>
       <element name="author">
         <attribute name="id"/>
         <ref name="name-element"/>
         <parentRef name="born-element"/>
         <optional>
           <ref name="died-element"/>
         </optional>
       </element>
     </start>
     <define name="name-element">
       <element name="name">
```

```
        <text/>
      </element>
    </define>
    <define name="died-element">
      <element name="died">
        <text/>
      </element>
    </define>
  </grammar>
</define>
<element xmlns="http://relaxng.org/ns/structure/1.0" name="university">
 <element name="name">
   <text/>
 </element>
 <grammar>
   <include href="flat.rng"/>
 </grammar>
</element>
```

Attributes

datatypeLibrary
> This attribute defines the default datatype library. The value is inherited.

ns This attribute defines the default namespace for the elements defined in a portion of a
    schema. The value is inherited.

group

```
element group
{
(
attribute ns { text }?,
attribute datatypeLibrary { xsd:anyURI }?,
attribute * - (rng:* | local:*) { text }*
),
(
( element * - rng:* { ... }* )
& (
element element { ... }
| element attribute { ... }
| element group { ... }
| element interleave { ... }
| element choice { ... }
| element optional { ... }
| element zeroOrMore { ... }
| element oneOrMore { ... }
| element list { ... }
| element mixed { ... }
| element ref { ... }
| element parentRef { ... }
| element empty { ... }
| element text { ... }
```

```
   | element value { ... }
   | element data { ... }
   | element notAllowed { ... }
   | element externalRef { ... }
   | element grammar { ... }
  )+
  )
}
```

Class

pattern

May be included in

attribute, choice, define, element, except, group, interleave, list, mixed, oneOrMore, optional, start, zeroOrMore

Compact syntax equivalent

pattern, pattern

Description

The group pattern defines an ordered group of subpatterns. Note that when attribute patterns are included in such a group, their order isn't enforced. group patterns are implicit with element and define patterns.

Example

```
<element name="name">
  <choice>
   <text/>
   <group>
    <element name="first"><text/></element>
     <optional>
       <element name="middle"><text/></element>
     </optional>
     <element name="last"><text/></element>
    </group>
  </choice>
 </element>
<element name="foo">
  <interleave>
   <element name="out"><empty/></element>
   <group>
    <element name="in1"><empty/></element>
    <element name="in2"><empty/></element>
   </group>
  </interleave>
 </element>
```

Attributes

datatypeLibrary
> This attribute defines the default datatype library. The value is inherited.

ns   This attribute defines the default namespace for the elements defined in a portion of schema. The value is inherited.

---

include   Grammar merge

```
element include
{
 attribute href { xsd:anyURI },
 (
 attribute ns { text }?,
 attribute datatypeLibrary { xsd:anyURI }?,
 attribute * - (rng:* | local:*) { text }*
 ),
 (
 ( element * - rng:* { ... }* )
 & (
 ( element start { ... } )
 | ( element define { ... } )
 | element div { ... }
 )*
 )
}
```

Class

grammar-content

May be included in

div, grammar

Compact syntax equivalent

include

Description

The include pattern includes a grammar and merges its definitions with the definitions of the current grammar. The definitions of the included grammar may be redefined and over-ridden by the definitions embedded in the include pattern. Note that a schema must contain an explicit grammar definition in order to be included.

Example

```
<grammar xmlns="http://relaxng.org/ns/structure/1.0">
 <start>
  <element name="library">
   <oneOrMore>
    <ref name="book-element"/>
```

```
    </oneOrMore>
   </element>
  </start>
  <include href="included.rng"/>
    ...
 </grammar>
 <grammar xmlns="http://relaxng.org/ns/structure/1.0">
  <include href="flat.rng">
    <define name="book-element">
      <element name="book">
        <attribute name="id"/>
        <attribute name="available"/>
        <ref name="isbn-element"/>
        <ref name="title-element"/>
        <ref name="description-element"/>
        <zeroOrMore>
          <ref name="author-element"/>
        </zeroOrMore>
      </element>
    </define>
  </include>
  <define name="description-element">
    <element name="description">
      <text/>
    </element>
  </define>
 </grammar>
```

Attributes

datatypeLibrary

    This attribute defines the default datatype library. The value is inherited.

href

    This attribute defines the location of the schema and specifies the grammar to be included.

ns   This attribute defines the default namespace for the elements defined in a portion of schema. The value is inherited.

---

interleave

```
element interleave
{
(
attribute ns { text }?,
attribute datatypeLibrary { xsd:anyURI }?,
attribute * - (rng:* | local:*) { text }*
),
(
( element * - rng:* { ... }* )
& (
element element { ... }
```

```
   | element attribute { ... }
   | element group { ... }
   | element interleave { ... }
   | element choice { ... }
   | element optional { ... }
   | element zeroOrMore { ... }
   | element oneOrMore { ... }
   | element list { ... }
   | element mixed { ... }
   | element ref { ... }
   | element parentRef { ... }
   | element empty { ... }
   | element text { ... }
   | element value { ... }
   | element data { ... }
   | element notAllowed { ... }
   | element externalRef { ... }
   | element grammar { ... }
   )+
   )
 }
```

Class

pattern

May be included in

attribute, choice, define, element, except, group, interleave, list, mixed, oneOrMore, optional, start, zeroOrMore

Compact syntax equivalent

pattern&pattern

Description

The interleave pattern "interleaves" subpatterns; it allows their leaves to be mixed in any order.

interleave does more than define unordered groups, as you can see in the following example. Consider element a and the ordered group of element b1 and b2. An unordered group of these two patterns allows only element a followed by elements b1 and b2 or elements b1 and b2 followed by element a. An interleave of these two patterns allows these two combinations, but also element b1 followed by a followed by b2. It allows any combination in which the element a has been interleaved between elements b1 and b2.

The interleave behavior is applied to attribute patterns even when they are embedded in (ordered) group patterns (the reason for this is that XML 1.0 specifies the relative order of attributes isn't significant).

Another case in which interleave patterns are often needed is to describe mixed content models in which text is interleaved between elements. A shortcut (the mixed pattern) has been defined for this case.

Restrictions

- The `interleave` pattern can't be used within a `list`.
- Elements within a `interleave` pattern can't have overlapping name classes.
- There can be at most one text pattern in each set of patterns combined by `interleave`.

Example

```
<element name="character">
  <interleave>
   <attribute name="id"/>
   <element name="name">
    <text/>
   </element>
   <element name="born">
    <text/>
   </element>
   <element name="qualification">
    <text/>
   </element>
  </interleave>
</element>
<element name="title">
 <interleave>
  <attribute name="xml:lang"/>
  <zeroOrMore>
   <element name="a">
    <attribute name="href"/>
     <text/>
   </element>
  </zeroOrMore>
  <text/>
 </interleave>
</element>
```

Attributes

datatypeLibrary
  This attribute defines the default datatype library. The value is inherited.

ns   This attribute defines the default namespace for the elements defined in a portion of schema. The value is inherited.

---

list   Text node split

```
element list
{
(
attribute ns { text }?,
attribute datatypeLibrary { xsd:anyURI }?,
attribute * - (rng:* | local:*) { text }*
),
(
```

```
      ( element * - rng:* { ... }* )
      & (
      element element { ... }
      | element attribute { ... }
      | element group { ... }
      | element interleave { ... }
      | element choice { ... }
      | element optional { ... }
      | element zeroOrMore { ... }
      | element oneOrMore { ... }
      | element list { ... }
      | element mixed { ... }
      | element ref { ... }
      | element parentRef { ... }
      | element empty { ... }
      | element text { ... }
      | element value { ... }
      | element data { ... }
      | element notAllowed { ... }
      | element externalRef { ... }
      | element grammar { ... }
      )+
      )
      }
```

Class

pattern

May be included in

attribute, choice, define, element, except, group, interleave, list, mixed, oneOrMore, optional, start, zeroOrMore

Compact syntax equivalent

list

Description

The list pattern splits a text node into tokens separated by whitespace. The splitting allows the validation of these tokens separately. This practice is most useful for validating lists of values.

Restrictions

- interleave can't be used within list.
- The content of a list is only about data: it's forbidden to define element, attribute, or text there.
- It's forbidden to embed list into list.

Example

```
<attribute name="see-also">
 <list>
  <zeroOrMore>
   <data type="token"/>
  </zeroOrMore>
 </list>
</attribute>
<attribute name="dimensions">
 <list>
  <data type="xs:decimal"/>
  <data type="xs:decimal"/>
  <data type="xs:decimal"/>
  <choice>
   <value>inches</value>
   <value>cm</value>
   <value>mm</value>
  </choice>
 </list>
</attribute>
```

Attributes

datatypeLibrary

This attribute defines the default datatype library. The value is inherited.

ns   This attribute defines the default namespace for the elements defined in a portion of schema. The value is inherited.

---

mixed   Pattern for mixed content models

```
element mixed
{
(
attribute ns { text }?,
attribute datatypeLibrary { xsd:anyURI }?,
attribute * - (rng:* | local:*) { text }*
),
(
( element * - rng:* { ... }* )
& (
element element { ... }
| element attribute { ... }
| element group { ... }
| element interleave { ... }
| element choice { ... }
| element optional { ... }
| element zeroOrMore { ... }
| element oneOrMore { ... }
| element list { ... }
| element mixed { ... }
| element ref { ... }
```

mixed

```
  | element parentRef { ... }
  | element empty { ... }
  | element text { ... }
  | element value { ... }
  | element data { ... }
  | element notAllowed { ... }
  | element externalRef { ... }
  | element grammar { ... }
  )+
  )
}
```

Class

pattern

May be included in

attribute, choice, define, element, except, group, interleave, list, mixed, oneOrMore, optional, start, zeroOrMore

Compact syntax equivalent

mixed

Description

The mixed pattern is a shortcut for interleave with an embedded text pattern. It describes unordered content models in which a text node may be included before and after each element. Note that RELAX NG doesn't allow the addition of constraints on these text nodes.

Restrictions

The limitations of interleave apply here:

- The mixed pattern can't be used within a list.
- Elements within a mixed pattern can't have overlapping name classes.
- There must no other text pattern in each set of patterns combined by mixed.

Example

```
<element name="title">
 <mixed>
  <attribute name="xml:lang"/>
  <zeroOrMore>
   <element name="a">
    <attribute name="href"/>
    <text/>
   </element>
  </zeroOrMore>
 </mixed>
</element>
```

This is equivalent to:

```
<element name="title">
 <interleave>
  <text/>
  <group>
    <attribute name="xml:lang"/>
    <zeroOrMore>
     <element name="a">
      <attribute name="href"/>
      <text/>
     </element>
    </zeroOrMore>
  </group>
 </interleave>
</element>
```

which itself is equivalent to:

```
<element name="title">
 <interleave>
  <text/>
  <attribute name="xml:lang"/>
  <zeroOrMore>
   <element name="a">
    <attribute name="href"/>
    <text/>
   </element>
  </zeroOrMore>
 </interleave>
</element>
```

Attributes

datatypeLibrary
>   This attribute defines the default datatype library. The value is inherited.

ns   This attribute defines the default namespace for the elements defined in a portion of a schema. The value is inherited.

---

name

```
element name
{
(
attribute ns { text }?,
attribute datatypeLibrary { xsd:anyURI }?,
attribute * - (rng:* | local:*) { text }*
),
xsd:QName
}
```

Class

name-class

May be included in

attribute, choice, element, except

Compact syntax equivalent

name

Description

The name name class defines a class with a single name.

Example

```
<element>
  <nsName ns="http://eric.van-der-vlist.com/ns/person"/>
    <except>
      <name>name</name>
    <except>
  </nsName>
  <ref name="anything"/>
</element>
<element>
  <choice>
    <name>lib:name</name>
    <name>hr:name</name>
  </choice>
 <ref name="name-content"/>
</element>
```

Attributes

datatypeLibrary
> This attribute defines the default datatype library. The value is inherited.

ns   This attribute defines the default namespace for the elements defined in a portion of schema. The value is inherited.

notAllowed

Not allowed

```
element notAllowed
{
 (
 attribute ns { text }?,
 attribute datatypeLibrary { xsd:anyURI }?,
 attribute * - (rng:* | local:*) { text }*
 ),
 ( element * - rng:* { ... }* )
}
```

Class

pattern

May be included in

attribute, choice, define, element, except, group, interleave, list, mixed, oneOrMore, optional, start, zeroOrMore

Compact syntax equivalent

notAllowed

Description

The notAllowed pattern always fails. It can provide abstract definitions that must be over-ridden before they can be used in a schema.

Example

```
<define name="isbn-element" combine="choice">
  <notAllowed/>
</define>
```

Attributes

datatypeLibrary
>   This attribute defines the default datatype library. The value is inherited.

ns   This attribute defines the default namespace for the elements defined in a portion of schema. The value is inherited.

---

nsName   Name class for any name in a namespace

```
element nsName
{
(
attribute ns { text }?,
attribute datatypeLibrary { xsd:anyURI }?,
attribute * - (rng:* | local:*) { text }*
),
( ( element * - rng:* { ... }* ) & element except { ... }? )
}
```

Class

name-class

May be included in

attribute, choice, element, except

Compact syntax equivalent

nsName exceptNameClass

Description

The nsName name class allows any name in a specific namespace.

Restrictions

Within the scope of an element, the name classes of attributes can't overlap. The same restriction applies to name classes of elements when these elements are combined by interleave. It is impossible to use nsName to produce empty name classes by including nsName in an except name class included in another nsName.

Example

```
<element>
  <choice>
    <nsName ns="http://eric.van-der-vlist.com/ns/library"/>
    <nsName ns="http://eric.van-der-vlist.com/ns/person"/>
  </choice>
  <ref name="anything"/>
</element>
<element>
  <nsName ns="http://eric.van-der-vlist.com/ns/person"/>
    <except>
      <name>name</name>
    <except>
  </nsName>
 <ref name="anything"/>
</element>
```

Attributes

datatypeLibrary
> The datatypeLibrary attribute defines the default datatype library. The value of datatypeLibrary is inherited.

ns
> The ns attribute defines the default namespace for the elements defined in a portion of a schema. The value of ns is inherited.

---

oneOrMore oneOrMore pattern

```
element oneOrMore
{
(
attribute ns { text }?,
attribute datatypeLibrary { xsd:anyURI }?,
attribute * - (rng:* | local:*) { text }*
),
(
( element * - rng:* { ... }* )
& (
element element { ... }
| element attribute { ... }
| element group { ... }
```

```
  | element interleave { ... }
  | element choice { ... }
  | element optional { ... }
  | element zeroOrMore { ... }
  | element oneOrMore { ... }
  | element list { ... }
  | element mixed { ... }
  | element ref { ... }
  | element parentRef { ... }
  | element empty { ... }
  | element text { ... }
  | element value { ... }
  | element data { ... }
  | element notAllowed { ... }
  | element externalRef { ... }
  | element grammar { ... }
  )+
  )
}
```

Class

pattern

May be included in

attribute, choice, define, element, except, group, interleave, list, mixed, oneOrMore, optional, start, zeroOrMore

Compact syntax equivalent

pattern+

Description

The oneOrMore pattern specifies that its subpatterns considered as an ordered group must be matched one or more times.

Restrictions

The oneOrMore pattern can't contain attribute definitions.

Example

```
<element name="library">
 <oneOrMore>
  <element name="book">
  ...
  </element>
 </oneOrMore>
</element>
```

Attributes

datatypeLibrary
> This attribute defines the default datatype library. The value is inherited.

ns This attribute defines the default namespace for the elements defined in a portion of
> schema. The value is inherited.

---

optional

```
element optional
{
(
attribute ns { text }?,
attribute datatypeLibrary { xsd:anyURI }?,
attribute * - (rng:* | local:*) { text }*
),
(
( element * - rng:* { ... }* )
& (
element element { ... }
| element attribute { ... }
| element group { ... }
| element interleave { ... }
| element choice { ... }
| element optional { ... }
| element zeroOrMore { ... }
| element oneOrMore { ... }
| element list { ... }
| element mixed { ... }
| element ref { ... }
| element parentRef { ... }
| element empty { ... }
| element text { ... }
| element value { ... }
| element data { ... }
| element notAllowed { ... }
| element externalRef { ... }
| element grammar { ... }
)+
)
}
```

Class

pattern

May be included in

attribute, choice, define, element, except, group, interleave, list, mixed, oneOrMore,
optional, start, zeroOrMore

Compact syntax equivalent

pattern?

Description

The optional pattern specifies that its subpatterns considered as an ordered group is optional, i.e., be matched zero or one times.

Example

```
<element name="author">
 <attribute name="id"/>
 <element name="name">
   <text/>
 </element>
 <element name="born">
   <text/>
   </element>
 <optional>
   <element name="died">
     <text/>
   </element>
  </optional>
 </element>

<element name="name">
 <choice>
  <text/>
  <group>
  <element name="first"><text/></element>
  <optional>
   <element name="middle"><text/></element>
  </optional>
   <element name="last"><text/></element>
  </group>
  </choice>
 </element>
```

Attributes

datatypeLibrary
> This attribute defines the default datatype library. The value is inherited.

ns This attribute defines the default namespace for the elements defined in a portion of schema. The value is inherited.

---

param

```
element param
{
 attribute name { xsd:NCName },
 (
```

```
        attribute ns { text }?,
        attribute datatypeLibrary { xsd:anyURI }?,
        attribute * - (rng:* | local:*) { text }*
        ),
        text
    }
```

Class

parameter

May be included in

data

Compact syntax equivalent

param

Description

The param element specifies parameters passed to the datatype library to determine whether a value is valid per a datatype. When the datatype library is the W3C XML Schema datatype, these parameters are the facets of the datatype and define additional restrictions to be applied. The name of the parameter is defined by the name attribute, and its value is the content of the param element.

Example

```
    <element name="book">
     <attribute name="id">
      <data type="NMTOKEN">
        <param name="maxLength">16</param>
      </data>
     </attribute>
     <attribute name="available">
      <data type="boolean"/>
     </attribute>
     <element name="isbn">
      <data type="NMTOKEN">
        <param name="pattern">[0-9]{9}[0-9x]</param>
      </data>
     </element>
     <element name="title">
      <attribute name="xml:lang">
       <data type="language">
        <param name="length">2</param>
       </data>
      </attribute>
      <data type="token">
        <param name="maxLength">255</param>
      </data>
     </element>
```

Attributes

datatypeLibrary
> This attribute defines the default datatype library. The value is inherited.

name
> This attribute specifies the name of the parameter.

ns This attribute defines the default namespace for the elements defined in a portion of schema. The value is inherited.

---

parentRef

Reference to a named pattern from the parent grammar

```
element parentRef
{
 attribute name { xsd:NCName },
 (
 attribute ns { text }?,
 attribute datatypeLibrary { xsd:anyURI }?,
 attribute * - (rng:* | local:*) { text }*
 ),
 ( element * - rng:* { ... }* )
}
```

Class

pattern

May be included in

attribute, choice, define, element, except, group, interleave, list, mixed, oneOrMore, optional, start, zeroOrMore

Compact syntax equivalent

parent

Description

The parentRef pattern is a reference to a named pattern belonging to the parent grammar—in other words, the grammar in which the current grammar is included. The scope of a named pattern is usually limited to the grammar in which they are defined. The parentRef pattern provides a way to extend this scope and refer to a named pattern defined in the parent grammar.

Example

```
<define name="born-element">
  <element name="born">
    <text/>
  </element>
</define>
<define name="author-element">
  <grammar>
```

```
    <start>
      <element name="author">
        <attribute name="id"/>
        <ref name="name-element"/>
        <parentRef name="born-element"/>
        <optional>
          <ref name="died-element"/>
        </optional>
      </element>
    </start>
    <define name="name-element">
      <element name="name">
        <text/>
      </element>
    </define>
    <define name="died-element">
      <element name="died">
        <text/>
      </element>
    </define>
  </grammar>
</define>
```

Attributes

datatypeLibrary
> This attribute defines the default datatype library. The value is inherited.

name
> This attribute specifies the name of the named pattern that is referenced.

ns   This attribute defines the default namespace for the elements defined in a portion of schema. The value is inherited.

---

ref

```
element ref
{
 attribute name { xsd:NCName },
 (
 attribute ns { text }?,
 attribute datatypeLibrary { xsd:anyURI }?,
 attribute * - (rng:* | local:*) { text }*
 ),
 ( element * - rng:* { ... }* )
}
```

Class

pattern

May be included in

attribute, choice, define, element, except, group, interleave, list, mixed, oneOrMore, optional, start, zeroOrMore

Compact syntax equivalent

Name without a colon

Description

The ref pattern defines a reference to a named pattern defined in the current grammar.

Example

```
<element name="book">
 <ref name="book-start"/>
 <ref name="book-end"/>
</element>

  <element name="library">
   <oneOrMore>
    <ref name="book-element"/>
   </oneOrMore>
  </element>
```

Attributes

datatypeLibrary
> This attribute defines the default datatype library. The value is inherited.

name
> This attribute specifies the name of the named pattern that is referenced.

ns   This attribute defines the default namespace for the elements defined in a portion of schema. The value is inherited.

---

start
Start of a grammar

```
element start
{
( attribute combine { "choice" | "interleave" }? ),
(
attribute ns { text }?,
attribute datatypeLibrary { xsd:anyURI }?,
attribute * - (rng:* | local:*) { text }*
),
(
( element * - rng:* { ... }* )
& (
element element { ... }
| element attribute { ... }
| element group { ... }
| element interleave { ... }
```

```
          | element choice { ... }
          | element optional { ... }
          | element zeroOrMore { ... }
          | element oneOrMore { ... }
          | element list { ... }
          | element mixed { ... }
          | element ref { ... }
          | element parentRef { ... }
          | element empty { ... }
          | element text { ... }
          | element value { ... }
          | element data { ... }
          | element notAllowed { ... }
          | element externalRef { ... }
          | element grammar { ... }
          )
        )
      }
```

Class

start-element

May be included in

div, grammar, include

Compact syntax equivalent

start

Description

The start pattern defines the "start" of a grammar. When this grammar is used to validate a complete document, the start pattern specifies which elements can be used as the document (root) element. When this grammar is embedded in another grammar, the start pattern specifies which pattern should be applied at the location where the grammar is embedded. Like named pattern definitions, start patterns may be combined by choice or interleave and redefined when they are included in include patterns.

Example

```
<start>
 <element name="library">
  <oneOrMore>
   <ref name="book-element"/>
  </oneOrMore>
 </element>
</start>
<start combine="choice">
  <ref name="book-element"/>
</start>
<define name="author-element">
  <grammar>
```

```
<start>
  <element name="author">
    <attribute name="id"/>
    <ref name="name-element"/>
    <ref name="born-element"/>
    <optional>
      <ref name="died-element"/>
    </optional>
  </element>
</start>
<define name="name-element">
  <element name="name">
    <text/>
  </element>
</define>
<define name="born-element">
  <element name="born">
    <text/>
  </element>
</define>
<define name="died-element">
  <element name="died">
    <text/>
  </element>
</define>
</grammar>
</define>
```

Attributes

combine

> This attribute specifies how multiple definitions of start pattern should be combined. The possible values are choice and interleave.
>
> When the combine attribute is specified and set to choice, multiple definitions of a start pattern are combined in a choice pattern. When the combine attribute is specified and set to interleave, multiple definitions of a start pattern are combined in an interleave pattern.
>
> Note that it is forbidden to specify more than one start with the same name and no combine attribute or multiple start with different values of combine attribute.

datatypeLibrary

> This attribute defines the default datatype library. The value is inherited.

ns   This attribute defines the default namespace for the elements defined in a portion of schema. The value is inherited.

---

text   Pattern-matching text nodes

```
element text
{
  (
  attribute ns { text }?,
```

```
    attribute datatypeLibrary { xsd:anyURI }?,
    attribute * - (rng:* | local:*) { text }*
    ),
    ( element * - rng:* { ... }* )
    }
```

Class

pattern

May be included in

attribute, choice, define, element, except, group, interleave, list, mixed, oneOrMore, optional, start, zeroOrMore

Compact syntax equivalent

text

Description

The text pattern matches zero or more text nodes. A match of more than one text node has no effect when it is used in ordered content models (the data model used by RELAX NG for XML documents is similar to the data model of XPath 1.0, and two text nodes can't be adjacent) but makes a difference when a text pattern is used in interleave. Adding a single text pattern in an interleave pattern has the effect of allowing any number of text nodes, which can interleave before and after each element (note that the mixed pattern is provided as a shortcut to define these content models).

Restrictions

No more than one text pattern can be included in an interleave pattern.

Example

```
<element name="first"><text/></element>
<element name="name">
 <choice>
  <text/>
  <group>
  <element name="first"><text/></element>
  <optional>
    <element name="middle"><text/></element>
  </optional>
  <element name="last"><text/></element>
  </group>
 </choice>
</element>
```

Attributes

datatypeLibrary
    This attribute defines the default datatype library. The value is inherited.

ns This attribute defines the default namespace for the elements defined in a portion of schema. The value is inherited.

value

```
element value
{
 attribute type { xsd:NCName }?,
 (
 attribute ns { text }?,
 attribute datatypeLibrary { xsd:anyURI }?,
 attribute * - (rng:* | local:*) { text }*
 ),
 text
}
```

Class

pattern

May be included in

attribute, choice, define, element, except, group, interleave, list, mixed, oneOrMore, optional, start, zeroOrMore

Compact syntax equivalent

datatypeName literal

Description

The value pattern matches a text node against a value using the semantic of a specified datatype to perform the comparison.

Restrictions

The value pattern is meant for data-oriented applications and can't be used in mixed-content models.

Example

```
<attribute name="see-also">
 <list>
  <oneOrMore>
   <choice>
    <value>0836217462</value>
    <value>0345442695</value>
    <value>0449220230</value>
    <value>0449214044</value>
    <value>0061075647</value>
   </choice>
  </oneOrMore>
 </list>
```

```
 </attribute>
 <attribute name="available">
  <data type="boolean">
   <except>
    <value>0</value>
    <value>1</value>
   </except>
  </data>
 </attribute>
 <attribute name="available">
  <data type="boolean">
   <except>
    <value type="boolean">false</value>
   </except>
  </data>
 </attribute>
```

Attributes

datatypeLibrary

This attribute defines the default datatype library. The value is inherited.

ns   This attribute defines the default namespace for the elements defined in a portion of a schema. The value is inherited.

type

This attribute specifies which datatype to use to perform the comparison. Note that this isn't an inherited attribute. When it isn't specified, the comparison is done using the default datatype, the token datatype of RELAX NG's built-in type library. Because of this, a string comparison is done on the values after space normalization.

zeroOrMore

zeroOrMore **pattern**

```
element zeroOrMore
{
 (
 attribute ns { text }?,
 attribute datatypeLibrary { xsd:anyURI }?,
 attribute * - (rng:* | local:*) { text }*
 ),
 (
 ( element * - rng:* { ... }* )
 & (
 element element { ... }
 | element attribute { ... }
 | element group { ... }
 | element interleave { ... }
 | element choice { ... }
 | element optional { ... }
 | element zeroOrMore { ... }
 | element oneOrMore { ... }
 | element list { ... }
 | element mixed { ... }
```

```
  | element ref { ... }
  | element parentRef { ... }
  | element empty { ... }
  | element text { ... }
  | element value { ... }
  | element data { ... }
  | element notAllowed { ... }
  | element externalRef { ... }
  | element grammar { ... }
  )+
 )
}
```

Class

pattern

May be included in

attribute, choice, define, element, except, group, interleave, list, mixed, oneOrMore, optional, start, zeroOrMore

Compact syntax equivalent

pattern*

Description

The zeroOrMore pattern specifies that its subpatterns are considered an ordered group that must be matched zero or more times.

Restrictions

The zeroOrMore pattern can't contain attribute definitions.

Example

```
<define name="book-element">
 <element name="book">
  <attribute name="id"/>
  <attribute name="available"/>
  <ref name="isbn-element"/>
  <ref name="title-element"/>
  <zeroOrMore>
   <ref name="author-element"/>
  </zeroOrMore>
  <zeroOrMore>
   <ref name="character-element"/>
  </zeroOrMore>
 </element>
</define>
```

Attributes

datatypeLibrary
    This attribute defines the default datatype library. The value is inherited.

ns This attribute defines the default namespace for the elements defined in a portion of schema. The value is inherited.

CHAPTER 18

Compact Syntax Reference

This reference follows the formal description of the compact syntax described as an EBNF (Extended Backus-Naur Form, a syntax that doesn't include annotation syntax) grammar. Each definition of the EBNF grammar is documented. When a definition includes a long list of alternatives (as is the case for `pattern`, `nameClass`, and `literalSegment`), each alternative is documented separately. The grammar from the specification has been slightly simplified to suppress definitions that were used only once; nevertheless, the meaning has been kept unchanged.

Here is the full EBNF grammar that's used as the basis for this reference:

```
topLevel                ::=
decl* (
pattern|
grammarContent*)
decl                    ::= "namespace"
identifierOrKeyword     "="
namespaceURILiteral

                        |"default" "namespace" [
identifierOrKeyword]    "="
namespaceURILiteral

                        |"datatypes"
identifierOrKeyword     "="
literal
pattern                 ::= "element"
nameClass "{"
pattern "}"

                        |"attribute"
nameClass "{"
pattern "}"

                        |
pattern (","
pattern)+

                        |
pattern ("&"
pattern)+

                        |
pattern ("|"
```

```
pattern)+
                        |
pattern "?"
                        |
pattern "*"
                        |
pattern "+"
                        |"list" "{"
pattern "}"
                        |"mixed" "{"
pattern "}"
                        |
identifier
                        |"parent"
identifier
                        |"empty"
                        |"text"
                        |[
datatypeName]
literal
                        |
datatypeName ["{"
param* "}"] [
exceptPattern]
                        |"notAllowed"
                        |"external"
literal [
inherit]
                        |"grammar" "{"
grammarContent* "}"
                        |"("
pattern ")"
param              ::=
identifierOrKeyword "="
literal
exceptPattern      ::= "-"
pattern
grammarContent     ::=
start
                        |
define
                        |"div" "{"
grammarContent* "}"
                        |"include"
literal [
inherit] ["{"
includeContent* "}"]
includeContent     ::=
define
                        |
start
                        |"div" "{"
includeContent* "}"
start              ::= "start"
```

```
assignMethod
pattern
define              ::=
identifier
assignMethod
pattern
assignMethod        ::= "="
                        |"|="
                        |"&="
nameClass           ::=
name

                        |

NCName ":*" [
exceptNameClass]
                        |"*" [

exceptNameClass]

                        |

nameClass "|"
nameClass
                        |"("

nameClass ")"
name                ::=
identifierOrKeyword

                        |

CName
exceptNameClass     ::= "-"
nameClass
datatypeName        ::=
CName
                        |"string"
                        |"token"
namespaceURILiteral ::=
literal
                        |"inherit"
inherit             ::= "inherit" "="
identifierOrKeyword
identifierOrKeyword ::=
identifier

                        |

keyword
identifier          ::= (
NCName -
keyword)

                        |

quotedIdentifier
quotedIdentifier    ::= "\"
NCName
CName               ::=
NCName ":"
NCName
literal              ::=
literalSegment ("~"
literalSegment)+
literalSegment       ::= """ (
```

```
          Char - (""""
          newline))* """
                                |"'" (

          Char - ("'"
          newline))* "'"

          Char - """))* """"""
                                |"""""" ([""""] [""""] (

                                |"'''" (["'"] ["'"] (
          Char - "'"))* "'''"
          keyword              ::= "attribute"
                                |"default"
                                |"datatypes"
                                |"div"
                                |"element"
                                |"empty"
                                |"external"
                                |"grammar"
                                |"include"
                                |"inherit"
                                |"list"
                                |"mixed"
                                |"namespace"
                                |"notAllowed"
                                |"parent"
                                |"start"
                                |"string"
                                |"text"
                                |"token"
```

Note that EBNF doesn't capture the restrictions applied after simplification. The simplification process and restrictions are described in detail in Chapter 15. The main restrictions are also mentioned for each element in the "Restrictions" section.

EBNF Production Reference

This reference lists the EBNF productions alphabetically and describes them.

"""" """"   **Literal segment enclosed in three double quotes**
   •••

```
     """""" ([""""] [""""] (
     Char - """))* """"""
```

Class
literalSegment

May be included in

datatypeName literal, datatypes, external, include

XML syntax equivalent

None

Description

The """...""" production describes literal segments enclosed in three double quotes. These segments can include any characters except a sequence of three double quotes.

Literal segment enclosed in double quotes

```
"""  (Char - ("""
newline))* """
```

Class

literalSegment

May be included in

datatypeName literal, datatypes, external, include

XML syntax equivalent

None

Description

The "..." production describes literal segments enclosed in double quotes. These segments can include any character except newlines and double quotes.

Literal segment enclosed in three single quotes

```
"'''"  (["'"] ["'"] (
Char - "'"))* "'''"
```

Class

literalSegment

May be included in

datatypeName literal, datatypes, external, include

XML syntax equivalent

None

Description

The '''...''' production describes literal segments enclosed in three single quotes. These segments can include any character except sequences of three single quotes.

```
"'" (Char - ("'"
newline))* "'"
```

Class

literalSegment

May be included in

datatypeName literal, datatypes, external, include

XML syntax equivalent

None

Description

The '...' production describes literal segments enclosed in single quotes. These segments can include any character except newlines and single quotes.

(nameClass)   Container

```
"(" nameClass ")"
```

Class

nameClass

May be included in

(nameClass),   *-nameClass,   attribute,   element,   nameClass|nameClass,   nsName
exceptNameClass

XML syntax equivalent

None

Description

The (nameClass) container is useful for grouping together name classes that have been combined using | (choice). This container is a name class and may be combined with other name classes.

Even when such a container isn't required, it is often used to improve the readability of a schema.

Example

```
element hr:* - ( hr:author | hr:name | hr:born | hr:died ) { anything }
```

(pattern)   Container

```
"(" pattern ")"
```

Class

pattern

May be included in

(pattern), attribute, datatypeName   param   exceptPattern, element, list, mixed,
pattern&pattern, pattern*, pattern+, pattern,pattern, pattern?, pattern|pattern

XML syntax equivalent

None

Description

The (pattern) container is useful when grouping together patterns combined using
, (ordered group), | (choice), or & (interleave). This container is treated itself as a pattern
and may be combined with other patterns or quantified using qualifiers.

The operator (, | &) used within the (pattern) container defines how the subpatterns are
combined, and different operators can't be mixed at the same level.

Even when such a container isn't required, it is often used to improve the readability of a
schema.

Example

```
element name {
text|(
 element first{text},
 element middle{text}?,
 element last{text}
)}

element foo {
 element out {empty} &
 (
  element in1 {empty},
  element in2 {empty}
 )
}
```

*-nameClass   Name class accepting any name

```
"*" [exceptNameClass]
```

Class

nameClass

May be included in

(nameClass), *-nameClass, attribute, element, nameClass|nameClass, nsName exceptNameClass

XML syntax equivalent

anyName

Description

The anyName name class matches any name from any namespace. This wide spectrum may be restricted by embedding except name classes.

The set of these names can be restricted using the optional exceptNameClass production.

Restrictions

Within the scope of an element, the name classes of attributes can't overlap. The same restriction applies to name classes of elements when these elements are combined by interleave.

Example

```
foreign-elements = element * - (local:* | lib:* | hr:*) { anything }*
```

-nameClass

Remove a name class from another

```
exceptNameClass ::= "-"
nameClass
```

May be included in

*-nameClass, nsName exceptNameClass

XML syntax equivalent

except

Description

The except name class is used to remove one name class from another.

Restrictions

It's impossible to use -nameClass to produce empty name classes by including anyName in an except name class, or nsName in an except name class included in another nsName.

Example

```
element hr:* - ( hr:author | hr:name | hr:born | hr:died ) { anything }
```

-pattern

Remove a set of values from a data pattern

```
exceptPattern ::= "-"
pattern
```

May be included in

datatypeName param exceptPattern

XML syntax equivalent

except

Description

The except pattern removes a set of values from a datatypeName param exceptPattern pattern.

Restrictions

The -pattern pattern can be used only in the context of data and can contain only data, value, and choice elements.

Example

```
attribute available {xs:boolean - (xs:boolean "false")}
```

CName

Colonized names

```
CName ::=
NCName ":"
NCName
```

May be included in

(nameClass), attribute, datatypeName literal, datatypeName param exceptPattern, element, nameClass|nameClass

XML syntax equivalent

None

Description

The CName production describes colonized names (names containing a colon) as two noncolonized names separated by a colon.

QuotedIdentifier

Quoted identifier

```
quotedIdentifier ::= "\"
NCName
```

May be included in

(pattern), attribute, datatypes, default namespace, element, list, mixed, namespace, parent, pattern&pattern, pattern*, pattern+, pattern,pattern, pattern?, pattern|pattern

XML syntax equivalent

None

Description

The QuotedIdentifier production describes quoted identifiers, which are noncolonized names preceded by a backslash. This is needed to allow names that are the same as the keywords of the compact syntax.

Top level Top level

```
topLevel ::=
decl* (
pattern|
grammarContent*)
```

XML syntax equivalent

None

Description

Start symbol for the RELAX NG compact syntax EBNF. The topLevel production describes the top-level structure of a RELAX NG compact syntax document composed of an optional declaration section and of the actual schema composed of either a single pattern or a more complete grammarContent.

---

assignMethod Defines how to assign content to start and named patterns

```
assignMethod ::= "="
 |"|="
 |"&="
```

May be included in

div, grammar, include

XML syntax equivalent

None

Description

The assignMethod describes how the content of start and named patterns are affected by a new definition. assignMethod may take the values: = (definition), &= (combination by interleave), or |= (combination by choice).

---

attribute

```
"attribute"
nameClass "{"
pattern "}"
```

Class

pattern

May be included in

(pattern), attribute, datatypeName   param   exceptPattern, element, list, mixed, pattern&pattern, pattern*, pattern+, pattern,pattern, pattern?, pattern|pattern

XML syntax equivalent

attribute

Description

The attribute pattern matches an attribute. The name of the attribute is defined using a nameClass, which may be either a single name or a name class. Note that, unlike the XML syntax, the content of an attribute doesn't default to text and must always be explicitly defined.

Restrictions

- After simplification, attribute patterns can contain only patterns relevant for text nodes.
- Attributes can't be duplicated, either directly or by overlapping name classes.
- Attributes that have an infinite name class (anyName or nsName) must be enclosed in a oneOrMore pattern (or zeroOrMore before simplification).

Example

```
attribute available { text }
attribute xml:lang { xsd:language }
attribute * - (local:* | lib:* | hr:*) { text }
```

---

datatypeName

```
datatypeName ::=
CName
```

```
|"string"
|"token"
```

May be included in

datatypeName literal, datatypeName param exceptPattern

XML syntax equivalent

None

Description

The datatypeName production defines a valid datatype name. CName (for colonized names) must be used for any datatype library except for the built-in type library, which has only two datatypes (string and token).

---

datatypeName literal   Matches a text node and a value

```
[datatypeName]
literal
```

Class

pattern

May be included in

(pattern), attribute, datatypeName   param   exceptPattern, element, list, mixed, pattern&pattern, pattern*, pattern+, pattern,pattern, pattern?, pattern|pattern

XML syntax equivalent

value

Description

The datatypeName literal pattern matches a text node against a value using the semantic of a specified datatype to perform the comparison.

When datatypeName is omitted, the default datatype (which is the token datatype from the RELAX NG built in library) is used.

Restrictions

The datatypeName literal pattern is meant for data-oriented applications and can't be used in mixed-content models.

Example

```
"0"

xs:integer "0"
xs:boolean "false"
attribute available {xs:boolean "true"}
```

---

datatypeName param exceptPattern

```
datatypeName ["{"
param* "}"] [
exceptPattern]
```

Class

`pattern`

May be included in

`(pattern)`, `attribute`, `datatypeName` `param` `exceptPattern`, `element`, `list`, `mixed`, `pattern&pattern`, `pattern*`, `pattern+`, `pattern,pattern`, `pattern?`, `pattern|pattern`

XML syntax equivalent

`data`

Description

The `datatypeName` `param` `exceptPattern` pattern matches a single text node and allows the possibility of restricting its values. It is different from the text pattern, which matches zero or more text nodes and doesn't allow the possibility of restricting the values of these text nodes.

In this construction, the restrictions are applied using datatypeName. It defines the datatype, the optional param that defines additional parameters passed to the datatype library (when the datatype library is W3C XML Schema datatypes, these parameters are the W3C XML Schema facets), and the optional exceptPattern. exceptPattern defines exceptions, a set of excluded values.

Restrictions

The `datatypeName` `param` `exceptPattern` pattern is meant for data-oriented applications and can't be used in mixed-content models.

Example

```
attribute available {xs:boolean - (xs:boolean "false")}

element born {xs:date {
  minInclusive = "1900-01-01"
  maxInclusive = "2099-12-31"
  pattern = "[0-9]{4}-[0-9]{2}-[0-9]{2}"
}}
```

datatypes

```
"datatypes"
identifierOrKeyword "="
literal
```

decl

Class

decl

XML syntax equivalent

xmlns:*name*

Description

The datatypes declaration assigns a prefix to a datatype library for the compact syntax, like xmlns:xxx attributes in XML. Note that unlike XML namespace declarations, declarations for the RELAX NG compact syntax in general (and datatypes declarations in particular) are global to a schema and can't be redefined. The prefix xsd is predefined and bound to *http://www.w3.org/2001/XMLSchema-datatypes*.

Example

```
datatypes xs = "http://www.w3.org/2001/XMLSchema-datatypes"
```

---

decl   Declarations

```
decl ::= "namespace"
identifierOrKeyword "="
namespaceURILiteral
  |"default" "namespace" [
identifierOrKeyword] "="
namespaceURILiteral
  |"datatypes"
identifierOrKeyword "="
literal
```

XML syntax equivalent

None

Description

decl contains the declarations section of a RELAX NG compact syntax schema. These declarations are global and common to the whole schema and include the namespace and datatype libraries declarations.

---

default namespace   Default namespace declaration

```
"default" "namespace" [
identifierOrKeyword] "="
namespaceURILiteral
```

Class

decl

XML syntax equivalent

xmlns

Description

The default namespace declaration defines the default namespace for the compact syntax–like xmlns attributes in XML. An optional prefix may be assigned to the default namespace and can then be explicitly referenced. Unlike XML default namespace declarations, declarations for the RELAX NG compact syntax in general (and default namespace declarations in particular) are global to a schema and can't be redefined. A prefix can be assigned to no namespace at all using the value "".

Example

```
default namespace = "http://eric.van-der-vlist.com/ns/library"
default namespace local = ""
```

---

div
Division (in the context of a grammar)

```
"div" "{"
grammarContent* "}"
```

Class

grammarContent

May be included in

div, grammar

XML syntax equivalent

div

Description

The div element is provided to define logical divisions in RELAX NG schemas. It has no effect on the validation. Its purpose is to define a group of definitions within a grammar that may be annotated as a whole.

In the context of a grammar, the content of a div element is the same as the content of a grammar (div elements may be embedded in other div elements).

Example

```
[
  xhtml:p [
    "The content of the book element has been split into two named patterns:"
  ]
]
div {
  book-start =
    attribute id { text },
```

```
        isbn-element,
        title-element,
        author-element*
      book-end =
        author-element*,
        character-element*,
        attribute available { text }
    }
```

---

element

```
    "element" nameClass "{"
    pattern "}"
```

Class

pattern

May be included in

(pattern), attribute, datatypeName   param   exceptPattern, element, list, mixed, pattern&pattern, pattern*, pattern+, pattern,pattern, pattern?, pattern|pattern

XML syntax equivalent

element

Description

The element pattern matches an element. The name of the element is defined by a name-Class, which may be either a single name or name class.

Example

```
    element isbn { text }
    element hr:born { text }
    element title { attribute xml:lang { text }, text }
    element * - (local:* | lib:* | hr:*) { anything }
```

---

empty

```
    "empty"
```

Class

pattern

May be included in

(pattern), attribute, datatypeName   param   exceptPattern, element, list, mixed, pattern&pattern, pattern*, pattern+, pattern,pattern, pattern?, pattern|pattern

---

XML syntax equivalent

empty

Description

The empty pattern is used to define empty pattern nodesets—for example elements without child elements, text, or attributes. Note that it is mandatory to use this pattern in such cases (element foo{ } isn't forbidden) and that there is no such thing as an empty attribute (an attribute such as foo="" is considered to have a value of the empty string rather than being empty—having no value).

Example

```
element foo {
 element out {empty} &
 (
  element in1 {empty},
  element in2 {empty}
 )
}
```

external

Reference to an external schema

```
"external"
literal [
inherit]
```

Class

pattern

May be included in

(pattern), attribute, datatypeName param exceptPattern, element, list, mixed, pattern&pattern, pattern*, pattern+, pattern,pattern, pattern?, pattern|pattern

XML syntax equivalent

externalRef

Description

The external pattern is a reference to an external schema. This has the same effect as replacing the external pattern by the external schema considered as a pattern.

Example

```
element university { element name { text }, external "flat.rnc" }
element book { external "book.rnc" }
```

grammar

```
"grammar" "{"
grammarContent* "}"
```

Class

pattern

May be included in

(pattern), attribute, datatypeName   param   exceptPattern, element, list, mixed, pattern&pattern, pattern*, pattern+, pattern,pattern, pattern?, pattern|pattern

XML syntax equivalent

grammar

Description

The grammar pattern encapsulates the definitions of start and named patterns.

The most common use of grammar is to validate XML documents. In this case, the start pattern specifies which elements can be used as the document root element. The grammar pattern may also be used to write modular schemas. Here, the start pattern specifies which nodes must be matched by the grammar at the location in which it appears in the schema.

In every case, the named patterns defined in a grammar are considered to be local to this grammar. Note that the top-level grammar is implicit for the compact syntax.

Example

```
grammar {
 author-element= element author {
  attribute id {text},
  name-element,
  born-element,
  died-element?
 }
 book-element = element book {
  attribute id {text},
  attribute available {text},
  isbn-element,
  title-element,
  author-element *,
  character-element*
 }
 born-element = element born {text}
 character-element = element character {
  attribute id {text},
  name-element,
  born-element,
  qualification-element
 }
```

```
    died-element = element died {text}
    isbn-element = element isbn {text}
    name-element = element name {text}
    qualification-element = element qualification {text}
    title-element = element title {attribute xml:lang {text}, text}
    start = element library {
     book-element +
    }
   }

   author-element =
     grammar
     {
        start =
          element author
          {
             attribute id { text },
             name-element,
             born-element,
             died-element?
          }
        name-element = element name { text }
        born-element = element born { text }
        died-element = element died { text }
     }
```

---

grammarContent

```
grammarContent ::=
start
 |
define
 |"div" "{"
grammarContent* "}"
 |"include"
literal [
inherit] ["{"
includeContent* "}"]
```

Class

pattern

May be included in

div, grammar

XML syntax equivalent

None

Description

The grammarContent production defines the content of a grammar.

---

identifier
Identifier

```
identifier ::= (
NCName -
keyword)
  |
quotedIdentifier
```

May be included in

(pattern), attribute, datatypeName param exceptPattern, datatypes, default namespace, div, element, external, grammar, include, list, mixed, namespace, parent, pattern&pattern, pattern*, pattern+, pattern,pattern, pattern?, pattern|pattern

XML syntax equivalent

None

Description

The identifier production describes valid identifiers for the compact syntax, either quoted identifiers or noncolonized names that aren't keywords.

---

identifier assignMethod pattern
Named pattern definition

```
define ::=
identifier
assignMethod
pattern
```

Class

pattern

May be included in

div, grammar, include

XML syntax equivalent

define

Description

When identifier assignMethod pattern is embedded in a grammar, it defines a named pattern or combines a new definition with an existing one. Named patterns are global to a grammar and can be referenced by ref in the scope of their grammar and by parentRef in the scope of the grammars directly embedded in their grammar.

When identifier assignMethod pattern is embedded in include, the new definition is a redefinition. It replaces the definitions from the included grammar unless a combine attribute is specified. If one is, the definitions are combined.

The combination is defined using the assignMethod, which may take the values: = (definition), &= (combination by interleave), or |= (combination by choice).

Restrictions

Named patterns are always global and apply only to patterns. It isn't possible to define or make reference to nonpatterns such as class names or datatype parameters.

Example

```
date-element = element born { xsd:data }

date-element |= element died { xsd:date }
```

identifierOrKeyword
Identifier or keyword

```
identifierOrKeyword ::=
identifier
  |
keyword
```

May be included in

(nameClass), attribute, datatypeName param exceptPattern, datatypes, default namespace, element, external, include, nameClass|nameClass, namespace

XML syntax equivalent

None

Description

The identifierOrKeyword production is either a valid identifier or a keyword.

include
Grammar merge

```
"include" literal [
inherit] ["{"
includeContent* "}"]
```

Class

grammarContent

May be included in

div, grammar

XML syntax equivalent

include

Description

The include pattern includes a grammar and merges its definitions with the definitions of the current grammar. The definitions of the included grammar may be redefined and over-ridden by the definitions embedded in the include pattern. Note that a schema must contain an explicit grammar definition in order to be included.

The optional inherit production specifies which namespaces are inherited from the included schema. includeContent allows you to redefine definitions from the included schema.

Example

```
include "included.rnc"
include "flat.rnc" { start = book-element }
```

---

includeContent   Content of an include pattern

```
includeContent ::=
define
 |
start
 |"div" "{"
includeContent* "}"
```

May be included in

include

XML syntax equivalent

None

Description

The includeContent production defines the content of an include. The only difference with grammarContent is that includeContent doesn't allow an embedded include.

---

inherit   Namespace inheritance

```
inherit ::= "inherit" "="
identifierOrKeyword
```

May be included in

external, include

XML syntax equivalent

None

Description

The inherit production is used in external and include statements. It specifies the prefixes of the namespaces that are inherited by the included file.

---

keyword

```
keyword ::= "attribute"
  |"default"
  |"datatypes"
  |"div"
  |"element"
  |"empty"
  |"external"
  |"grammar"
  |"include"
  |"inherit"
  |"list"
  |"mixed"
  |"namespace"
  |"notAllowed"
  |"parent"
  |"start"
  |"string"
  |"text"
  |"token"
```

May be included in

(pattern), attribute, datatypeName param exceptPattern, datatypes, default namespace, element, external, include, list, mixed, namespace, parent, pattern&pattern, pattern*, pattern+, pattern,pattern, pattern?, pattern|pattern

XML syntax equivalent

None

Description

The keyword production gives the list of keywords for the RELAX NG compact syntax. Note that these keywords are reserved only when there is a risk of confusion. They can be used, for instance, as element or attribute names without being quoted. When they are reserved, they can still be used as identifiers, but they need to be quoted.

list

```
"list" "{"
pattern "}"
```

Class

pattern

May be included in

(pattern), attribute, datatypeName param exceptPattern, element, list, mixed, pattern&pattern, pattern*, pattern+, pattern,pattern, pattern?, pattern|pattern

XML syntax equivalent

list

Description

The list pattern splits a text node into tokens separated by whitespace to allow the validation of these tokens separately. This item is most useful for validating lists of values.

Restrictions

- interleave can't be used within list.
- The content of a list is only about data: it's forbidden to define element, attribute or, text there.
- It's forbidden to embed list into list.

Example

```
attribute see-also {list {token*}}

attribute dimensions {list {xsd:decimal, xsd:decimal, xsd:decimal,
  ("inches"|"cm"|"mm")}}
```

literal

```
literal ::=
literalSegment ("~"
literalSegment)+
```

May be included in

datatypeName literal, datatypeName param exceptPattern, datatypes, default namespace, external, include, namespace

XML syntax equivalent

None

Description

The literal production describes literals as several segments of literals contained by the tilde (~) symbol.

literalSegment

```
literalSegment ::= """ (
Char - ("""
newline))* """
 |"'" (
Char - ("'"
newline))* "'"
 |"""""" ([""""] ["""] (
Char - """))* """"""
 |"'''" ([""'"] ["'"] (
Char - "'"))* "'''"
```

May be included in

datatypeName literal, datatypeName param exceptPattern, datatypes, default namespace, external, include, namespace

XML syntax equivalent

None

Description

The literalSegment production describes literal segments as strings enclosed either in single or double quotes or enclosed in three single or three double quotes using a Python-like syntax.

mixed

```
"mixed" "{"
pattern "}"
```

Class

pattern

May be included in

(pattern), attribute, datatypeName param exceptPattern, element, list, mixed, pattern&pattern, pattern*, pattern+, pattern,pattern, pattern?, pattern|pattern

XML syntax equivalent

mixed

Description

The mixed pattern is a shortcut for interleave with an embedded text pattern. It describes unordered content models in which a text node may be included before and after each element. Note that RELAX NG doesn't allow adding constraints to these text nodes.

Restrictions

The limitations of interleave apply here:

- The mixed pattern can't be used within a list.
- Elements within a mixed pattern can't have overlapping name classes.
- There must no other text pattern in each set of patterns combined by mixed.

Example

```
element title {
 mixed {
  attribute xml:lang {text}&
  element a {attribute href {text}, text} *
 }
}
is equivalent to:
element title {
 ( text & (
  attribute xml:lang {text}&
  element a {attribute href {text}, text} *
 )
}
which itself is equivalent to:
element title {
  text &
  attribute xml:lang {text}&
  element a {attribute href {text}, text} *
}
```

---

name

Define a set of names that must be matched by an element or attribute

```
name ::=
identifierOrKeyword
 |
CName
```

May be included in

(nameClass), *-nameClass, attribute, element, nameClass|nameClass, nsName exceptNameClass

XML syntax equivalent

None

Description

The name name class defines sets of names that are singletons: they match only one name. There is no restriction other than those of XML 1.0 and namespaces in XML 1.0 on such names. They can be either CName or identifierOrKeyword (in particular, even keywords can be used as names).

---

nameClass
Define a set of names that must be matched by an element or attribute

```
nameClass ::=
name
 |
NCName ":*" [
exceptNameClass]
 |"*" [
exceptNameClass]
 |
nameClass "|"
nameClass
 |"("
nameClass ")"
```

May be included in

(nameClass), *-nameClass, attribute, element, nameClass|nameClass, nsName exceptNameClass

XML syntax equivalent

None

Description

The nameClass production defines sets of names that must be matched by elements and attributes. Its simplest expression is to define a single name, but specific wildcards can also be expressed as nameClass.

---

nameClass|nameClass
Choice between name classes

```
nameClass "|"
nameClass
```

Class

nameClass

May be included in

(nameClass), *-nameClass, attribute, element, nameClass|nameClass, nsName exceptNameClass

---

XML syntax equivalent

choice

Description

The nameClass|nameClass production performs a choice between two name classes. A name matches nameClass|nameClass if, and only if, it matches at least one of the two alternatives.

Example

```
element lib:* | hr:* { anything }
```

---

namespace   Namespace declaration

```
"namespace"
identifierOrKeyword "="
namespaceURILiteral
```

Class

decl

May be included in

XML syntax equivalent

xmlns

Description

The namespace declaration defines namespace prefixes for the compact syntax, like xmlns:*xxx* attributes in XML. Note that unlike XML namespace declarations, declarations for the RELAX NG compact syntax in general (and namespace declarations in particular) are global to a schema and can't be redefined. A prefix can be assigned to the lack of namespace using the value "". The xml prefix is predefined.

Example

```
namespace hr = "http://eric.van-der-vlist.com/ns/person"
namespace local = ""
```

---

namespaceURILiteral   Namespace URI Literal

```
namespaceURILiteral ::=
literal
 |"inherit"
```

May be included in

default namespace, namespace

XML syntax equivalent

None

Description

The `namespaceURILiteral` production specifies a namespace URI. It can be either a `literal` or the value `inherit` to specify that the namespace URI is inherited from the including file.

---

notAllowed

Not allowed

```
"notAllowed"
```

Class

`pattern`

May be included in

`(pattern)`, `attribute`, `datatypeName` `param` `exceptPattern`, `element`, `list`, `mixed`, `pattern&pattern`, `pattern*`, `pattern+`, `pattern,pattern`, `pattern?`, `pattern|pattern`

XML syntax equivalent

`notAllowed`

Description

The `notAllowed` pattern always fails. It can provide abstract definitions that must be over-ridden before they can be used in a schema.

Example

```
isbn-element |= notAllowed
```

---

nsName exceptNameClass

Name class for any name in a namespace

```
NCName ":*" [
exceptNameClass]
```

Class

`nameClass`

May be included in

`(nameClass)`, `*-nameClass`, `attribute`, `element`, `nameClass|nameClass`, `nsName` `exceptNameClass`

XML syntax equivalent

`nsName`

Description

The `nsName exceptNameClass` name class allows any name in a specific namespace.

The namespace is defined by the `nsName` production, and the set of these names can be restricted using the `exceptNameClass` production.

Restrictions

Within the scope of an element, the name classes of attributes can't overlap. The same restriction applies to name classes of elements when these elements are combined by `interleave`. It's impossible to use `nsName exceptNameClass` to produce empty name classes by including `nsName exceptNameClass` in an except name class that's included in another `nsName`.

Example

```
element lib:* { anything }

element hr:* - ( hr:author | hr:name | hr:born | hr:died ) { anything }
```

---

param

Datatype parameter

```
param ::=
identifierOrKeyword "="
literal
```

Class

`parameter`

May be included in

`datatypeName param exceptPattern`.

XML syntax equivalent

`param`

Description

The `param` production defines parameters passed to the datatype library to determine whether a value is valid per a datatype. When the datatype library is the W3C XML Schema datatype set, these parameters are the facets of the datatype, and they define additional restrictions to be applied. The name of the parameter is defined by `identifierOrKeyword` and its value is defined by `literal param`.

Example

```
element born {xs:date {
  minInclusive = "1900-01-01"
  maxInclusive = "2099-12-31"
  pattern = "[0-9]{4}-[0-9]{2}-[0-9]{2}"
}}
```

---

parent

Reference to a named pattern from the parent grammar

> "parent" *identifier*

Class

pattern

May be included in

(pattern), attribute, datatypeName   param   exceptPattern, element, list, mixed, pattern&pattern, pattern*, pattern+, pattern,pattern, pattern?, pattern|pattern

XML syntax equivalent

parentRef

Description

The parent pattern is a reference to a named pattern belonging to the parent grammar, the grammar in which the current grammar is included. The scope of named patterns is usually limited to the grammar in which they are defined. The parent pattern provides a way to extend this scope and refer to named patterns defined in the parent grammar.

Example

```
born-element = parent born-element

start =
    attribute id { parent id-content },
    attribute available { parent available-content },
    element isbn { parent isbn-content },
    element title { parent title-content },
    element author { parent author-content }*,
    element character { parent character-content }*
```

pattern

Pattern

```
pattern ::= "element"
nameClass "{"
pattern "}"
 |"attribute"
nameClass "{"
pattern "}"
 |
pattern (","
pattern)+
 |
pattern ("&"
pattern)+
 |
pattern ("|"
```

```
pattern)+
 |
pattern "?"
 |
pattern "*"
 |
pattern "+"
 |"list" "{"
pattern "}"
 |"mixed" "{"
pattern "}"
 |
identifier
 |"parent"
identifier
 |"empty"
 |"text"
 |[
datatypeName]
literal
 |
datatypeName ["{"
param* "}"] [
exceptPattern]
 |"notAllowed"
 |"external"
literal [
inherit]
 |"grammar" "{"
grammarContent* "}"
 |"("
pattern ")"
```

Class

pattern

May be included in

(pattern), attribute, datatypeName param exceptPattern, div, element, grammar, include, list, mixed, pattern&pattern, pattern*, pattern+, pattern,pattern, pattern?, pattern|pattern

XML syntax equivalent

None

Description

A pattern is an atom of RELAX NG schema. It is matched against nodes from the instance document (elements, attributes, text nodes, or tokens resulting from a split through list).

pattern&pattern

```
pattern ("&"
pattern)+
```

Class

pattern

May be included in

(pattern), attribute, datatypeName   param   exceptPattern, element, list, mixed, pattern&pattern, pattern*, pattern+, pattern,pattern, pattern?, pattern|pattern

XML syntax equivalent

interleave

Description

The interleave pattern "interleaves" subpatterns; it allows their leaves to be mixed in any relative order.

interleave is about more than defining unordered groups, as can be seen in the following example. Consider element a and the ordered group of element b1 and b2. An unordered group of these two patterns allows only element a followed by elements b1 and b2 or elements b1 and b2 followed by element a. An interleave of these two patterns does allow these two combinations but also element b1 followed by a followed by b2: a combination in which element a has been interleaved between elements b1 and b2.

The interleave behavior is the behavior applied to attribute patterns even when they are embedded in (ordered) group patterns. The reason for this is that XML 1.0 specifies that the relative order of attributes isn't significant.

Another case where interleave patterns are often needed is to describe mixed-content models: content models where text is interleaved between elements. A shortcut (the mixed pattern) has been defined for this case.

Any number of patterns may be combined using the & operator when using this construct; however, different operators (, | &) can't be mixed at the same level.

Restrictions

- The pattern&pattern pattern can't be used within a list.
- Elements within a pattern&pattern pattern can't have overlapping name classes.
- There must be at most one text pattern in each set of patterns combined by the pattern&pattern.

Example

```
element character {
 attribute id {text}&
 element name {text}&
```

```
  element born {text}&
  element qualification {text}}

  element foo {
   element out {empty} &
   (
   element in1 {empty},
   element in2 {empty}
   )
  }
```

---

pattern*   zeroOrMore pattern

pattern `"*"`

Class

pattern

May be included in

(pattern), attribute, datatypeName   param   exceptPattern, element, list, mixed, pattern&pattern, pattern*, pattern+, pattern,pattern, pattern?, pattern|pattern

XML syntax equivalent

zeroOrMore

Description

A pattern qualified as zeroOrMore must be matched zero or more times (i.e., any number of times).

Restrictions

The pattern* pattern can't contain attribute definitions.

Example

```
element author {
  attribute id {text},
  element name {text},
  element born {text},
  element died {text}?}*

book-element = element book {
  attribute id {text},
  attribute available {text},
  isbn-element,
  title-element,
   uthor-element *,
  character-element*
}
```

pattern+

oneOrMore pattern

> *pattern* "+"

Class

pattern

May be included in

(pattern), attribute, datatypeName   param   exceptPattern, element, list, mixed, pattern&pattern, pattern*, pattern+, pattern,pattern, pattern?, pattern|pattern

XML syntax equivalent

oneOrMore

Description

A pattern qualified as oneOrMore must be matched one or more times.

Restrictions

The pattern+ pattern can't contain attribute definitions.

Example

```
start = element library {
 book-element +
}

attribute see-also {list
       {("0836217462"|"0345442695"|"0449220230"|"0449214044"|"0061075647")+}}
```

pattern,pattern

pattern,pattern pattern

pattern (","

pattern)+

Class

pattern

May be included in

(pattern), attribute, datatypeName   param   exceptPattern, element, list, mixed, pattern&pattern, pattern*, pattern+, pattern,pattern, pattern?, pattern|pattern

XML syntax equivalent

group

Description

The group pattern defines an ordered group of subpatterns (note that when `attribute` patterns are included in such a group, their order can't be guaranteed). Any number of patterns may be combined through the `,` operator using this construct; however different operators (`,` | `&`) can't be mixed at the same level.

Example

```
element author {
  attribute id {text},
  element name {text},
  element born {text},
  element died {text}?}*

element lib:title { attribute xml:lang { text }, text }

attribute dimensions {list {token, token, token, ("inches"|"cm"|"mm")}}
```

pattern?   optional pattern

```
pattern "?"
```

Class

pattern

May be included in

(pattern), attribute, datatypeName   param   exceptPattern, element, list, mixed, pattern&pattern, pattern*, pattern+, pattern,pattern, pattern?, pattern|pattern

XML syntax equivalent

optional

Description

A pattern qualified as optional is optional. It must be matched zero or one times.

Example

```
element died {text}?

attribute see-also {list {token, token?, token?, token?}}
```

pattern|pattern   choice pattern

```
pattern ("|"
pattern)+
```

Class

pattern

May be included in

(pattern), attribute, datatypeName   param   exceptPattern, element, list, mixed,
pattern&pattern, pattern*, pattern+, pattern,pattern, pattern?, pattern|pattern

XML syntax equivalent

choice

Description

The choice pattern defines a choice between different patterns; it matches a node if, and
only if, at least one of its subpatterns matches this node.

Any number of patterns may be combined using the | operator when using this construct;
however, different operators (, | &) can't be mixed at the same level.

Example

```
element name {
 text|(
  element first{text},
  element middle{text}?,
  element last{text}
 )}

attribute available {"true"|"false"|"who knows?"}
```

---

start

Start of a grammar

```
start ::= "start"
assignMethod
pattern
```

May be included in

div, grammar, include

XML syntax equivalent

start

Description

The start pattern defines the "start" of a grammar. When this grammar validates a complete
document, the start pattern specifies which elements may be used as the document (root)
element. When this grammar is embedded within another grammar, the start pattern specifies which pattern should be applied at the location where the grammar is embedded. Like

named pattern definitions, start patterns may be combined by choice or interleave and redefined when they are included in include patterns.

The combination is defined by the assignMethod, which may take the values: = (definition), &= (combination by interleave), or |= (combination by choice).

Example

```
start = element library {
 book-element +
}

start |= book-element
```

---

text   Pattern matching text nodes

```
"text"
```

Class

pattern

May be included in

(pattern), attribute, datatypeName   param   exceptPattern, element, list, mixed, pattern&pattern, pattern*, pattern+, pattern,pattern, pattern?, pattern|pattern

XML syntax equivalent

text

Description

The text pattern matches zero or more text nodes. The fact that a text pattern matches more than one text node has no effect when it is used in ordered-content models (the data model used by RELAX NG for XML documents is similar to the data model of XPath 1.0, and two text nodes can't be adjacent), but makes a difference when a text pattern is used in interleave. Adding a single text pattern in an interleave pattern allows any number of text nodes that can interleave before and after each element. Note that the mixed pattern is provided as a shortcut to define these content models.

Restrictions

No more than one text pattern can be included in an interleave pattern.

Example

```
element author {
 attribute id {text},
 element name {text},
 element born {text},
 element died {text}?}?
```

CHAPTER 19

Datatype Reference

This chapter provides a quick reference to all the datatypes the W3C XML Schema defines. Each datatype is listed along with its RELAX NG datatype parameters. The list corresponds to the W3C XML Schema facets available for the datatype, with the exception of the whiteSpace facet (which isn't supported by RELAX NG). It also provides information about what the facets represent and how they do it. For the secondary datatypes (the W3C XML Schema builtin types that are derived from another builtin type), the synopsis shows the formal definition of the type using W3C XML Schema syntax. Examples are given for all these datatypes.

xsd:anyURI

URI (Uniform Resource Identifier)

```
<xsd:simpleType name="anyURI" id="anyURI">
 <xsd:restriction base="xsd:anySimpleType">
 <xsd:whiteSpace value="collapse" fixed="true"/>
 </xsd:restriction></xsd:simpleType>
```

Derived from

xsd:anySimpleType

Primary

xsd:anyURI

Known subtypes

None

Data parameters (facets)

enumeration, length, maxLength, minLength, pattern

Description

This datatype corresponds normatively to the XLink href attribute. Its value space includes the URIs defined by RFCs 2396 and 2732, but its lexical space doesn't require the character escapes needed to include non-ASCII characters in a URIs.

Restrictions

Relative URIs aren't absolutized by the W3C XML Schema. A pattern defined as:

```
<data type="xsd:anyURI">
  <choice">
    <value type="xsd:anyURI">http://www.w3.org/TR/xmlschema-0/</value>
    <value type="xsd:anyURI">http://www.w3.org/TR/xmlschema-1/</value>
    <value type="xsd:anyURI">http://www.w3.org/TR/xmlschema-2/</value>
  </choice>
</data>
```

shouldn't match the href attribute in this instance element:

```
<a xml:base="http://www.w3.org/TR/" href="xmlschema-1/">
  XML Schema Part 2: Datatypes
</a>
```

The Recommendation states that "it is impractical for processors to check that a value is a context-appropriate URI reference," thus freeing schema processors from having to validate the correctness of the URI.

Example

```
<define name="httpURI">
  <data type="xsd:anyURI">
    <param name="pattern">http://.*<param>
  </data>
</define>
```

xsd:base64Binary   Binary content coded as "base64"

```
<xsd:simpleType name="base64Binary" id="base64Binary">
 <xsd:restriction base="xsd:anySimpleType">
 <xsd:whiteSpace value="collapse" fixed="true"/>
 </xsd:restriction>
</xsd:simpleType>
```

Derived from

xsd:anySimpleType

Primary

xsd:base64Binary

Known subtypes

None

Data parameters (facets)

enumeration, length, maxLength, minLength, pattern.

Description

The value space of xsd:base64Binary is the set of arbitrary binary contents. Its lexical space is the same set after base64 coding. This coding is described in Section 6.8 of RFC 2045.

Restrictions

RFC 2045 describes the transfer of binary contents over text-based mail systems. It imposes a line break at least every 76 characters to avoid the inclusion of arbitrary line breaks by the mail systems. Sending base64 content without line breaks is nevertheless a common usage for applications such as SOAP and the W3C XML Schema Working Group. After a request from other W3C Working Groups, the W3C XML Schema Working Group decided to remove the obligation to include these line breaks from the constraints on the lexical space. (This decision was made after the publication of the W3C XML Schema Recommendation. It is now noted in the errata.)

Example

```
<define name="picture">
  <attribute name="type">
    <ref name="graphicalFormat"/>
  </attribute>
  <data type="xsd:base64Binary">
</define>
```

xsd:boolean

Boolean (true or false)

```
<xsd:simpleType name="boolean" id="boolean">
 <xsd:restriction base="xsd:anySimpleType">
 <xsd:whiteSpace value="collapse" fixed="true"/>
 </xsd:restriction>
</xsd:simpleType>
```

Derived from

xsd:anySimpleType

Primary

xsd:boolean

Known subtypes

None

Data parameters (facets)

pattern

Description

The value space of xsd:boolean is true and false. Its lexical space accepts true, false, and also 1 (for true) and 0 (for false).

Restrictions

This datatype can't be localized—for instance, it can't accept the French *vrai* and *faux* instead of the English *true* and *false*.

Example

```
<book id="b0836217462" available="true"/>
```

---

xsd:byte   Signed value of 8 bits

```
<xsd:simpleType name="byte" id="byte">
 <xsd:restriction base="xsd:short">
 <xsd:minInclusive value="-128"/>
 <xsd:maxInclusive value="127"/>
 </xsd:restriction>
</xsd:simpleType>
```

Derived from

xsd:short

Primary

xsd:decimal

Known subtypes

None

Data parameters (facets)

enumeration, fractionDigits, maxExclusive, maxInclusive, minExclusive, minInclusive, pattern, totalDigits

Description

The value space of xsd:byte includes the integers between −128 and 127—the signed values that can fit in a word of 8 bits. Its lexical space allows an optional sign and leading zeros before the significant digits.

Restrictions

The lexical space doesn't allow values expressed in other numeration bases (such as hexadecimal, octal, or binary).

Example

Valid values for byte include 27, −34, +105, and 0.

Invalid values include 0A, 1524, and INF.

---

xsd:date

```
<xsd:simpleType name="date" id="date">
 <xsd:restriction base="xsd:anySimpleType">
 <xsd:whiteSpace value="collapse" fixed="true"/>
 </xsd:restriction>
</xsd:simpleType>
```

Derived from

xsd:anySimpleType

Primary

xsd:date

Known subtypes

None

Data parameters (facets)

enumeration, maxExclusive, maxInclusive, minExclusive, minInclusive, pattern

Description

This datatype is modeled after the calendar dates defined in Chapter 5.2.1 of ISO (International Organization for Standardization) 8601. Its value space is the set of Gregorian calendar dates as defined by this standard; i.e., a one-day-long period of time. Its lexical space is the ISO 8601 extended format:

```
[-]CCYY-MM-DD[Z|(+|-)hh:mm]
```

with an optional time zone. Time zones that aren't specified are considered undetermined.

Restrictions

The basic format of ISO 8601 calendar dates, CCYYMMDD, isn't supported.

The other forms of dates available in ISO 8601 aren't supported: ordinal dates defined by the year, the number of the day in the year, dates identified by calendar week, and day numbers.

As the value space is defined by reference to ISO 8601, there is no support for any calendar system other than Gregorian. Because the lexical space is also defined using a reference to ISO 8601, there is no support for any localization such as different orders for date parts or named months.

The order relation between dates with and without time zone is partial: they can be compared beyond a +/− 14 hour interval.

There is a difference between ISO 8601, which defines a day as a 24-hour period of time, and the W3C XML Schema, which indicates that a date is a "one-day-long, non-periodic instance ... independent of how many hours this day has." Even though technically correct, some days don't last exactly 24 hours because of leap seconds; this definition doesn't concur with the definition of xsd:duration that states that a day is always exactly 24 hours long.

Example

Valid values include: 2001-10-26, 2001-10-26+02:00, 2001-10-26Z, 2001-10-26+00:00, -2001-10-26, or -20000-04-01.

The following values would be invalid: 2001-10 (all the parts must be specified), 2001-10-32 (the days part—32—is out of range), 2001-13-26+02:00 (the month part—13—is out of range), or 01-10-26 (the century part is missing).

xsd:dateTime   Instant of time (Gregorian calendar)

```
<xsd:simpleType name="dateTime" id="dateTime">
<xsd:restriction base="xsd:anySimpleType">
<xsd:whiteSpace value="collapse" fixed="true"/>
</xsd:restriction>
</xsd:simpleType>
```

Derived from

xsd:anySimpleType

Primary

xsd:dateTime

Known subtypes

None

Data parameters (facets)

enumeration, maxExclusive, maxInclusive, minExclusive, minInclusive, pattern.

Description

This datatype describes instances identified by the combination of a date and a time. Its value space is described as a combination of date and time of day in Chapter 5.4 of ISO 8601. Its lexical space is the extended format:

    [-]CCYY-MM-DDThh:mm:ss[Z|(+|-)hh:mm]

The time zone may be specified as Z (UTC) or (+|-)hh:mm. Time zones that aren't specified are considered undetermined.

Restrictions

The basic format of ISO 8601 calendar datetimes, CCYYMMDDThhmmss, isn't supported.

The other forms of date-times available in ISO 8601—ordinal dates defined by the year, the number of the day in the year, dates identified by calendar week, and day numbers—aren't supported.

As the value space is defined by reference to ISO 8601, there is no support for any calendar system other than Gregorian. As the lexical space is also defined in reference to ISO 8601, there is no support for any localization such as different orders for date parts or named months.

The order relation between date-times with and without time zone is partial: they can be compared only outside of a +/– 14 hours interval.

Example

Valid values for `xsd:dateTime` include: `2001-10-26T21:32:52`, `2001-10-26T21:32:52+02:00`, `2001-10-26T19:32:52Z`, `2001-10-26T19:32:52+00:00`, `-2001-10-26T21:32:52`, or `2001-10-26T21:32:52.12679`.

The following values are invalid: `2001-10-26` (all the parts must be specified), `2001-10-26T21:32` (all the parts must be specified), `2001-10-26T25:32:52+02:00` (the hours part—25—is out of range), or `01-10-26T21:32` (all the parts must be specified).

xsd:decimal

Decimal numbers

```
<xsd:simpleType name="decimal" id="decimal">
 <xsd:restriction base="xsd:anySimpleType">
 <xsd:whiteSpace value="collapse" fixed="true"/>
 </xsd:restriction>
</xsd:simpleType>
```

Derived from

xsd:anySimpleType

Primary

xsd:decimal

Known subtypes

xsd:integer

Data parameters (facets)

enumeration, fractionDigits, maxExclusive, maxInclusive, minExclusive, minInclusive, pattern, totalDigits.

Description

xsd:decimal is the datatype that represents the set of all decimal numbers with arbitrary lengths. Its lexical space allows any number of insignificant leading and trailing zeros (after the decimal point).

Restrictions

The decimal separator is always a point (.), and no separation at the thousand mark may be added. There is no support for scientific notation.

Example

Valid values include: 123.456, +1234.456, -1234.456, -.456, or -456.

The following values are invalid: 1 234.456 (spaces are forbidden), 1234.456E+2 (scientific notation—E+2—is forbidden), + 1234.456 (spaces are forbidden), or +1,234.456 (delimiters between thousands are forbidden).

---

xsd:double   IEEE 64-bit floating-point

```
<xsd:simpleType name="double" id="double">
 <xsd:restriction base="xsd:anySimpleType">
 <xsd:whiteSpace value="collapse" fixed="true"/>
 </xsd:restriction>
</xsd:simpleType>
```

Derived from

xsd:anySimpleType

Primary

xsd:double

Known subtypes

None

Data parameters (facets)

enumeration, maxExclusive, maxInclusive, minExclusive, minInclusive, pattern

Description

The value space of xsd:double is double (64 bits) floating-point numbers as defined by the IEEE (Institute of Electrical and Electronics Engineers). The lexical space uses a decimal format with optional scientific notation. The match between lexical (powers of 10) and value (powers of 2) spaces is approximate and done on the closest value.

This datatype differentiates positive (0) and negative (–0) zeros, and includes the special values –INF (negative infinity), INF (positive infinity) and NaN (Not a Number).

Note that the lexical spaces of xsd:float and xsd:double are exactly the same; the only difference is the precision used to convert the values in the value space.

Restrictions

The decimal separator is always a point (.), and no thousands separator may be used.

Example

Valid values include: 123.456, +1234.456, -1.2344e56, -.45E-6, INF, -INF, or NaN.

The following values are invalid: 1234.4E 56 (spaces are forbidden), 1E+2.5 (the power of 10 must be an integer), +INF (positive infinity doesn't expect a sign), or NAN (capitalization matters in special values).

xsd:duration

```
<xsd:simpleType name="duration" id="duration">
 <xsd:restriction base="xsd:anySimpleType">
 <xsd:whiteSpace value="collapse" fixed="true"/>
 </xsd:restriction>
 </xsd:simpleType>
```

Derived from

xsd:anySimpleType

Primary

xsd:duration

Known subtypes

None

Data parameters (facets)

enumeration, maxExclusive, maxInclusive, minExclusive, minInclusive, pattern

Description

Duration may be expressed using all the parts of a date-time (from year to fractions of second) and are, therefore, defined as a six-dimensional space. Because the relation between some of date parts isn't fixed (such as the number of days in a month), the order relationship between durations is only partial, and the result of a comparison between two durations may be undetermined.

The lexical space of xsd:duration is the format defined by ISO 8601 under the form:

PnYnMnDTnHnMnS

The capital letters are delimiters and can be omitted when the corresponding member isn't used.

Some durations are undetermined, until a starting point is determined for the duration. The W3C XML Schema relies on this feature to define the algorithm to compare two durations. Four date-times have been chosen that produce the greatest deviations when durations are added. A duration is considered bigger than another when the result of its addition to these four dates is consistently bigger than the result of the addition of the other duration to these same four date-times. These date-times are: 1696-09-01T00:00:00Z, 1697-02-01T00:00:00Z, 1903-03-01T00:00:00Z, and 1903-07-01T00:00:00Z.

Restrictions

The lexical space can't be customized.

Example

Valid values include PT1004199059S, PT130S, PT2M10S, P1DT2S, -P1Y, or P1Y2M3DT5H20M30.123S.

The following values are invalid: 1Y (leading P is missing), P1S (T separator is missing), P-1Y (all parts must be positive), P1M2Y (parts order is significant and Y must precede M), or P1Y-1M (all parts must be positive).

---

xsd:ENTITIES
Whitespace-separated list of unparsed entity references

```
<xsd:simpleType name="ENTITIES" id="ENTITIES">
<xsd:restriction>
<xsd:simpleType>
<xsd:list>
<xsd:simpleType>
<xsd:restriction base="xsd:ENTITY"/>
</xsd:simpleType>
</xsd:list>
</xsd:simpleType>
<xsd:minLength value="1"/>
</xsd:restriction>
</xsd:simpleType>
```

Derived from

xsd:ENTITY

Primary

None

Known subtypes

None

Data parameters (facets)

enumeration, length, maxLength, minLength

Description

xsd:ENTITIES is derived by a list from xsd:ENTITY. It represents lists of unparsed entity references. Each part of this entity reference is a nonqualified name (xsd:NCName) and must be declared as an unparsed entity in an internal or external DTD.

Restrictions

Unparsed entities have been defined in XML 1.0 as a way to include non-XML content in an XML document. Still, most of the applications prefer to define links (such as those defined in (X)HTML to include images or other multimedia objects).

The W3C XML Schema doesn't provide alternative ways to declare unparsed entities; a DTD is needed to do so.

xsd:ENTITY

```
<xsd:simpleType name="ENTITY" id="ENTITY">
 <xsd:restriction base="xsd:NCName"/>
</xsd:simpleType>
```

Derived from

xsd:NCName

Primary

xsd:string

Known subtypes

xsd:ENTITIES

Data parameters (facets)

enumeration, length, maxLength, minLength, pattern

Description

xsd:ENTITY is an entity reference. It is a nonqualified name (xsd:NCName) that has been declared as an unparsed entity in an internal or external DTD.

Restrictions

Unparsed entities are defined in XML 1.0 as a way to include non-XML content in an XML document, but most of the applications prefer to define links (such as those defined in (X)HTML to include images or other multimedia objects).

The W3C XML Schema doesn't provide alternative ways to declare unparsed entities; a DTD is needed to do so.

xsd:float

```
<xsd:simpleType name="float" id="float">
 <xsd:restriction base="xsd:anySimpleType">
 <xsd:whiteSpace value="collapse" fixed="true"/>
 </xsd:restriction>
</xsd:simpleType>
```

Derived from

xsd:anySimpleType

Primary

xsd:float

Known subtypes

None

Data parameters (facets)

enumeration, maxExclusive, maxInclusive, minExclusive, minInclusive, pattern

Description

The value space of xsd:float is "float," 32-bit floating-point numbers as defined by the IEEE. The lexical space uses a decimal format with optional scientific notation. The match between lexical (powers of 10) and value (powers of 2) spaces is approximate and maps to the closest value.

This datatype differentiates positive (0) and negative (–0) zeros, and includes the special values –INF (negative infinity), INF (positive infinity), and NaN (Not a Number).

Note that the lexical spaces of xsd:float and xsd:double are exactly the same; the only difference is the precision used to convert the values in the value space.

Restrictions

The decimal separator is always a point (.), and no thousands separator may be added.

Example

Valid values include: 123.456, +1234.456, -1.2344e56, -.45E-6, INF, -INF, and NaN.

The following values are invalid: 1234.4E 56 (spaces are forbidden), 1E+2.5 (the power of 10 must be an integer), +INF (positive infinity doesn't expect a sign), or NAN (capitalization matters in special values).

---

xsd:gDay   Recurring period of time: monthly day

```
<xsd:simpleType name="gDay" id="gDay">
 <xsd:restriction base="xsd:anySimpleType">
 <xsd:whiteSpace value="collapse" fixed="true"/>
 </xsd:restriction>
</xsd:simpleType>
```

Derived from

xsd:anySimpleType

Primary

xsd:gDay

Known subtypes

None

Data parameters (facets)

enumeration, maxExclusive, maxInclusive, minExclusive, minInclusive, pattern

Description

The value space of xsd:gDay is the period of one calendar day recurring each calendar month (such as the third day of the month); its lexical space follows the ISO 8601 syntax for such periods (i.e., -- -DD) with an optional time zone.

When needed, days are reduced to fit in the length of the months, so ---31 would occur on the 28th of February of nonleap years.

Restrictions

The period (one month) and the duration (one day) are fixed, and no calendars other than Gregorian are supported.

Example

Valid values include ---01, ---01Z, ---01+02:00, ---01-04:00, ---15, and ---31.

The following values are invalid: --30- (the format must be ---DD), ---35 (the day is out of range), ---5 (all the digits must be supplied), or 15 (missing leading ---).

---

xsd:gMonth
Recurring period of time: yearly month

```
<xsd:simpleType name="gMonth" id="gMonth">
 <xsd:restriction base="xsd:anySimpleType">
 <xsd:whiteSpace value="collapse" fixed="true"/>
 </xsd:restriction>
</xsd:simpleType>
```

Derived from

xsd:anySimpleType

Primary

xsd:gMonth

Known subtypes

None

Data parameters (facets)

enumeration, maxExclusive, maxInclusive, minExclusive, minInclusive, pattern

Description

The value space of xsd:gMonth is the period of one calendar month recurring each calendar year (such as the month of April). Its lexical space should follow the ISO 8601 syntax for such periods (i.e., `-- MM`) with an optional time zone.

 There's a typo in the W3C XML Schema Recommendation, in which the format is defined as `-- MM -- --`. Even though an erratum should be published to bring the W3C XML Schema inline with ISO 8601, most current schema processors expect the (bogus) `-- MM -- --` format.

In the example, I follow the correct ISO 8601 format.

Restrictions

The period (one year) and the duration (one month) are fixed, and no calendars other than Gregorian are supported.

Because of the typo in the W3C XML Schema Specification, you must choose between a bogus format, which works on the current version of the tools, or a correct format, which conforms to ISO 8601.

Example

Valid values include `--05`, `--11Z`, `--11+02:00`, `--11-04:00`, and `--02`.

The following values are invalid: `-01-` (the format must be `--MM`), `--13` (the month is out of range), `--1` (both digits must be provided), or `01` (leading `--` are missing).

---

xsd:gMonthDay

Recurring period of time: yearly day

```
<xsd:simpleType name="gMonthDay" id="gMonthDay">
 <xsd:restriction base="xsd:anySimpleType">
 <xsd:whiteSpace value="collapse" fixed="true"/>
 </xsd:restriction>
</xsd:simpleType>
```

Derived from

xsd:anySimpleType

Primary

xsd:gMonthDay

Known subtypes

None

Data parameters (facets)

enumeration, maxExclusive, maxInclusive, minExclusive, minInclusive, pattern

---

Description

The value space of xsd:gMonthDay is the period of one calendar day recurring each calendar year (such as the third of April); its lexical space follows the ISO 8601 syntax for such periods (i.e., -- MM-DD) with an optional time zone.

When needed, days are reduced to fit in the length of the months, so --02-29 would occur on the 28th of February of nonleap years.

Restrictions

The period (one year) and the duration (one day) are fixed, and no calendars other than Gregorian are supported.

Example

Valid values are --05-01, --11-01Z, --11-01+02:00, --11-01-04:00, --11-15, and --02-29.

The following values are invalid: -01-30- (the format must be --MM-DD), --01-35 (the day part is out of range), --1-5 (the leading zeros are missing), or 01-15 (the leading -- are missing).

---

xsd:gYear   Period of one year

```
<xsd:simpleType name="gYear" id="gYear">
 <xsd:restriction base="xsd:anySimpleType">
 <xsd:whiteSpace value="collapse" fixed="true"/>
 </xsd:restriction>
</xsd:simpleType>
```

Derived from

xsd:anySimpleType

Primary

xsd:gYear

Known subtypes

None

Data parameters (facets)

enumeration, maxExclusive, maxInclusive, minExclusive, minInclusive, pattern

Description

The value space of xsd:gYear is the period of one calendar year (such as the year 2003); its lexical space follows the ISO 8601 syntax for such periods (YYYY) with an optional time zone.

Restrictions

The duration (one year) is fixed, and no calendars other than Gregorian are supported.

Example

Valid values include 2001, 2001+02:00, 2001Z, 2001+00:00, -2001, and -20000.

The following values are invalid: 01 (the century part is missing) or 2001-12 (month parts are forbidden).

---

xsd:gYearMonth   Period of one month

```
<xsd:simpleType name="gYearMonth" id="gYearMonth">
 <xsd:restriction base="xsd:anySimpleType">
 <xsd:whiteSpace value="collapse" fixed="true"/>
 </xsd:restriction>
</xsd:simpleType>
```

Derived from

xsd:anySimpleType

Primary

xsd:gYearMonth

Known subtypes

None

Data parameters (facets)

enumeration, maxExclusive, maxInclusive, minExclusive, minInclusive, pattern

Description

The value space of xsd:gYearMonth is the period of one calendar month in a specific year (such as the month of February 2002); its lexical space follows the ISO 8601 syntax for such periods (i.e., YYYY-MM) with an optional time zone.

Restrictions

The duration (one month) is fixed, and no calendars other than Gregorian are supported.

Example

Valid values are 2001-10, 2001-10+02:00, 2001-10Z, 2001-10+00:00, -2001-10, and -20000-04.

The following values are invalid: 2001 (the month part is missing), 2001-13 (the month part is out of range), 2001-13-26+02:00 (the month part is out of range), or 01-10 (the century part is missing).

xsd:hexBinary

```
<xsd:simpleType name="hexBinary" id="hexBinary">
<xsd:restriction base="xsd:anySimpleType">
<xsd:whiteSpace value="collapse" fixed="true"/>
</xsd:restriction>
</xsd:simpleType>
```

Derived from

xsd:anySimpleType

Primary

xsd:hexBinary

Known subtypes

None

Data parameters (facets)

enumeration, length, maxLength, minLength, pattern

Description

The value space of xsd:hexBinary is the set of all binary contents; its lexical space is a simple coding of each octet as its hexadecimal value.

Restrictions

This datatype shouldn't be confused with another encoding called BinHex, which isn't supported by the W3C XML Schema. Other popular binary text encodings (such as Quote Printable, uuXXcode, BinHex, aencode, or base85, to name a few) aren't supported by the W3C XML Schema.

The expansion factor is high because each binary octet is coded as two characters (i.e., four octets if the document is encoded with UTF-16).

Example

A UTF-8 XML header such as:

```
"<?xml version="1.0" encoding="UTF-8"?>"
```

encoded is:

```
"3f3c6d78206c657673726f693d6e3122302e20226e656f636964676e6223d54552d4622383e3f"
```

xsd:ID

```
<xsd:simpleType name="ID" id="ID">
<xsd:restriction base="xsd:NCName"/>
</xsd:simpleType>
```

Derived from

xsd:NCName

Primary

xsd:string

Known subtypes

None

Data parameters (facets)

enumeration, length, maxLength, minLength, pattern

Description

The purpose of the xsd:ID datatype is to define unique identifiers that are global to a document and emulate the ID attribute type available in the XML DTDs.

Unlike their DTD counterparts, W3C XML Schema ID datatypes can be applied to not only attributes but also simple element content.

For both attributes and simple element content, the lexical domain of these datatypes is the lexical domain of XML nonqualified names (xsd:NCName).

Identifiers defined using this datatype are global to a document and provide a way to uniquely identify their containing element, whatever its type and name is.

The constraint added by this datatype, beyond the xsd:NCName datatype from which it is derived, is that the values of all the attributes and elements that have an ID datatype in a document must be unique.

Note that the behavior of this datatype depends on whether the RELAX NG implementation supports RELAX NG DTD compatibility datatype library, in which case, the uniqueness of the identifiers will be checked. This datatype can be used both for elements and for defining multiple type assignment to attributes defined as ID, depending on their location in the schema.

Restrictions

Applications that need to maintain a level of compatibility with DTDs shouldn't use this datatype for elements but should reserve it for attributes.

The lexical domain (xsd:NCName) of this datatype doesn't allow the definition of numerical identifiers or identifiers containing whitespace.

Example

```
<element name="book">
  <element name="isbn">
    <data type="xsd:int"/>
  </element>
  <element name="title">
    <data type="xsd:string"/>
  </element>
```

```
<element name="author-ref">
  <attribute name="ref">
    <data type="xsd:IDREF"/>
  </attribute>
</element>
<element name="character-refs">
  <data type="xsd:IDREFS"/>
</element>
<attribute name="identifier">
  <data type="xsd:ID"/>
</attribute>
</element>
```

xsd:IDREF

Definition of references to unique identifiers

```
<xsd:simpleType name="IDREF" id="IDREF">
 <xsd:restriction base="xsd:NCName"/>
</xsd:simpleType>
```

Derived from

xsd:NCName

Primary

xsd:string

Known subtypes

xsd:IDREFS

Data parameters (facets)

enumeration, length, maxLength, minLength, pattern

Description

The xsd:IDREF datatype defines references to the identifiers defined by the ID datatype. It emulates the IDREF attribute type of XML DTDs, even though it can be used for simple content elements as well as for attributes.

The lexical space of xsd:IDREF is, like the lexical space of xsd:ID, nonqualified XML names (NCName).

RELAX NG implementations supporting the DTD compatibility feature add a constraint for this datatype beyond the xsd:NCName datatype from which it is derived; the values of all the attributes and elements that have a xsd:IDREF datatype must match an ID defined within the same document.

Restrictions

Applications that need to maintain compatibility with DTDs shouldn't use this datatype for elements, but should instead reserve it for attributes.

The lexical domain (NCName) of this datatype doesn't allow definition of numerical key references or references containing whitespace.

Example

```
<element name="book">
  <element name="isbn">
    <data type="xsd:int"/>
  </element>
  <element name="title">
    <data type="xsd:string"/>
  </element>
  <element name="author-ref">
    <attribute name="ref">
      <data type="xsd:IDREF"/>
    </attribute>
  </element>
  <element name="character-refs">
    <data type="xsd:IDREFS"/>
  </element>
  <attribute name="identifier">
    <data type="xsd:ID"/>
  </attribute>
</element>
```

xsd:IDREFS

Definition of lists of references to unique identifiers

```
<xsd:simpleType name="IDREFS" id="IDREFS">
 <xsd:restriction>
 <xsd:simpleType>
 <xsd:list>
 <xsd:simpleType>
 <xsd:restriction base="xsd:IDREF"/>
 </xsd:simpleType>
 </xsd:list>
 </xsd:simpleType>
 <xsd:minLength value="1"/>
 </xsd:restriction>
</xsd:simpleType>
```

Derived from

xsd:IDREF

Primary

None

Known subtypes

None

Data parameters (facets)

enumeration, length, maxLength, minLength

Description

xsd:IDREFS is derived as a list from xsd:IDREF. It represents whitespace-separated lists of references to identifiers that are defined using the ID datatype.

The lexical space of xsd:IDREFS is the lexical space of a list of xsd:NCName values with a minimum length of one element (xsd:IDREFS can't be empty lists).

For RELAX NG implementations that support the DTD compatibility library, xsd:IDREFS emulates the IDREFS attribute type of the XML DTDs, even though it can define simple content elements as well as attributes.

Restrictions

Applications that need to maintain compatibility with DTDs shouldn't use this datatype for elements, but instead should reserve it for attributes.

The lexical domain (lists of xsd:NCName) of this datatype doesn't allow the definition of lists of numerical key references or references containing whitespace.

Example

```
<element name="book">
  <element name="isbn">
    <data type="xsd:int"/>
  </element>
  <element name="title">
    <data type="xsd:string"/>
  </element>
  <element name="author-ref">
    <attribute name="ref">
      <data type="xsd:IDREF"/>
    </attribute>
  </element>
  <element name="character-refs">
    <data type="xsd:IDREFS"/>
  </element>
  <attribute name="identifier">
    <data type="xsd:ID"/>
  </attribute>
</element>
```

xsd:int   32-bit signed integers

```
<xsd:simpleType name="int" id="int">
 <xsd:restriction base="xsd:long">
 <xsd:minInclusive value="-2147483648"/>
 <xsd:maxInclusive value="2147483647"/>
 </xsd:restriction>
</xsd:simpleType>
```

Derived from

`xsd:long`

Primary

`xsd:decimal`

Known subtypes

`xsd:short`

Data parameters (facets)

`enumeration, fractionDigits, maxExclusive, maxInclusive, minExclusive, minInclusive, pattern, totalDigits`

Description

The value space of `xsd:int` is the set of common single-size integers (32 bits), the integers between −2147483648 and 2147483647. Its lexical space allows any number of insignificant leading zeros.

Restrictions

The decimal point (even when followed only by insignificant zeros) is forbidden.

−0 and +0 are considered equal, which is different from the behavior of `xsd:float` and `xsd:double`.

Example

Valid values include `-2147483648`, `0`, `-000000000000000000005`, or `2147483647`.

Invalid values include `-2147483649` and `1..`.

---

xsd:integer
Signed integers of arbitrary length

```
<xsd:simpleType name="integer" id="integer">
 <xsd:restriction base="xsd:decimal">
 <xsd:fractionDigits value="0" fixed="true"/>
 </xsd:restriction>
</xsd:simpleType>
```

Derived from

`xsd:decimal`

Primary

`xsd:decimal`

Known subtypes

`xsd:nonPositiveInteger, xsd:long, xsd:nonNegativeInteger`

Data parameters (facets)

enumeration, fractionDigits, maxExclusive, maxInclusive, minExclusive, minInclusive, pattern, totalDigits

Description

The value space of xsd:integer includes the set of all the signed integers, with no restriction on range. Its lexical space allows any number of insignificant leading zeros.

Restrictions

The decimal point (even when followed only by insignificant zeros) is forbidden.

−0 and +0 are considered equal, which is different from the behavior of xsd:float and xsd:double.

Example

Valid values for xsd:integer include -12345678901234567890123456789012345678 90, 2147483647, 0, or -000000000000000000000005.

Invalid values include 1., 2.6, and A.

---

xsd:language

```
<xsd:simpleType name="language" id="language">
 <xsd:restriction base="xsd:token">
 <xsd:pattern
 value="([a-zA-Z]{2}|[iI]-[a-zA-Z]+|[xX]-[a-zA-Z]{1,8})(-[a-zA-Z]{1,8})*"
 />
 </xsd:restriction>
</xsd:simpleType>
```

Derived from

xsd:token

Primary

xsd:string

Known subtypes

None

Data parameters (facets)

enumeration, length, maxLength, minLength, pattern

Description

The lexical and value spaces of xsd:language are the set of language codes defined by RFC 1766.

Restrictions

Although the schema for schema defines a test to perform expressed as patterns (see the definition), the lexical space is the set of existing language codes.

Example

Some valid values for this datatype are: en, en-US, fr, or fr-FR.

xsd:long

```
<xsd:simpleType name="long" id="long">
 <xsd:restriction base="xsd:integer">
 <xsd:minInclusive value="-9223372036854775808"/>
 <xsd:maxInclusive value="9223372036854775807"/>
 </xsd:restriction>
</xsd:simpleType>
```

Derived from

xsd:integer

Primary

xsd:decimal

Known subtypes

xsd:int

Data parameters (facets)

enumeration, fractionDigits, maxExclusive, maxInclusive, minExclusive, minInclusive, pattern, totalDigits

Description

The value space of xsd:long is the set of common double-size integers (64 bits)—the integers between −9223372036854775808 and 9223372036854775807. Its lexical space allows any number of insignificant leading zeros.

Restrictions

The decimal point (even when followed only by insignificant zeros) is forbidden.

Example

Valid values for xsd:long include -9223372036854775808, 0, -0000000000000000000005, and 9223372036854775807.

Invalid values include 9223372036854775808 and 1..

xsd:Name

```
<xsd:simpleType name="Name" id="Name">
 <xsd:restriction base="xsd:token">
 <xsd:pattern value="\i\c*"/>
 </xsd:restriction>
</xsd:simpleType>
```

Derived from

xsd:token

Primary

xsd:string

Known subtypes

xsd:NCName

Data parameters (facets)

enumeration, length, maxLength, minLength, pattern

Description

The lexical and value spaces of xsd:Name are the tokens (NMTOKEN) that conform to the definition of a name in XML 1.0.

Restrictions

Following XML 1.0, those names may contain colons, but no special meaning is attached to them. Another datatype (xsd:QName) should be used for qualified names when they use namespace prefixes.

Example

Valid values include Snoopy, CMS, and _1950-10-04_10:00.

Invalid values include 0836217462 (a xsd:Name can't start with a number) and bold,brash (commas are forbidden).

xsd:NCName

```
<xsd:simpleType name="NCName" id="NCName">
 <xsd:restriction base="xsd:Name">
 <xsd:pattern value="[\i-[:]][\c-[:]]*"/>
 </xsd:restriction>
</xsd:simpleType>
```

Derived from

xsd:Name

Primary

`xsd:string`

Known subtypes

`xsd:ID, xsd:IDREF, xsd:ENTITY`

Data parameters (facets)

`enumeration, length, maxLength, minLength, pattern`

Description

The lexical and value spaces of `xsd:NCName` are the names (`Name`) that conform to the definition of a `NCName` in the Recommendation "Namespaces in XML 1.0." These are all the XML 1.0 names that don't contain colons.

Restrictions

This datatype allows characters such as hyphens and may need additional constraints to match the notion of name in your favorite programming language or database system.

Example

Valid values include Snoopy, CMS, `_1950-10-04_10-00`, and `bold_brash`.

Invalid values include `_1950-10-04:10-00` and `bold:brash` (colons are forbidden).

---

xsd:negativeInteger   Strictly negative integers of arbitrary length

```
<xsd:simpleType name="negativeInteger" id="negativeInteger">
 <xsd:restriction base="xsd:nonPositiveInteger">
 <xsd:maxInclusive value="-1"/>
 </xsd:restriction>
</xsd:simpleType>
```

Derived from

`xsd:nonPositiveInteger`

Primary

`xsd:decimal`

Known subtypes

None

Data parameters (facets)

`enumeration, fractionDigits, maxExclusive, maxInclusive, minExclusive, minInclusive, pattern, totalDigits`

Description

The value space of xsd:negativeInteger includes the set of all the strictly negative integers (excluding zero), with no restriction of range. Its lexical space allows any number of insignificant leading zeros.

Restrictions

The decimal point (even when followed only by insignificant zeros) is forbidden.

Example

Valid values for xsd:negativeInteger include -123456789012345678901234567890, -1, and -0000000000000000000000005.

Invalid values include 0 or -1..

---

xsd:NMTOKEN   XML 1.0 name token (NMTOKEN)

```xsd
<xsd:simpleType name="NMTOKEN" id="NMTOKEN">
 <xsd:restriction base="xsd:token">
 <xsd:pattern value="\c+"/>
 </xsd:restriction>
</xsd:simpleType>
```

Derived from

xsd:token

Primary

xsd:string

Known subtypes

xsd:NMTOKENS

Data parameters (facets)

enumeration, length, maxLength, minLength, pattern

Description

The lexical and value spaces of xsd:NMTOKEN are the set of XML 1.0 name tokens, tokens composed of characters, digits, period, colons, hyphens, and the characters defined by Unicode, such as "combining" or "extender."

Restrictions

This type is usually called a token.

Example

Valid values include Snoopy, CMS, 1950-10-04, and 0836217462.

Invalid values include brought classical music to the Peanuts strip (spaces are forbidden) and bold,brash (commas are forbidden).

---

xsd:NMTOKENS

List of XML 1.0 name tokens (NMTOKEN)

```
<xsd:simpleType name="NMTOKENS" id="NMTOKENS">
<xsd:restriction>
<xsd:simpleType>
<xsd:list>
<xsd:simpleType>
<xsd:restriction base="xsd:NMTOKEN"/>
</xsd:simpleType>
</xsd:list>
</xsd:simpleType>
<xsd:minLength value="1"/>
</xsd:restriction>
</xsd:simpleType>
```

Derived from

xsd:NMTOKEN

Primary

None

Known subtypes

None

Data parameters (facets)

enumeration, length, maxLength, minLength

Description

xsd:NMTOKENS is derived by list from xsd:NMTOKEN and represents whitespace-separated lists of XML 1.0 name tokens.

Restrictions

None

Example

Valid values include Snoopy, CMS, 1950-10-04, 0836217462 0836217463, and brought classical music to the Peanuts strip (note that, in this case, the sentence is considered to be list of words).

Invalid values include "brought classical music to the Peanuts" "strip" (quotes are forbidden) and bold,brash (commas are forbidden).

xsd:nonNegativeInteger

```
<xsd:simpleType name="nonNegativeInteger" id="nonNegativeInteger">
 <xsd:restriction base="xsd:integer">
 <xsd:minInclusive value="0"/>
 </xsd:restriction>
</xsd:simpleType>
```

Derived from

xsd:integer

Primary

xsd:decimal

Known subtypes

xsd:unsignedLong, xsd:positiveInteger

Data parameters (facets)

enumeration, fractionDigits, maxExclusive, maxInclusive, minExclusive, minInclusive, pattern, totalDigits

Description

The value space of xsd:nonNegativeInteger includes the set of all the integers greater than or equal to zero, with no restriction of range. Its lexical space allows any number of insignificant leading zeros.

Restrictions

The decimal point (even when followed only by insignificant zeros) is forbidden.

Example

Valid values include +123456789012345678901234567890, 0, 0000000000000000000005, and 2147483647.

Invalid values include 1. and -1..

xsd:nonPositiveInteger

```
<xsd:simpleType name="nonPositiveInteger" id="nonPositiveInteger">
 <xsd:restriction base="xsd:integer">
 <xsd:maxInclusive value="0"/>
 </xsd:restriction>
</xsd:simpleType>
```

Derived from

xsd:integer

Primary

`xsd:decimal`

Known subtypes

`xsd:negativeInteger`

Data parameters (facets)

`enumeration, fractionDigits, maxExclusive, maxInclusive, minExclusive, minInclusive, pattern, totalDigits`

Description

The value space of `xsd:nonPositiveInteger` includes the set of all the integers less than or equal to zero, with no restriction of range. Its lexical space allows any number of insignificant leading zeros.

Restrictions

The decimal point (even when followed only by insignificant zeros) is forbidden.

Example

Valid values include `-123456789012345678901234567890`, `0`, `-000000000000000000000005`, and `-2147483647`.

Invalid values include `-1.` and `1.`.

---

xsd:normalizedString   Whitespace-replaced strings

```
<xsd:simpleType name="normalizedString" id="normalizedString">
<xsd:restriction base="xsd:string">
<xsd:whiteSpace value="replace"/>
</xsd:restriction>
</xsd:simpleType>
```

Derived from

`xsd:string`

Primary

`xsd:string`

Known subtypes

`xsd:token`

Data parameters (facets)

`enumeration, length, maxLength, minLength, pattern`

Description

The lexical space of `xsd:normalizedString` is unconstrained (any valid XML character may be used). Its value space is the set of strings after whitespace replacement—i.e., after any occurrence of #x9 (tab), #xA (linefeed), and #xD (carriage return) have been replaced by an occurrence of #x20 (space) without any whitespace collapsing.

Restrictions

This is the only datatype that performs whitespace replacement without collapsing. When whitespace isn't significant, `xsd:token` is preferred.

This datatype corresponds neither to the XPath function `normalize-space()` (which performs whitespace trimming and collapsing) nor to the DOM normalize method (which is a merge of adjacent text objects).

Example

The value of the element:

```
<title lang="en">
  Being a Dog Is
  a Full-Time Job
</title>"
```

is the string: " Being a Dog Is a Full-Time Job ", in which all whitespace has been replaced by spaces, if the title element is a type `xsd:normalizedString`.

---

xsd:NOTATION   Emulation of the XML 1.0 feature

```
<xsd:simpleType name="NOTATION" id="NOTATION">
 <xsd:restriction base="xsd:anySimpleType">
 <xsd:whiteSpace value="collapse" fixed="true"/>
 </xsd:restriction>
</xsd:simpleType>
```

Derived from

xsd:anySimpleType

Primary

xsd:NOTATION

Known subtypes

None

Data parameters (facets)

enumeration, length, maxLength, minLength, pattern

Description

For the W3C XML Schema, the value and lexical spaces of xsd:NOTATION are references to notations declared though the xsd:notation element. This element doesn't exist in RELAX NG; there, this datatype can be seen as a synonym for xsd:QName with backward compatibility for the W3C XML Schema.

Restrictions

Notations are seldom used in real-world applications.

---

xsd:positiveInteger
Strictly positive integers of arbitrary length

```
<xsd:simpleType name="positiveInteger" id="positiveInteger">
 <xsd:restriction base="xsd:nonNegativeInteger">
 <xsd:minInclusive value="1"/>
 </xsd:restriction>
</xsd:simpleType>
```

Derived from

xsd:nonNegativeInteger

Primary

xsd:decimal

Known subtypes

None

Data parameters (facets)

enumeration, fractionDigits, maxExclusive, maxInclusive, minExclusive, minInclusive, pattern, totalDigits

Description

The value space of xsd:positiveInteger includes the set of the strictly positive integers (excluding zero), with no restriction of range. Its lexical space allows any number of insignificant leading zeros.

Restrictions

The decimal point (even when followed only by insignificant zeros) is forbidden.

Example

Valid values include 123456789012345678901234567890, 1, and 000000000000000000000005.

Invalid values include 0 and 1.

xsd:QName

```
<xsd:simpleType name="QName" id="QName">
 <xsd:restriction base="xsd:anySimpleType">
 <xsd:whiteSpace value="collapse" fixed="true"/>
 </xsd:restriction>
</xsd:simpleType>
```

Derived from

xsd:anySimpleType

Primary

xsd:QName

Known subtypes

None

Data parameters (facets)

enumeration, length, maxLength, minLength, pattern

Description

The lexical space of xsd:QName is a qualified name according to Namespaces in XML. It is a local name (which is an xsd:NCName) with an optional prefix (itself an xsd:NCName), separated by a colon. The prefix is declared a namespace prefix in the scope of the element carrying the value. Its value space comprises the pairs (namespace URI, local name) in which the namespace URI is the URI associated to the prefix in the namespace declaration.

Restrictions

It is impossible to apply a pattern on the namespace URI.

The usage of QNames in elements and attributes is controversial because it creates a dependency between the content of the document and its markup. However, the official position of the W3C doesn't discourage this practice.

Example

W3C XML Schema itself has already provided some examples of QNames. When I wrote "<xsd:attribute name="lang" type="xsd:language"/>", the type attribute was a xsd:QName, and its value was the tuple {"http://www.w3.org/2001/XMLSchema", "language"}, because the URI "http://www.w3.org/2001/XMLSchema" had been assigned to the prefix "xsd:". If there is no namespace declaration for this prefix, the type attribute is considered invalid.

xsd:short

```
<xsd:simpleType name="short" id="short">
 <xsd:restriction base="xsd:int">
```

```
    <xsd:minInclusive value="-32768"/>
    <xsd:maxInclusive value="32767"/>
    </xsd:restriction>
  </xsd:simpleType>
```

Derived from

xsd:int

Primary

xsd:decimal

Known subtypes

xsd:byte

Data parameters (facets)

enumeration, fractionDigits, maxExclusive, maxInclusive, minExclusive, minInclusive, pattern, totalDigits

Description

The value space of xsd:short is the set of common short integers (16 bits)—the integers between −32768 and 32767. Its lexical space allows any number of insignificant leading zeros.

Restrictions

The decimal point (even when followed only by insignificant zeros) is forbidden.

Example

Valid values include -32768, 0, -0000000000000000000005, and 32767.

Invalid values include 32768 and 1..

---

xsd:string

Any string

```
    <xsd:simpleType name="string" id="string">
     <xsd:restriction base="xsd:anySimpleType">
     <xsd:whiteSpace value="preserve"/>
     </xsd:restriction>
    </xsd:simpleType>
```

Derived from

xsd:anySimpleType

Primary

xsd:string

Known subtypes

xsd:normalizedString

Data parameters (facets)

enumeration, length, maxLength, minLength, pattern

Description

The lexical and value spaces of xsd:string are the set of all possible strings composed of any character allowed in a XML 1.0 document without any treatment done on whitespace.

Restrictions

This is the only datatype that leaves all the whitespace. When whitespace isn't significant, xsd:token is preferred.

Example

The value of the following element:

```
<title lang="en">
  Being a Dog Is
  a Full-Time Job
</title>
```

is the full string Being a Dog Is a Full-Time Job, with all its tabulations, and CR/LF if the title element is a xsd:string type.

xsd:time

Point in time recurring each day

```
<xsd:simpleType name="time" id="time">
 <xsd:restriction base="xsd:anySimpleType">
 <xsd:whiteSpace value="collapse" fixed="true"/>
 </xsd:restriction>
</xsd:simpleType>
```

Derived from

xsd:anySimpleType

Primary

xsd:time

Known subtypes

None

Data parameters (facets)

enumeration, maxExclusive, maxInclusive, minExclusive, minInclusive, pattern

Description

The lexical space of xsd:time is identical to the time part of xsd:dateTime (hh:mm:ss[Z|(+|-)hh:mm]), and its value space is the set of points in time recurring daily.

Restrictions

The period (one day) is fixed, and no calendars other than Gregorian are supported.

Example

Valid values include 21:32:52, 21:32:52+02:00, 19:32:52Z, 19:32:52+00:00, and 21:32:52.12679.

Invalid values include 21:32 (all the parts must be specified), 25:25:10 (the hour part is out of range), -10:00:00 (the hour part is out of range), and 1:20:10 (all the digits must be supplied).

---

xsd:token   Whitespace-replaced and collapsed strings

```
<xsd:simpleType name="token" id="token">
 <xsd:restriction base="xsd:normalizedString">
 <xsd:whiteSpace value="collapse"/>
 </xsd:restriction>
</xsd:simpleType>
```

Derived from

xsd:normalizedString

Primary

xsd:string

Known subtypes

xsd:language, xsd:NMTOKEN, xsd:Name

Data parameters (facets)

enumeration, length, maxLength, minLength, pattern

Description

The lexical and value spaces of xsd:token are the sets of all strings after whitespace replacement; i.e., after any occurrence of #x9 (tab), #xA (linefeed), or #xD (carriage return). These are replaced by an occurrence of #x20 (space) and collapsing. Collapsing is when contiguous occurrences of spaces are replaced by a single space, and leading and trailing spaces are removed.

More simply, xsd:token is the most appropriate datatype to use for strings that don't care about whitespace.

Restrictions

The name xsd:token is misleading, as whitespace is allowed within xsd:token. xsd:NMTOKEN is the type corresponding to what are usually called tokens.

Example

The element:

```
<title lang="en">
  Being a Dog Is
  a Full-Time Job
</title>
```

is a valid xsd:token, and its value is the string Being a Dog Is a Full-Time Job, in which all the extra whitespace has been replaced by single spaces. Leading and trailing spaces have been removed, and contiguous sequences of spaces have been replaced by single spaces.

---

xsd:unsignedByte

Unsigned value of 8 bits

```
<xsd:simpleType name="unsignedByte" id="unsignedBtype">
<xsd:restriction base="xsd:unsignedShort">
<xsd:maxInclusive value="255"/>
</xsd:restriction>
</xsd:simpleType>
```

Derived from

xsd:unsignedShort

Primary

xsd:decimal

Known subtypes

None

Data parameters (facets)

enumeration, fractionDigits, maxExclusive, maxInclusive, minExclusive, minInclusive, pattern, totalDigits

Description

The value space of xsd:unsignedByte is the range of integers between 0 and 255—the unsigned values that can fit in a word of 8 bits. Its lexical space allows an optional + sign and leading zeros before the significant digits.

Restrictions

The lexical space doesn't allow values expressed in other numeration bases (such as hexadecimal, octal, or binary).

The decimal point (even when followed only by insignificant zeros) is forbidden.

Example

Valid values include 255, 0, +00000000000000000000005, and 1.

Invalid values include -1 and 1..

---

xsd:unsignedInt

Unsigned integer of 32 bits

```xml
<xsd:simpleType name="unsignedInt" id="unsignedInt">
 <xsd:restriction base="xsd:unsignedLong">
 <xsd:maxInclusive value="4294967295"/>
 </xsd:restriction>
</xsd:simpleType>
```

Derived from

xsd:unsignedLong

Primary

xsd:decimal

Known subtypes

xsd:unsignedShort

Data parameters (facets)

enumeration, fractionDigits, maxExclusive, maxInclusive, minExclusive, minInclusive, pattern, totalDigits

Description

The value space of xsd:unsignedInt is the range of integers between 0 and 4294967295—the unsigned values that can fit in a word of 32 bits. Its lexical space allows an optional + sign and leading zeros before the significant digits.

Restrictions

The decimal point (even when followed only by insignificant zeros) is forbidden.

Example

Valid values include 4294967295, 0, +00000000000000000000005, and 1.

Invalid values include -1 and 1..

---

xsd:unsignedLong

Unsigned integer of 64 bits

```xml
<xsd:simpleType name="unsignedLong" id="unsignedLong">
 <xsd:restriction base="xsd:nonNegativeInteger">
 <xsd:maxInclusive value="18446744073709551615"/>
 </xsd:restriction>
</xsd:simpleType>
```

Derived from

`xsd:nonNegativeInteger`

Primary

`xsd:decimal`

Known subtypes

`xsd:unsignedInt`

Data parameters (facets)

`enumeration, fractionDigits, maxExclusive, maxInclusive, minExclusive, minInclusive, pattern, totalDigits`

Description

The value space of `xsd:unsignedLong` is the range of integers between 0 and 18446744073709551615—the unsigned values that can fit in a word of 64 bits. Its lexical space allows an optional + sign and leading zeros before the significant digits.

Restrictions

The decimal point (even when followed only by insignificant zeros) is forbidden.

Example

Valid values include 18446744073709551615, 0, +0000000000000000000005, and 1.

Invalid values include -1 and 1.

---

xsd:unsignedShort

Unsigned integer of 16 bits

```
<xsd:simpleType name="unsignedShort" id="unsignedShort">
 <xsd:restriction base="xsd:unsignedInt">
 <xsd:maxInclusive value="65535"/>
 </xsd:restriction>
</xsd:simpleType>
```

Derived from

`xsd:unsignedInt`

Primary

`xsd:decimal`

Known subtypes

`xsd:unsignedByte`

Data parameters (facets)

enumeration, fractionDigits, maxExclusive, maxInclusive, minExclusive, minInclusive, pattern, totalDigits

Description

The value space of xsd:unsignedShort is the range of integers between 0 and 65535—the unsigned values that can fit in a word of 16 bits. Its lexical space allows an optional + sign and leading zeros before the significant digits.

Restrictions

The decimal point (even when followed only by insignificant zeros) is forbidden.

Example

Valid values include 65535, 0, +0000000000000000000005, and 1.

Invalid values include -1 and 1..

Appendixes

DSDL

Although RELAX NG started as a standalone project under the auspices of the Organization for the Advancement of Structured Information Standards (OASIS), RELAX NG is now being standardized at ISO (ISO/IEC JTC1 SC34 WG1, to be precise) as a part of a multipart standard named DSDL (see *http://dsdl.org*).

DSDL (Document Schema Definition Languages) recognizes that the validation of XML documents is a subject too wide and complex to be covered by a single language. It also acknowledges that the industry needs a set of simple and dedicated languages to perform different validation tasks—as well as a framework in which these languages may be used together.

Validating (or schematizing) XML documents may involve:

- Validating the structure of the document: i.e., checking the containment of elements and attributes (this is the domain in which RELAX NG is very good).

- Validating the content of each text node and attribute independently of each other (this is where datatype libraries are needed).

- Validating integrity constraints between different elements and attributes.

- Validating any other rules (often called *business rules*).

Throughout this book, you've seen that RELAX NG is simple and efficient because it stays focused on solving one—and only one—problem. There are huge gaps that can't be covered by RELAX NG. For instance, if an XML vocabulary includes mixed-content models, you can't restrict the content of your documents to ASCII; neither can you define that the content of your modeling element must be spell-checked. The goal of DSDL is to provide a means to fill out these gaps and to cover the whole domain of document validation.

DSDL can be seen as a framework and set of languages that checks the quality of XML documents, a crucial issue for any XML based application. Recent works such as the presentation given by Simon Riggs at XML Europe 2003 or the work of Isabelle Boydens (*Informatique, normes et temps,* Bruxelles, Éditions E. Bruylant, 1999.)

about the quality of large databases have shown that about 10% of XML documents (or data records) contain at least one error. This level of quality is unacceptable for many applications; and so DSDL can be an absolutely indispensable technology for many XML applications.

A Multipart Standard

DSDL is still a work in progress. It is a multipart specification, with each of the parts presenting a different schema language (except Part 1, which is an introduction, and Part 10, which is the description of the framework itself).

Part 1: Overview

This part is a roadmap describing DSDL and introducing each of the parts.

Part 2: Regular Grammar-Based Validation

This part covers RELAX NG; it rewrites the RELAX NG OASIS Technical Committee specification to meet the requirements of ISO publications. Its wording is more formal than the OASIS specification, but the features of the language are the same. Any RELAX NG implementation that conforms to either of these two documents is also conformant to the other.

DSDL Part 2 is now a Final Draft International Standard (FDIS); i.e., an official ISO standard.

Part 3: Rule-Based Validation

This part of DSDL describes the next release of the rule-based schema language known as Schematron. The current version of Schematron has been defined by Rick Jelliffe and other contributors as a language that expresses sets of rules as XPath expressions (or more accurately, as XSLT expressions because XSLT functions such as document( ) are also supported in XPath expressions). Its home page is *http://www. ascc.net/xml/schematron/*.

Without going into the details of the language, a Schematron schema is composed of sets of rules named *patterns* (these patterns shouldn't be confused with RELAX NG patterns). Each pattern includes one or more rules. Each rule sets the context nodes under which tests are performed, and each test is performed either as an assert or as a report. An assert is a test that raises an error if it is not verified, while a report is a test that raises an error if it is specified.

A fragment of a Schematron schema for our library could be:

```
<sch:schema xmlns:sch="http://www.ascc.net/xml/schematron">
<sch:title>Schematron Schema for library</sch:title>
```

```
<sch:pattern>
 <sch:rule context="/">
  <sch:assert test="library">The document element should be "library".</sch:assert>
 </sch:rule>
 <sch:rule context="/library">
  <sch:assert test="book">There should be at least a book!</sch:assert>
  <sch:assert test="not(@*)">No attribute for library, please!</sch:assert>
 </sch:rule>
 <sch:rule context="/library/book">
  <sch:report test="following-sibling::book/@id=@id">
     Duplicated ID for this book.</sch:report>
  <sch:assert test="@id=concat('_', isbn)">
     The id should be derived from the ISBN.</sch:assert>
 </sch:rule>
 <sch:rule context="/library/*">
  <sch:assert test="self::book or self::author or self::character">
     This element shouldn't be here...</sch:assert>
 </sch:rule>
 </sch:pattern>
</sch:schema>
```

You can see from this simple example that it would be verbose to write a full schema with Schematron because it means writing a rule for each element. In this rule writing, all the individual tests that check the content model, and eventually the relative order between child elements, must be specified. You can also see that it does very well expressing what are often called business rules, such as:

```
<sch:assert test="@id=concat('_', isbn)">The id should be derived
   from the ISBN.</sch:assert>
```

This example checks that the id attribute of a book is derived from its ISBN element by adding a leading underscore.

DSDL Part 3, the next version of Schematron, will keep this structure and add still more power by allowing it to use not only XPath 1.0 expressions, but also expressions taken from other languages such as EXSLT (a standard extension library for XSLT), XPath 2.0, XSLT 2.0, and even XQuery 1.0.

Part 4: Selection of Validation Candidates

Although RELAX NG provides a way to write and combine modular schemas, it is often the case that you need to validate a composite document against existing schemas that might be written using different languages; you might want, for instance, to validate XHTML documents with embedded RDF statements. In this case, you need to split your documents into pieces and validate each piece against its own schema.

The first contribution to Part 4 was an ISO specification known as RELAX Namespace by Murata Makoto. This contribution was followed by Modular Namespaces (MNS) by James Clark, and Namespace Switchboard by Rick Jelliffe. The latest contribution, Namespace Routing Language (NRL), was made by James

Clark in June 2003 and builds on previous proposals. Although it is too early to say whether NRL will become DSDL Part 4, it will most likely influence it heavily. NRL is implemented in the latest versions of Jing.

The first example given in the specification (*http://www.thaiopensource.com/relaxng/nrl.html*) shows how NRL can validate a SOAP message containing one or more XHTML documents:

```
<rules xmlns="http://www.thaiopensource.com/validate/nrl">
  <namespace ns="http://schemas.xmlsoap.org/soap/envelope/">
    <validate schema="soap-envelope.xsd"/>
  </namespace>
  <namespace ns="http://www.w3.org/1999/xhtml">
    <validate schema="xhtml.rng"/>
  </namespace>
</rules>
```

This example splits the SOAP messages into two parts. The SOAP envelope is validated against the W3C XML Schema *soap-envelope.xsd*. The one or more XHTML documents found in the body of the SOAP message are validated against the RELAX NG schema *xhtml.rng*.

More advanced features are available including namespace wildcards, validation modes, open schemas, transparent namespaces, and NRL. These features seem to be able to handle the most complex cases until the basic assumption that instance documents may be split according to the namespaces of its elements and attributes is met.

Part 5: Datatypes

The goal of this part is to define a set of primitive datatypes with their constraining facets and the mechanisms to derive new datatypes from this set. It is fair to say that it's probably the least developed, yet most complex part of DSDL. While people agree on what shouldn't be done, it is difficult to get beyond the criticism of existing systems such as W3C XML Schema datatypes to propose something better.

Some interesting ideas were raised during the last DSDL meeting in May 2003 that tend to converge with threads on the XML-DEV mailing list in June. This may lead to something more constructive in future DSDL meetings.

Part 6: Path-Based Integrity Constraints

The goal of this part is basically to define a feature covering W3C XML Schema's xs:unique, xs:key and xs:keyref. Part 6 hasn't had any contributions yet.

Part 7: Character Repertoire Validation

Part 7 allows you to specify which characters can be used in specific elements and attributes or within entire XML documents. The W3C note "A Notation for

Character Collections for the WWW" (*http://www.w3.org/TR/charcol/*), is used as an input for Part 7. The first contribution is "Character Repertoire Validation for XML" (CRVX) (*http://dret.net/netdret/docs/wilde-crvx-www2003.html*).

A simple example of CRVX is:

```
<crvx xmlns="http://dret.net/xmlns/crvx10">
  <restrict structure="ename aname pitarget" charrep="\p{IsBasicLatin}"/>
  <restrict structure="ename aname" charrep="[^0-9]"/>
</crvx>
```

In this proposal, the structure attribute contains identifiers for element names (ename), attribute names (aname), Processing Instruction targets (pitarget), and other XML constructions including element and attribute contents. This example thus requires that element and attribute names and Processing Instruction targets must use characters from the BasicLatin block and that element and attribute names must not use digits.

There is some overlap between Part 7 and other schema languages such as Part 2 (RELAX NG). You need to take care that your names match the rules defined in both places, and you can use the data pattern to check the content of attributes and simple content elements. However, Part 7 gives you a more focused way to express these rules independently of other schemas. It fills some gaps in such constraints: RELAX NG can't express such constraints on name classes nor on mixed content elements.

Part 8: Declarative Document Architectures

This section is still in development. The idea here is to allow you to add information (such as default values) to documents depending on the structure of the document. The only input considered for Part 8 so far is known as Architectural Forms, an old technology with strong adherents but limited use.

Part 9: Namespace- and Datatype-Aware DTDs

There were plenty of good things in DTDs, especially in SGML DTDs. Many people are still using them and question the need to put them in the trash and then define new schema languages to support namespaces and datatypes. DSDL Part 9 is for these people who would like to rely on years DTD experience without losing all the goodies of newer schema languages. Despite a burst of discussion in April 2002, this part hasn't advanced yet.

Part 10: Validation Management

Last but not least, Part 10 (formerly known as Part 1: *Interoperability Framework*) is the cement that lets you use the different parts from DSDL together with external tools such as XSLT, W3C XML Schema, or your favorite spell checker, to reuse an example given in the introduction to this chapter.

Here again, different contributions have been made, including my own "XML Validation Interoperability Framework" XVIF and Rick Jelliffe's Schemachine. The latest contribution is known (and implemented) as *xvif/outie* (see *http://downloads.xmlschemata.org/python/xvif/outie/about.xhtml*).

A simple example of a xvif/outie document is:

```
<?xml version="1.0" encoding="utf-8"?>Declarative Document Architectures

<framework>
 <rule>
  <instance>
   <transform transformation="normalize.xslt"/>
  </instance>
  <assert>
   <isValid schema="schema.rng"/>
   <isValid schema="schema.sch"/>
  </assert>
 </rule>
</framework>
```

This document defines a rule that checks on the result of the XSLT transformation *normalize.xslt* that is applied to the instance document. This rule states that the result of the transformation must be valid for both *schema.rng* and *schema.sch*.

What DSDL Should Bring You

As a RELAX NG user, DSDL should bring you all that RELAX NG ignored in its relentless focus on the validation of the structure of XML documents, and even more:

- You are already using Part 2 (RELAX NG).

- Part 3 (*Schematron*) gives you the ability to add highly flexible business rules to your schemas.

- Part 4 (*Selection of Validation Candidates*) lets you write and reuse schemas written in any language and combine them to validate composite documents.

- Part 5 (*Datatypes*) should provide a better alternative to W3C XML Schema datatypes.

- Part 6 (*Path-Based Integrity Constraints*) lets you specify integrity constraints between elements and attributes.

- Part 7 (*Character Repertoire Validation*) will let you specify which characters may be used in your documents.

- Part 8 (*Declarative Document Architectures*) lets you make explicit information that was previously only implicit to your documents before validation.

- Part 9 (*Namespace- and Datatype-Aware DTDs*) lets you upgrade and reuse your DTDs in the context of newer applications.

- Part 10 (*Validation Management*) lets you combine these parts and plug in other transformation and validation tools.

If you like RELAX NG, I am sure that you'll enjoy the other members of the DSDL family. They share the same principles of focusing on solving very specific issues. This focus keeps them powerful and easy to use.

The GNU Free Documentation License

Published editions of this book are being released under the GNU Free Documentation License, a copy of which is provided in this appendix. The online version of this document is maintained at *http://dubinko.info/writing/xforms/*. In addition, updates, examples, and other things that didn't make it into the printed version of the book can be found there.

GNU Free Documentation License

Version 1.2, November 2002

```
Copyright (C) 2000,2001,2002 Free Software Foundation, Inc.
59 Temple Place, Suite 330, Boston, MA 02111-1307 USA
Everyone is permitted to copy and distribute verbatim copies
of this license document, but changing it is not allowed.
```

0. Preamble

The purpose of this License is to make a manual, textbook, or other functional and useful document "free" in the sense of freedom: to assure everyone the effective freedom to copy and redistribute it, with or without modifying it, either commercially or noncommercially. Secondarily, this License preserves for the author and publisher a way to get credit for their work, while not being considered responsible for modifications made by others.

This License is a kind of "copyleft", which means that derivative works of the document must themselves be free in the same sense. It complements the GNU General Public License, which is a copyleft license designed for free software.

We have designed this License in order to use it for manuals for free software, because free software needs free documentation: a free program should come with manuals providing the same freedoms that the software does. But this License is not limited to software manuals; it can be used for any textual work, regardless of subject matter or whether it is published as a printed book. We recommend this License principally for works whose purpose is instruction or reference.

1. APPLICABILITY AND DEFINITIONS

This License applies to any manual or other work, in any medium, that contains a notice placed by the copyright holder saying it can be distributed under the terms of this License. Such a notice grants a world-wide, royalty-free license, unlimited in duration, to use that work under the conditions stated herein. The "Document", below, refers to any such manual or work. Any member of the public is a licensee, and is addressed as "you". You accept the license if you copy, modify or distribute the work in a way requiring permission under copyright law.

A "Modified Version" of the Document means any work containing the Document or a portion of it, either copied verbatim, or with modifications and/or translated into another language.

A "Secondary Section" is a named appendix or a front-matter section of the Document that deals exclusively with the relationship of the publishers or authors of the Document to the Document's overall subject (or to related matters) and contains nothing that could fall directly within that overall subject. (Thus, if the Document is in part a textbook of mathematics, a Secondary Section may not explain any mathematics.) The relationship could be a matter of historical connection with the subject or with related matters, or of legal, commercial, philosophical, ethical or political position regarding them.

The "Invariant Sections" are certain Secondary Sections whose titles are designated, as being those of Invariant Sections, in the notice that says that the Document is released under this License. If a section does not fit the above definition of Secondary then it is not allowed to be designated as Invariant. The Document may contain zero Invariant Sections. If the Document does not identify any Invariant Sections then there are none.

The "Cover Texts" are certain short passages of text that are listed, as Front-Cover Texts or Back-Cover Texts, in the notice that says that the Document is released under this License. A Front-Cover Text may be at most 5 words, and a Back-Cover Text may be at most 25 words.

A "Transparent" copy of the Document means a machine-readable copy, represented in a format whose specification is available to the general public, that is suitable for revising the document straightforwardly with generic text editors or (for images composed of pixels) generic paint programs or (for drawings) some widely available drawing editor, and that is suitable for input to text formatters or for automatic translation to a variety of formats suitable for input to text formatters. A copy made in an otherwise Transparent file format whose markup, or absence of markup, has been arranged to thwart or discourage subsequent modification by readers is not

Transparent. An image format is not Transparent if used for any substantial amount of text. A copy that is not "Transparent" is called "Opaque".

Examples of suitable formats for Transparent copies include plain ASCII without markup, Texinfo input format, LaTeX input format, SGML or XML using a publicly available DTD, and standard-conforming simple HTML, PostScript or PDF designed for human modification. Examples of transparent image formats include PNG, XCF and JPG. Opaque formats include proprietary formats that can be read and edited only by proprietary word processors, SGML or XML for which the DTD and/or processing tools are not generally available, and the machine-generated HTML, PostScript or PDF produced by some word processors for output purposes only.

The "Title Page" means, for a printed book, the title page itself, plus such following pages as are needed to hold, legibly, the material this License requires to appear in the title page. For works in formats which do not have any title page as such, "Title Page" means the text near the most prominent appearance of the work's title, preceding the beginning of the body of the text.

A section "Entitled XYZ" means a named subunit of the Document whose title either is precisely XYZ or contains XYZ in parentheses following text that translates XYZ in another language. (Here XYZ stands for a specific section name mentioned below, such as "Acknowledgements", "Dedications", "Endorsements", or "History".) To "Preserve the Title" of such a section when you modify the Document means that it remains a section "Entitled XYZ" according to this definition.

The Document may include Warranty Disclaimers next to the notice which states that this License applies to the Document. These Warranty Disclaimers are considered to be included by reference in this License, but only as regards disclaiming warranties: any other implication that these Warranty Disclaimers may have is void and has no effect on the meaning of this License.

2. VERBATIM COPYING

You may copy and distribute the Document in any medium, either commercially or noncommercially, provided that this License, the copyright notices, and the license notice saying this License applies to the Document are reproduced in all copies, and that you add no other conditions whatsoever to those of this License. You may not use technical measures to obstruct or control the reading or further copying of the copies you make or distribute. However, you may accept compensation in exchange for copies. If you distribute a large enough number of copies you must also follow the conditions in section 3.

You may also lend copies, under the same conditions stated above, and you may publicly display copies.

3. COPYING IN QUANTITY

If you publish printed copies (or copies in media that commonly have printed covers) of the Document, numbering more than 100, and the Document's license notice requires Cover Texts, you must enclose the copies in covers that carry, clearly and legibly, all these Cover Texts: Front-Cover Texts on the front cover, and Back-Cover Texts on the back cover. Both covers must also clearly and legibly identify you as the publisher of these copies. The front cover must present the full title with all words of the title equally prominent and visible. You may add other material on the covers in addition. Copying with changes limited to the covers, as long as they preserve the title of the Document and satisfy these conditions, can be treated as verbatim copying in other respects.

If the required texts for either cover are too voluminous to fit legibly, you should put the first ones listed (as many as fit reasonably) on the actual cover, and continue the rest onto adjacent pages.

If you publish or distribute Opaque copies of the Document numbering more than 100, you must either include a machine-readable Transparent copy along with each Opaque copy, or state in or with each Opaque copy a computer-network location from which the general network-using public has access to download using public-standard network protocols a complete Transparent copy of the Document, free of added material. If you use the latter option, you must take reasonably prudent steps, when you begin distribution of Opaque copies in quantity, to ensure that this Transparent copy will remain thus accessible at the stated location until at least one year after the last time you distribute an Opaque copy (directly or through your agents or retailers) of that edition to the public.

It is requested, but not required, that you contact the authors of the Document well before redistributing any large number of copies, to give them a chance to provide you with an updated version of the Document.

4. MODIFICATIONS

You may copy and distribute a Modified Version of the Document under the conditions of sections 2 and 3 above, provided that you release the Modified Version under precisely this License, with the Modified Version filling the role of the Document, thus licensing distribution and modification of the Modified Version to whoever possesses a copy of it. In addition, you must do these things in the Modified Version:

- A. Use in the Title Page (and on the covers, if any) a title distinct from that of the Document, and from those of previous versions (which should, if there were any, be listed in the History section of the Document). You may use the same title as a previous version if the original publisher of that version gives permission.

- B. List on the Title Page, as authors, one or more persons or entities responsible for authorship of the modifications in the Modified Version, together with at least five of the principal authors of the Document (all of its principal authors, if it has fewer than five), unless they release you from this requirement.
- C. State on the Title page the name of the publisher of the Modified Version, as the publisher.
- D. Preserve all the copyright notices of the Document.
- E. Add an appropriate copyright notice for your modifications adjacent to the other copyright notices.
- F. Include, immediately after the copyright notices, a license notice giving the public permission to use the Modified Version under the terms of this License, in the form shown in the Addendum below.
- G. Preserve in that license notice the full lists of Invariant Sections and required Cover Texts given in the Document's license notice.
- H. Include an unaltered copy of this License.
- I. Preserve the section Entitled "History", Preserve its Title, and add to it an item stating at least the title, year, new authors, and publisher of the Modified Version as given on the Title Page. If there is no section Entitled "History" in the Document, create one stating the title, year, authors, and publisher of the Document as given on its Title Page, then add an item describing the Modified Version as stated in the previous sentence.
- J. Preserve the network location, if any, given in the Document for public access to a Transparent copy of the Document, and likewise the network locations given in the Document for previous versions it was based on. These may be placed in the "History" section. You may omit a network location for a work that was published at least four years before the Document itself, or if the original publisher of the version it refers to gives permission.
- K. For any section Entitled "Acknowledgements" or "Dedications", Preserve the Title of the section, and preserve in the section all the substance and tone of each of the contributor acknowledgements and/or dedications given therein.
- L. Preserve all the Invariant Sections of the Document, unaltered in their text and in their titles. Section numbers or the equivalent are not considered part of the section titles.
- M. Delete any section Entitled "Endorsements". Such a section may not be included in the Modified Version.
- N. Do not retitle any existing section to be Entitled "Endorsements" or to conflict in title with any Invariant Section.
- O. Preserve any Warranty Disclaimers.

If the Modified Version includes new front-matter sections or appendices that qualify as Secondary Sections and contain no material copied from the Document, you may at your option designate some or all of these sections as invariant. To do this, add their titles to the list of Invariant Sections in the Modified Version's license notice. These titles must be distinct from any other section titles.

You may add a section Entitled "Endorsements", provided it contains nothing but endorsements of your Modified Version by various parties--for example, statements of peer review or that the text has been approved by an organization as the authoritative definition of a standard.

You may add a passage of up to five words as a Front-Cover Text, and a passage of up to 25 words as a Back-Cover Text, to the end of the list of Cover Texts in the Modified Version. Only one passage of Front-Cover Text and one of Back-Cover Text may be added by (or through arrangements made by) any one entity. If the Document already includes a cover text for the same cover, previously added by you or by arrangement made by the same entity you are acting on behalf of, you may not add another; but you may replace the old one, on explicit permission from the previous publisher that added the old one.

The author(s) and publisher(s) of the Document do not by this License give permission to use their names for publicity for or to assert or imply endorsement of any Modified Version.

5. COMBINING DOCUMENTS

You may combine the Document with other documents released under this License, under the terms defined in section 4 above for modified versions, provided that you include in the combination all of the Invariant Sections of all of the original documents, unmodified, and list them all as Invariant Sections of your combined work in its license notice, and that you preserve all their Warranty Disclaimers.

The combined work need only contain one copy of this License, and multiple identical Invariant Sections may be replaced with a single copy. If there are multiple Invariant Sections with the same name but different contents, make the title of each such section unique by adding at the end of it, in parentheses, the name of the original author or publisher of that section if known, or else a unique number. Make the same adjustment to the section titles in the list of Invariant Sections in the license notice of the combined work.

In the combination, you must combine any sections Entitled "History" in the various original documents, forming one section Entitled "History"; likewise combine any sections Entitled "Acknowledgements", and any sections Entitled "Dedications". You must delete all sections Entitled "Endorsements."

6. COLLECTIONS OF DOCUMENTS

You may make a collection consisting of the Document and other documents released under this License, and replace the individual copies of this License in the various documents with a single copy that is included in the collection, provided that you follow the rules of this License for verbatim copying of each of the documents in all other respects.

You may extract a single document from such a collection, and distribute it individually under this License, provided you insert a copy of this License into the extracted document, and follow this License in all other respects regarding verbatim copying of that document.

7. AGGREGATION WITH INDEPENDENT WORKS

A compilation of the Document or its derivatives with other separate and independent documents or works, in or on a volume of a storage or distribution medium, is called an "aggregate" if the copyright resulting from the compilation is not used to limit the legal rights of the compilation's users beyond what the individual works permit. When the Document is included in an aggregate, this License does not apply to the other works in the aggregate which are not themselves derivative works of the Document.

If the Cover Text requirement of section 3 is applicable to these copies of the Document, then if the Document is less than one half of the entire aggregate, the Document's Cover Texts may be placed on covers that bracket the Document within the aggregate, or the electronic equivalent of covers if the Document is in electronic form. Otherwise they must appear on printed covers that bracket the whole aggregate.

8. TRANSLATION

Translation is considered a kind of modification, so you may distribute translations of the Document under the terms of section 4. Replacing Invariant Sections with translations requires special permission from their copyright holders, but you may include translations of some or all Invariant Sections in addition to the original versions of these Invariant Sections. You may include a translation of this License, and all the license notices in the Document, and any Warranty Disclaimers, provided that you also include the original English version of this License and the original versions of those notices and disclaimers. In case of a disagreement between the translation and the original version of this License or a notice or disclaimer, the original version will prevail.

If a section in the Document is Entitled "Acknowledgements", "Dedications", or "History", the requirement (section 4) to Preserve its Title (section 1) will typically require changing the actual title.

9. TERMINATION

You may not copy, modify, sublicense, or distribute the Document except as expressly provided for under this License. Any other attempt to copy, modify, sublicense or distribute the Document is void, and will automatically terminate your rights under this License. However, parties who have received copies, or rights, from you under this License will not have their licenses terminated so long as such parties remain in full compliance.

10. FUTURE REVISIONS OF THIS LICENSE

The Free Software Foundation may publish new, revised versions of the GNU Free Documentation License from time to time. Such new versions will be similar in spirit to the present version, but may differ in detail to address new problems or concerns. See http://www.gnu.org/copyleft/.

Each version of the License is given a distinguishing version number. If the Document specifies that a particular numbered version of this License "or any later version" applies to it, you have the option of following the terms and conditions either of that specified version or of any later version that has been published (not as a draft) by the Free Software Foundation. If the Document does not specify a version number of this License, you may choose any version ever published (not as a draft) by the Free Software Foundation.

Addendum: How to use this License for your documents

To use this License in a document you have written, include a copy of the License in the document and put the following copyright and license notices just after the title page:

```
Copyright (c)  YEAR  YOUR NAME.
Permission is granted to copy, distribute and/or modify this document
under the terms of the GNU Free Documentation License, Version 1.2
or any later version published by the Free Software Foundation;
with no Invariant Sections, no Front-Cover Texts, and no Back-Cover Texts.
A copy of the license is included in the section entitled "GNU
Free Documentation License".
```

If you have Invariant Sections, Front-Cover Texts and Back-Cover Texts, replace the "with...Texts." line with this:

```
with the Invariant Sections being LIST THEIR TITLES, with the
Front-Cover Texts being LIST, and with the Back-Cover Texts being LIST.
```

If you have Invariant Sections without Cover Texts, or some other combination of the three, merge those two alternatives to suit the situation.

If your document contains nontrivial examples of program code, we recommend releasing these examples in parallel under your choice of free software license, such as the GNU General Public License, to permit their use in free software.

Glossary

A

ambiguous

A pattern is ambiguous when a fragment of an instance document can be valid against using several alternatives in its choice patterns. RELAX NG allows ambiguous patterns, but they can be a problem for annotation and datatype assignment.

C

chameleon design

Specifying a namespace in include, externalRef, or parentRef to give a namespace to grammars or patterns defined without a namespace is known as chameleon design, because the imported grammar or pattern takes on the new namespace like a chameleon takes on the color of the environment in which it is placed.

character class

In a regular expression, a character class is an atom that matches a set of characters. Character classes may be classical Perl character classes, Unicode character classes, or user-defined character classes.

classical Perl character class

A set of character classes designated by a single letter, for which upper- and lower-cases of the same letter are complementary (for instance, \d is all the decimal digits, and \D is all the characters that aren't decimal digits).

compositor

A compositor is a pattern that can be used to combine other patterns. RELAX NG has three basic compositors: group, choice, and interleave. A fourth compositor, mixed, is a shortcut for interleave with an embedded text pattern.

content model

A description of the structure of child elements and text nodes (independent of attributes). The content model is *simple* when there is a text node but no elements, *complex* when there are element nodes but no text, *mixed* when there are text and element nodes, and *empty* when there are neither text nor element nodes.

D

datatype

A term used by RELAX NG to qualify the content of a simple content element or attribute. Datatypes shouldn't be confused with XML 1.0 element types; those are called *element names* by RELAX NG.

deterministic

A pattern is deterministic if a schema processor can always determine which path through the schema to follow by looking only at the current element under validation. Unlike W3C XML Schema, RELAX NG doesn't require deterministic patterns.

DOM

Document Object Model. An object oriented model of XML documents, including the definition of the API allowing its manipulation. The third version of DOM (DOM Level 3) includes an API called Abstract Schemas, which facilitate schema-guided editions of XML documents; also see *http://www.w3.org/TR/DOM-Level-3-Core*).

DSDL

Document Schema Definition Languages (DSDL) is a project undertaken by ISO (ISO/IEC JTC 1/SC 34/WG 1, to be precise) whose objective is "to create a framework within which multiple validation tasks of different types can be applied to an XML document to achieve more complete validation results than just the application of a single technology"; see *http://dsdl.org*.

DTD

Document Type Definition. XML 1.0 DTDs are inherited from SGML, in which rules were included that allow the customization of the markup itself and played a very central role. Because of the syntactical rules included in their DTDs, SGML applications need a DTD to read an SGML document. One of the simplifications of XML is to state that a XML parser should be able to read a document without needing a DTD. DTDs have therefore been simplified from their SGML ancestors and remain the first incarnation of what is today called an XML Schema Language.

E

element

One of the basic type of nodes in the tree represented by an XML document. An element is delimited by start and end tags. In the corresponding tree, an element is a nonterminal node, which may have subnodes of type element, character (text), namespace, and attribute, as well as comment and processing instruction nodes.

element type

Term used in the XML 1.0 Recommendation, which is equivalent to the notion of element names in W3C XML Schema and shouldn't be confused with the simple or complex datatype of an element.

empty content

An element that has neither child elements nor text nodes (with or without attributes).

F

facet

A constraint added to the lexical or value space of a simple datatype of the W3C XML Schema datatype system. The list of facets that can be used depends on the simple datatype. W3C XML Schema's facets can be used as parameters in RELAX NG data patterns.

G

Grammar

A grammar is a pattern that acts a container for a start pattern and any number of named patterns.

I

Infoset

XML Information Set. A formal description of the information that may be found in a well-formed XML document.

instance document

A XML document that is a candidate for being validated by a schema. Any well-formed XML 1.0 document that conforms to the Namespaces in XML 1.0 Recommendation can be considered a valid or invalid instance document.

L

lexical space

The set of all representations (after parsing and whitespace processing) allowed for a simple datatype.

local name

The name of a component within its namespace. It's the part of the qualified name that comes after the namespace prefix and colon.

M

mixed content

The content of an element that contains both child element and text nodes.

N

Named pattern

Named patterns are globally defined in a grammar. These patterns may be referenced from anywhere in this grammar or in the child grammars.

namespace

A unique identifier that can be associated with a set of XML elements and attributes. This identifier is a URI that isn't required to point to an actual resource but must "belong" to the author of these elements and attributes. Because the full URI can't be included in the name of each element and attribute, a namespace prefix is assigned to the namespace URI using a namespace declaration. This prefix is added to the local name of the elements and attributes to form a qualified name. Namespaces are optional, and elements and attributes may have no namespaces attached.

P

pattern

Any part of a RELAX NG schema that can be matched against a set of attributes and a sequence of elements and strings is a pattern. With the exception of name classes, all parts (including the whole schema) of a RELAX NG schema are patterns.

piece

Regular expressions (or patterns) are composed of pieces. Each piece is itself composed of an atom describing a condition on a substring and an optional quantifier defining the expected number of occurrences of the atom.

Q

qualified name

The complete name of a component, including the prefix associated with its target namespace if one is defined.

R

Recursive content models

Recursive content models are content models in which elements can be included directly or indirectly within themselves (such as XHTML div or span elements).

recursive patterns

Recursive patterns are named patterns that include direct or indirect references to themselves. RELAX NG allows only recursive patterns that describe recursive content models—those for which the definition of the named pattern is isolated from its reference by an element pattern.

regular expression

A syntax that expresses conditions on strings. The syntax used by the W3C XML Schema for its patterns is very close to the syntax introduced by the Perl programming language. A regular expression is composed of elementary pieces.

RELAX

A grammar-based XML Schema language developed by Murata Makoto and published in March 2000 as a Japanese ISO Standard; see *http://www.xml.gr.jp/relax*.

RELAX NG

A grammar-based XML Schema language resulting from a merger between RELAX and TREX; see *http://relaxng.org*.

Russian doll design

A schema in which the definitions of elements and attributes are embedded one inside the other without using named patterns.

S

SAX

Simple API for XML. A streaming, event-based API used between parsers and applications. Its streaming nature means that pipelines of XML processing may be created using SAX; see *http://www. saxproject.org.*

Schematron

A rule-based XML Schema language, developed by Rick Jelliffe, using XPath expressions to describe validation rule; see *http://www.ascc.net/xml/resource/schematr on/schematron.html.*

SGML

Standard Generalized Markup Language, the ancestor of XML. XML was designed as a simplified subset of SGML to be used on the Web.

simple content

An element has a simple-content model when it has a child text node only (and no subelements). A simple content element has a simple type if it has no attributes; it has a complex type if it has any attributes.

simplification

The process of simplifying and normalizing a RELAX NG schema to remove the syntactical variations and use only a few basic patterns and name classes.

special character

A character that may be used as an atom after a slash (\) to accept a specific character, either for convenience or because this character is interpreted differently in the context of a regular expression.

start pattern

When a grammar validates an instance document, its start pattern is matched against the root element of the instance document. When a grammar is embedded in another grammar, the embedded grammar is replaced by its start pattern during the implementation of the schema.

T

Trang

A tool for converting among RELAX NG syntax, RELAX NG Compact Syntax, DTDs, W3C XML Schema, and simple instance documents. Available at *http:// thaiopensource.com/relaxng/trang.html.*

TREX

A grammar-based XML Schema language developed by James Clark; see *http:// www.thaiopensource.com/trex.*

U

unambiguous

A pattern is unambiguous when any fragment of an instance document that is valid per this pattern is valid for precisely one of the choices in the schema. RELAX NG doesn't require the use of unambiguous patterns, but they can be considered good practice for annotation and datatype assignment, especially when conversion from RELAX NG to another schema language is necessary.

Unicode block

A set of characters classified by their localization (Latin, Arabic, Hebrew, Tibetan, and even Gothic or musical symbols).

Unicode category

A set of characters classified by their usage (letters, uppercase, digit, punctuation, etc.).

Unicode character class

A set of character classes based on the Unicode blocks and categories.

URI

Uniform Resource Identifier. Defined by RFCs 2396 and 2732. URIs were created to extend the notion of URLs (Uniform Resource Locators) to include abstract identifiers that don't necessarily need to locate a resource.

URL

Uniform Resource Locator, a common identifier used on the Web. URLs are absolute when the full path to the resource is indicated, and relative when a partial path is given that needs to be evaluated in relation with a base URL.

V

valid

An XML document that is well-formed and conforms to a schema (RELAX NG, DTD, W3C XML Schema, etc.) of some kind.

value space

The set of all the possible values for a simple datatype, independent of their actual representation in the instance documents.

W

W3C

World Wide Web Consortium. Originally created to settle HTML and HTTP as de facto standards. The main specification body for the core specifications of the World Wide Web and the keeper of the core XML specifications; see *http://www.w3.org*.

well-formed

An XML document that meets the conditions defined in the XML 1.0 Recommendation: it must be readable without ambiguity. Syntax errors are detected by an XML parser even without schema of any type.

whitespace

Characters #x9 (tab), #xA (linefeed), #xD (carriage return), and #x20 (space). These are often used to indent the XML documents to make them more readable, and are filtered by an operation called *whitespace processing*.

X

XInclude

A W3C specification defining a general purpose inclusion mechanism for XML documents; see *http://www.w3.org/TR/xinclude*.

XML

Extensible Markup Language. A subset of SGML created to be used on the Web. Its core specification (XML 1.0) was published by the W3C in February 1998. New XML specifications have been added since this date, and the W3C considers that, with the addition of W3C XML Schema, the core specifications are now complete.

XPath

A query language that identifies a set of nodes within an XML document. Originally defined to be used with XSLT, it's also used by other specifications such as Schematron, XPointer, W3C XML Schema or XForms; see *http://www.w3.org/TR/xpath*.

XSLT

Extensible Stylesheet Language Transformations. A programming language specialized for the transformation of XML documents; for more information, see *http://www.w3.org/TR/xslt*.

Index

We'd like to hear your suggestions for improving our indexes. Send email to *index@oreilly.com.*

mixed element, 351–353
mixed pattern, 54, 396
    pattern normalization, 284
Modular Namespaces (MNS), 453
Multi-Schema Validator (MSV), 6, 246
Murata, Makoto, 12, 453
    foreword, xi–xii

N

\n character, 107
name classes, 13
    abiguity, 312–314
    combining using choice element, 207
    defining for any name from "lib"
        namespace, 207
    first example of, 172
    normalization and simplification, 283
    operating on specific element or attribute
        names, 208
    overlap, 300
    pattern normalization, 284
    patterns and, 173
Name datatype (W3C XML Schema), 82
name element, 353
name name class, 397
*-nameClass, 377
-nameClass, 378
(nameClass) container, 376
nameClass production, 397
nameClass|nameClass production, 398
named patterns
    combining, 146
    defining, 33, 35
    defining for content rather than
        elements, 196–200
    escaping identifiers in compact syntax, 44
    extensibility of, 197
    glossary definition, 469
    referencing, 34
    referencing in compact syntax, 34
    strict scoping, 128
Namespace- and Datatype-Aware DTDs
        (DSDL Part 9), 455
Namespace Routing Language (NRL), 453
    validating SOAP message containing one
        or more XHTML documents, 454
Namespace Switchboard, 453
namespaces, 160–187
    applying to elements, 161
    assigning prefixes to, 163
    attributes, 164

challenges of, 165–179
declaed using xmlns attribute, 163
declarations, 398
declaring in schemas, 166–171
default, 163
default (see default namespace)
elements, 164
foreign (see foreign namespaces)
glossary definition, 469
goals of, 161, 164
independent vocabularies, 164
introduction, 160–165
mixing default and nondefault, 168
removing from anyName using except and
        nsName, 207
to manage translation to W3C XML
        Schema, 242
namespaceURILiteral production, 398
native datatypes and whitespace, 70–72
native types versus W3C XML Schema
        datatypes, 101
NCName datatype (W3C XML Schema), 82
negativeInteger datatype, 86
newline, 107
newline character, escaping, 73
NMTOKEN datatype (W3C XML
        Schema), 82
NMTOKENS datatype (W3C XML
        Schema), 82
nodes, 8
    occurrence constraints on, 21
noncolonized name, 82
non-deterministic schemas, 7
nonNegativeInteger datatype, 86
nonPositiveInteger datatype, 86
normalization
    simplification and, 277
    suppressing, 72
    whitespace, 71
normalizedString datatype (W3C XML
        Schema), 82
normalize-space( ) function (XPath), 71
notAllowed element, 354
notAllowed patterns, 399
    simplification, 294
NOTATION (W3C XML Schema), 85
ns, 180
nsName element, 355
nsName exceptNameClass name class, 400
numeric datatypes, 85
numeric types, 116

pieces, glossary definition, 469
pivot format, 240
positiveInteger datatype, 86
Post-Schema Validation Infoset (PSVI), 9
prefixes, applying to namespaces, 163
preprocessing annotations, 211, 238–240
primitive types (W3C XML Schema), 81
processing instructions (PIs), 53
    compact syntax, 24
    lack of namespace support, 221
PSVI (Post-Schema Validation Infoset), 9
PUBLIC identifier (XML), 160
Python type library, 80

Q

QName datatypes, 84, 441
qualification element, 49
qualified names
    glossary definition, 469
    versus syntax, 214
quantifiers, using to limit the number of
    leading zeros, 107
QuotedIdentifier production, 380
quotes
    double, 374
    single, 375

R

\r character, 107
RDDL documents
    generating from annotated RELAX NG
        schemas, 263–264
recursive content models, glossary
    definition, 469
recursive models, 32, 43
recursive patterns, glossary definition, 469
redundancy and maintenance of schema, 31
ref element, 362
regular expressions
    ambiguity, 307–309
    glossary definition, 469
    in pattern facets, 97
Regular Grammar–Based Validation (DSDL
    Part 2), 452
regular hedge grammars,
    ambiguous, 310–312
relative order between subelements, 201
relative order of child elements
    other schema languages and, 202
RELAX, glossary definition, 469
RELAX Namespace, 453

RELAX NG
    datatype assignment and, 7
    downside to, 7
    DTD compatibility comments, 228–231
    glossary definition, 469
    key area related to more functionality, 63
    main rival, 5
    mathematical backgound, 12
    overview, xiii, 3–7
    patterns (see patterns)
    schemas (see schemas)
    specification simplification, 276
    XML Processing Instructions and, 13
    XSLT and, 5
report, 452
Resource Directory Description Language
    (RDDL), 161
    annotations, 236–238
restricting schemas, 206
restrictions, 295–304
    removal of, 42
RFC 2045, 85, 411
Riggs, Simon, 451
root elements
    as grammar elements, 190
    definition of in Russian doll–style, 35
Rule-Based Validation (DSDL Part 3), 452
rules, 9
Russian doll design, glossary definition, 469
Russian doll schemas, 23
    definition of root element, 35
    modeling documents with, 31
    structure of, 31
    using external references with, 120–122
russian-doll.rnc file, 191
russian-doll.rng file, 190

S

\S Perl character class, 109
\s Perl character class, 109
SAX (Simple API for XML), 8
    glossary definition, 470
Scalable Vector Graphics (SVG)
    annotations, 234
Schema Adjunct Framework (SAF), 243
schemas
    adding SQL-based processing information
        to, 244
    ambiguous (see ambiguity)
    annotating (see annotations)
    chameleon (see chameleon schemas)
    complete, creating, 36–42

Z

About the Author

Eric van der Vlist is an independent XML consultant, developer, trainer, and writer. He is involved in many XML projects for the French administration, most of them related to the publication of XML vocabularies.

Eric is the editor of the ISO DSDL Part 10 specification (work in progress, see *http://dsdl.org*) describing Validation Management. He is also the author of Examplotron (*http://examplotron.org*) and one of the editors of RSS 1.0. (*www.purl.org/rss/1.0/*).

He is a contributing editor to XML.com and xmlhack.com; creator and chief editor of XMLfr.org, the main web site dedicated to XML in French; and works to encourage the adoption of XML by the French community. Eric is also the author of O'Reilly's *XML Schema*.

He lives in Paris, but you may find him at one of the many international conferences where he delivers tutorials and presentations. He welcomes your comments at *vdv@dyomedea.com*.

Colophon

Our look is the result of reader comments, our own experimentation, and feedback from distribution channels. Distinctive covers complement our distinctive approach to technical topics, breathing personality and life into potentially dry subjects.

The animal on the cover of *RELAX NG* is a blood pheasant (*Ithaginis cruentus*). Unlike other pheasants, the blood pheasant resembles a partridge in size and shape. Its crest is grey, and the male's forehead, face, and throat are red. A female's upper features are more rust-colored. Both males and females have grey to light brown bodies.

The blood pheasant lives in the coniferous forests of the Himalayas, from Nepal through Tibet into northern Burma to northwest China. It lives in flocks of 4–20 in nonbreeding season, up to 40 in winter. Between late April and early May, the female fills a shallow saucer nest of dry twigs lined with leaves with up to 14 eggs. Chicks are born in mid-June and able to follow mother to feed at two days old.

The blood pheasant picks up food with its bill and seldom digs with its claws, although it sometimes jumps up to shrubs to feed. It's considered a good runner but a poor flier. When threatened, it rushes down hills and hides under stones. Because it lives in such remote regions, however, the blood pheasant population remains stable and unthreatened by man.

Mary Anne Weeks Mayo was the production editor, and Nancy Wolfe Kotary was the copyeditor for *RELAX NG*. Reg Aubry and Colleen Gorman provided quality control. Julie Hawks wrote the index.

Emma Colby designed the cover of this book, based on a series design by Edie Freedman. The cover image is a 19th-century engraving from *Cuvier's Animals*. Emma produced the cover layout with QuarkXPress 4.1 using Adobe's ITC Garamond font.

Melanie Wang designed the interior layout, based on a series design by David Futato. This book was converted by Joe Wizda to FrameMaker 5.5.6 with a format conversion tool created by Erik Ray, Jason McIntosh, Neil Walls, and Mike Sierra that uses Perl and XML technologies. The text font is Linotype Birka; the heading font is Adobe Myriad Condensed; and the code font is LucasFont's TheSans Mono Condensed. The illustrations that appear in the book were produced by Robert Romano and Jessamyn Read using Macromedia FreeHand 9 and Adobe Photoshop 6. The tip and warning icons were drawn by Christopher Bing. This colophon was compiled by Mary Anne Weeks Mayo.

Related Titles Available from O'Reilly

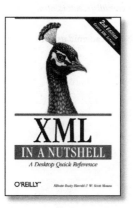

XML

Content Syndication with RSS

Java and XML

Java and XSLT

Learning XML, *2nd Edition*

Learning XSLT

Perl & XML

Practical RDF

Programming Jabber

Programming Web Services with SOAP

Python & XML

SAX2

SVG Essentials

Web Services Essentials

XForms Essentials

XML CD Bookshelf, *Version 1.0*

XML in a Nutshell, *2nd Edition*

XML Pocket Reference, *2nd Edition*

XML Schema

Xpath and Xpointer

XSL-FO

XSLT

XSLT Cookbook

O'REILLY®

Our books are available at most retail and online bookstores.
To order direct: 1-800-998-9938 • *order@oreilly.com* • *www.oreilly.com*
Online editions of most O'Reilly titles are available by subscription at *safari.oreilly.com*

Keep in touch with O'Reilly

1. Download examples from our books

To find example files for a book, go to:

www.oreilly.com/catalog

select the book, and follow the "Examples" link.

2. Register your O'Reilly books

Register your book at *register.oreilly.com*

Why register your books?
Once you've registered your O'Reilly books you can:

- Win O'Reilly books, T-shirts or discount coupons in our monthly drawing.
- Get special offers available only to registered O'Reilly customers.
- Get catalogs announcing new books (US and UK only).
- Get email notification of new editions of the O'Reilly books you own.

3. Join our email lists

Sign up to get topic-specific email announcements of new books and conferences, special offers, and O'Reilly Network technology newsletters at:

elists.oreilly.com

It's easy to customize your free elists subscription so you'll get exactly the O'Reilly news you want.

4. Get the latest news, tips, and tools

www.oreilly.com

- "Top 100 Sites on the Web"—PC Magazine
- CIO Magazine's Web Business 50 Awards

Our web site contains a library of comprehensive product information (including book excerpts and tables of contents), downloadable software, background articles, interviews with technology leaders, links to relevant sites, book cover art, and more.

5. Work for O'Reilly

Check out our web site for current employment opportunities:

jobs.oreilly.com

6. Contact us

O'Reilly & Associates, Inc.
1005 Gravenstein Hwy North
Sebastopol, CA 95472 USA

TEL: 707-827-7000 or 800-998-9938
(6am to 5pm PST)

FAX: 707-829-0104

order@oreilly.com
For answers to problems regarding your order or our products. To place a book order online, visit:

www.oreilly.com/order_new

catalog@oreilly.com
To request a copy of our latest catalog.

booktech@oreilly.com
For book content technical questions or corrections.

corporate@oreilly.com
For educational, library, government, and corporate sales.

proposals@oreilly.com
To submit new book proposals to our editors and product managers.

international@oreilly.com
For information about our international distributors or translation queries. For a list of our distributors outside of North America check out:

international.oreilly.com/distributors.html

adoption@oreilly.com
For information about academic use of O'Reilly books, visit:

academic.oreilly.com

O'REILLY®

Our books are available at most retail and online bookstores.
To order direct: 1-800-998-9938 • *order@oreilly.com* • *www.oreilly.com*
Online editions of most O'Reilly titles are available by subscription at *safari.oreilly.com*